MONOPOLIES

AND

THE PEOPLE.

By D. C. CLOUD,
MUSCATINE.

THIRD EDITION.

"THE ENUMERATION IN THE CONSTITUTION, OF CERTAIN RIGHTS, SHALL NOT BE CONSTRUED TO DENY OR DISPARAGE OTHERS RETAINED BY THE PEOPLE."

"THE POWERS NOT DELEGATED TO THE UNITED STATES BY THE CONSTITUTION, NOR PROHIBITED BY IT TO THE STATES, ARE RESERVED TO THE STATES RESPECTIVELY, OR TO THE PEOPLE."—*Articles IX. and X. of the Constitution of the United States.*

DAVENPORT, IOWA:
DAY, EGBERT, & FIDLAR;
MUSCATINE, IOWA:
ALLEN BROOMHALL,
1873.

TO THE

Patrons of Husbandry,

WHO HAVE BECOME THE PIONEER CORPS IN THE EFFORTS BEING MADE TO REFORM THE ABUSES NOW OPPRESSING THE COUNTRY, AND WHO ARE EARNESTLY AND EFFICIENTLY LABORING FOR THE RESTORATION OF THE RIGHTS OF THE PEOPLE, WITH THE HOPE THAT IT MAY AID THEM IN THEIR PATRIOTIC WORK, THIS BOOK IS RESPECTFULLY DEDICATED

BY

THE AUTHOR.

The Granger at Home. The Granger abroad.

PREFACE.

TO THE READER.

FOR two years past the author has awaited the auspicious moment for presenting to the public his views upon the oppressions and abuses practiced by corporations and combinations of men who are apparently getting a controlling influence over the commerce, finances, and government of the contry. Recent action on the part of the people has convinced him that his opportunity has come, and he embraces it. He has aimed to present a true history of the operations of the different monopolies.

Since he began the preparation of his work, some events have taken place not noticed by him. Oakes Ames and James Brooks, two prominent characters among railroad men, and whom he has had occasion to name, have died. Some changes in the laws of congress have been made affecting the interests of corporations. The law requiring the secretary of the treasury to retain but one-half of the earnings from the government of the Pacific roads to apply on the interest due to government on subsidy bonds, has been repealed, and he may now retain and apply the whole amount. Suit has also been brought against the Union Pacific company because of its dishonest practices.

On the whole, however, combinations of corporations, and other rings and organizations, at war with the best interests of the people, have acquired new strength and more power within the last few months.

The reader will notice the fact, that while the author

has quoted liberally from the statutes and resolves of congress to show the great privileges and powers conferred upon railroad companies, and familiarized the reader with their financial and other transactions for a clear understanding of their manner of doing business, he has not pretended to give a full history; satisfying himself with such chapters as would place before the public the true character of these monopolies.

The author has sought to present truthful statements of matters in connection with the various *interests* now so hostile to the *rights* of the people, and he believes he has embodied the facts as they exist.

D. C. C.

MUSCATINE, IOWA, July 28, 1873.

Since the publication of former editions of this work some additions have been made to the chapter on banking; on the legal tender decisions; on the control of railroad corporations; on water transportation, and a chapter added to the appendix on the financial policy of the government, as illustrated by the present crisis in monetary affairs. Of other changes introduced, an index has been prepared, a superior quality of paper is used, and the work is stereotyped.

The book is now presented to the public in the enlarged and improved form, with the hope that the efforts of the author and publishers to aid in reforming the abuses under which the country is suffering may be appreciated.

D. C. C.

September 26, 1873.

TABLE OF CONTENTS.

CHAPTER VIII.

CHAPTER IX.

CHAPTER X.

CHAPTER XI.

CHAPTER XII.

CHAPTER XIII.

CHAPTER XIV.

CHAPTER XV.

CHAPTER XVI.

CHAPTER XVII.

CHAPTER XVIII.

CHAPTER XIX.

CHAPTER XX.

CHAPTER XXI.

CHAPTER XXII.

CHAPTER XXIII.

CHAPTER XXIV.

CHAPTER XXV.

CONCLUSION.

APPENDIX.

CHAPTER I.

CHAPTER II.

CHAPTER III.

CHAPTER IV.

CHAPTER V.

CHAPTER VI.

CHAPTER VII.

ERRATA.

Page 230, nineteenth line from top, for "twelve" read *six*.
346, seventh line from top, for "arrest" read *wrest*.
346, seventh line from bottom, for "in" read *is*.
347, in eighth and tenth lines from top, for "imports" read *imposts*.
350, second line from top for "it" read *they*.

MONOPOLIES

—AND—

THE PEOPLE.

INTRODUCTORY CHAPTER.

IN treating of the topics discussed in this work the author addresses himself to the task with no partisan bias. His purpose is to draw aside the veil, and let the facts speak for themselves. He writes, as he believes, in the performance of duty. Serious dangers are threatening the people. There is a power in the land, possessing elements destructive not only of the industrial and producing public, but of the very form and spirit of republican government. It will be the aim of the author to show forth the progress and present attitude of this power in its relations with the people; and to suggest, if not to advocate, such measures of relief and protection as the exigency demands.

It is a fact to be admitted by every candid thinker, that of late years, corporations, rings, and single speculators have, by united and persistent efforts, obtained control of the government; that their interests are guarded, and protected by the legislative, executive, and judicial departments of the government, both state and national.

The men who are thus combined in opposition to the people do not belong to any one political division; they are found in all parties; they are firmly united for the purpose of grasping power, of controlling the government in their own interest, of fastening upon the people oppressive monopolies, and of enriching themselves at the expense of the public. To accomplish these ends they procure donations of land, money subsidies, protective tariffs, continue a depreciated currency, and by arbitrary rules and by-laws of their own hold the whole people at their mercy. To such an extent have these monopolies been fostered and protected that at the present time the farmer pays in freights, taxes, and duties, at least one-half of his farm products for their support.

A silent or passive acquiescence in, and submission to, these abuses and oppressions, have given a controlling strength and power to monopolies that cannot now be overcome without a united, long, and hard struggle.

These evils cannot be corrected, nor the rights of the people restored, save by concerted action on their part, not only in securing proper legislation, but in asserting and maintaining in their business, at elections, and in the courts, their rights as free and independent citizens of the United States. The taxing of the people for the purpose of aiding private enterprises, the donation of the public land or of the public money to individuals or companies, or the enactment of laws by which the people are compelled to pay a part of their hard-earned substance to aid private parties in accumulating wealth, are oppressions not to be tolerated in a republic. Yet it is true that we are now taxed for the purpose of paying the interest on many millions of money given or loaned to railroad corporations, that we pay large duties on goods for the benefit of wealthy manufacturers, that extortionate rates are exacted for transportation of products to market, that we are taxed to build railroads for private owners, and these things are all pronounced legal and constitutional—not because they are so, but because these private interests have become so powerful that they control the country. The *antiquated* idea that the government was instituted by the people, and for the people, has become entirely obsolete, and the new doctrine has obtained that the whole duty of the government is to foster, protect, and support monopolies, and that these monopolies own the people.

In no country of the civilized world are the people more directly connected with all the questions affecting their well-being than they are in the United States. It follows that all should be familiar with such measures as tend to fix and establish the general policy of the government—not only in respect to its general administration, but especially in those matters that directly or indirectly give to corporations, associations, companies, or individuals, exclusive grants, donations or privileges, detrimental to the interests of those who are not of the "favored few."

A republican government can only exist when it is controlled by the people, and administered in their interest. When special or class legislation, for the benefit of certain limited interests, or in favor of certain parties, becomes the rule of action in the administration of either the state or national government, accompanied by grants of land, money, or taxes, to be returned to the government by levies made upon the people without their consent, that government ceases to be republican.

In our country, with its vast extent of territory, its diverse interests, and variety of products and manufactures, it is but natural for different localities and interests to ask governmental aid; nor is it always an abuse of power for the government to give this aid. In some instances it is the duty of the government to use its power and the public money in matters that in some degree, at least, are in their nature local — such, for instance, as the improvement of rivers, harbors, etc. In these cases it is not an abuse of power, but a legitimate exercise of the delegated authority for the benefit of the people.

But there is another species of legislation, approved by the executive and judicial departments of the general government, and endorsed and supported by the legislatures and courts of many of our States, that is, in its operation, anti-republican and oppressive to the people. We refer to the current special legislation in favor of railroad corporations, our protective tariff, and the banking system, and financial policy of the government.

No one will accuse the author of indulging in a partisan

view of these matters. The history of our country shows that men of all parties have sought for and obtained special grants and privileges. Our aim is to direct the attention of the reader to some of the facts connected with, and resulting from, special legislation on the above named subjects, and show their effect upon the people generally.

The assertion that the government is now committed to the policy of donating the public lands to railroad corporations may be thought untrue, yet if we look through the acts of congress for the last few years we will find that more than two hundred million acres have been donated to such corporations, and from the number of bills asking for further grants introduced during the last congress these donations have but just begun. It will not be claimed that the people asked for these grants, or that the necessities of the government demanded them. Nor will it be contended that the people derive any direct benefit from them. On the contrary, the lands and the roads are owned and controlled by private corporations, and not even the government can use these roads for purposes of transportation without compensation. Now, these lands do not belong to the government, but to the people. Those persons filling the different departments of government are but the agents or servants of the people, and have no more right to give the public lands to railroad corporations than to tax the people and donate the money received as taxes to these companies. The policy is bad and oppressive in its effects. If one owns lands and employs an agent to sell it at a given price per acre, this agent has no right to convey one-half of it to himself and friends, and mark up the remaining half to a double price, and leave it on the owner's hands. This is what congress has done with the public lands, and in every instance the grants or donations have been made to aid monopolies, corporations, and powerful companies, who disregard the interests of the public, and use their power and these immense gifts for the purpose of securing further grants by corrupting legislators, judges, and executive officers. If we scale their efforts at corruption by their apparent success, they have not always failed. The interests of these monopolies are adverse to those of the people. The privileges granted them are taken from the people. The wealth of the nation, held by the government in trust for the people, has been and is now being misapplied by the people's trustees, and given to these anti-republican monopolies, and unless something is done to arrest this species of dishonest and unconstitutional legislation, it is only a question of time, and that time not distant, when this government, called republican, will deny to the common people those *unalienable rights* guaranteed to them by the constitution. How is it now? Discriminations are made against the public in favor of these monopolies in payment of taxes, in special legislation for their benefit, and the aid and protection afforded them by the courts.

Corporations and joint stock companies should have such legislation and judicial aid afforded them as is necessary to give them a legal being, and place them on an equal plane with individuals, and no more. All privileges, immunities, and favors granted to them, beyond such as are necessary for the above enumerated purposes, are in conflict with the spirit and genius of our government. The granting of exclusive privileges to individuals or companies tends to build up an aristocracy of wealth, to array capital against labor, and to divide the people into classes. While we have no titled aristocracy in this country, under the fostering care of the government an aristocracy of wealth has sprung up among us more despotic in its nature than exists in the old world. It holds in its grasp the labor of the country; it compels the whole people to pay tribute to it; it is constantly asking, claiming, and receiving additional strength at the expense of the people. So great has its power become throughout the country as to alarm all who have considered the subject. For the purpose of self-protection, the laboring community throughout the country are banding together to resist this monopoly. The Patrons of Husbandry are moving in the same direction, all feeling assured that no time must be lost, and that the welfare of the country, the perpetuity of our free institutions, and the privilege of owning and enjoying the fruits of thrift and labor, without giving at least one-half of them to support these monopolies, demand prompt, united, and efficient action.

We propose discussing the different matter referred to in the following order :—

I. Donations of land and government subsidies, and their effect upon the people and the country.

II. The oppressions practiced, and unjust discriminations made by railroad companies in the transportation, shipping, and storage of freights.

III. The unjust system of taxation and discrimination made by legislatures and congress in favor of railroad companies.

IV. The financial policy of the government, and the aid afforded by it to corporations and monopolies.

V. The tendency of the courts of the country to uphold special or class legislation in favor of monopolies and corporations, at the sacrifice of the interests and rights of the people.

VI. The banking system of the country with its useless burdens imposed upon the public.

VII. The policy of protective tariff, and its effect upon the people and the interests of the country.

VIII. The evils incident to the patent laws of the country.

IX. The author will present his views respecting the means to be used for redressing the grievances considered by him.

In treating of these different subjects, it will be our design to cite and quote such acts of congress, of the state legislatures, and decisions of the courts as will sustain the views presented, in order that the reader may fully understand how these giant monopolies are in fact aided and supported by the government; and we shall try to demonstrate that the only way to arrest and correct these evils is by united and persistent action on the part of the industrial and farming communities, and that the remedy for all improper legislation for, and governmental aid to, these monopolies is in the hands and under the control of the people.

CHAPTER I.

A PRELIMINARY SURVEY.

NOTHING in this country has contributed so much to the subversion of our republican institutions as Land Grants, made by congress to railroad corporations, and congressional legislation in their favor. The policy has opened a wide field for reckless speculation and corrupt legislation. It has reversed the old rule, that "the people are sovereign," and has given to "the favored few" the absolute control of the nation. The reckless giving of lands to railroad corporations, by congress, is without excuse, or even apology. When grants were first made to states, it was pretended that railroads could not be built without this aid. Subsequent developments exploded this idea. Take Iowa as an example: In 1856 four leading railroads crossing the state from east to west, received grants of lands sufficient to pay at least one-half of the entire cost of their construction across the state, yet they were not built until long years after the grants were made, nor were they constructed as rapidly as roads built exclusively by private enterprise and private capital. The effect of the grants was to retard the settlement and development of the wealth and resources of the state, by demanding from those who wished to settle upon the lands so granted, an extortionate, or at least a greatly appreciated price therefor. It does not require a great stretch of the imagination to arrive at the conclusion that but for these grants the population and wealth of Iowa (the taxable wealth) would be quite one-fourth greater now. The grant of lands to certain railroad companies in Iowa reach eight thousand acres per mile; this, at $1.25 per acre, amounts to $10,000 per mile; much more than one-half of the actual entire cost of their construction. Yet, as a matter-of-fact, some, if not all, of them became insolvent, and either before, or soon after their completion, their roads were sold to other parties — the original companies becoming bankrupt. But while the companies became bankrupt, the officers and few stockholders who controlled the corporation retired with immense wealth. These are the men who, at the inception of the land grant system of building railroads, inaugurated the theory which has since been practiced, that all lands thus granted were to be treated as donations to the men who controlled the roads receiving the grants. The result has been demoralizing. It has opened a field to adventurers, stock jobbers, and unscrupulous men, who have gone to the national capital and organized themselves into squads, rings, and companies, for the purpose of robbing the people. Not unfrequently the men elected by the people to look after their interests in congress, have themselves become leaders and partners in these raids upon the public treasurer; and so powerful are these organizations that all the departments of government have yielded to them, and the rule, with but few exceptions, is, to plunder the treasury upon all occasions, and for every conceivable object. But as these matters will be treated in detail in the following pages, we dismiss them for the present.

The rule has been, with few exceptions, in granting lands, to provide that the railroad company shall select alternate sections; that the residue shall be for sale at $2.50 per acre; that it shall not be subject to settlement under the pre-emption or homestead law. By these provisions, those persons who enter the remaining alternate sections, pay back to government the value of the lands donated to the railroad company. This plan of aiding monopolies is at variance with every principal of right and justice. The people themselves are the governing power. They are the government. Those who fill the various offices are not rulers, but agents and servants of the people. The public lands are the property of the people, and these agents or servants representing them in congress have no more right to give these lands to corporations than to vote a part of each citizen's private fortune to the same corporations.

When, in addition to these grants, embracing territory eight or ten times larger than the state of Iowa, large subsidies of money are also voted to accompany the lands, the people should become alarmed, and, if possible, arrest such abuses.

Every acre of land given to railroad companies is a direct robbery of the people, and the fact that whenever a grant is made the people are required to make good the amount taken from them by paying a double price for the moiety that is left to them, but adds insult to injury. The citizen who wishes to live upon and improve his quarter section, instead of claiming it as a homestead, or even purchasing it at the government price of $1.25 per acre, must pay $2.50 per acre before he will be permitted to occupy it. Nor is this all; he must be taxed to pay the interest on the subsidy bonds issued to the same companies that have received the grants of land, and all the benefit he derives from these unjust burdens imposed upon him, is the privilege of traveling upon railroads, or of shipping his produce over them, after he has paid to their officers whatever sum they choose to demand for the privilege.

To show more fully the extent to which the people are being plundered under the plea of assisting railroads in their efforts to develop the country, we desire to direct the reader's attention to some of the acts of congress covering "railroad legislation." Let us, for an example, take the Union and Central Pacific railroad, beginning at Council Bluffs and terminating at San Francisco. The charter for this road was granted in 1862, at a time when the country was at war; when it would be natural to presume that the government had no surplus capital, and when reason and common prudence demanded strict integrity and rigid economy in every department. In chartering the company, all idea of economy, integrity, or even *common honesty* seems to have been abandoned. The demand for the road as a national necessity in time of war, for direct communication between the Atlantic and Pacific States, and the immense cost of the road, with its great length, were the arguments used in favor of liberal aid. All these reasons were plausible — perhaps valid. They were seized upon, and the action of congress besought in the premises by a ring that was formed for the purpose of making immense fortunes out of the enterprise. A noticeable feature in the matter is, that members of congress, in the senate and house, as soon as the act was passed granting the charter became large stockholders and managers in the corporations. The aid granted by congress to this company was sufficient, if honestly applied, to construct a double track road the entire distance, and leave a large margin for distribution among the stockholders. The act of congress granting the charter, with subsequent amendments, opened a wide field for plunder, and the way the corporators availed themselves of their opportunity shows that they had determined to plunder the people of the last available dollar. A reference to this act and amendments, as published by congress, will fully sustain all we have asserted. Selecting the charter of this road as an apt illustration of all others receiving aid from the government, we ask the reader's attention to some of its more remarkable features.

CHAPTER II.

THE PACIFIC RAILROAD INIQUITY.

ON the first day of July, A. D. 1862, the charter of the Union Pacific railroad was passed. It contains, among others, the following provisions, to-wit:

"SECTION 2. That the right of way through the public lands be, and the same is hereby, granted to said company for the construction of said railroad and telegraph line, and the right, power and authority, are hereby given to said company to take from the public lands adjacent to the line of said road, earth, stone, timber, and other materials, for the construction thereof. Said right of way is granted to said railroad to the extent of two hundred feet in width on each side of said railroad, where it may pass over the public lands, including all necessary grounds for stations, buildings, workshops, and depots, machine shops, switches, side tracks, turn-tables, and water stations."

The right of way was reduced to one hundred feet for each side of the railroad, by act of congress of July 2, 1864, and the right to take material for the construction of the road was limited to ten miles on each side thereof, by the same act. By this section the company is allowed to take from the public lands all the material needed in the construction of the road; to strip the lands and leave them naked for the people. The real value of the lands is given to the company; the refuse left for the American people.

A part of the third section reads as follows:

"That there be, and is hereby, granted to the said company, for the purpose of aiding in the construction of said railroad and telegraph line, and to secure the safe and speedy transportation of the mails, troops, munitions of war, and public stores thereon, every alternate section of land, designated by odd numbers, to the amount of five alternate sections per mile, on each side of said road, on the line thereof, and within the limits of ten miles on each side of said road, not sold, reserved, or otherwise disposed of, by the United States, and to which a pre-emption or homestead lien may not have attached at the time the line of said road is definitely fixed. Provided, that all mineral lands shall be exempted from the operation of this act; but when it shall contain timber, the timber is hereby granted to said company."

By the act of congress, of July 2, 1864, this act was so amended as to grant ten alternate sections on each side of the road, and to grant to the company the iron and coal found within ten miles of the road. The reader will notice the reasons given for this grant. 1st. To aid in the construction of the road; a legitimate reason. 2d. *To secure the safe and speedy transportation of the mail, troops, munitions of war*, etc. Twenty sections of land per mile are given to the company for the purpose of securing the safe and speedy transportation of troops, and above enumerated articles. It has been said that a poor reason is better than no reason. Of all poor reasons given for an act, this appears to be one of the weakest. The reader will not be able to discover its force. As we progress, we will find that from its inception this Pacific railroad charter, and amendments, were "conceived in sin, and brought forth in iniquity;" that, in its provisions and grants, it presents a state of facts which stamps the whole scheme as a base fraud upon the public, planned by men who were seeking to enrich themselves at the expense of their country; and that congress, either from inattention to the interests of the people, or because the spoils were to be divided, granted the company the precise charter that was to enable it to plunder the public without hindrance.

That we may not be regarded as treating the subject captiously, let us concede that the reason given was a good one, and that the grant of lands would give security to the transportations of the mails; still the thought presents itself that a grant of lands to the value of $15,500 per mile would be ample aid for the people to give this company, in the construction of its road. It is not a government work, owned by the public, operated and controlled by the government. It is a private enterprise, and while all persons see the necessity of a railroad connection between the Atlantic and Pacific States, but few will indorse the policy of the government giving to this private company more aid in lands and money than the entire cost of the road, or more than it would have cost if built by private capital. And when it is found that this large grant is made without any equivalent, that not even the mails, troops, or munitions of war, can be transported over the road without the payment of just such rates as this private corporation chooses to charge, the conclusion is inevitable that the good, not of the public, but of the corporation, was the controlling motive in affording it aid: that the untold millions of subsidy bonds, and vast tracts of lands wrongfully taken from the public, and given to this company, was but placing the interests of the whole people, in their social and business intercourse across the continent, at the mercy of a soulless corporation.

The donations we have already noticed are the "right of way;" the right to take all building material within ten miles of the road, and the grant of twenty sections of land per mile. But this is not all. Section five of the act provides: "That for the purposes herein mentioned, the secretary of the treasury shall, upon the certificate in writing, of said commissioners, of the completion and equipment of forty consecutive miles of said railroad and telegraph line, in accordance with the provisions of this act, issue to said company bonds of the United States of one thousand dollars each, payable in thirty years after date, bearing six per centum per annum interest (said interest payable semi-annually) which interest may be paid in United States treasury notes, or in any other money or currency which the United States have, or shall, declare lawful money, and legal tender, to the amount of sixteen of said bonds per mile; and to secure the repayment to the United States, as hereinafter provided, of the amount of said bonds so issued and delivered to said company, together with all interest thereon which shall have been paid by the United States, the issue of said bonds and delivery to the company shall *ipse facto* constitute a first mortgage on the whole line of the railroad and telegraph, together with the rolling stock, fixtures, and property of every kind and description, and in consideration of which said bonds may have been issued." As we shall hereafter see, this section was amended by act of July 2d, 1864, so as to allow the company to issue its own bonds to the same amount per mile issued by the government, and to subrogate the government bonds to those issued by the company, thus making the bonds issued by the company the first mortgage bonds.

Section six provides for the transmission of messages by telegraph, and the transportation of the mails, troops, munitions of war, supplies, and public stores of the government, giving it the preference at all times, "at fair and reasonable rates of compensation, and not to exceed the amount paid by private parties for the same kind of service."

Section eleven reads as follows:

"That for three hundred miles of said road, most mountainous and difficult of construction, to wit: One hundred and fifty miles westwardly from the eastern base of the Rocky mountains, and one hundred and fifty miles eastwardly from the western base of the Sierra Nevada mountains, said points to be fixed by the president of the United States, the bonds to be issued in aid of the construction thereof shall treble the number per mile hereinbefore provided, and the same shall be issued, and the lands herein granted be set apart, upon the construction of every twenty miles thereof, upon certificate of the commissioners as aforesaid, that twenty consecutive miles of the same are completed; and between the sections last named, of one hundred and fifty miles each, the bonds to be issued to aid in the construction thereof shall be double the number per mile first mentioned, and the same shall be issued, and the lands herein granted be set apart, upon the construction of every twenty miles thereof, upon the certificate of the commissioners as aforesaid, that twenty consecutive miles of the same are completed; provided that no more than fifty thousand of said bonds shall be issued under this act to aid in constructing the main line of said railroad and telegraph."

This vast amount of bonds was issued to the main line of the road, which, as will be seen by an examination of the first section of the act, terminates at the western boundary of Nevada territory. This company, under its charter, gets $50,000,000 in bonds; its charter does not authorize it to construct the whole road to the Pacific, but to the western boundary of Nevada, where it meets the Central Pacific railroad, built by a company chartered by the legislature of California. Fifty millions in bonds, with the privilege of subrogating the security for their payment to a like amount issued by the company as first mortgage bonds on the road, with the grant of lands above named, the right of way, and the right to all building material within ten miles of the line of the road; this is deemed a fair provision for one company. In order that no charge of selfishness, or want of charity should be brought against congress, it next turned its attention to other companies. Perhaps it was thought promotive of the interest of this corporate power, now controlling the government, that there should be unity of action and purpose; that its strength should be so great, and its ramifications so extensive, that neither private persons nor the public would dare to resist its demands. The necessity for a railroad from the Atlantic to the Pacific states was not the only consideration influencing the law-making power of the country. This fact is clearly apparent from the provisions of the charter, for numerous branch or spike roads are included in the charter, and provided for in the land grants and subsidy bonds.

Let us look at the "Central Pacific railroad company," of California. This company received its charter from that state, was duly organized, and as we are informed, was at work on its road when the charter was granted by congress to the "Union Pacific." But congress, not to show partiality, in the ninth section of the charter of the Union Pacific, provides for the Central Pacific as follows:

"The Central Pacific railroad company, of California, a corporation existing under the laws of California, is hereby authorized to construct a railroad and telegraph line from the Pacific coast, at or near San Francisco, or the navigable waters of the Sacramento river, to the eastern boundary of California, upon the same terms and conditions, in all respects, as are contained in this act for the construction of said railroad and telegraph line first mentioned, and to meet and connect with the first mentioned railroad and telegraph line on the eastern boundary of California."

Here is a company building its road exclusively in a single state, under a charter derived from a state having the exclusive control of its own affairs, and not subject to the legislation of congress, or the administration of the general government, like the territories; yet congress, that it may aid a great monopoly, assumes control of the matter, reaches out its hand laden with the people's land, and the people's money, and says to this California company: "If you will unite with and become a part of this giant monopoly we are creating to crush the people, and will accept the provisions of this act and render fealty to the general government as the 'higher power,' we will give you twenty sections of land, and subsidy bonds to the amount of sixteen thousand dollars per mile, with the privilege of issuing your own first mortgage bonds for an additional sixteen thousand dollars per mile for every mile of road you build in the state of California." Of course this California company accepts this tempting offer, and in addition to the fifty thousand of subsidy bonds for sixteen thousand dollars each to the Union Pacific, an additional sixteen thousand dollars per mile is issued to the Central Pacific, all of which, as we will show, principal and interest, will in the end come out of the pockets of the people. The uniting of these two companies, and the completion of their roads and telegraph lines, afforded to the country and the government (provided in all cases they paid to the companies the amounts they charged therefor) a road for the purpose of travel, and transportation of freights, and secured a "*safe and speedy transportation of the mails, troops, munitions of war, and public stores thereon,*" and if the construction of the road was aided for that purpose, it would seem to have been accomplished, and as a matter of justice to the public, no further burdens should have been imposed upon the public. Two companies had been provided for at the people's expense, and all that was demanded for the prosecution of the public business had been effected. But there was danger that other through lines of railroad might be constructed across the territories that might become rivals of this giant monopoly. The Hannibal & St. Joseph railroad company were across the state of Missouri, looking to the west. The Leavenworth, Pawnee, & Western company were preparing for action. A road was crossing Minnesota and Iowa to strike the Missouri river at Sioux City. Any or all of these roads might become rivals. To prevent such a catastrophe, and to retain for all time to come an absolute and exclusive monopoly, these companies must be absorbed, or at least rendered harmless. To assist this scheme, congress is called upon for further aid from the public lands and treasury. The response is all that could be desired. It gave the final blow to competition, and left the people powerless in the grasp of this, the greatest monopoly in the country. A monopoly created by the servants of the people, and enriched with spoils taken from the people, in violation of every principle of right and justice, had been created by act of congress, and to insure it the absolute control of the country, anything promising competition must be absorbed. To accomplish this object the same act, section nine, provides: "That the Leavenworth, Pawnee, & Western railroad company of Kansas, is hereby authorized to construct a railroad and telegraph from the Missouri river, at the mouth of the Kansas river, on the south side, so as to connect with the Pacific railroad of Missouri to the aforesaid point, on the one hundredth meridian of longitude west from Greenwich, as herein provided, upon the same terms and conditions in all respects as are provided in this act for the construction of the railroad and telegraph line first mentioned, and to meet and connect with the same at the meridian of longitude aforesaid; and in case the general line or route of the road from the Missouri river to the Rocky mountains should be so located as to require a departure northwardly from the proposed line of said Kansas railroad before it reaches the meridian of longitude aforesaid, the location of said Kansas road shall be made so as to conform thereto; and said railroad through Kansas shall be so located between the mouth of Kansas river as aforesaid, and the aforesaid point, on the hundredth degree of longitude, that the several railroads from Missouri and Iowa herein authorized to connect with the same can make connections within the limits prescribed by this act, provided the same can be done without deviating from the general direction of the whole line to the Pacific coast."

It will be seen that one of the rival lines is given a premium of lands and bonds to intersect with the Union Pacific near the east end thereof; it becomes, for a consideration, a part of this great monopoly, and abandons all idea of competition.

Section ten provides for a union or consolidation of the Union Pacific, the Central Pacific, the Leavenworth, Pawnee & Western, and the Hannibal & St. Joseph companies; and section thirteen provides: "That the Hannibal & St. Joseph railroad company, of Missouri, may extend its road from St. Joseph, via Atchison, to connect and unite with the road through Kansas, upon filing its assent to the provisions of this act, upon the same terms and conditions in all respects, for one hundred miles in length next to the Missouri river, as are provided in this act for the construction of the railroad and telegraph line first mentioned, and may for this purpose use any railroad charter which has been or may be granted by the legislature of Kansas." The section also provides for connecting this road with the main line. This company promised to be a rival, but when congress is appealed to, $1,600,000 in subsidy bonds, and two thousand sections of land are given it as its share of the spoils, provided it will accept this trifle as an inducement to combine its interest with this great corporation. This disposes of all rivals south of Omaha. True the people have paid dearly for it. They, through their servants in congress, have enriched a lot of unscrupulous men, banded together for the purpose of plundering the public, and given to these corporations the power to oppress the people for all time to come; but as it affords a safe means of transporting the mails, etc., for a consideration which the people must pay as the services are rendered, the public should not complain.

Congress thought the matter so important as to require the gift of vast sums of the public moneys, and princely donations out of the public domain, and as our legislators acted for the people, and the companies have built their roads; the public must submit.

But there was danger that the roads crossing Iowa and Minnesota might compete with the Union Pacific. Sioux City was an objective point on the Missouri river. West of that city, across the then territory of Nebraska, a road could be constructed at comparatively small cost. This line might become a rival, and it also must be absorbed. To effect this object, the following provision was made a part of the fourteenth section of this act: "And whenever there shall be a line of railroad completed through Minnesota or Iowa to Sioux City, then the said Pacific railroad company is hereby authorized and required to construct a railroad and telegraph line from said Sioux City, upon the most direct and practicable route, to a point on, and so as to connect with, the branch railroad and telegraph line in this section hereinbefore mentioned, or with the said Union Pacific railroad, said point of junction to be fixed by the president of the United States, not farther west than the one-hundredth meridian of longitude aforesaid, and on the same terms and conditions as provided in this act for the construction of the Union Pacific railroad, as aforesaid, to complete the same at the rate of one hundred miles per year." The amendment made to this part of the act in 1864, to which we shall refer in another chapter, materially changes its provisions; and as we examine these provisions, we will discover that all the unjust donations made of the public lands and moneys are exceeded in this amendment.

Now, if the reader will take a map on which the railroads are marked, he will discover that from Leavenworth to Sioux City all the railroads running west are concentrated into one line, after leaving the one-hundredth degree of longitude—the Burlington & Missouri railroad company being made by the act of 1864 a part of the same great monopoly. By the exclusive franchises and imperial wealth conferred upon it by congress, this great corporation is given control, absolute control of the business interests of the great west. This grand system of railroads looks well on the map, and lends color to the plea that the wants of the public and of the government justified this large outlay of money and lands; but an inspection of the act chartering the companies, consolidating them, and by law giving them unlimited control of the interests of the public, will convince the impartial reader that the interests of the companies, rather than the needs of the government, or the welfare of the people, controlled the action of congress.

Grants of lands and exclusive privileges have been made to other corporations, as also to states, for the purpose of aiding in the construction of railroads; but our aim being to combat the policy itself, as involving gross injustice and oppression, and to show its effects upon the public, we have selected the Union Pacific and its branches as the best illustration of the action of congress in making these grants, and the companies owning this road and its branches as a fair sample of the class of professed benefactors of the people.

CHAPTER III.

THE MONOPOLISTS "HELP THEMSELVES."

THE Pacific companies are such a deep mine of iniquity, we must sink our shaft somewhat deeper if we would see the true quality of the corruption. In order to fully comprehend the injustice done to the people, it will be necessary to examine the further legislation of congress in their favor.

A perusal of the act from which we have quoted will convince the reader that these companies received all that was necessary for the successful completion and operation of their road, and its numerous branches, and to enable them to extort from the government and the people all that the most grasping and avaricious could desire. But, like Oliver Twist, they still asked "for more," and they got it; not in more lands and money, but in being relieved, by act of congress, from the restrictions and duties imposed upon them by their charter.

The act of congress chartering the Union Pacific railroad, and its numerous branches, was amended by the act of July 2, 1864, in many particulars, to some of which we have already referred. The fourth section amends the third section of the original charter by increasing the number of sections of land granted per mile to said road, from ten to twenty, and allowing the selection of the lands to be made within twenty miles of the line of road, instead of ten, as provided in the original charter; and also provides that the secretary of the interior shall withdraw from sale and pre-emption all the land within twenty-five miles of the line of the road, until the company has selected its twenty sections. The original charter limited the withdrawal to fifteen miles. The amendment also qualified the term "mineral lands," contained in the original act, so as to except from the lands reserved by the government all coal and iron lands; thus enabling the company to select coal and iron lands to the full amout of twenty sections per mile, giving to said railroad company, or companies, a monopoly of the coal trade in a country where coal is, and will continue to be, the greatest desideratum; and the same section gives the company the right to use, in fact grants to the company, all the timber found on each side of the road within ten miles thereof. The company can, under its charter, take all the timber from the land it does not select, and then take its twenty sections in coal lands, when they can be found. This it has done, and in addition, bought of the government other large tracts of coal land; not in the name of the company, perhaps, but in the name of the individual stockholders. By this means, all who settle along the line, in the vicinity of this Union Pacific road, are placed in the power of this great corporation, and must pay for its fuel and transportation whatever sum may be demanded, because the charter does not restrict the company in the matter of charges for transportation.

Section seventeen of the original charter provided that twenty-five per centum of the subsidy bonds should be retained by the government until the entire line of the road was completed. Section seven, of the act of July 2, 1864, repealed this provision.

Other amendments are made for the benefit of the corporation, as to time and manner of payment; but as it is not our intention to examine all of its provisions in detail, we pass to the tenth section.

By the original charter, the subsidy bonds issued to the company were to be and remain first mortgage bonds upon the road and property of the company, the company paying six per cent. interest (payable semi-annually) on said bonds, and the principal in thirty years. The tenth section of the amendment reads as follows :

" That section five of said act be so modified and amended that the Union Pacific railroad company, the Central Pacific railroad company, and any other companies authorized to participate in the construction of said road, may, on the completion of each section of said road, as provided in this act, and the act to which this act is an amendment, issue their first mortgage bonds on their respective railroad and telegraph lines, to an amount not exceeding the bonds of the United States, and of even tenor, time of maturity, rate and character of interest, with the bonds authorized to be issued to said railroad companies, respectively. And the lien of the United States bonds shall be subordinate to that of the bonds of any or either of said companies, hereby authorized to be issued on their respective roads, property, and equipments, except as to the sixth section of said act, to which this is an amendment, relating to the transmission of dispatches, and the transportation of mails, troops, munitions of war, supplies, and public stores for the United States."

By this amendment, the public money appropriated to private corporations, to the amount of about $65,000,000, for which security had been taken, on all the property of the companies, was left in the hands of the companies without any security; or, in other words, the servants of the people made an absolute gift of this great sum of money. The history of the country, in connection with railroad corporations, demonstrates the fact that these corporations by "watering" their stock, and characteristic management, show, if they so desire it, no margin from the business of their roads. They permit the interest on their bonds to accumulate, until a foreclosure and sale on first mortgage bonds are necessary, and then, under a new name, but with the same persons as stockholders, the road is bought in and becomes profitable. In this case the amount of $65,000,000, and the accrued interest must be first paid, or the property of the corporation must be sold, and the public money advanced by the govenment will be lost. Even at the present time (as we shall show hereafter) the people are paying the interest on these subsidy bonds, and the only security they have for its repayment is the *honor* of the company; for all precedents prove that as a rule second mortgage bonds, when a large sum of first mortgage bonds is to be paid, are of no real value.

Sections fifteen and sixteen provide for a division of earnings, and a consolidation of the various companies. Sections eighteen, nineteen and twenty, provide for the admission of the Burlington and Missouri river railroad company as a branch of the Union Pacific, with a grant of land in Nebraska. But the greatest outrage upon the rights and interests of the people in this Pacific railroad law, will be found in the seventeenth section of this amendment. By the original act, the Union Pacific company was required to construct a branch road from Sioux City (on the most direct and practicable route) to some point on its road to be fixed by the President of the United States (but not beyond the one-hundredth parallel) when a railroad should be constructed through Minnesota or Iowa to Sioux City. This new road was to unite with and form a part of the great monopoly, and was to receive the same amount of lands, and subsidy bonds, per mile, as the main line received. The building of this road from Sioux City west, to a proper point of connection with the main line, would have cost but little, comparatively, because of the favorable character of the country through which it would pass.

For some reason, unknown to the public, it was decided to make a change in respect to this branch, not only as to its location, but also as to the company whose *duty* it should be to build it. To effect this object, this seventeenth section contains the following provisions:

"That so much of section fourteen of said act as relates to a branch from Sioux City, be, and the same is hereby, amended so as to read as follows: That whenever a line of railroad shall be completed through the State of Iowa or Minnesota, to Sioux City, such company now organized, or as may be hereafter organized, under the laws of Iowa, Minnesota, Dakota, or Nebraska, as the President of the United States, by its request, may designate, or approve for the purpose, shall construct and operate a line of railroad and telegraph from Sioux City, upon the most direct and practicable route to such point on, and so as to connect with, the Iowa branch of the Union Pacific railroad as such company may select, and on the same terms and conditions as are provided in this act, and the act to which this is an amendment, for the construction of said Union Pacific railroad and telegraph line, and branches; and said company shall complete the same at the rate of fifty miles per year. Provided, that said Union Pacific railroad company shall be, and is hereby, released from the construction of said branch. And said company constructing said branch shall not be entitled to receive in bonds, an amount larger than the said Union Pacific railroad company would be entitled to receive if it had constructed the branch under this act, and the act to which this is an amendment; but said company shall be entitled to receive alternate sections of land for ten miles in width on each side of the same, along the whole length of said branch; and provided further, that if a railroad shall not be completed to Sioux City, across Iowa or Minnesota, within eighteen months from the date of this act, then said company designated by the President as aforesaid, may commence and complete the construction of said branch, as contemplated by the provisions of this act. Provided, however, that if the company so designated by the President as aforesaid, shall not complete the said branch from Sioux City to the Pacific railroad within ten years from the passage of this act, then, and in that case, all of the railroad that shall have been constructed by said company, shall be forfeited to, and become the property of, the United States."

Now if the reader will take a late map, having the lines of railroads upon it, he will discover that a road from Sioux City to Columbus in Nebraska, would be about one hundred miles in length, on a line running nearly west; and at this latter point it would intersect and unite with the Iowa branch of the Union Pacific; or a line running southwest for a less distance would unite with the Union Pacific at Fremont, in Nebraska. In the original charter it was contemplated to occupy one of these lines, and, in fact, a branch road was commenced from Sioux City to Fremont. The directors of this branch, and the Union Pacific are in part the same, to-wit: Oakes Ames, of Boston, and G. M. Dodge, of Iowa. It would seem that this road, running southwest to Fremont, and there uniting with the Pacific, would afford all necessary facilities for securing the transportation of the mails, troops, etc., and that upon no pretext whatever could another grant of land and subsidy bonds be asked. Yet congress thought otherwise, and in the section last quoted, authorized any company organized under the laws of Iowa, Minnesota, Dakota, or Nebraska, that might be designated by the President of the United States, on application to him for that purpose, to construct a railroad to unite with the Union Pacific, leaving it with the new company to fix the point at which it would so unite, but requiring it to commence at Sioux City. Taking advantage of this act, two companies, the Sioux City & Missouri Valley, and the Chicago & Northwestern, constructed a line of road from Sioux City to Council Bluffs, there to unite with the Pacific; the Sioux City & Missouri Valley constructing the road from Sioux City to Missouri Valley, and the Chicago & Northwestern from Missouri Valley to Council Bluffs. This line of road was constructed ostensibly as a part of the Pacific road. It is presumed to run west. Look at the map and you will see that from Sioux City to Council Bluffs, instead of going west, it runs on a line east of south, to the extent of thirty miles, Council Bluffs being thirty miles east of Sioux City. The company constructing this last named road received from the government a grant of one hundred sections of land per each mile, and $16,000 in subsidy bonds for each mile of road. This road runs along the east side of the Missouri river, and in truth, is of no use as a route for the transportation of mails, troops, etc., unless the government prefers to use the longest, least expeditious, and most expensive line of road. Indeed, it seems to be a road that is under the especial care and protection of congress. It is called in the *Railroad Manual*, "The Sioux City & Pacific Railroad." It was a "nice and fat" job. It has one feature not often found in these railroad jobs carried through congress. It appears to have been gotten up for the benefit of congressmen. After repeated efforts to learn who were the incorporators of this company, we addressed a letter to the secretary of state of Iowa, and received the following answer:

DES MOINES, December 7, 1872.

DEAR SIR:—In answer to yours of the 6th inst., I will say that there is no line of railroad from Sioux City to Council Bluffs, run as one road or by one company. The Sioux City

& Pacific railroad runs from Sioux City to Missouri Valley, and the Chicago & Northwestern (Cedar Rapids & Missouri River) from Missouri Valley to Council Bluffs. The incorporators of the Sioux City & Pacific company were L. B. Crocker, M. K. Jessup, James F. Wilson, A. W. Hubbard, Chas. A. Lombard, Frank Schuchardt, W. B. Allison, and John I. Blair.

Yours Truly, ED. WRIGHT,
Secretary of State

Among the present directors, are to be found the names of Oakes Ames, John I. Blair, D. C. Blair, and G. M. Dodge. Ames was a member of the late congress, and G. M. Dodge is an ex-member. Among the directors of the Cedar Rapids & Missouri River company appear the names of John B. Alley and James F. Wilson, who were members of congress when the act of July, 1864, was passed, amending the charter of the Union Pacific, and making the large grants to the company designated by the president to build the Sioux City branch of the Union Pacific railroad. William B. Allison has been a member of congress almost continuously from 1860 to the present time.

This Sioux City branch seems to have been a special favorite with certain congressmen. It received the lion's share of lands, getting five times as many sections per mile as the main lines, and this, too, for the purpose of building a railroad running east of south, instead of west—the direction of the main line—following the course of the Missouri river on the east side thereof for the entire length of this branch, and crossing on the bridge to the Nebraska shore at Omaha.

In addition to the road from Sioux City to Omaha, and for the purpose of getting all the land and money possible out of the government, the conspirators organized another company, under the laws of Nebraska, to wit: The Fremont, Elkhorn & Missouri Valley company, and built a road running from Missouri Valley to Fremont in Nebraska—about fifty miles—and these two roads, from Sioux City to Missouri Valley, and from Missouri Valley to Fremont, are now called the Sioux City & Pacific. We do not know who were the incorporators of the Fremont, Elkhorn & Missouri Valley company, but we find among the present directors, John I. Blair, D. C. Blair, and ex-congressman John B. Alley. The two companies are consolidated. The grant of one hundred sections of land, and bonds to the amount of $16,000 per mile, with the privilege of issuing first mortgage bonds to the amount of $16,000 per mile, altogether comprise one of the most remunerative jobs ever conceived and consummated by incorporating, stockholding, and "direct"-ing congressmen in the companies receiving the aid. When it is remembered that the actual cost of the construction of the road was less than $30,000 per mile (as shown by the *Railroad Manual*), and that it is of no value to the government because of its course, save for carrying local mails (its entire earnings for government transportation being less than $1,000 per annum), it will not be uncharitable to conclude that this *fat* little slice of the Pacific railroad job was put through congress, and nursed and petted by government for the exclusive benefit of congressmen, their friends and relatives.

We do not deny the right to congressmen to become and remain stockholders and directors in railroad corporations, but we do deny their right to vote lands and money to companies in which they are stockholders and directors. They are elected to represent the people, to attend to and protect the public interests. When they form themselves into companies and vote the lands and moneys of the people to themselves, they violate their trust, and instead of protecting the people, plunder them, and divide the spoils. To give these unjust practices some color of right, or in some manner to excuse themselves for thus appropriating the wealth of the country and dividing it with their friends, they assert in the laws thus enacted that it is done to aid in the construction of railroads, and "to secure the safe and speedy transmission of the mails, troops, munitions of war, and government supplies," etc. It is no part of the duties of congressmen to construct railroads, nor are the people under obligations to furnish them the means for that purpose. When members of congress form themselves into private companies, and, to procure the means for prosecuting their private enterprises, agree to divide among themselves a part of the money and property belonging to the public, because the position they occupy enables them to do so, they manifest the same disregard for the rights of others, and the same disregard of law that is shown by the class of men who follow theft and robbery for a livelihood.

But let us follow still further the course of this Pacific railroad company. It would occupy too much space, and weary the reader were we to state in detail all the acts of congress passed in aid of this gigantic combination. In speaking of the Pacific railroad we are apt to look upon it as simply a line of road extending from the Missouri river to the Pacific ocean, to consider its great length, the character of the country through which it passes, the sparse settlements, the necessity for direct and speedy communication between the Atlantic and Pacific states, and we yield a ready assent to the action of congress in voting lands and subsidy bonds for its construction. But when we find that the charters of the Union Pacific and Central Pacific companies, and their various amendments, together with the several acts of congress making many other companies branches of the Pacific road, virtually consolidates all the railroads between the cities of St. Louis and St. Paul, on the Mississippi river, and all the railroads running west from Chicago, into one vast corporation, uniting all in one track from Fort Kearney to the Pacific ocean, the people will begin to realize that while they thought congress was appropriating lands and moneys solely for the purpose of opening a highway across the territories, it was in fact aiding a combination of men and corporations in their attempt to control the commerce of the great west; and when we further learn that this great railroad interest is already virtually consolidated, and that the whole people are placed at the mercy of this great monopoly, we see at a glance the extent of the power vested in it by act of congress.

Among the railroad companies that are included in this combination are the following: Chicago & Northwestern; Iowa Falls & Sioux City; Cedar Rapids & Missouri River; Leavenworth, Atchison & Northwestern; Kansas Pacific; Union Pacific; Burlington & Missouri River; Sioux City & Pacific; Missouri River; Chicago, Iowa & Nebraska; Hannibal & St. Joseph, and the St. Paul & Sioux City. Most of the above roads received grants of lands; some of them received subsidy bonds, ostensibly for the public benefit, but in reality for the purpose of combining in one the interests of all these combinations. Whatever may have been the intention of congress in granting exclusive privileges to these companies and permitting them to unite, the effect has been to fasten upon the great west a monopoly that for all time to come will be an instrument of oppression. With its vast power and wealth, it can but control the fortune of the laboring and producing classes inhabiting the richest portion of our common country. The further fact that this great corporate power is the particular pet of congressmen, and that among its directors and stockholders are members and ex-members of congress, render the hope of any change in favor of the people remote, if at all attainable. If the reader is desirous of learning who are the directors and managers of the Pacific railroad and branches, he has only to consult *Poor's Railroad Manual* for 1872–3. He will find among the present directors the men who, in congress, voted the lands and subsidies to the companies in which they are now directors, and also that some of these directors are now holding the offices of congressmen and of United States senators.

By the acts of congress granting and amending the charters of the Pacific railroad companies and branches, it is made the duty of the president of the United States to appoint five directors, "who shall be denominated directors on the part of the government," and these acts forbid such directors being stockholders in said Pacific railroad companies. It is made the duty of these government directors to exercise a general supervision of the Pacific road and branches, and to report its condition from time to time to the secretary of the interior. In contemplation of law they are to have no pecuniary interest in the companies or in the roads. The present government directors are B. F. Wade, of Ohio; Hiram Price and J. F. Wilson, of Iowa; J. C. S. Harrison, of Indiana; and D. S. Ruddock, of Connecticut. By act of congress of June 2d,

1864, the Cedar Rapids & Missouri River railroad was authorized to connect with the Iowa branch of the Union Pacific road, and sections fifteen and sixteen of the acts of July 2d, 1864, place all roads connecting with the Union Pacific on an equality as to charges for freights and passengers, and permits them to consolidate if they elect so to do. The Cedar Rapids & Missouri River company has leased its road to the Chicago & Northwestern company, and it is operated in connection with the Union Pacific, uniting with it at Council Bluffs, and it virtually becomes a branch of the Union Pacific road. The reader can look over the list of directors, as shown in the *Railroad Manual*, before referred to, and learn if any of the government directors of the Union Pacific are directors in the Cedar Rapids & Missouri River company. The reports made of the cost, condition, and other matters connected with Pacific railroad enterprises, disclose such utter disregard of the rights and interests of the people, and such a gross betrayal of the public good for the benefit of a ring (in part a congressional ring) as to leave it without precedent.

The fact that the men who formed this ring have become a powerful moneyed aristocracy, able by their votes and influence in congress to convert the public lands and money to their own use, and are now boldly taxing the people with the interest on the money appropriated to build up these oppressive monopolies, should arouse the country to a sense of its imminent peril.

CHAPTER IV.

HOW CONGRESS BETRAYED THE PEOPLE.

IN order to fully realize the great power of what is known as the Pacific railroad companies, it will be necessary to look at the Central Pacific company, and its control of the transportation of freights and passengers from the Pacific country. This company, organized under the laws of California, was, by act of congress of July 1st, 1862, admitted into the grand combination known as the Pacific roads, and granted equal privileges with the Union Pacific and branches. The Central Pacific extends from the Pacific ocean to Ogden, a distance of eight hundred and eighty-one miles. The acts of congress of April 4th, 1864, and July 2d, 1864, granted to this company additional privileges and powers, including the right of consolidating with all the companies on the Pacific coast. In 1870 the following companies, to-wit: The Western Pacific railroad company; the San Francisco, Oakland & Alameda railroad company; the San Joaquin railroad company; the California & Oregon railroad companies were consolidated.

The state of California at that date had but one thousand and thirteen miles of road within its borders. Of this number of miles, about one-half became a part of the Central Pacific, by the consolidation as above stated. All the roads pointing towards the east were combined in this one great corporation, forming a solid body, with one common and general object and interest, viz.: a monopoly of the travel and traffic with the eastern states. And congress, by appropriating lands and subsidy bonds, and granting exclusive rights and privileges to this monster monopoly, has given it the key not only to the overland commerce of the country, but also to the commerce of our country with other nations upon the Pacific coast. This giant monopoly, by the aid of congress, has obtained the absolute control of the best interests of the whole people for all time to come—a control that is now being used, and will continue to be used, to enrich its own members and stockholders by oppressive levies for transportation over its roads.

To fully comprehend the cost to the country of these munificent gifts by congress to the Union and Central Pacific corporations, let us examine the expense somewhat in detail.

First. A grant is made of all the material needed in the construction of the roads, found within ten miles of the line of said roads.

Second. A grant of thirty-five million acres of the public lands, amounting, at $1.25 per acre, to $43,750,000. This vast amount of land is taken from the people and given to companies by congressmen who in some instances are members of the companies, and receive their *pro rata* share of the grants.

Third. Aid voted by congress in shape of subsidy bonds, $65,000,000, payable in thirty years, with six per cent. per annum. The theory was that the companies would pay the interest as it matured (semi-annually) and eventually the principal. But that this was not the intent of the companies, nor of congress, is apparent from the different acts regulating the matter, and as the case stands, the government is actually paying the interest and collecting the amount from the people in tariffs and excise taxes. The payment of the amount of these bonds, with the interest according to their terms, will require about $200,000,000. This amount, or nearly all of it, will be paid by the people, and not by the companies. The report of the secretary of the treasury shows that the amount of interest annually due on these subsidy bonds is $3,875,000, of which the Pacific railroad companies have paid about $750,000, and the government the balance, say $3,125,000. The original charter of the companies provided that the charges for carrying done for the government should be credited to the companies in liquidation of these bonds, and also that five per cent. of the net earnings of the road should be applied to the same object. The secretary of the treasury of the United States insisted that these companies should be bound by this provision of their charters, refused to pay them their earnings for government services, and also demanded the five per cent. under the law. The companies refused to pay the five per cent. of their net nearings, and demanded pay for transportation. If we remember that congress had already so amended the charters of these companies as to permit them to issue $65,000,000 of their own bonds as "first mortgage bonds," and provided that the subsidy bonds obtained from government should be subordinate or junior to the bonds issued by the companies, and also bear in mind that these amendments also provided that whenever twenty miles of road was completed the patent for twenty sections of land per mile was to issue to the companies, so that when the roads were completed they would have title to all their lands, we will see good reason for the stand taken by the United States secretary of the treasury.

The security which the United States had for the payment of the principal and interest of the bonds, under the charter, was destroyed by subsequent legislation, and unless the secretary could retain the amounts due from government for transportation, and collect the five per cent., the whole amount of the subsidy bonds, would be lost to the government and the people. The facts of the case being well known to congress, who are supposed to be the representatives of the people, and to legislate in their interest and for their benefit, it would hardly be supposed that an act would pass both branches, and receive the approval of the president, compelling the secretary of the treasury to yield to the demands of these corporations. Honest legislation, and a decent regard for the public welfare, would seem to forbid any attempt on the part of any one of the departments of the government to aid the companies in their dishonest endeavor to avoid the provisions of a charter which had been enacted for their special benefit. And when it is remembered that at the time the application was made to congress (March, 1871,) certain members were stockholders and directors in these same companies, one would not think it possible that an act could be passed relieving the companies from these requirements of their charters, or only possible because of the practice being so long established for congressmen to appropriate public lands and moneys to their own use, that they had arrived at the point where they deemed the property and money of the government lawful plunder, and that their first duty was to provide for the rings and corporations in which they had a personal interest. It seems to have required some strategy for the friends of these corporations to grant them the aid they asked. Afraid to take issue with the secretary of the treasury, and unwilling to hazard the success of their scheme by an attempt to pass an act for the *relief* of these railroad companies independently of any other measure, to insure the safe passage of the legislation and its approval by the president, congress, by an amendment, tacked it to the army appropriation bill, (which passed March 3d, 1871,) secured the relief asked for.

Section nine of the army appropriation bill reads as follows: "That, in accordance with the fifth section of the act approved July 2, 1864, entitled 'An act to amend an act to aid in the construction of a railroad and telegraph line from the Missouri river to the Pacific ocean, and to secure the same for postal, military and other purposes, approved July 1, 1862,' the secretary of the treasury is hereby directed to pay over in money to the Pacific railroad companies mentioned in said act, and performing services for the United States, one-half of the compensation, at the rate provided by law for such services heretofore or hereafter to be rendered: *Provided*, that this section shall not be construed to affect the legal rights of the government or the obligations of the companies, except as hereinafter specifically provided."

This act was approved by the President, and the question at issue between the secretary of the treasury and the companies was settled by congress in favor of the latter — absolutely relieving them from the payment of any part of the $65,000,000 of subsidy bonds, except such sums as may be paid by allowing the government to retain one-half of the earnings of the roads for carrying mails, etc., which sums, as shown by the companies themselves, amount to less than one-fourth of the annual interest accruing on the bonds. The people must pay all the balance, principal and interest. These companies have received in lands and bonds, from the general government, about $109,000,000, to aid in the construction of their roads, and all that government receives in return is one-half of the fare levied on government transportation over these roads, "at the price fixed by law." The only provision as to price is, that after having donated to the companies sufficient to pay the entire cost of the construction of the roads, government shall pay such reasonable prices as may be agreed upon, not exceeding the rate the companies charge to other parties. When we we say "entire cost," we do not mean the full cost claimed by the companies, for it is not policy for them to make a correct showing in this matter; we mean the real actual cost. We cannot find a statement of the cost of the Union Pacific, and do not know what the company claim to be its cost per mile, or the aggregate cost. The Central Pacific puts the costs of its roads at $120,000,000 or about $136,000 per mile. It shows a paid-up capital stock of $54,000,000, and a funded debt of about $82,000,000, making its indebtedness about $16,000,000 more than the entire cost of its road, including rolling stock and equipments. Making a liberal margin for the value of these last named items, and allowing the Central Pacific to cost nearly double the ordinary cost of other roads, and the reader must conclude that there has been, in this case, a watering of stock and an excessive issue of bonds for the benefit of the company and at the expense of the people. The statement of the capital stock and funded debt of the Union Pacific shows about the same condition for its road as to indebtedness; but the estimated cost of the road is not given.

For proof that we are not mistaken in our estimated cost of these roads, and that the companies have received from the government a sum more than sufficient to defray the entire expense of their construction, we turn to reports of the cost of railroads generally, in the country, made by men who are in sympathy with our present railroad system. These men say that the cost of railroads in this country, from their first introduction, is about $50,000 per mile, and that those constructed recently will average about $30,000 per mile. We are apt to think that the cost of the Pacific roads would exceed that of most other roads. Such is not the fact. On the contrary, taking the entire road into consideration, the line was more favorable than any other in the country. It is thus described in the *Railroad Manual* before referred to:

"The route for the eastern portion of the line is up the valley of the Platte, which has a course nearly due east from the base of the mountains. Till these are reached, this valley presents, probably, the finest line ever adopted for such a work for an equal distance. It is not only straight, but its slope is very nearly uniform toward the Missouri, at the rate of about ten feet to the mile. The soil on the greater part of the line forms an admirable road bed. The road, after leaving the mountains, has very few affluents, the only constructed bridges for the distance being one over the Loup Fork and the North Platte. The base of the mountains is assumed to be at Cheyenne, five hundred and seventeen miles from the Missouri river. This part is elevated six thousand and sixty-two feet above the sea, and five thousand and ninety-five feet above Omaha. From Cheyenne to the summit of the mountains, which is elevated eight thousand two hundred and forty-two feet above the sea, the distance is thirty-two miles. The grades for reaching the summit do not exceed eighty feet to the mile. The elevation of the vast plain from which the Rocky Mountains arise, is so great, that the mountains, when they are reached, present no obstacles so formidable as those offered by the Alleghany ranges to several lines of railroads which cross them. * * * * The line of the railroad up the eastern slope of the Rocky Mountains is not so difficult as those upon which several great works have been constructed in the eastern states. After crossing the eastern crest of the mountains, the line traverses an elevated table land for about four hundred miles, to the western crest of the mountains, which forms the eastern rim of the Salt Lake basin, and which has an elevation of seven thousand five hundred and fifty feet above the sea. Upon this elevated table land is a succession of extensive plains, which present great facility for the construction of the road. The whole line is a very favorable one when its immense length is considered. More than one-half of it is practically level, while the mountain ranges are surmounted by grades not in any case exceeding those now worked upon some of most successful roads."

The description of the line of the Central Pacific, or western six hundred and sixty-seven miles, from Ogden to Sacramento, will not vary much from that given of the Union Pacific. It is not quite so favorable. Taking the character of the route as given, with the facilities for building the road, and it is not probable the actual cost of construction averaged more than $30,000 per mile, or $57,000,000 for the whole line. Taking the highest rate, as given, viz.: $50,000,000, and apply to the whole road, the entire cost would be $94,000,000.

To aid in the construction of this road, the government issued subsidy bonds at the rate of $48,000 per mile for three hundred miles, $32,000 per mile for nine hundred and four miles, and $16,000 per mile for the balance of the main road and branches. The funded debt of the companies owning and operating the road (not including the debts of the branches), after deducting the amount of bonds they received from the government, to-wit: $65,000,000, is, as shown by their own report, $93,000,000. How much their floating debt amounts to we cannot tell. The stock on their road cannot cover one-tenth of the amount of their debts. The companies report a paid up capital stock of $91,028,190. The statement of account would be about as follows:

CREDIT ACCOUNT.

Paid up capital	$91,028,190
Bonds from government	65,000,000
Funded debt	93,000,000
Total invested	$249,028,190

CONTRA.

Actual cost of construction	$94,000,000
Balance	$155,028,190
Deduct for 37,500,000 acres of land at $1.25 per acre	46,875,000
Balance against road	$108,153,190

Thus, after placing the land received from the government to the credit of the road, still a small balance of more than

$108,000,000 has disappeared and the companies are not able to pay the interest on the government bonds. The reports of these companies show, for the year 1871, that the net earnings of their roads (over and above all expenses, including taxes, repairs, damages to property and persons, cost of snow sheds, and all other items of expense) amounted to about $9,000,000, and yet because these companies asked it, congress released them from the payment of the interest on the subsidy bonds.

The conclusion to be drawn from the facts of the case, as they develop themselves, is, that these Pacific railroad companies have used the Federal offices, and the public moneys, and lands, for enriching themselves; that a company of men, in congress, and out of it, have combined and confederated together for the purpose of robbing the people, and controlling the government. We have selected the Union and Central Pacific companies for illustrations, and attempted to state the facts in their case, not because of any exception that they present to the general rule, but to show the manner in which the people are duped and defrauded by congressmen voting government aid to railroad companies, under the pretext of developing the country, and the equally false necessity of providing speedy and secure transportation for the mails, troops, supplies, and munitions of war.

One peculiar feature about the whole matter is, that congressmen have deemed it necessary for the accomplishment of their object, to become personally interested in their own legislation by subscribing stock, and becoming directors in the companies to which they voted these aids. We can name congressmen who, if they were not stockholders in these Pacific roads, at the time the bonds and lands were voted, certainly were stockholders and directors when these companies were relieved from the payment of the interest on the bonds issued to them by the government, to-wit: Oakes Ames and James Brooks. How many more held stock we cannot tell; but the fact that members were stockholders and directors must have been known to the different departments, for, under the charter of these companies, the directors, and especially the government directors, are required to report in detail the condition of the companies, and the names of the directors once each year to the secretary of the interior, at Washington. If the reader would know the extent of congressional legislation in favor of the rings, and combinations of men, plundering the people, he need only look over the different acts of congress passed directly for their benefit during the last twelve years. He will arise from their perusal feeling that the chief duty of the government is to foster, protect, and enrich these rings at the expense of the people.

These Pacific companies are required, by their charters, to construct telegraph lines along the route of their roads, and to transmit messages for the government at such rates as they charge other parties. The appropriations by congress show that $40,000 have been voted annually to pay for telegraphic dispatches, between the Atlantic and Pacific, but there is nothing to show that any such sum was due from the government for telegraphing. Among the appropriations is an item for the mileage of the government engineer for travel, from Cincinnati to Omaha, and from Omaha to Washington, and thence to New York; but the charters of the companies required *them* to pay the expenses incurred on account of the services of persons appointed by the president to inspect these roads. Indeed, the action of congress is such as to induce the belief, that these roads, if not owned by the general government, are owned by congress, or congressmen, and that it is perfectly legitimate and proper for government to pay the cost of their construction, and of the telegraph lines, and also their running expenses. The energy and zeal manifested by congress, in aid of these corporations, and the great number and variety of acts passed for their benefit, demonstrate the fact that while the representatives of the people assemble at Washington ostensibly to legislate for the public generally, they devote their time to legislation for their own benefit, and that of the numerous corporations and companies of which they are members.

CHAPTER V.

CONGRESS BECOMES A STOCK EXCHANGE.

IN scanning the names of the directors of the railroad corporations which have received large grants of lands, subsidies, and special and exclusive privileges, we find many ex-members of congress in whose terms of service these grants were voted. We also find members of congress who were directors at the time their relief and aid bills were passed. We find one member who is now a director in three of the companies receiving the largest sums from government, and which are considered the best of all, because of the opportunity they present to *enterprising* men of legislative and financial ability; and in order that proper provision should be made for his kindred, one of the brothers of this same congressman is a director in five of these land grant subsidy corporations. These jobs are "nice and fat," made so by the unjust legislation of congress, and being "nice and fat," the division and distribution of the spoils is made among these congressmen and their friends. The practice of voting the money and lands of the public to these corporations has become so common that it is considered legitimate to bribe or buy the votes and influence of certain congressmen in favor of certain grants. Large bribes have been offered, and perhaps accepted for these purposes. So common is the practice of lobbying these jobs through congress that it excites but little attention save in extraordinary cases, and elicits but little comment. The power and corrupting influence of these corporations have grown to such proportions that they and their friends in congress can disregard and defy public opinion, and compel all the departments of the government to yield to their demands. They plunder the people with impunity. They have transformed the government; while we are in name a republic, and theorectically the people govern, we are in fact an oligarchy, and corporations rule the country. If the reader has followed us thus far he will have seen that while the idea of public necessity has been put prominently forth as the excuse for the great donations made to railroad companies, and the apology for the special privileges granted to them, in fact, the real object has been to create by special charter a privileged class with facilities to amass fortunes, and by the power granted to this class of perpetual succession and exclusive right under the law, to compel the whole people to pay tribute to it. This power is so great at this time, that it controls the whole commerce of the country; and as we will hereafter demonstrate, it controls not only the financial, but also the judicial department, and reigns supreme in the general politics of the country. Looking at these charters the thought is presented to the mind, and the idea is incorporated in the charter, that the people of the whole country are petitioning congress to grant aid to these companies for the purpose of developing the country; that by a spontaneous movement on the part of the whole people congress is called upon to incorporate these different companies, and to grant lands and money to aid in the different enterprises as they are presented. To give color to this idea, the names of men from most of the states and territories are included among the incorporators, some fifteen or twenty of whom are named as provisional directors who are to hold their places until the first regular meeting of the company, and the election of officers. Congress fixes the time and place of meeting and the notice to be given to the stockholders, and to carry out the idea that it is to be a company in which all can participate, the charter provides that any person can subscribe stock and become a stockholder who desires to do so. In fact, though, no petitions have been presented to congress, nor do any considerable number of the persons named as corporators know of the organization, or that their names have been used; nor is it intended that they should know; the fifteen or twenty interested parties who have formed their plan for a raid upon the treasury, are the only ones, besides their particular friends in congress, who are supposed to know anything about it. These fifteen or twenty men who have gotten up the scheme, meet and elect themselves directors, and are then ready for action. Having obtained their charters, and organized under them, the work of robbing the people begins. With their friends, and some of their directors in congress, they have been able thus far to obtain all they demanded. There is no authority for the assumption that the chartering of these companies is in obedience to the wish of the people, either expressed or implied. On the contrary, this action of congress has uniformly been in opposition to public opinion, and indeed it has excited popular remonstrance. None but the few who wish to get their hands into the public treasury have asked the interference of congress, or desired the government to aid in these enterprises. So great is their anxiety to aid in the development of the country that substantially the same companies undertake to construct all the roads for which congress will grant sufficient aid. All these railroad schemes which have received the special attention of congress were planned by a set of unscrupulous men, who combined to plunder the treasury.

The system of aiding in the construction of railroads by grants of land was inaugurated in 1850, by grants to the Illinois Central, and did not develop itself fully until 1862, when the plan of obtaining charters from congress, connected with grants of land and subsidies, was systematically adopted. Since the latter date the practice has increased with fearful rapidity, and within the last four or five years it has assumed such immense proportions as to threaten the entire subversion of the government.

The greatest raid made upon congress for these grants and special charter privileges during any one term was at the session closing March 4th, 1868. When it is remembered that the public business did not require these roads, and that the people had not asked congress to aid in their construction, it seems incredible that in the fortieth congress representatives and senators should have introduced more than *one hundred and fifty bills and resolutions* to aid railroad companies. Yet such is the fact. A gentleman who spent much time in Washington, and examined into this matter, writes as follows:

"The latest developments show that in the grandeur and number of their schemes of spoil and plunder, the congressional rings of railroad jobbers throw into the shade all other rings of the lengthy catalogue of confederate treasury robbers. * * * One hundred and fifty-nine railroad bills and resolutions have been introduced into the fortieth congress, and twice as many more are in preparation in the lobby; one hundred millions of acres of the public lands, and two hundred millions of United States bonds would not supply the demands of these cormorants. In other words, this stupendous budget of railway jobs would require sops and subsidies in lands and bonds, which, reduced to a money valuation, would swell up to the magnificent figure of half of the national debt!" He continues: "Among the jobs of this schedule is the Atchison & Pike's Peak railroad company, or Union Pacific Central branch, which, after having received government sops to the extent of six millions, puts in for seven millions more. Next comes the Denver Pacific & Telegraph company, which, having feathered its nest to the tune of *thirty-two millions*, puts in for a little more, and this company is reported to be a mere gang of speculators, without any known legal organization whatever—a set of mythical John Does and Richard Roes, who cannot be found when called for. Next, we have the Leavenworth, Pawnee & Western railroad, now known as the Union Pacific, eastern division, chartered by the Kansas territorial legislature in 1855, subsidized with Delaware Indian Reserve lands in 1861, and then in 1862, by a rider on the Pacific railroad law, granted sixteen thousand dollars per mile in United States bonds, and every alternate section of land within a certain limit on each side of the line of the road, and the privilege of a first mortgage (by subsequent amendment) to secure bonds issued by the company to the amount of sixteen thousand dollars per mile. It further appears that a clique of seceders from the old company illegally formed a new company, and having by force of arms taken possession of the the road, are pocketing the spoils which legally belong to the old company. All this, too, with the consent of the president, the secretary of the treasury, and congress. From another source we learn that some half dozen Pacific branch or main stem railroads, northern and southern, are on the anvil, involving lands and bonds by tens and twenties, and hundreds of millions; that Senator Pomeroy of Kansas, has seven of these jobs on the docket; Senator Ramsey, of Minnesota, four; Senator Connors, of California, five; and Senator Harlan, of Iowa, four. Senator Pomeroy, however, distances all competitors in the number and extent of his jobs, for, as it appears, they in-include a line from Kansas to Mexico, three bills for roads, from Fort Scott to Santa Fe, in Texas, a South Carolina road through to the Sea Island cotton section, two or three lines from the Mississippi river through to Texas, and a little private Atchison Pacific—one of the nicest and fattest speculations ever worked through. Is not this a magnificent budget, and is not the audacity of these railroad jobs and jobbers positively sublime?"

We do not vouch for the entire accuracy of the statements above quoted, but we know that much contained in them is absolutely true. If the congressional committee now investigating the alleged Credit Mobilier frauds, perform their duty honestly and faithfully, we will probably learn that the John Does and Richard Roes referred to were Ames, Alley, and other distinguished persons in congress and out of it. An *exposé* by this committee of the sum total voted to this eastern division of the Union Pacific, and the actual cost of the road and telegraph lines, would show a large margin for division, a goodly portion of which found its way into the pockets of members of congress. Can it be claimed that the needs of government required these large subsidies of lands and money? Had the people requested congress to make these grants? Has the development of this country returned to the people a tithe of the wealth thus recklessly given away by congress? The people are now groaning under the burdens imposed upon them by reckless or dishonest legislation at Washington. We might well stop and inquire from what source the power for this kind of legislation is derived. Mr. Washburn of Illinois, now United States minister at Paris, in a speech in congress, in the winter of 1868, seems to have comprehended the situation, and in opposition to the system of plundering the public treasury, spoke as follows:

"With the unreconstructed states admitted into the Union, with full and equal protection for all men, in all of the states, and with manhood suffrage secured by legislation or constitutional amendments, the minds of the people will turn to questions of finances, of taxes, of economy, of decreased expenditures, and honest and enlightened legislation—to questions of tariff, and to questions of railroads, telegraphs, and express monopolies which are sucking the very life-blood of the people—to the administration of the revenue laws and to the robberies and plunderings of the treasury by dishonest office holders. Already the eyes of the people of this country are upon congress. I may say they are upon the Republican majority in congress, for that majority is now responsible before the country for the legislation of congress. It can make and unmake laws in defiance of executive vetoes. The Republican party triumphed because it was pledged to honesty and economy, to the upholding of public faith and credit, and to the faithful execution of the laws. * * * The condition of the country, the vast public debt, the weight of taxation, the depreciated and fluctuating currency, the enormous expenditure of public money, maladministration of the government, the extortion of monopolies press upon our attention with most crushing force. The people elected General Grant to the presidency—not only on account of the great and inestimable services he had rendered the country, in subduing the rebellion, not only on account of his devotion to the great principles of the Republican party—but because they believed him to be emphatically an honest man, and an enlightened statesman who would faithfully administer the laws without fear, favor or affection. The time has come when we are imperatively called upon to take a new departure. Added to the other terrible evils brought upon the country by the war for the suppression of the great rebellion, in the demoralization incident to all great wars, and to the expenditure of vast and unheard of amounts of public money; to the giving out of immense contracts, by which sudden and vast fortunes were made; the inflation of the currency, which engendered speculation, profligacy, extravagance, and corruption, by the intense desire to get suddenly rich out of the government, and without labor, and the inventions and schemes generally to get money out of the treasury for the benefit of individuals without regard to the interest of the government. While the restless and unpausing energies of a patriotic and incorruptible people were devoted to the salvation of their government, and were pouring out their blood and treasure in its defense, there was a vast army of the base, the venal, and unpatriotic who rushed to take advantage of the misfortune of their country, and to plunder its treasury. The statute books are loaded with legislation which will impose burdens on future generations. Public land enough to make empires has been voted to private railroad corporations; subsidies of untold millions of bonds, for the same purposes, have become a charge upon the people, while the fetters of vast monopolies have been fastened closer and still closer upon the public. It is time that the representatives of the people were admonished that they are the servants of the people, and are paid by the people; that their constituents have confided to them the great trust of guarding their rights and protecting their interests; that their position and their power is to be used for the benefit of the people whom they represent, and not for their own benefit and the benefit of the lobbyists, the gamblers and the speculators who have come to Washington to make a raid upon the treasury."

The above shows the light in which Mr. Washburn, four years ago, viewed the matters of which we are now treating. Since the delivery of that speech act after act has been passed by congress in favor of these corporations, giving them greater privileges, releasing them from their obligations to government, discharging their liability to government for many millions of money; and to accomplish this, imposing upon the people additional burdens and taxes for which no equivalent has been or ever will be given. The determination to plunder the government and people seems to control not only the adventurers, who go to Washington to lobby their schemes through congress, but also congressmen themselves, who become chiefs among this class of money and land grabbers. They vote to the corporations, of which they are a part, large sums in money and lands, and then use the means thus obtained for the purpose of bribing and corrupting their fellow members in favor of other and larger robberies

CHAPTER VI.

HOW THE LAND GRANT RAILROADS "DEVELOP" A COUNTRY.

THE ostensible object in granting lands to railroad companies was to aid new and undeveloped portions of the country in procuring necessary railroad facilities for communication with the rest of the world; and to assist, by donations of alternate sections, in their development and settlement.

Whether these ends have been achieved is a matter of doubt. It is scarcely to be hoped that the people will ever be reimbursed for the vast extent of lands, and large amount of bonds, which have been so recklessly lavished upon so many railroad companies. When the proposition to grant lands to railroad companies was brought before congress, the right to donate them to private corporations was not admitted; the right of the states to have control of the lands was not questioned. Recognizing this latter right, the lands were granted to the states for the purpose of aiding in the construction of certain roads within their borders. It was not until 1862 that congress came to the front, created private railroad corporations, and endowed them with lands and money. Nor did these corporations commence their wholesale raid upon the public treasury until after congress went into the business of creating railroad companies. Is it true that the country has been benefited in proportion to the grants made? Are the people richer because of these grants? Has the country, as a general rule, been more rapidly settled and improved by this railroad legislation? We are aware that the idea is commonly entertained that the people receive an equivalent for these railroad grants in the increased facilities for travel and transportation of freights. Were it true that the roads receiving grants of land were more speedily constructed, or that transportation over them was less expensive, then we would admit that the benefits derived would in some degree be an equivalent for the aid afforded them. To ascertain the facts, let us see how this legislation has affected the west, taking Iowa and Kansas as illustrations.

In the first place, for every acre of land given to railroads in these states the people have paid $1.25, inasmuch as they are charged $2.50 for the reserved alternate sections. Taking the land granted in Iowa, the amount charged to the people of this state is $9,009,841; or, taking the grants already certified to, the people are charged with $4,387,303. This sum, amounting to about $4.00 per head, has been taken from the people of Iowa and given to railroad companies, and must be charged against the benefits received. The construction of about eleven hundred miles of railroad in Iowa was aided by land grants. The cost, at $30,000 per mile, would be less than $33,000,000. The amount the people are obliged to pay into the public treasury for the *reserved sections*, in making up the account should be charged to the land grant roads, as also the increased price they are compelled to pay the companies for the donated lands, which range from $5.00 to $50.00 per acre; and this, too, of lands that under the general laws they could have entered at $1.25 per acre.

The amount taken from the people who settle in and improve the state and develop its resources, which they must pay to the government and these railroad companies before getting title to their lands, is about $25,000,000 more than would have been demanded of them but for these land grants. What have they received in return? The companies in Iowa receiving grants of land have not extended their lines across the state more rapidly than companies receiving no grants. In fact, roads built entirely with private means have been constructed more rapidly than these land grant roads. The companies receiving the grants did not keep pace with the settlement of the country; the people, as pioneers, were always in advance of the roads. It was only when the population of the country was sufficient to afford a paying business that the roads were extended. The excuse paraded by congress for making these grants was that the companies would advance their roads so as to draw after them an agricultural population. This has not been done. On the contrary, the lands outside of the boundaries of the railroad grants were the first settled, and the most rapidly developed. Has the result been different in Kansas? The number of miles of railroad in this state in 1870, was about seventeen hundred, of which nearly one thousand received grants of land, and the Kansas Pacific company $6,303,000 in subsidy bonds. Companies constructing these roads received land grants to the amount of 5,420,000 acres. At $1.25 per acre the grants amount to $6,775,000. This sum is charged upon the reserved sections, as in Iowa, and must be paid by the people of Kansas. Add to this the $6,303,000 subsidy bonds, and the Kansas railroads have cost the people of that state and the public treasury $13,000,000, outside of the immense local aid voted to them by the different cities, towns and counties. The population of this state in 1860, was 107,206. In 1870, it was 362,872. Saying nothing about the increased prices to be paid to the railroad companies for the lands granted to them, or the large amount of subsidy bonds, and leaving out the immense amounts of local aid afforded to the different railroads, and the sum to be charged to the railroads for the extra price of the reserved sections is about $20.00 per head for the entire population. Looking at the facts as they are developed, we conclude that the people have not been benefited by these grants of lands, that railroad companies are the only parties benefited, that the people are not richer because of these grants, but on the contrary they would have made money by giving to the railroad companies the actual cost of the roads.

Has the country been more rapidly settled and improved by reason of this special legislation? The leading idea advanced in favor of grants to railroad companies, has been their necessity in developing the new states and territories. We are pointed to the new states of Iowa, Minnesota, Nebraska, Kansas and Nevada, and the territories of Colorado, Utah and Wyoming, and referred to the fact that these states have a population of 2,874,000, and 9,000 miles of railroad; and from this exhibit an argument is deduced in favor of these grants. The theory is that the population has followed the roads. Is this theory correct? In 1850 Iowa had a population of 676,913, and in 1870 a population of 1,191,729. In 1860 there were 655 miles of railroad, about three-fourths of which had received grants of land. In 1870 the number of miles of railroad had increased to 2,668. Of this increase not more than one-third was aided by land grants, private enterprise having constructed at least two-thirds of it; and the same kind of enterprise is still at work, and since 1870 has increased the number of miles to 3,250. The land grants were nearly all made to Iowa in 1856, yet the energetic and rapid building of roads was not shown until after the close of the war, nor until the people had advanced beyond the roads, and their necessities demanded them. Kansas, in 1860, had a population of 107,209. In 1870 it had increased to 364,400. Prior to 1864 it had no railroads. In 1870 it had 1,501 miles, all of which, save forty miles, was built in four years. Nearly all of the Kansas roads were aided by grants, and some of them by subsidy bonds. In 1870 there was one mile of railroad in Kansas for every 242 inhabitants. To construct these railroads in Kansas, counties, cities and towns have taxed themselves by vote to the amount of $4,400,000, or about $9.00 to each inhabitant. This debt must be charged to the railroad account, and a similarly voted indebtedness in Iowa to the amount of about $6,000,000. The valuation of property in Iowa, in 1860, was $205,166,000, and in 1870, $302,515,000. Thus, while the population of the state had nearly doubled, and the lines of railroad had more than quadrupled, the valuation had increased less than fifty per cent., and at least one-half of this increase was in the value of railroads. Deducting from the increased valuation of property in Kansas the value of railroads there, and about the same state of facts appears. The figures in these two states will show that so far from the donations of land and money adding to their wealth, the reverse is true. And this position is supported by the exhibit of other states. In Pennsylvania the population has increased since 1860, 600,000. The mileage of railroads has nearly doubled in this time, and the valuation of property has increased from $717,253,000 to $1,318,236,000. In that state, where no government aid has been voted to railroads, the wealth of the state has nearly doubled, while in the same time in the state of Iowa it has not increased fifty per cent., land grants included.

The population of Nebraska has increased from 7,000 to 42,000 in the last decade. This state has 593 miles of railroad, or one mile of railroad to each seventy of its population, nearly all aided by grants.

California had a population in 1860 of 380,000. In 1870 it had increased to 560,000.

Colorado in the last decade increased from 34,000 to 40,000. In this territory there are 392 miles of railroad, all built by grants of lands and bonds.

Of course the roads through the territories are the Pacific roads, but as the states and territories were both cited as illustrations of the wisdom of congress in making grants to companies for the construction of railroads, we have examined the matter somewhat in detail to show the weakness of the argument. If we take the census of 1860 and that of 1870 and observe the increase in population, wealth and railroad building, we will discover that the laws of trade, of supply and demand have controlled the whole matter, and that the growth of the country has not been increased because of these grants from government. In all cases where the construction of railroads has approached the frontier line of settlement, it has drawn but little population after it, aside from the employes of the road. The real pioneer immigration, that which opens and improves the country, is doing now what it has done for the last generation, moving steadily to the west, followed and surrounded by railroad sharks and jobbers, who, after getting all they can from the government, prey upon the people; and the people of the new states, instead of being blessed with the means of adding to their wealth, find themselves burdened with debt and taxes, fastened upon them by the construction of railroads, many of which are of doubtful utility. As a necessary consequence of the railroad taxes upon their lands, and the excessive charges imposed for the transportation of their produce their farms do not appreciate in value, and the anticipated rapid increase in population and wealth of the locality is not realized. From a view of the whole situation, regarding the benefits accruing to the people from these grants to railroad companies, with what the people have paid for them, the withholding of these railroad lands from market, and the high prices charged per acre by the companies, together with the unjust privileges granted to these corporations, we conclude that the people of the new states and territories have not received an equivalent for the grants made to railroad companies. We are aware that a different opinion prevails, and that our conclusions will be controverted; but when it is remembered that thousands of people have left Iowa, or, coming from the east have refused to settle in Iowa, because of the fact that lands could only be had by purchase from railroad companies at extravagant prices, and that for this reason vast tracts of Iowa lands are yet unimproved which would now be settled upon and cultivated had they not thus been withdrawn from the market, it must be admitted that Iowa would have had a greater population, and greater wealth, had her railroad companies received no land grants. And what is true of Iowa is also true, as a general rule, of other states and territories. Perhaps an exception exists in the far western territories, whose gold and silver mines are in themselves an exception to the general rule, and where agriculture has but few followers.

The advocates of the railroad land grant and subsidy bond system for the settlement of a country have the following to say in its favor. We quote from the *Railroad Manual* before referred to: "One of the most remarkable things connected with the progress of this country is the construction of railroads in advance even of the lines of settlement of our people. Such result is largely due to the grants made by government of lands for the encouragement of these works. Never was a policy more wise or more beneficent." No instances can be shown where railroads have been built in advance of the line of settlement, save when the objective point could only be reached by passing over an unsettled country, as in the case of the road from the Atlantic to the Pacific states. In all other cases, railroad companies have awaited the settlement and development of the country, and followed, not led, our pioneer corps. Of the wisdom and beneficence of these grants the people can judge from their acquaintance with the workings of the system, and the wholesale robberies and frauds practiced by the companies, to some of which we have already referred. Again the author says: "The government has been greatly the gainer in a pecuniary point of view, as it was enabled to sell the land reserved at twice the established rate." It is not clearly seen how this *gain* is made. The people, who are the government, give away one-half of their lands, and then pay into their treasury just money enough for the remaining half to make up the value of the lands they have given away. The only gain the government has made (and this is not a pecuniary one) is the reflection that the men who have received these large grants have become rich, while the people have been deprived of their lands at the original price; they must pay for one-half of them a double price, and for the residue just what they can buy it for from the corporations to whom their servants have donated it. This author says: "That the public has reaped the advantage of the construction of some ten thousand miles of railroads, that otherwise would not have been built." Is this true? In Iowa the land grant roads were not built as fast as other roads having no grants, and the companies finally completed them because they were about to lose their lands by longer delay. And in other states and territories some of these land grant roads are dragging their slow length along, and are being constructed only as fast as the lines are settled with a sufficient number of inhabitants to make the business of the roads profitable. After showing that in certain states and territories there is now one mile of railroad for each three hundred inhabitants, the author adds: "This is certainly a most wonderful exhibit, and is one no other nation can display, and which in our case has only been secured by the wise, benevolent policy of our government, which in this way did more to give remunerative employment to the poorer classes than any other legislation could adopt." It is certainly a "*most wonder-*

ful exhibit." It is one that "*no other nation can display;*" but its wisdom and benevolence are matters of grave doubt. If we add to this "wonderful exhibit" the $65,000,000 stolen from the people by corrupt men and interested legislation, with the $3,126,000 annual interest that the whole people are taxed to pay, because the Pacific railroad companies and the congressional Credit Mobilier have wrongfully appropriated this vast sum to their own use, it presents truly "a *most* wonderful exhibit," without a parallel in any country in the world, but its wisdom and benevolence are certainly wanting.

CHAPTER VII.

THE CREDIT MOBILIER, AND A VILLAINOUS CONTRACT

WE now approach one of the grandest schemes for defrauding a people ever conceived in the breast of the speculator. Before considering the Credit Mobilier, and to show the utter rottenness of the policy of affording congressional aid to railroads, indulge us in a brief re-survey of the subsidy bonds issued to the Pacific railroad corporations. We may concede that at the date of the original charter of these companies, there were no congressmen interested in the grand scheme, and that it was planned by outside combinations. The charter received various amendments with additional aids and privileges after members of congress had become interested; these amendments were made while directors of, and contractors for, these Pacific roads were occupying seats in congress. Whether or not they voted for these amendments does not appear, but it is certain they did not oppose them. As we have already shown, the aid voted by congress was ample to build and equip these roads, taking the statements of the *Railroad Manual* upon the character of the country through which they pass, and the average cost of railroads as the basis for our conclusion. The companies could have built the roads without using the capital stock they reported as paid up. The Union Pacific has made no public exhibit of the cost of its portion of the roads, and from this fact we are at liberty to infer that an honest exhibit would present a bad look. Facts enough have been disclosed to prove that the stockholders and directors of the Union Pacific company had formed a combination for the purpose of defrauding the government and the people. The letting of the contract for the construction of its division of the roads presents one of the most perfect combinations for private speculation at the expense of the public that was ever planned or executed. When this division was completed, according to the statements of the company, it was indebted in the sum of $112,911,512. The cost of the whole line of road, at the highest price per mile given, to wit: $50,000, would amount to less than one-half of the reported indebtedness of the company, including the paid-up capital reported as $37,000,000. To show what was done with the subsidy bonds issued to this company, we must look at the contract made by the directors with Oakes Ames for the construction of six hundred and sixty-seven miles of the road, and the subsequent transfer of this contract to the Credit Mobilier of America. Let us remember that, in addition to the bonds issued by the government to the amount of $16,000 per mile for a part of the road, $32,000 per mile for a part, and $48,000 per mile for a part, congress, by a subsequent amendment to the charter, allowed the company to issue its own bonds for a like amount per mile, as first mortgage bonds, and that at the time of making the contract now under consideration, the directors of the company and of the Credit Mobilier were the same persons, some of whom were at that time and since members of congress. With these facts before us, we can see the reason for the excess of the debts over the cost of the road, as well as for many of the peculiar features of this singular contract. The executive committee of the company was composed of the following named persons: Oliver Ames (brother of Oakes Ames, contractor and member of congress), C. S. Bushnell, Springer Harbaugh, and Thomas C. Durant. The seven directors of the company who were made trustees, and who signed the transfer of the contract to the Credit Mobilier, were Thomas C. Durant, Oliver Ames, John B. Alley (a member of congress), Sidney Dillon, C. S. Bushnell, H. S. McComb, and Benjamin E. Bates; and the president of the Credit Mobilier was Sidney Dillon.

The grant of lands and bonds was made to the railroad company, as well as the right to issue their first mortgage bonds. All of the contracting parties were directors in the railroad company, and in the Credit Mobilier. As a body they controlled the whole matter. If a desire to protect the best interests of the company, and to deal honestly with the public, had actuated these men, and not a determination to plunder the public, no reason can be shown for this strange contract; but it it was the intent of a combination of men to defraud the public and the government, then the contract and its assignments can easily be accounted for. All of the stockholders of the company, at the time the contract was made with Oakes Ames, by indorsement on the back of their certificates of stock, appointed the above named seven trustees, irrevocably to represent their stock at all business meetings and elections of directors, during the existence of the Ames contract. The following is a correct copy of the contract and assignments:

THE "OAKES AMES CONTRACT"—ITS ASSIGNMENTS TO THE CREDIT MOBILIER.

Agreement made this 16th day of August, 1867, between the Union Pacific railroad company, party of the first part, and Oakes Ames, party of the second part, witnesseth:

That the party of the first part agrees to let and contract, and the party of the second part agrees to contract as follows, to wit:

First. The party of the second part agrees and binds himself, his heirs, executors, administrators, and assigns to build and equip the following named portions of the railroad and telegraph line of the party of the first part, commencing at the one hundredth meridian of longitude, upon the following terms and conditions, to wit:

1. One hundred miles at and for the rate of $42,000 per mile.

2. One hundred and sixty-seven miles at and for the rate of $45,000 per mile.

3. One hundred miles at and for the rate of $96,000 per mile.

4. One hundred miles at and for the rate of $80,000 per mile.

5. One hundred miles at and for the rate of $90,000 per mile.

6. One hundred miles at and for the rate of $96,000 per mile.

Second. At least three hundred and fifty miles shall be, if possible, completed and ready for acceptance before the first day of January, 1868, provided the Union Pacific railroad company transport the material. The whole to be constructed in a good and workmanlike manner, upon the same general plan and specifications as adopted east of the one hundredth meridian of longitude. The party of the second part shall erect all such necessary depots, machine shops, machinery, tanks, turn tables, and provide all necessary machinery and rolling stock at a cost of not less than $7,500 per mile, in cash, and shall construct all such necessary side tracks as may be required by the party of the first part, not exceeding six per cent. of the length of the road constructed, and to be constructed under this contract. The kind of timber used for ties and in the bridges, and in its preparation, shall be such as from time to time may be ordered or prescribed by the general agent, or the company, under the rules and regulations and standard as recommended by the secretary of the interior, of the date of February —, 1866.

Third. Whenever one of the above named sections of the road shall be finished to the satisfaction and the acceptance of the government commissioners, the same shall be delivered into the possession of the party of the first part, and upon such portions of the road as well as on that part east of the one hundredth meridian now completed, the party of the first part shall transport, without delay, all men and material to be used in construction at a price to be agreed upon by the party of the second part, his heirs, executors, administrators or assigns, and the general agent, but not less than cost to the party of the first part.

Fourth. The party of the second part, his heirs, executors, administrators or assigns, shall have the right to enter upon all lands belonging to the company, or upon which the company may have any rights, and take therefrom any material used in the construction of the road, and may have the right to change the grade and curvature within the limits of the provisions of the act of congress for the temporary purpose of hastening the completion of the road; but the estimated cost of reducing the same to grade and curvatures, as established by the chief engineer, or as approved from time to time by the company, shall be deducted and detained by the party of the first part, until such grade and curvature is so reduced.

Fifth. The party of the second part, his heirs, executors, administrators, or assigns, is to receive from the company and enjoy the benefits of all existing contracts, and shall assure all such contracts and all liabilities of the company accrued or arising therefrom for work done or to be done, and material furnished or to be furnished, for or on account of the road west of the one hundredth meridian, crediting, however, the party of the first part on this contract all moneys heretofore paid or expended on account thereof.

Sixth. The party of the second part, for himself, his heirs, executors, administrators, and assigns, stipulates and agrees that the work shall be prosecuted and completed with energy and all possible speed, so as to complete the same at the earliest practicable day, it being understood that the speed of construction and time of completion is the essence of this contract, and at the same time the road to be a first-class road, with equipments; and if the same, in the opinion of the chief engineer, is not so prosecuted, both as regards quality and dispatch, that then the said party of the first part shall and may, through its general agent or other officer detailed for that purpose, take charge of said work and carry the same on at proper cost and expense of the party of the second part.

Seventh. The grading, bridging, and superstructure to be completed under the supervision of the general agent of the company, to the satisfaction of the chief engineer, and to be of the same character as to the workmanship and materials as in the construction of the road east of the one hundredth meridian.

It is, however, understood th[illegible] all iron hereafter purchased or contracted for, shall be of the we[illegible]ht of not less than fifty-six pounds to the yard, and to be fish ba[illegible] joints.

Eighth. All the expenses of the engin[illegible]ering are to be charged and paid by the party of the second part, except the pay and salary of the chief engineer and consulting engineer, and their immediate assistants, and the expenses of the general survey of the route.

Ninth. The depot buildings, machine shops, water tanks, and also bridges shall be of the most approved pattern, and they, as well as the kind of masonry and other material used, shall be previously approved by the general agent and chief engineer of the company, and all tunnels shall be arched with brick or stone, when necessary for the protection of the same.

Tenth. Payments to be made as the work progresses, upon the estimates of the chief engineer, in making which the engineer shall deduct from each section its proportion of the cost of equipment not then furnished, station buildings, superstructure, and cost of telegraph, but all materials delivered or in transit for the account of the company may be estimated for.

Eleventh. Payments hereon shall be made to the party of the second part, his heirs, executors, administrators, or assigns, in cash; but if the government bonds received by the company cannot be converted into money at their par value net, and the first mortgage bonds of the company at ninety cents on the dollar net, then the said party of the second part, his heirs, executors, administrators, and assigns, shall be charged thereon the difference between the amount realized and the above-named rates; provided the first mortgage bonds are not sold for less than eighty cents on the dollar, and if there shall not be realized from the sale of such bonds an amount sufficient to pay the party of the second part, his heirs, executors, administrators, or assigns, for work, as stipulated in this contract, and according to the terms thereof, then such deficiency shall from time to time be subscribed by said party of the second part, his heirs, executors, administrators, or assigns, to the capital stock of said company, and proceeds of such subscriptions shall be paid to said party of the second part, his heirs, executors, administrators, or assigns, on this contract.

Twelfth. On the first one hundred miles on this contract, there shall be added to the equipment now provided for and intended to apply on this section as follows, viz.: Six locomotives, fifty box cars, four passenger cars, two baggage cars, and a proportionate amount of equipment of like character be supplied to the second section of one hundred miles, after the same is completed.

Thirteenth. The amount provided to be expended for equipment, station buildings, etc., shall be expended under the direction of the party of the first part, and in such proportion for cars, locomotives, machine shops, station buildings, etc., and at such points as they may determine; the party of the first part to have the full benefit of such expenditures without profit to the contractor, or they may, in their option, purchase the equipment and expend any portion of said amount provided at any point on the road where they may deem the same most advantageous to the company, whether on the section on which said reservation occurs or not.

Fourteenth. The telegraph line is included herein under the term "railroad," and is to be constructed in the same manner and with similar materials as in the line east of the one hundredth meridian.

That said parties hereto, in consideration of the premises and of their covenants herein, do mutually agree, severally, to perform and fulfill their several and respective agreements above written.

This contract having been submitted to the executive committee by resolution of the board of directors, August 16, 1867, and we having examined the details of the same, recommend its execution by the proper officers of the company with the Hon. Oakes Ames, the party named as the second part.

OLIVER AMES,
C. S. BUSHNELL,
SPRINGER HARBAUGH,
THOMAS C. DURANT,
Executive Committee Union Pacific Railroad Company.

Resolved, The foregoing contract between the Union Pacific railroad company and Oakes Ames, referred to the executive committee by a resolution of the board, August 16, 1867, to settle the details, be approved, and that the proper officers of the company be instructed to execute the same, subject, however, to the written approval of the stockholders of the company, as understood by the board of directors when the same was voted upon.

Resolved, That the option to extend this contract to Salt Lake be referred to the board, with recommendations that said option be accepted.

ASSIGNMENT OF CONTRACT TO SEVEN TRUSTEES.

MEMORANDUM OF AGREEMENT—IN TRIPLICATE: Made this 15th day of October, 1867, between Oakes Ames, of North Easton, Massachusetts, party of the first part; Thomas C. Durant, of the city of New York; Oliver Ames, of North Easton, Massachusetts; John B. Alley, of Lynn, Massachusetts; Sidney Dillon, of the city of New York; Cornelius S. Bushnell, of New Haven, Connecticut; Henry S. Mc Comb, of Wilmington, Delaware; and Benjamin E. Bates, of Boston, Massachusetts, parties of the second part; and the Credit Mobilier of America, party of the third part; that

WHEREAS, The party of the first part has undertaken a certain large contract for the construction of certain portion therein named of the railroad and telegraph line of the Union Pacific railroad company over the plains and through and over the Rocky mountains, which will require a very large and hazardous outlay of capital, which capital he is desirous to be assured of raising, at such times, and in such sums as will enable him to complete and perform the said contract according to its terms and conditions; and

WHEREAS, The Credit Mobilier of America, the party of the third part, a corporation duly established by law, is empowered by charter to advance and loan money in aid of such enterprises, and can control large amounts of capital for such purposes, and is willing to loan to said party of the first part such sums as may be found necessary to complete said contract, provided sufficient assurance may be made to said party of the third part therein, that said sums shall be duly expended in the work of completing said railroad and telegraph line, and that the payments for the faithful performance of said contract by said railroad company shall be held and applied to reimburse said party of the third part for their loans and advances, together with a reasonable interest for the use of the money so loaned and advanced; and

WHEREAS, Said party of the third part fully believes that said contract, if honestly and faithfully executed, will be both profitable and advantageous to the parties performing the same, and therefore willing to guarantee the performance and execution of the same for a reasonable commission to be paid therefor; and

WHEREAS, Both parties of the first and third parts have confidence and reliance in the integrity, business capacity, and ability of the several persons named as parties of the second part hereto, and confidently believe that said persons have large interests as well in the Union Pacific railroad company as in the Credit Mobilier of America, they will execute and perform the said contract, and faithfully hold the proceeds thereof to the just use and benefit of the parties entitled thereto:

Therefore, It is agreed by and between the said parties of the first, second, and third parts hereto as follows; that is to say:

That said Oakes Ames, party of the first part hereto, hereby, for and in consideration of $1.00 lawful money of the United States, to him duly paid by the party of the second part, and for divers other good and valuable considerations herein, thereunto moving, doth hereby assign, set over, and transfer unto the said Thomas C. Durant, Oliver Ames, John B. Alley, Sidney Dillon, Cornelius S. Bushnell, Henry S. McComb, and Benjamin E. Bates, parties of the second part, all the right, title and interest of, in, and to, the said certain contract heretofore made and executed by and between the Union Pacific railroad company and the said Oakes Ames, bearing date the 16th day of August, 1867, for the construction of portions of the railroad and telegraph line of said railroad company, to which contract reference is herein made for them, the said parties of the second part, to have and to hold the same to them and their survivors and successors forever in trust.

Nevertheless, Upon the following trusts and conditions and limitations, to-wit:

1. That they, the said parties of the second part, shall perform all the terms and conditions of said contract so assigned in all respects which in and by the terms and conditions thereof is undertaken and assumed and agreed to be done and performed by the said party of the first part herein named.

2. That they, the said parties of the second part, shall hold all the avails and proceeds of the said contract, and therefrom shall reimburse themselves and the party of the third part hereto, all moneys advanced and expended by them, or either of them, in executing or performing the said contract, with interest and commission thereon as hereinafter provided.

3. Out of the said avails and proceeds to pay unto the parties of the second part a reasonable sum as compensation for their service, as such trustees, for executing and performing the terms and conditions of this agreement, which compensation shall not exceed $3,000 per annum to each and every one of the parties of the second part.

4. To hold all the rest and residue of the said proceeds and avails for the use and benefit of such of the several persons holding and owning shares in the capital stock of the Credit Mobilier of America on the day of the date hereof, in proportion to the number of shares which said stockholders now severally hold and own, and for the use and benefit of such of the assignees and holders of such shares of stock at the times herein set forth, for the distribution of said residue and remainder of said avails and proceeds, who shall comply with the provisions, conditions, and limitations herein contained, which are on their part to be complied with.

5. To pay over on or before the first Wednesday of June and September each year, or within thirty days thereafter, his just share and proportion of the residue and remainder of the said proceeds and avails as shall be justly estimated by the said trustees to have been made and earned as net profit on said

contract, during the preceding six months, to each shareholder only in said Credit Mobilier of America, who being a stockholder in the Union Pacific railroad shall have made and executed his power of attorney or proxy, irrevocable, to said several parties of the second part, their survivors and successors, empowering them, the said parties of the second part, to vote upon at least six tenths of all the stock owned by said shareholders of the Credit Mobilier of America, in the capital stock of the Union Pacific railroad company, on the day of the date hereof, and six tenths of any stock in said Union Pacific railroad company he may have received a dividend, or otherwise, because or by virtue of having been a stockholder in said Credit Mobilier of America, or which may appertain to any shares in said Union Pacific railroad company, which had been so assigned to him at the time or times of the distribution of the said profits as herein provided; and this trust is made and declared upon the express condition and limitation that it shall not enure in any manner or degree to the use or benefit of any stockholder of the Credit Mobilier of America who shall neglect or refuse to execute and deliver unto the said parties of the second part his proxy or power of attorney, in the manner and for the purpose hereinbefore provided, or who shall in any way, or by any proceeding, knowingly hinder, delay, or interfere with any execution or performance of the trust and conditions herein declared and set forth.

And the above transfer and conveyance of said contract is made upon these further trusts and conditions, to-wit:

1. The said parties of the second part, their survivors and successors, trustees as aforesaid, in all their acts and doings in the execution and performance of said contract, and in the execution of their several trusts and conditions herein set forth, shall act by the concurrent assent of four of their number, expressed in writing, or by yea and nay vote, at a meeting of said trustees, either or both of which shall be recorded in a book of proceedings of said trustees, kept for the purpose by their secretary, and not otherwise.

2. Said parties of the second part shall keep an office in

the city of New York for the transaction of the business incidental to said trust. Meetings of said trustees may be held on call of the secretary on request of any two of their number; such call may be made personally or by mail.

3. The said trustees shall appoint a competent person as secretary, who shall keep a faithful record of all their acts, proceedings, and contracts, in books to be provided for that purpose, and shall cause to be kept suitable books of accounts and vouchers of all their business transactions, which books shall at all times be open to the inspection of any of said trustees.

4. The said trustees shall cause a monthly statement to be made, showing the amount due from the Union Pacific railroad company on account of work done or equipment or material furnished under the contract, according to the estimates of the engineer of the Union Pacific railroad company, as provided in said contract, a copy of which statement shall be furnished to the Credit Mobilier of America.

And the above transfer and conveyance of said contract is made upon the further trust and condition:

1. That in case of death, declination, disability, by reason of sickness or absence from the country for the space of six months, or neglect to fulfill the duties and obligations of said trust for the same time by either of said trustees, the remaining or surviving trustees may declare the place of said trustee to be vacant, and to fill such vacancy by vote in manner aforesaid.

2. That in case any one of said trustees shall wilfully neglect or evade the performance of his duties as such trustee, or shall wilfully attempt to hinder, delay, obstruct, or interfere with the execution or performance of said contract, or the due execution or performance of said trust and conditions, according to the true intent thereof, or shall appropriate to his own use or benefit any money or other valuable thing belonging or appertaining to said trust, fund, or property, he shall not be entitled further to act as such trustee, or to receive any of the benefits of said trusts, either as shareholder in said Credit Mobilier of America, or otherwise.

The parties of the second part do hereby accept the said

trust, and agree faithfully to execute and perform the same according to the terms, conditions, and limitations herein set forth.

The party of the third part, in consideration of the premises, hereby agree to advance, as upon a loan, to the said parties of the second part, their survivors and successors, all such sums of money, and at such times as may be necessary, to enable said trustees, economically and promptly, to execute and perform the conditions of said contract, upon the call of said parties of the second part, their survivors and successors, such sums never to exceed in the whole the amount provided for in said contract, to be paid by the Union Pacific railroad company, for the execution and performance thereof, and to receive therefor interest at the rate of seven per cent. per annum, payable semi-annually, on each sum so advanced, until the same are repaid.

And said party of the third part do further agree, for the consideration aforesaid, and for an amount equal to two and one-half per cent. on the amount to be by them advanced, to be paid to them as commission, do hereby guarantee unto the parties of the first part and second part, the due performance and execution of the said contract, according to its terms and conditions, and do indemnify and hold harmless the said parties of the first and second part of and from all cost, liability, loss or damage to them, or either of them, arising from or on account of said contract, and to the faithful performance of the agreement, contracts and conditions herein above specified to be done and performed by each.

And this conveyance and transfer is made upon the further trust and condition—

That the trustees shall adjust and pay over to the Credit Mobilier of America such portion of the net profits of the work done and material furnished on the first one hundred miles west of the one hundredth meridian as was done and performed prior to January, 1, 1867.

In witness whereof the party of the first part, the several parties of the second part, in their own proper persons, have hereunto set their hands and seals, and the party of the third part has caused these presents to be executed by its president, attested by its secretary with the seal of the said company, on the day and year above written.

OAKES AMES,
THOMAS C. DURANT,
OLIVER AMES.
JOHN B. ALLEY,
SIDNEY DILLON,
CORNELIUS S. BUSHNELL,
H. S. MCCOMB,
BENJAMIN E. BATES.

Signed, sealed, and delivered in presence of CLARK BELL.
The Credit Mobilier of America, by its president,
SIDNEY DILLON.

Attest: BENJAMIN F. HAM,
Assistant Secretary.

The first noticeable feature of this instrument is that the directors of the company contract with one of their own body to build six hundred and sixty-seven miles of its road.

Second, that they agree to pay to one of their own body nearly double the actual cost of the work. Aside from these facts, nothing striking appears in the contract. It is dated August 16, 1867. It was approved by the directors, and on the 15th of October following, only two months after its execution, it was assigned to the seven trustees for the consideration of one dollar and divers other good and valuable considerations. These trustees agree to perform Oakes Ames' contract, but upon consideration that they shall hold all the avails and proceeds of the contract, reimburse themselves and the Credit Mobilier for all money expended on said contract, with interest and commission, and reserve to each of themselves $3,000 per year for services. The trustees are to hold all of the residue for the several persons possessing and owning stock in the Credit Mobilier, or to their assigns, but upon condition that all stockholders in the Pacific railroad company, who own stock in the Credit Mobilier, shall give an irrevocable proxy for their railroad stock to the trustees named in the agreement. The Credit Mobilier is to advance at seven per cent. the money necessary for the prosecution of the work, and for a commission of two and one-half per cent., agrees to save harmless the parties of the first and second part from all loss or damages to them, or either of them, arising from, or on account of said contract. The contracting parties are all stockholders and directors in the railroad company, and in the Credit Mobilier, (whatever that may be,) they are trustees for themselves. They loan to themselves the money they receive as a grant from government, (voted to the railroad corporation while a part of their own members were members of congress;) they pay themselves seven per cent. interest for loaning to themselves their own money; also two and one-half per cent. commission for furnishing this money, donated by government, to themselves, besides $3,000 per year each to themselves for their services in this most extraordinary transaction. In order to have funds with which to compensate themselves, they issue the first mortgage bonds on the road of the Union Pacific company to the amount of many millions, and then ask congress to relieve them from interest on the bonds received from government; and congress, composed in part of the persons signing the above quoted contract and assignment, relieves the company from $3,125,000. per year, for thirty years, and taxes the people with this vast sum, because the government requires "a *more safe and speedy* transmission of the mails, troops, etc., across the territories to the Pacific coast." We have nothing to do with the financial operations of this company, only as far as the people are affected by them. Bearing in mind that the eight persons concerned in and signing this contract and assignment, were all directors of the Union Pacific railroad company; that four of them were the executive committee; that one of them was the contractor, and all of them stockholders in the Credit Mobilier, probably at that time constituting that entire corporation; and that seven of them were trustees for some persons, company, or corporation, or what appears still more probable, for themselves, and Oakes Ames. the contractor, and we can account for the wholesale robbery of the people, perpetrated by these eight men, with the aid of congress, as above shown.

But how the five non-stockholding directors, appointed by the president, who are presumed to act for the government and its interest, could have been ignorant of the whole matter, is not so easily understood. The act of congress of July 2, 1864, section 13, provides:

"That at least one of said government directors shall be placed on each of the standing committees of said company, and at least one on every special committee that may be appointed. The government directors SHALL, from time to time, report to the secretary of the interior, in answer to inquiries he may make of them touching the condition, management, and progress of the work, and shall communicate to the secretary of the interior, at the same time, such information as should be in the possession of the department. They shall, as often as may be necessary for a full knowledge of the condition and management of the line, visit all portions of the line of road, whether built or surveyed, and while absent from home, attending to their duties as directors, shall be paid their actual traveling expenses, and be allowed and paid such reasonable compensation for their time actually employed as the board of directors may decide."

If these government directors and the company observed the law, then one of them was on the executive committee of the Union Pacific company and must have known of this fraudulent contract and its assignment. If no one of them was placed on the executive committee, then, in the discharge of their duty, they should have reported the facts to the secretary of the interior. One of two inferences is irresistible: 1st, That they were ignorant of what it was their duty to know, or 2d, That they were unfaithful to the public trust confided in them.

Follow us a little further into this Credit Mobilier organization. It was first organized in Pennsylvania, as the Pennsylvania Fiscal Agency for the buying and selling of railroad bonds, advancing loans to railroads and contractors, and to do almost any kind of business except banking. The charter was granted in 1860 to Duff Green and some fifteen others, but included none of the Credit Mobilier company. In 1864, (the corporation having done nothing up to this time,) the secretary of the company supposing Duff Green, (the president,) to be dead, sold out the charter to George Francis Train, Thomas C. Durant, Oakes Ames, Oliver Ames, and others, and Train baptized it with the new name of, "The Credit Mobilier of America;" and then George Francis seems to have disappeared. It does not appear that any considerable amount of the capital stock was ever paid in, (the whole capital stock being $5,000,000;) perhaps just sufficient to legalize their operations, to-wit, $25,000. The first business done, of which there is any record, was a contract made by the directors of the Union Pacific company with one Hoxie, of Iowa, for building 247 miles of the road, at what price per mile we cannot learn. It was not intended that Hoxie should build this road, but, as the directors of the company could not contract with themselves, it was arranged to contract with Hoxie, and then to set the Credit Mobilier to "running," and divide the spoils. With the consent of the executive committee of the company, Hoxie assigned his contract to the Credit Mobilier. The first mortgage bonds of the company were sold, and sufficient realized to build forty miles of road in 1865, and in 1866 to complete the Hoxie contract. From the subsidy bonds received from government, or from some other and unknown source, the Credit Mobilier, in the year 1867, reported a paid up capital stock of $3,750,000, and were ready for extensive operations. In pursuance of the plan formed by the executive committee of the railroad company and the owners and directors of the Credit Mobilier, the contract with Oakes Ames, herein copied, was made, and then assigned. The Credit Mobilier was so used as to *do good.* It was "placed where it would do the most good." It does not appear that this corporation had any considerable financial transactions, or did any particular business save in connection with the Pacific road; yet it proved to the holders the most prolific stock of any on record. The Ames contract was assigned to Sidney Dillon, and others, trustees, on the 15th of October, 1867. It declared dividends as follows:

Dec. 12, 1867, Union Pacific R. R. bonds, valued at	$2,700,000
Jan. 3, 1868, " " " " "	637,500
June 17, 1868, " " " " "	525,000
June 17, 1868, cash	2,250,000
July 8, 1868, "	1,125,000
Total of dividends in seven months	$7,237,500

In addition to the above, another dividend was declared July 3d, 1868, of $2,390,625 in bonds, which were pronounced bogus or worthless. It is thus seen that the directors of the Pacific railroad company, who were also the Credit Mobilier—trustees for themselves, and some of them members of congress—by the aid of congressional legislation, and the fiction of the Credit Mobilier, contracted with themselves, agreeing to pay themselves extravagant prices for building their own road, and getting their pay as a donation from the public treasury, and were able in seven months to declare dividends to themselves of nearly two hundred per cent upon the reported paid up capital, which capital was also obtained from the government. If the reader has followed us in the statements we have made relative to the land bond subsidies granted to the Pacific railroad companies, he will not wonder that the indebtedness of these companies, after the completion of the road, and after the receipt from the government of more than their entire cost, nearly doubles the amount necessary to build them, had honesty and economy been used in their construction.

We might pursue this subject further, but we think enough has been shown to convince the impartial reader, that whatever the pretence for making these grants, the real object has been to enrich unscrupulous and dishonest men at the expense of the public; and that this corrupting power has become so great that those who occupy high and responsible places in the government have become partners in these wholesale robberies of the people. This conclusion becomes irresistible when we find members of congress voting government aid to railroad companies in which they are stockholders and directors at the time the aid is voted.

CHAPTER VIII.

HAS CONGRESS THE POWER, UNDER THE CONSTITUTION, TO CREATE OR ENDOW PRIVATE CORPORATIONS?

TO answer this question intelligently, we must examine the the powers granted to the United States, as well as the rights, powers and relative duties of the state governments. The state governments are supreme in all matters affecting the public and the people, save in those which, by the expressed provisions of the constitution, are delegated to, or conferred upon the general government. The powers thus delegated to the general government are all of a public character, such as the states individually could not control or execute, and such as were deemed essential to our national existence. All the privilges, rights, and powers, not deemed essential to the successful administration of the national government, were reserved to the states and to the people. It follows that the general government is one of limited powers; that while it is supreme in all matters delegated to it by the constitution, and while in its several departments it can exercise all such implied powers as are necessary for the complete execution of those expressly delegated, neither the executive, legislative, nor judicial departments can assume the exercise of powers not conferred upon them by the express provisions of the constitution; and that while the state governments can exercise all powers not expressly prohibited in their constitutions, because of their general sovereign character, the general government is limited to such as are expressly granted. If these propositions are correct, then the general government has no authority for creating private corporations.

We are aware that congress has assumed the negative of these propositions, and has granted charters to some of the most gigantic corporations of the country, under which charters they have organized and are doing business in states which, according to our interpretation of the constitution, as above stated, should have the absolute control of such companies. We shall attempt to demonstrate that the acts of congress granting charters to railroads and other private corporations are usurpations of power, in conflict with the provisions of the constitution, destructive of the rights of the people and of republican government.

What are the powers delegated to the general government by the constitution in questions of this character? Article I. Section 8, contains, among others, the following, as some of the powers conferred upon congress: "To regulate commerce with foreign nations, and among the several states, and with the Indian tribes;" "To establish post-offices and post-roads;" "To make all laws which shall be necessary and proper for carrying into execution the foregoing powers and all other powers vested by this constitution in the government of the United States, or in any department or office thereof." The same section gives congress power to provide for organizing the army, etc.; and, in time of war, extraordinary powers, controlled only by the necessities of the case, are vested in congress. If congress has power under the constitution to charter private corporations, it must be derived from, or contained in, the provisions above quoted. Article IX. of the constitution reads as follows: "The enumeration in the constitution of certain rights shall not be construed to deny or disparage others retained by the people." And Section 10 reads as follows: "The powers not delegated to the United States by the constitution, nor prohibited by it to the states, are reserved to the states respectively or to the people." And the framers of the constitution it would seem, for the purpose of making the line of demarcation between the powers of the states and the general government still more plain and definite, provided as follows: Article IV., Section 2: "The citizens of each state shall be entitled to all privileges and immunities of citizens in the several states."

We think that the above quotations from the constitution (and we have quoted all having any relation to the question we are discussing) prove conclusively that the powers conferred upon congress by the constitution are limited; that while within the scope of the delegated powers its action is supreme, there is inherent in it no general power to legislate upon subjects not named in constitution, or not included by necessary implication. On the contrary, all the powers not expressly given are reserved to the states or the people.

Is the authority to charter private corporations necessarily included in the delegated power to regulate commerce among the several states, or to establish post roads? We think not. What do we understand by the word "commerce?" Webster defines it as follows: "1st. *In a general sense*, an interchange or mutual change of goods, wares, productions, or property of any kind between nations or individuals, either by barter, or by purchase and sale—trade, traffic. Commerce is *foreign, or inland.* Foreign commerce is the trade which one nation carries on with another; inland commerce, or inland trade, is the trade in the exchange of commodities between citizens of the same nation or state. 2d. Intercourse between individuals; interchange of work, business, civilities, or amusements; mutual dealings in life." And again: "To traffic; to carry on trade." In the absence of any definition given to it in the constitution, we must accept the above general definition of its meaning as being the sense in which it is used in the constitution.

Respecting trade with foreign nations or the Indian tribes, it can only relate to the interchange of commodities, or purchase or sale of articles of traffic. As incidental to this power, congress can prescribe rules for the regulation of navigation upon the high seas, including police regulations on board of vessels, because the oceans are the common or public highways of all nations, and each nation navigating the same is bound to protect not only its commerce, but its citizens or subjects. Nations hold commerce with nations across and upon the high seas, the citizens and subjects of each being protected by their own government. This commerce with foreign nations is not regulated by grants of private charters, but by acts of congress is open to all alike, save where, for the encouragement of certain branches of trade, certain bounties or privileges have been granted to particular parties for a specified time. But all such grants have been to parties navigating the high seas. The control of navigable streams within the United States does not depend alone upon the powers given to congress to regulate the commerce of the country, but depends also upon the further power vesting in the general government exclusive maritime jurisdiction. If we concede that the power to regulate commerce among the several states gives congress the exclusive right to regulate the commerce carried on upon our rivers, it would not follow that the power to charter railway companies is conferred. Navigable streams are *public highways*, open to the travel of all. No man, set of men, or corporations, can claim the exclusive right to navigate these rivers, nor could congress grant such exclusive right. The duty of protecting the rights of the citizen, and of making river transportation safe, and of protecting the rights of property, demand that the national, and not the state legislature, should be supreme in this particular jurisdiction, and hence this branch of commerce is placed in the custody of the nation. But keeping in mind the definition of the word "commerce," let us see what is meant by the term as applied to dealings between the states. We insist that it has no reference to the construction of roads, railroads, canals, or any other ways upon which commerce might be carried, or over which articles of trade or traffic might pass, but that it refers only to the dealing of the people of one state with another; that while the people of each state are under the supreme control of their state authority, all the privileges enjoyed by the citizens of any one of the states as to residence or traffic with the citizens of another state, are to be the same. No distinction can be made, and for the purpose of carrying out this provision of the constitution, and preventing the levy of tariffs or taxes by one state upon the citizens of another state, and for the purpose of guaranteeing to all citizens of the United States immunity from these unjust discriminations, the power to regulate commerce among the states was delegated to congress. Nor does it follow that, for the purpose of regulating commerce among the states, congress can grant exclusive privileges and monopolies in any business not confined to one state. When the constitution was adopted, each state was independent; each had all the powers and prerogatives of a nation; each was supreme within its geographical limits; each might prescribe its own rules in relation to immigrants, and to trade and traffic with other states; it might discriminate in favor of its own citizens; it might impose tariffs on foreign imports, and deal with its sister states as with foreign nations. To prevent this, and to secure to all citizens of the United States equal privileges and immunities in all parts of the United States, the provisions of the constitution we have quoted were adopted. While the independence of the States was recognized and preserved, the power to regulate commerce, among them, was delegated to congress; not the power to withdraw from the state its right to legislate upon the subject of commerce among its own citizens, or the right to protect its own citizens in their dealings with the citizens of other states; but simply providing that no discriminations should be made on account of residence, and establishing equal rights and privileges of all citizens of the United States in all the states, free from discriminations sought to be enforced under local or state statutes and regulations. Should any one state attempt to deny to the people of another state the privileges guaranteed by the constitution, then it would be the plain duty of congress to interfere and "*regulate commerce*" between these states. But while a general national law might constitutionally be enacted upon this subject, it certainly cannot be claimed that upon the pretext of regulating commerce among the states, congress can charter railroad companies, or any other companies organized for pecuniary profit. Nor can this power be claimed under the constitutional provision for the establishment of post offices and post roads. We admit that the grant of this power carries with it all such as are incidental; that by implication it includes within its terms the carrying and distribution of the mails, and all other matter necessarily connected therewith; and that congress might build, own, and control post roads, so far as the same might be found necessary for the transportation of the mails over the territory belonging to the United States, and to provide for the use of public roads for government purposes. Public highways are free to all. Over these highways, whether on land or water, congress can provide for the transportation of the mails, troops, army stores, munitions of war, and other public property. These highways are at all times open to the public. But while this is true, it does not follow that the government of the United States can take the absolute control of these public highways, and, by act of congress, deny the states a control over those within their borders respectively. The location and establishment of public roads within a state is a part of the local or police regulation, and while these roads are free to the passage of all, they are, by the provisions of the constitution, and the universally accepted custom of the country, recognized as being under the exclusive control of the states within which they are situated. The fact that congress never has taken the control of the public roads of the country is a full recognition of the exclusive right of the states to control them. Then how can it be claimed that congress, under the constitution, possesses the power to charter railroad companies? Until within the last few years no attempt was made to grant charters to railroad companies by the general government, nor indeed were charters granted for any purpose save in relation to the financial departments, as in the case of United States banks, fiscal agencies, etc., which were chartered for the public benefit, and not as private institutions. We are not positive that the constitutionality of these railroad charters has been determined by the courts of the United States, but we are aware of the fact that congress has deemed it necessary, in almost every instance where charters have been granted and aid voted, to declare, and place upon the record as a part of the charter, the reasons for granting it. The following are the reasons assigned in some of the charters, to wit: In the charter of the Union Pacific railroad company—"For the purpose of aiding in the construction of said railroad and telegraph line, and to secure *the safe and speedy transportation of the mails, troops, munitions of war, and public stores thereon.*"

In the charter of the Northern Pacific railroad company: "For the purpose of aiding in the construction of said railroad and telegraph line to the Pacific coast, and to secure *the safe and speedy transportation of the mails, troops, munitions of war, and public stores.*" In all other cases the above quoted statement of cause is inserted in the charters, as though the right or authority to make these grants was so doubtful that it became necessary in every case to state the reason for the grant. If the present necessities of the government demand such special legislation, then the same reasons existed from the organization of our government; and if congress possesses the power under the constitution to make these grants, and to assume the absolute control of public or private roads through the states, then from the adoption of that constitution congress could have taken absolute control of all the public roads in all the states of the Union. Before railroads were constructed, all overland transportation of mails, troops, munitions of war, etc., was over the public highways—highways that were and still are under the exclusive control of the states in which they lie. Over these public roads and such private ways as may be selected, government has a right to transport the mails, troops, and public property, and no state has the right to prohibit or restrict this right. Still, no power is given by the constitution, nor is there any implied, under which congress can, under the plea of rendering more safe and speedy the transportation of mails, troops, etc., grant exclusive charters and privileges to private corporations. In the nature of things, as our government is organized, the right to charter and control all corporations organized for pecuniary profit remains with the states. This power has never been delegated to the general government, nor prohibited to the states, or people. There can be no doubt upon this point, when we remember that the general government is limited to the delegated powers; and that it is supreme only in those matters which are delegated to and vested in it by the constitution. This position is fully sustained by the adjudication of the supreme court of the United States. In Marshall on the Federal Constitution, page 164, we find the following: "This government is acknowledged by all to be one of enumerated powers. The principle that it can exercise only the powers granted to it, would seem too apparent to have required to be enforced by all those arguments which its enlightened friends while it was depending before the people found it necessary to urge. That principle is now universally admitted." Again, on page 301, the author says: "In our complex system presenting the rare and difficult scheme of one general government whose action extends over the whole, but which possesses only certain enumerated powers and of numerous state governments, which retain and exercise all powers not delegated to the union, contests respecting power must arise. Were it otherwise, the measures taken by the respective governments to execute their acknowledged powers would often be of the same description, and might sometimes interfere. This, however, does not prove that one is exercising, or has the right to exercise, the power of the other."

As to the power of congress to create corporations, an argument has been drawn in its favor from the provision of the constitution which declares that congress shall have the power of making "all laws which shall be necessary and proper for carrying into execution the foregoing powers, and all other powers vested by this constitution in the government of the United States, or in any department thereof." The question before the court arose out of the attempt of the state of Maryland to tax the United States bank, a corporation chartered by congress. In this case the power was upheld on the ground that the bank was necessary in the administration of the finances of the government, that being one of the matters vested in or delegated to the general government, the power to charter the bank was incidental to the granted power. But on the question of the power of congress to create corporations, Mr. Marshall says, page 167: "The creation of a corporation, it is said, appertains to sovereignty. This is admitted. But to what portion of sovereignty does it appertain? Does it belong to one more than another? In America the powers of sovereignty are divided between the government of the Union, and those of the states. They are each sovereign with respect to the objects committed to it, and neither sovereign with respect to the objects committed to the other. We cannot comprehend a train of reasoning which would maintain that the extent of power granted by the people is to be ascertained, not by the nature and terms of the grant, but by its date. Some state constitutions were formed before, some since that of the United States. We cannot believe that their relation to each other is in any degree dependent upon this circumstance. Their respective powers must, we think, be precisely the same as if they had been formed at the same time. Had they been formed at the same time, and had the people conferred on the general government the power contained in the constitution and on the states the whole residium of power, would it have been asserted that the government of the union was not sovereign with respect to those objects which were entrusted to it, in relation to which its laws were declared to be supreme? If this could have been asserted, we cannot well comprehend the process of reasoning which maintains that a power appertaining to sovereignty cannot be connected with that vast portion of it which is granted to the general government, so far as it is calculated to subserve the legitimate objects of that government. The power of creating the corporation, though appertaining to sovereignty, is not like the power of making war, or levying taxes, or of regulating commerce, a great substantive and independent power which cannot be implied as incidental to other powers, or used as a means of executing them. It is never the end for which other powers are exercised, but the means by which these objects are accomplished. No contributions are made to charity for the sake of an incorporation, but a corporation is created to administer the charity. [illegible] nary of learning is instituted in order to be incorpora[illegible] the corporate character is conferred to subserve the p[illegible] of education. No city was ever built with the sole obj[illegible] being incorporated, but it is incorporated as the best [illegible] being well governed. The power of creating a corp[illegible] never used for its own sake, but for the purpos[illegible] something else. No sufficient reason is therefore perceived why it may not pass as incidental to those powers which are expressly given if it be the direct mode of executing them."

Taking the above definition of corporations, and their use, in the administration of the government, we can have no difficulty in distinguishing the cases in which congress can grant charters to any company or association. It is only when some of the delegated powers require the aid of corporate acts in their administration, that the right exists in congress to grant charters, as incidental to the grants. The grants of charters to railroad companies cannot be claimed as incidental to any express delegation of power to the general government. If railroads are private property, they cannot be chartered or controlled by congress. If they are to be taken and treated as public highways, then they are as exclusively under and subject to the control of the respective state governments, as common highways. The state legislatures have exclusive control of them in either case. If they are treated as private corporations, then under the rights reserved to the states, as well as by long usage, their exclusive control is retained by the states. If they are public roads, the same local or state laws apply to them as to all other public roads. Admit that congress has the right to grant charters for railroads, then it follows that it can control them. Admit that they are public roads, and that they are to be taken and treated as common highways, and congress at once assumes the local and police regulations of all the public roads in all of the United States.

To this doctrine we cannot subscribe, but insist that the exclusive power to charter and control railroad corporations remains with the people to be exercised by and under the exclusive control of the state governments. Nor can congress, rightfully, under the constitution, charter railroad corporations in the territories. The power vested in congress "to dispose of and make all needful rules respecting the territory or other property belonging to the United States," does not authorize the creation of private monopolies. When territorial governments are formed, they are clothed with many of the attributes of sovereignty. These governments are at liberty to legislate and to provide for the well-being of the people, and subject to the provisions of their "organic law," have the complete control of local and police regulations. They can construct highways, erect public buildings, impose taxes, grant charters, including charters to railroad companies. That territorial governments can charter railroad companies, and that general government has so acknowledged is proven by the acts of congress in donating lands and bonds to companies chartered by territorial legislation. This was done in the case of the Leavenworth, Pawnee & Western railroad company, chartered by the territorial legislature of Kansas; and other instances are common. The power to grant charters cannot vest in the states, and territorial governments, and at the same time exist in the general government, for the reason that the supreme power must exist in one or the other. If this were not so, one government could destroy what the other had created. The privileges acquired by a corporation under one could be entirely annulled by the other. Private rights would be subject to the adjudication of two separate and distinct tribunals, created and sustained by distinct governments, the one claiming to be supreme, because the right to exercise the power had been granted to it, and the other denying such grant, and because of this denial claiming the power as still remaining with the state government. This course would be destructive of the rights of the people, as well as of our system of government. Concede to congress the right to charter railroad companies, and there is no limit to the monopolies that can be forced upon the people of the whole country. Land companies, loan, and interest companies, manufacturing companies, and in short all conceivable projects of speculation can obtain charters from congress, and our government becomes entirely personal in character, without restraint or constitutional limit. The assumption by congress of the power to create private corporations is a fatal stab at our system of government, destructive of state rights, and a wanton violation of the constitution.

CHAPTER IX.

STATE RIGHTS AT THE BAR OF A CORRUPT CONGRESS.

NONE of the subjects of legislation have tended to destroy constitutional safeguards and debase public morals so much as congressional legislation, with its grants of land and bonds, and other special benefits in favor of railroad corporations. This species of legislation has well nigh destroyed republican institutions. While our government is republican in name it is in fact controlled by an oligarchy. The whole government has become a prey to the class of corporations above named, and is administered in their interest. Their influence controls the legislative department, the courts of the country and its finances. This is a sweeping assertion, but who will deny it? Further, the very men who by their votes in congress, have created these monopolies, have themselves, in many instances, received pecuniary consideration for their votes, either in corporate stock or direct payment. This last assertion is now, (January 9, 1873,) being supported by results arrived at by committees appointed to investigate charges of corruption made against members of both branches of congress.

Having assumed the right to grant charters and aid to these corporations in violation of the constitution, it was but one step further in the same direction for congress to enact other unconstitutional laws, regulating and combining railroads receiving their charters from state legislatures, laws which enable these roads to so combine their operations as to control the entire interests of the country. These acts are numerous in the published laws of congress. We will refer to some of them, and direct the reader to the following, of a general nature: On the 15th of June, 1866, congress passed the following unconstitutional act in the interest and for the benefit of railroad corporations: See Second Brightley's Digest, page 528, "That every railroad company in the United States, whose road is operated by steam, its successors and assigns, be and is hereby authorized to carry upon and over its road, boats, bridges, and ferries, all passengers, troops, government supplies, mails, freight, and property, on their way from one state to another state, and to receive compensation therefor, and to connect with roads of other states so as to form continuous lines for the transportation of the same to the place of destination. Provided that this act shall not affect any stipulations between the government of the United States and any railroad company for transportation and fares without compensation, nor impair or change the conditions imposed by the terms of the acts granting lands to any such company to aid in the construction of its road, nor shall it be construed to authorize any railroad company to build any new road, or connection with any other road without authority from the state in which said railroad, or connection, may be proposed." Commenting upon this extraordinary statute, the editor says: "In the preamble to this extraordinary assumption of power, on the part of the federal congress, they prefer to base their authority for it on the power to regulate commerce among the several states, to establish post-roads, and to raise and support armies. But it has been decided that the constitutional power to establish post-roads is confined to such as are regularly laid out under state authority; the government of the United States cannot construct a post-road within a state of the Union without its consent. The post-roads of the United States are the property of the states through which they pass. The United States have the mere right of transit over them for the purpose of carrying the mails; the government could not have an injunction to prevent the destruction of a mail-road." Citing the case of the Cleveland, Painesville & Ashtabula Railroad Company *vs.* The Franklin Canal Company, in the circuit court of the United States, the editor adds: "Congress certainly can confer no rights on a railroad company incorporated by a state government which are withheld from it by the charter of its creator."

The above quoted act assumes that congress has full power to regulate the connection of railroads in the different states, as well as the carrying trade upon the same. It strips the several state governments of all power to interfere, and in case of any controversy, takes from the state courts the power to determine the rights of the respective parties; the act of congress could be pleaded, and, as a necessary consequence, the United States courts would have exclusive jurisdiction. It cannot be claimed that this act can be supported under any express delegation of power to the general government, nor can it be supported as being incidental to any express grant. It is an usurpation not warranted or sustained by any part of the constitution. This one section quoted destroys the right of any state of the Union, or of two or more of them, to legislate upon the subject of uniting or connecting railroads meeting on the lines dividing them, and also takes from the states the right to regulate the carrying trade within their own respective borders. Congress had no more authority under the constitution to enact this law than to provide by statute for the construction of public highways when they meet upon the line dividing states, or to provide for the passage of teams from one state to another, and the transportation of freights over the common highways within or across a state. The whole power under the constitution is reserved to the states. Prior to the creation of these great railroad monopolies by congress, an attempt at such legislation would have been deemed unconstitutional, but as soon as the whole affairs of government passed into the hands of the few, and when the protection of their interests demanded it, the act was passed, and has remained upon the statute book as one of the laws of the land. This act is about the only one that openly and broadly covers the whole ground, and assumes to regulate the internal affairs of the states, but there are numerous acts passed in relation to land grants and the companies chartered by congress which have the same effect. In some cases the absolute control of roads constructed under charters obtained from state legislatures, or under state laws, has been taken from the states by acts of congress, and placed under the jurisdiction of the general government. In most instances where this has been done, members of congress, or their near relatives, were large owners of stock in the companies to be benefited by the act. To speak more plainly, the acts granting special privileges to particular companies, and placing them under the jurisdiction of the federal government, were passed for the benefit of congressmen and others in high official position. Let us examine some of these acts. Among the stockholders and directors of the Union Pacific and its branches there are found at least eight persons who were members of congress at the date of the act of congress creating the corporation, and also at the date of the material amendments to the charter. Some of these congressmen are still stockholders and directors, and were directors when congress released these companies from payment of interest on the bonds they had received from the government. Another land grant company having congressmen among its stockholders and directors, is the Leavenworth, Lawrence & Galveston; also, the Iowa Falls & Sioux City; also, the Cedar Rapids & Missouri River; also, the Burlington & Missouri River; also, the Atlantic & Pacific; also, the New Orleans, Mobile & Texas; also, the Northern Pacific; also, Sioux City & Pacific; also, the Fremont, Elkhorn & Missouri Valley. The number might be extended, but enough is given to sustain our charge. Most of the above named companies were organized under state laws, or received their charters from state or territorial legislatures. For the purpose of consummating certain speculative ends, congress has treated with contempt state laws and state authority. Where charters have been granted under state authority, and the companies were rightfully under the control of the states within which their roads were located, acts like the following have been passed by congress: "That the Leavenworth, Pawnee & Western railroad company of Kansas, are hereby authorized to construct a railroad and telegraph line from the Missouri river, at the mouth of the Kansas river, on the south side thereof, so as to connect with the Pacific railroad of Missouri;" and then follow the details for constructing and operating the road, and placing it under the control of the general government. In the case of the Central Pacific company, chartered by the state of California, congress passed the following act:

"The Central Pacific railroad company of California, a corporation existing under the laws of the state of California, are hereby authorized to construct a railroad and telegraph line from the Pacific coast, at or near San Francisco, or the navigable waters of the Sacramento river, to the eastern boundary of California."

Substantially the same provision is found for most of the corporations above named, and in all these cases the authority to construct the road is followed by a provision for aid by the general government.

It might be pertinent to inquire why it became necessary for congress to assume the control of railroads already chartered under state authority. It cannot be claimed that the states acted without authority in granting the charter; nor can the authority of the general government to take from the states the control of railroads within their border, be supported by any grant of power contained in the constitution. On the contrary, the power is reserved to the states, and its exercise is denied to the general government. It cannot be urged that the interests of the people are subserved by this assumption of power; on the contrary, these acts of congress take from the public its rights reserved by the constitution. But one answer can be given—*these acts were passed for the promotion of selfish and corrupt ends.* In support of this, we need only state the fact that in almost every instance where congress has attempted to re-charter companies organized under state authority, and granted them aid, members of congress who were members at the date of the passage of the acts were stockholders, and not unfrequently directors. Some congressmen who have been members for the last ten or twelve years, are stockholders in several of the companies, and at least one member of congress of twelve years standing is now a director in at least three companies that received grants of land, one of them getting large amounts of subsidy bonds, for all of which he voted, and for which, as often as occasion served, he has used his vote and influence in procuring additional privileges. We do not claim that every member of congress is interested in railroads; but we do assert that there are many senators and representatives who are personally interested, and that the proportion is so great that whenever it is desirable to have legislation it can be obtained without difficulty. To prove that the chartering and endowing of railroad companies is one of the principal occupations of the national legislature, we have only to look through the acts of congress the last two or three sessions. At the first session of the forty-second congress, fourteen railroad bills were passed, some of them conferring grants to companies yet in embryo, having no being save upon paper, but presenting "great expectations" to our congressmen, who combine the business of granting charters and building railroads, and who find no indelicacy in becoming stockholders and directors in the corporations to which they, as congressmen, have voted lands and money. Some of these roads, under the acts of congress, present great inducements for investments, and in due time will receive proper attention. The effect of this species of legislation has been most baneful. The national congress, once the most pure and patriotic body in the world, has become the headquarters of all the unscrupulous men of the nation. It is under the control of dishonest and reckless men. Elections to seats in that body have become of such value that to secure them men do not hesitate to pay more than the salary for the entire term. Nor do candidates always pay their own money. It is often furnished by rings and interests which require special legislation. It is now well understood that senators and representatives are in the market like other commodities. The purchase is made either in large donations of $10,000, $20,000, $30,000, or more from single corporations, or by shares, stocks, or bonds in companies chartered by congress, and afterwards fostered and protected by congressmen. So common has this practice become that it is not now considered disreputable. What in former years would have been deemed bribery and corruption are now nothing but fair business transactions. We recall a case which illustrates the purity of former legislation compared

with what we see in our own day. Some thirty years ago, certain parties desired a charter for a denominational college. A Rev. Mr. Strong was appointed to visit the capital and interest the legislature in behalf of the charter. He was introduced to a Mr. Cushing, to whom he presented his case, and whom he sought to interest in favor of the grant. The grant of the charter was likely to meet with opposition, and to remove certain objections, Mr. Strong was anxious to have Mr. Cushing examine into the matter fully, and as an inducement for making such an examination he was told that the friends of the measure would compensate him liberally for the time he might spend in such examination. This Mr. Cushing interpreted as an offer to bribe a member of a legislative body, and he felt bound to resist it. Accordingly he laid the matter before the house. That body, by unanimous vote, ordered the sergeant-at-arms to arrest Mr. Strong and bring him to the bar of the house. After an investigation into the truth of the charge, Mr. Strong was found guilty, and publicly reprimanded by the speaker. This happened before legislators had learned to speculate upon their official position. It was in simple times, when those elected to office supposed their first duty was to serve their country, and when it was an irrecoverable disgrace to receive a bribe. It was at a time when our law-makers had too much self-respect to purchase their election with tens of thousands of dollars, and then reimburse themselves by taking stock in, and dividends from, giant corporations chartered and created by themselves. How is it now? Let the facts answer. Class or personal legislation, for special combinations, or in certain interests, is the rule, and legislation for the benefit of the whole people is the exception to that rule. Congressmen, to secure an election, expend large sums of money, and when elected their first care is to *get even.* To accomplish their purpose, they resort to unconstitutional legislation such as granting exclusive privileges or jobs to individuals, for which indirect pecuniary consideration is received. But this alone would not suffice to reimburse them for their great outlay. The greatest source of profit to congressmen has been—and, unless it is checked, will continue to be—found in railroad legislation.

CHAPTER X.

AN UNSETTLED ACCOUNT—A GUILTY DIRECTORY.

WE now invite the attention of the reader to the account as it now stands with the subsidy bonds voted by congressmen to companies in which many who voted were stockholders and directors.

As the law stood prior to April, 1871, all railroad companies that had received government lands were required to pay the interest once in six months as it accrued. This interest had not been paid, and the secretary of the treasury withheld, to apply on the accrued interest, the amount earned by the different companies by the transportation of the mails, troops, etc., for government. Congress, composed in part of stockholders and directors in these same companies, passed a law ordering the secretary to pay in money to the different companies one-half of the amount thus earned, and left it optional with the companies to pay, or not to pay the interest on their bonds. This they have not done, and the interest account of these companies with the government stands about as follows:

Central Pacific, paid........	$ 527,025	Balance	due...	$5,841,351
Kansas Pacific, paid........	973,905	"	" ...	995,448
Union Pacific, paid.........	2,181,989	"	" ...	4,779,763
Central Branch, U. P., paid..	15,839	"	" ...	477,969
Western Pacific, " paid..	9,350	"	" ...	358,329
Sioux City & Pacific, paid..	826	"	" ...	388,780

Making the total amount of payments the sum of $3,708,935, and the amount that these companies owe government, as the accrued interest on subsidy bonds, $12,861,640. This is the amount due in July, 1872. Add the interest accruing since that date and these companies owe the government not less than $16,000,000 interest on their bonds. This amount, as well as future interest, and the principal of the bonds was at one time secured to the government; but when congressmen and their friends get a controlling interest in the companies, they procured the passage of an act, supported by their own votes, which destroyed the security held by the government, and relieved the companies of the payment of this large amount of interest, thereby compelling the people to pay it, while the stockholders, including some of the same congressmen who had voted in favor of the act, received dividends on their stock and on their *Credit Mobilier* stock to the amount of two and three hundred per cent.; thus, by the abuse of the power vested in themselves as members of congress, compelling the people to pay the interest the companies should have paid, and pocketing in the shape of dividends the money so dishonestly obtained. If we needed any further proof to establish the fact that these Pacific railroads were in fact congressional jobs, that members of congress were looking to their own interests rather than to the interests of the people, we need but glance at the interest account of the Sioux City & Pacific company. The excuse pleaded of the "necessities of government," will not avail in this instance. While the interest account of this company is about $400,000, the account for the transportation of troops, mails, etc., over its road, amounts to the sum of $1,642, one half of which has been applied on the interest account of the company, and the other half, under the act of congress, has been paid by the secretary of the treasury to the company. The conclusion is irresistible, that the personal interest of congressmen, rather than the wants of the public, has controlled their action.

Connect with the incorporation of railroad companies, and special legislation in their favor, the legislation in favor of "Indian rings," "whisky rings," "patent right combinations," and the numerous other kinds of special legislation, with the advantages presented to legislators to make personal gain from all these sources, and we can well understand why men are willing to spend such large sums to secure an election to the United States senate, or house of representatives. The baneful effects of the modern code of political morality are not seen in the legislative department of the government only. The same disregard of the rights of the people, and a determination to protect and aid combinations in their efforts toward self-aggrandizement, made at a sacrifice of those principles which are supposed to govern all persons holding places of trust, honor, or confidence, seem to influence to a great degree those holding high position in other departments of the government. The acts of congress chartering the Pacific railroad companies make it the duty of the president of the United States to appoint five government directors for these roads. Under the statutes these directors cannot own stock in the companies; nor have in them any personal interest whatever. They are supposed to be free from any bias for or against the companies; but they are appointed to represent the government, and to guard against and report to the secretary of the interior all abuses on the part of the companies, and at such times as they are required to so report, to also make such suggestions as in their opinion shall best subserve the interest of the public. It is made their duty to personally inspect the roads, during their building and after their completion. At least two of these government directors must have a place on all important committees appointed by the companies for the management and prosecution of their business. Any dishonesty on the part of the companies in letting contracts for the construction of their roads, or any misapplication of the grants made by congress, must have been known to these five government directors, or some of them, if they had properly discharged the duties imposed upon them by law. The formation of an inside ring, under the title of "The Credit Mobilier of America," composed entirely of the directors and stockholders of the Union Pacific company, the letting of the contract for the construction of the road to one of the directors of the railroad company, who was also a director in the Credit Mobilier (and a member of congress), at more than double its actual cost, the transfer of this contract to certain trustees who were directors in both companies, in a manner stated in a preceding chapter in this work, and the declaration of large dividends on the stock of the companies at a time when the work on the road was barely begun, and before any dividends could possibly have been earned,—all these facts must have been known to the government directors, and concealed by them from the government. When it is remembered that some of these government directors were members of congress at the date of the passage of the acts chartering the roads, there is but little question that the same influences controlling them in voting these large subsidies to the companies also controlled them as government directors in their supervision of the roads. This conclusion is strengthened on seeing that some of them became owners of stock in the Credit Mobilier.

The same corrupting influences have been felt in other departments of the government. The abuses practiced in the collection of customs by the officers of the different ports of entry, as shown at the recent investigations made by authority of congress, are but the natural sequence of the questionable course of the legislative department. The great frauds practiced by parties having contracts for furnishing supplies to the Indian tribes are traceable to the same source. This assumption by congress of the power to grant charters to private monopolies, its unconstitutional interference in matters reserved to state control, its determination to foster these gigantic corporations by princely grants, with the corruption incident to these selfish and greedy combinations, are the direct cause of the dishonesty prevailing everywhere among our public officers, and besides other rank growth have led to the imposition of burdens upon the people, oppressive to the last degree. The controlling purpose of a large portion of those elected or appointed to government offices seems to be to accumulate wealth without regard to the propriety or honesty of the means employed. In their eagerness to benefit themselves, all consideration for the public good, or respect for their obligations as sworn servants of the people, are of secondary importance. They accept office from purely selfish motives, and enter upon their duties with the same object in view animating those who embark in trade, manufactures, or commerce, viz.: private gain. Seemingly viewing the offices they hold as being their own private property, they use them as the banker uses his money—for purposes of speculation. Not unfrequently they permit themselves to be bought and sold, like any other articles of merchandise. While we do not claim that all public officers were pure prior to the legislative creation of monopolies we have been examining, we do claim that previous to that sad departure, honesty was the rule, and not the exception. It was when congress entered upon the business of chartering railroad companies, donating public lands to them, and voting them money from the public treasury, that the rule changed; and when, in addition, congressmen became principal owners and directors in these companies, while still retaining their seats in congress, they placed themselves upon the record as unfaithful to their trust, and struck a blow at public morality which will be fatal to our popular government, unless resisted by the whole moral power of the nation.

And here we might well pause and ask, what security have the people for the continuance of republican government? These gigantic corporations are in their nature anti-republican; they tend to a centralization of power; they compel the people to submit to their demands; they are under the protection of congress, under whose special legislation they are permitted to disregard state laws; their ramifications extend throughout the country; their artifices and money control the votes of the people; they elect their friends to both the senate and house; they organize and send strong bodies of men to the lobby of congress and state legislatures, well supplied with money to obtain the passage of laws in their interest, and to prevent such legislation as would be detrimental to them, and in favor of the people; they have their friends and emissaries in every department of the government, and throughout the country, and they exercise a controlling influence not only at Washington, but at almost all the seats of state government. The offices filled by appointment of the executive and confirmation of the senate are too often the agencies of this same influence. We would not be understood as saying that the president acts corruptly in these appointments; we mean that the influences that secure many of the presidential nominations are the same as used by these corporations in the election of *their* senators and representatives. The appointment of judges of the supreme court of the United States has, in at least two instances, within the last few years, been made through the influence and in the interest of these monopolies. These corporations are also represented in the cabinet. It is well understood that the removal of Attorney-General Ackerman, and the appointment of his successor, was done by these corporate influences. The fact that the secretary of the interior, to whom reports should have been regularly made of the progress and condition of the Pacific railroad, was silent, while private fortunes were being fraudulently taken from the public treasury, proves that he also was under the same influence. It can be accepted as an established fact, that all the departments of the government are to a great extent controlled by corporations and combinations of speculators whose interests are adverse to those of the people, and the result is, that statutes are enacted, executive officers appointed, and decisions of court rendered in the favor of these powerful classes, while the rights guaranteed to the people by the constitution are disregarded.

The influence of corporations is also powerful in the administration of state governments. While no such gigantic monopolies as the Pacific railroad have been organized in any state yet, either by special charters granted by state legislatures, or under general incorporation laws, railroad corporations in large numbers have been organized, and by combining their influence have obtained control of most of the state governments; they have been granted special and exclusive privileges, and by the use of money and patronage have been able to control state conventions, state legislatures and state courts. As a logical result, the people are taxed, while railroad companies are practically free from taxation; subsidies to corporations are authorized and declared to be constitutional, and the people are obliged to submit to rates of charges for transportation of freight that amount to a confiscation of the farm products of the country. We need not enter into a history of state grants to railroad companies, for it is familiar to all; the same corrupt practices incident to national, attend state, legislation. In many instances, corporations have organized under state statutes, or obtained special charters from state legislatures, located their roads, procured local aid, and then obtained from congress land grants for their roads, and have thus become powerful in the states where they are located, while other companies have built their roads exclusively with the means afforded by local aid voted under state laws, and loans of money or sale of bonds; but in every instance so planning and contriving that the entire road shall pass into the exclusive control of a select few, leaving to those who furnished the local aid no rights or privileges in connection with the company or the road, save that of paying extortionate freights and burdensome taxes.

CHAPTER XI.

THE SOLE PURPOSES OF TAXATION.

TAXES can only be levied, and collected for public purposes; but all the property of the country can be taxed to its entire value, when the public good requires it. The exigency demanding high rates of taxation is left to the determition of the legislatures of the states, and of the general government. No taxes can be legally levied or collected save for the support of the government, state and national, and subject to the restrictions incorporated in the constitution. All other taxes imposed upon the people are unconstitutional, illegal, and oppressive, and should be declared absolutely void. Direct taxation, for the support of the general government, has never been practiced in time of peace. The usual method for raising a sufficient revenue for its support has been by duties, or tariff imposed by acts of congress upon imports. This has always been deemed the best method for raising the revenue necessary for the support of the government. The powers and duties of the general government are limited and restricted by the constitution of the United States; and as its legislative, executive, and judicial powers are thus limited, it follows that its power to impose taxes upon the people is limited in the same manner, and that it can tax for no purpose save for defraying the expense of its different departments in the exercise of the powers delegated by the federal constitution. This conceded, all that can be claimed by those who administer the affairs of the nation, unless they transcend the constitutional limit, is conceded. The power to appropriate the lands or money of the public to private parties or corporations not being found in the constitution, nor implied in any of the granted powers, all such appropriations are usurpations; they are donations of the people's money and property to private corporations and individuals in violation of the constitutional restrictions; and no authority is vested in congress to tax the people either directly or indirectly, for the purpose of making return of the money and property thus wrongfully taken from them. A private corporation is not a public necessity; its franchises are private property and even if the United States owned the whole of its stock, and took the entire control of its business, it could not become a public corporation for the reason that congress does not possess the power, under the constitution, to create private corporations. The fact that the United States owned the stock and controlled the corporation would not impart to it any of the attributes of sovereignty, but in so far as the general government was interested in the corporation, it would be treated as any other private party, and would be amenable to the same law and subject to the same jurisdiction as private parties or individuals. If the action of the general government can confer none of the attributes of sovereignty upon a private corporation — if it has no constitutional authority to donate lands or money to railroad companies — how can it lawfully collect taxes from the people, either by direct levies, or in duties upon articles of commerce, for the purpose of reimbursing the government for the lands donated to corporations, or to pay either the principal or interest on the bonds given to these corporations? As well might congress levy a direct tax upon the property of the people for the purpose of donating to a private party sufficient means to build a residence; there is not found in the constitution any warrant for either of such levies. Both alike are unwarranted usurpations of power, not to be justified under any grant of power from the people to the federal government. To admit that the congress of the United States possesses the power to tax the people for any purpose save for the support of the general government, is to admit that the constitution is elastic, subject to any congressional construction, and liable to be used as an instrument for promoting personal and private ends. Congress had no power to vote subsidy bonds to railroad corporations as we have already shown; nor could it release these corporations from the payment of these bonds, and the interest as it accrues, and collect the amount from the people in duties on imports or in any other kind of taxes. No such power was ever delegated to the general government by the people. This power cannot be found in any part of the constitution. While this is true, the people are now taxed annually to the amount of many millions of dollars to pay the interest on the bonds issued to the Pacific railroads. Taxes are also collected to the amount of $18,000,000 or $20,000,000 to pay the interest on the banking capital of the country, the stock of a gigantic corporation, chartered by congress, but in the hands and under the control of private parties and companies. While the general government, under the constitution, has the control of the money of the country, and its coinage, value, etc., and can provide such means as shall be deemed best for the administration of the national or public finances, it has no power to enter into private banking; and because it has not this power, it cannot create private banking institutions and tax the people for their support. Any tax levied upon the citizen by the general government for any purpose whatsoever, save for the necessary expenses in the administration of the same, in all of its departments, in accordance with the letter and spirit of the constitution, is without authority, and violates the fundamental law. The levy of taxes in aid of private corporations subserves none of the purposes of the government, and is the exercise of a power not possessed by congress. Our position is fully sustained by legal adjudications, and the writings of eminent jurists. Chief-Justice Marshall, in his writings upon the constitution, has considered this point. He says, on page 345 of his work: "It is, we think, a sound principle, that when government becomes a partner in a trading company, it divests itself, so far as concerns the transactions of the company, of its sovereign character, and takes that of a private citizen. Instead of communicating to the company its privileges and its prerogatives, it descends to a level with those with whom it associates itself, and takes the character which belongs to its associates, and to the business which it transacts. * * * As a member of a corporation, a government never exercises its sovereignty. It acts merely as a corporator, and exercises no other powers in the management of the affairs of the corporation than are expressly given by the incorporation act. The government of the Union held shares in the old Bank of the United States, but the privileges of the government were not imparted by that circumstance to the bank."

If there exists any authority in the general government to create a corporation for any purpose, it is in relation to the finances of the country. The necessity of a fiscal agent of some kind would seem to warrant the creation of a banking corporation. But if the power is conceded, it does not follow that the people should be taxed to provide a bounty payable semi-annually, to the private companies who are engaged in banking, and who alone receive the profits arising from the business. Yet the act of congress creating the banks provides for the payment of semi-annual interest on the capital invested; and this interest is collected from the people. All railroad corporations, created by act of congress, are absolutely private corporations. The insertion in the charter of the words, "to secure the more safe and speedy transportation of the mails, troops, munitions of war, and government supplies," found in all of these charters, does not change the character of the corporations. The grants are made to private parties; the roads are under their control; they receive aid from the general government, but in their own names own and control the roads, and can, at any time, dispose of the roads and franchises, and the general government has no power to prevent any action the companies may choose to adopt so long they regard the provisions of their charters. No statesman or jurist of our country has at any time until within the last few years, claimed that congress could create corporations for private purposes. On the contrary, in all of the earlier decisions of the federal courts, it was uniformly conceded that congress did not possess the power to create such corporations. Chancellor Kent, Chief Justice Marshall, and other eminent writers are all agreed that, under the constitution, congress cannot create a private corporation. If congress had no constitutional right to create railroad corporations, how can it possess the power to tax the people to pay their debts? The people are now paying at least $8,000,000 per annum in shape of taxes for the purpose of liquidating the interest due from railroads chartered by congress in violation of the fundamental law of the land. This large amount of taxes is collected and applied by the general government in payment of interest due from railroad companies, because the influence of congressmen and their friends in these companies was sufficiently powerful to override constitutional barriers, and to procure the passage of an act enabling the parties holding the stock to pocket the earnings of their roads, and make good the deficit in their interest account by taxing the people.

The whole history of congressional legislation does not present a case of such entire disregard of the provisions of the constitution, and such dishonest and corrupt legislation as is contained in the acts of congress relating to the Pacific rail roads. It is questionable whether another instance can be found in this or any other country having a constitutional government, where legislators, by direct vote, have taken millions ot money from the public treasury, and given it to private corporations of which they were members and directors, and to make good the amount thus taken from the treasury have provided *by law* for its collection from the people in the shape of taxes and duties! When we remember that congress does not possess the power to charter private corporations, that in so doing it violates the letter and spirit of the constitution, upon what principle can it claim the right to tax the people for the benefit of these private corporations? We repeat, no country in the world, governed by a written constitution, offers a parallel case. Not even in France, under the personal government of the late emperor, would such an unwarranted act have been attempted.

We are aware that it is claimed that railroad corporations are public corporations—and this granted, taxes may be rightfully levied and collected for their benefit. But we do *not* grant this, and shall, in the following pages, essay to demonstrate that all railroad corporations are private, being owned and controlled by private citizens, and not by the state or national government. But admitting they are public and not private corporations, the general government even then cannot legally charter or control them, because the power for that purpose has never been delegated by the states or the people; and it follows that the general government cannot rightfully impose taxes upon the people for the support of corporations over which it can have no control. If congress can levy taxes for the construction and support of railroads, and take the management and control of them, it certainly can take the entire supervision of all the highways in all the states, provide for their construction, and tax the people at will for that purpose. This being admitted, no local or police regulation in any of the states is exclusively under the jurisdiction of the state governments; but the general government may at any time take the absolute control of the governmental affairs of the several states, and thus complete the centralization of power now so rapidly developing in all the departments at Washington. The assumption of the right to tax the people for any and every purpose that to congress shall seem expedient, irrespective of constitutional prohibition, is at once destructive of the rights that were supposed to be guaranteed and preserved to the whole people by the constitution. If the will of those men who happen to occupy seats in congress (and that will too often controlled by personal interest) is to govern, then all constitutional government is at an end, and the liberty and property of the citizen have no constitutional safeguard. Taxes to the entire value of all the wealth in the country may be levied by the general government, and the citizen of this republic holds his entire estate at the will of the persons who fill the offices of the country. Under the system of congressional legislation that now obtains, the laboring and producing classes are being rapidly reduced to a state of servitude that would grace the most despotic government.

CHAPTER XII.

THE RIGHT OF EMINENT DOMAIN—UNCONSTITUTIONALITY OF MUNICIPAL AID TO RAILROADS.

THE question of taxation for the benefit of private corporations has agitated the public mind since the construction of railroads became one of the admitted necessities of the country. For the purpose of justifying and legalizing governmental aid to railroad corporations, in the various forms in which such aid has been afforded, the doctrine has obtained among the advocates of the measure that railroads are public highways, as well as a public necessity; and such being the fact, that aid in the shape of grants, taxes, and subsidies, are legal, legitimate, and proper. They draw an argument in favor of this doctrine, from the fact that legislatures, state and national, have provided by law for the condemnation of private property, for the use of the companies, respectively, upon paying the assessed value thereof; and that thus the right of *eminent domain* is vested in these corporations; that the right of eminent domain is an attribute of sovereignty, and that the granting of this attribute to corporations imparts to them the character of public highways. They reason that because they are public highways, and the companies owning them are common carriers, taxes may be legally levied and collected for the exclusive use of these companies. They claim that because the United States, states, counties, cities, towns, and townships, have authority to construct, or to aid in constructing, common highways, they have the same right to construct or aid in constructing railroads.

If it were not that precedent has tended to sustain this "false doctrine," we would not think it profitable to combat it. The only point in the argument in favor of this doctrine that has any real foundation is that railroad companies are allowed to locate their roads where they please, upon payment of the damages assessed in the manner prescribed by statute. The answer to this is, that railroads could not be built, unless the companies had permission to pass over the lands of private citizens. If the title from each land owner could be procured only by negotiation and purchase, no railroad could be constructed, for the reason that a direct or continuous line for a road could rarely be secured. Railroads are constructed to aid in the transportation of freight and passengers from one part of the country to another; to promote commerce throughout the whole country; to supply the wants of a people just as a mill or factory supplies the wants of a particular locality. The miller constructs his dam across a stream, and under the statutes of most of the states, he can procure the condemnation of the land of his neighbor overflowed by his dam, to his own use, upon payment of the damages assessed. It is not a condemnation for the use of the public, but for the use and benefit of the owner of the mill. The mill itself, while it is owned by a private individual, and can be sold and transferred by him at any time, is also a public benefit. Can it be said that the right of eminent domain attaches to the mill or its owner? So with railroads—they are owned by private companies; are built and controlled by them; they are of public benefit, but not owned or controlled by the public or by the state, or local authority, as in the case of public highways. Their private owners can sell them, with all their franchises, rights, and privileges. The rules for their operation, rates of charges, and all other matters affecting their government, are exclusively under the control of the parties owning them. Only that the companies may become the owners of the necessary grounds over which to build their roads, have legislatures provided that they may enter upon lands owned by private persons, and upon the payment of the appraised value thereof, appropriate a narrow strip (the width being fixed by statute) for the purpose of locating their road upon it. It is not condemned for public use, as in the case of a public highway, or where land is needed for public buildings, or any other public purpose. The assessed value is not paid by the government, or from the public fund, nor by individuals for the public; but by the private corporation out of its own purse, and for its own gain.

This is what is called, by the advocates of the measure, "the right of eminent domain," a right that only belongs to the supreme government. This power cannot be exercised by local or subordinate governments, unless it is delegated to them by the supreme or superior government. While the courts in some of the states, Iowa included, have, by decisions, made this right of eminent domain attach to railroad companies, it cannot be supported on principle. To allow it to obtain is to clothe private corporations with the attributes of sovereignty. But conceding that this right attaches to these corporations, upon no principle of constitutional law or justice can the right to levy taxes upon private citizens to aid in the construction of railroads, either by acts of congtess, by state statutes, or by local municipal government, be supported. And it matters not in what form these taxes are imposed upon the people, whether in the shape of municipal subscriptions of stock, to be paid by assessments upon the people; by donations of land or money, to be repaid by imposing a larger price upon lands sold to the citizen; by indirect taxation, or by special local elections held in cities, towns, or counties,—the compulsory taxation of the property of individuals, under our system of government, can only be imposed for governmental or public purposes. Taxes are levied for the support of the government in all its departments; for the construction and repairing of highways; for the building of school houses and all other edifices of a public character; for the support of schools; for the necessities of local municipal governments, and for other objects having the public weal for their sole consideration. These taxes are legitimate and proper, because the end sought to be reached by such taxation are for the use and benefit of the whole people, and for the protection of their rights. For all of these purposes the legislature can provide an uniform system of taxation. But when the government attempts to compel A to pay a tax to assist B and C in building a railroad, it enters upon the exercise of a despotic and oppressive power, that is in conflict with the letter and spirit of our constitutions, both state and national. The legislature, by the passage of such a statute, says, in substance, to the tax payer: "A company is formed for the purpose of building a railroad which passes through the county in which you reside. This company has not sufficient means for constructing and stocking its road. That the necessary means may be furnished to it for that purpose, you must pay a tax upon your property, amounting to one tenth or one twentieth of its value; this amount you must donate to the company. True, you will have no interest in this road when it is completed; you will not be a stockholder; you cannot ride in its cars, or ship your freights over the road without paying the same price as other persons. It may cause you to sacrifice a part of your property to pay this tax, but the road will be of great advantage to the public, and you must make this donation to help the enterprise." The consequences flowing from this unjust and oppressive system of taxation are appalling. It has no foundation in right or justice. The legislature has no inherent right to impose taxes for any purpose. The authority to levy taxes is dependent upon the power delegated by the people as contained in the fundamental law. In a republic even a majority of the people do not possess the inherent right to tax the minority for private purposes. Such taxation can be imposed by no other government than a despotic one, where the will of the despot is the supreme law, and where might rather than right is the controlling power. So conscious are the advocates of this species of taxation of the fact that taxes can be levied for public purposes alone, that they deem it all-important to connect and blend in one—the right of eminent domain and taxation.

But this position is not tenable. Bouvier defines the term, "Eminent Domain," as follows: "The right which the people or government retains over the estate of individuals, to resume the same for public use." Taxes are defined to be burdens or charges imposed by the legislative power of a state, upon persons or property, to raise money for public purposes. It will be seen that there is a wide distinction between the taxing power and the right of eminent domain; that while they both appropriate private property for public uses, they differ in degree. While the right of eminent domain takes from the private citizen the absolute title to property upon just and fair compensation, taxation exacts from each property owner a contribution for the support of the government, or for the benefit of the public, without any other compensation than the protection the government affords him in life, liberty, and property. Contribution for this purpose is a duty imposed upon all who are under the protection of government. A complete power to procure a regular and adequate supply of revenue forms an indispensable article in our constitution; and provisions for levying and collecting this revenue is a charge laid upon the legislative department. The levy and collection of all taxes deemed necessary for the administration of the government and for the public good, is an incident of sovereignty; but this does not extend to the levy and collection of taxes to aid private interests or enterprises. The taxing power is limited; the needs of the public fix this limit. When this is passed, the citizen is subject to continual plunder. The value of his property is destroyed; he is but a trustee holding his property subject to the will of an arbitrary power, that can at any moment call for a part or all of it. He had entered into a governmental contract for the purpose of appealing to the strong arm of constitutional law when his rights are assailed, but finds, instead of the protection he had reason to expect, an irresponsible, arbitrary power, compelling him to divide his property with railroad corporations, or other private parties, without any consideration; not only without consideration, but the taxes illegally and forcibly taken from him are used to build up and protect a monopoly that is blasting the fruit of his labor, while it is as surely destroying constitutional and republican government. His property is taken from him by what can only be termed a superior, despotic power, and appropriated without his consent for the benefit of a private corporation.

It is not difficult to distinguish what are proper objects of public support and for which taxes can be levied and collected from those that are not, if we keep in sight the fundamental or organic law. In the formation of a republic no new rights are created. The adoption of a constitution is but declaratory of pre-existing rights and laws; its object is to define and limit the powers of the government, and to guard and protect the rights of the citizens. An eminent jurist, in speaking of the constitution, uses the following clear and forcible language: "It is not the beginning of a community, nor the origin of private rights; it is not the fountain of law, nor the incipient state of government; it is not the cause, but the consequence, of personal and political freedom; it grants no rights to the people, but is the creation of their power, the instrument of their convenience, designed for their protection in the enjoyment of the rights and powers which they possessed before the constitution was made; it is but the frame-work of the political government, and necessarily based upon the pre-existing condition of laws, rights, habits, and modes of thought. There is nothing primitive in it; it is all derived from a known source. It pre-supposes an organized society, law, order, property, personal freedom, a love of political liberty, and enough of cultivated intelligence to know how to guard it against the encroachments of tyranny. A written constitution is, in every instance, a *limitation* upon the powers of the government in the hands of agents, for there never was a written republican constitution which delegated to functionaries all the *latent powers* which lie *dormant* in every nation, and are boundless in extent, and incapable of definitions." Keeping in mind the distinction existing between measures of a governmental or public nature, and those that are private, and applying the above quoted definition of constitutional power, we cannot find it difficult to determine what are, and what are not, constitutional levies and collection of taxes.

Another thought having weight in connection with the constitutional right to tax the people in aid of railroads, is, that minorities have the right to live, and to own and enjoy property; and the majority has no right to compel the minority to contribute aid to railroad corporations. It has always been conceded that in a republican government the majority should rule, and that their will expressed in a constitutional and legal manner should be the law of the land; yet no one claiming to respect constitutional law will contend that this will of the majority can act outside or independent of constitutional restrictions. If this doctrine should obtain, constitutional government is at an end; private rights are destroyed, and the unrestricted will of a bare majority becomes supreme; all the guarantees of the constitution are annulled; life, liberty and property are all dependent upon the popular will; constitutional safeguards are destroyed, and the stability of the government is lost. The first step in this direction is fraught with the greatest danger. When the restrictions embodied in the constitution are overridden and disregarded in one instance, it affords a precedent for a second step in the same direction. Acquiescence in encroachments upon constitutional restriction by the people, undermine and absolutely destroy republican institutions and the government itself. If, for the accomplishment of some private purpose, a community, a state, or the general government disregard the provisions of the constitution, and assume powers not granted them by that instrument, they arbitrarily act the part of the absolute tyrant. And it makes no difference whether the course pursued, or the measure adopted, proves beneficial to the public, or oppressive. In the fact that it is the usurpation of an unauthorized power, lies the danger. The disregard of the limits fixed by the constitution, in the administration of the government, destroys the only guarantee the people have for the protection of their private rights. Among all the unconstitutional measures which now obtain throughout the country, the affording of aid to railroads, by the government, state and national, has proved the most burdensome to the people. Of this class of subsidies, that afforded by local municipal subscription, with or without a vote of the people, has caused the greatest injury. A local or municipal government can lawfully impose taxes for the support of its administration, and for contribution to the general comfort and happiness of the people. It can tax for the purpose of laying out and constructing streets and public highways, because these objects are intended to be, and in fact are open to the use of the whole people; all can use them on equal terms; they are made for the benefit of the public; each citizen has undertaken to contribute his just proportion of the expense of providing for the common, public benefit. But when a county, a city, town, or township, organized for the convenience of the people, and to more effectually protect their rights, attempts to become a stockholder in a railroad corporation, it attempts the exercise of a power it does not and cannot possess under the constitution. Municipal corporations were not created for the purpose of private speculation or private gain, but for purely and strictly government purposes. No power is granted, (nor can it be implied,) to county judges, commissioners, or supervisors, nor to township trustees, or city boards, to take stock in railroad corporations, or to issue bonds of the municipality in payment for such stock, for the reason that such power is not necessary for the administration of these several governments, and does not come within the limit of the powers granted by the people. We know there are many decisions of courts sustaining the position that municipal corporations can become stockholders in railroads, and may issue bonds in payment therefor, and that it is within the scope of the powers vested in such corporations to levy taxes for the payment of the bonds so issued; but we have yet to see a decision that is sustained by any provision of the constitution. Many of these decisions admit that the right to subscribe stock is not contained in the constitution and cannot be justified on constitutional grounds. Of these decisions we shall speak hereafter, and we leave them for the present. We insist that there is no authority in the constitution, state or national, under which any department of any of the governments can become stockholders in a railroad corporation; nor is the right to take such stock in accordance with the genius or spirit of republican government. The distinction that exists between cities and towns acting under charters, and counties, townships, school and road districts, is marked, and should be kept in mind in considering the nature of the powers possessed by each. County, township, school, and road district organizations are necessary in the administration of the laws of the state. They are at most but *quasi* corporations; all their powers are derived from, and executed under the general statutes of the state. They have no special grants or privileges, but are the chosen means for executing state laws. In the distribution of the powers and duties vested in and imposed upon the state governments, the duties of administering the local affairs of the counties, townships, and districts, are delegated to, and imposed upon these *quasi* corporations respectively. They can only exercise such powers as are necessary for the accomplishment of the objects of their creation. Their acts are the acts of the state government as applied to their respective localities. They are not clothed with any extraordinary power; nor can the state government delegate to them a power it does not itself possess. When the constitution of a state, (as in the case of Iowa and other states,) prohibits the state from subscribing stock, loaning its credit, or issuing its bonds to private corporations, we would at once conclude that it could [illegible]gate authority to one of its subordinate departments to do an act forbidden to itself by the constitution. But this is what it has done, if these *quasi* corporations possess the power to afford aid to railroad or other private enterprises. Municipal corporations, such as cities, towns, etc., act under special charters, and in some respects are sovereign. But they are governed and controlled as absolutely by the provisions of their charters as is the state by its constitution. They can only act within the scope of their delegated powers, and in all doubtful questions the presumption is against their right and in favor of the public, for the reason that only special privileges are conferred upon them. Nor can the legislature confer upon them privileges or powers not possessed by itself under the constitution. It is then absolutely certain that neither counties, cities, nor towns, can aid private corporations, or become stockholders in such corporations, unless the power has been delegated to them by the state legislature. It is equally certain that unless the state, in its sovereign capacity, possesses this power, it cannot delegate it to either counties or cities, and that when the constitution of a state forbids the exercise of a power, it includes the legislature, all the departments of the state gov ernment, all counties, cities and towns, and all the people. All these corporations are agencies in the administration of the affairs of the public. Being political in their nature, they are entirely distinct from private corporations organized for the purpose of pecuniary profit. They are established for public purposes exclusively. Judge Dillon, in his valuable work on municipal corporations, says that "They can exercise the following powers and no others: First, those granted in express words. Second, those necessarily or fairly implied, or incident to the powers expressly granted. Third, those essential to the declared objects and purposes of the corporation — not simply convenient, but indispensable." The same author, in treating upon aid to railroads, while admitting that the current of judicial decision is in favor of the principle that in the absence of special constitutional restrictive provisions, it is competent for the legislature to grant this power to municipal corporations, says that "Notwithstanding the opinions of so many learned and eminent judges, there remains serious thought as to the soundness of the principle, viewed simply as one of constitutional law. Regarded in the light of its effects, however, there is little hesitation in affirming that this invention to aid private enterprises has proved itself baneful in the last degree," and he adds: "Taxes, it is everywhere agreed, can only be imposed for public objects, and taxation to aid in building the roads of private railway companies is hardly consistent with a proper respect for the inviolability of private property and individual rights. Fraud usually accompanies its exercise, and extravagant indebtedness is the result, and sooner or later the power will be denied either by constitutional provision, (as in Pennsylvania, Ohio, and Illin[illegible] it already is,) or by legislative enactment."

As we are now dealing with constitutional [illegible] with judicial decisions, we think [illegible] public or municipal [illegible] constitution [illegible] issue of bonds, and [illegible] people to pay for such stock or bonds; and if it be [illegible] counties and cities are not, and cannot be clothed with the power to aid in the prosecution of private enterprises, it is equally true that the legislature cannot delegate to the majority of the voters of a county, city, township, or district, the authority to tax the minority for the same purpose. Legislatures cannot create new powers; they can only exercise such as they possess under the constitution. The powers not delegated by the people in the fundamental law, are retained by them. If the people are sovereign, they are the source of power, and all that is not vested in some department of the government remains vested exclusively in the sovereign. If the legislative, executive or judicial department of the government can act independently of the restrictions and prohibitions contained in the constitution, then the will of the servants of the people is the supreme law, and the sovereign power supposed to reside in the people is destroyed, and constitutional government is at an end. Oppressive taxation imposed without authority, for private and selfish ends, if persisted in, will eventually subvert our republican institutions. This, and other unconstitutional legislation, to some of which we have already referred, has caused such a departure from the old landmarks that it is questionable if we now have, in fact, a republican government. Under the rules adopted in legislation, and the pliant decisions of courts, constitutions are made to yield to the demands of combinations, stock-jobbers, and private corporations, until we cease, as a people, to revere and respect these safeguards of our liberty

CHAPTER XIII.

THE FATAL POLICY OF MORTGAGING CITIES AND COUNTIES FOR THE CONSTRUCTION OF RAILROADS.

THE justification for the munificent grants and lavish taxation of the people in aid of railroads has been, that these roads afford the necessary facilities for transportation of freight, promote speedy communication throughout the country, provide ready markets for the products of husbandry, increase the value of property in their vicinity, and assist in improving and developing the new portions of our country. While some, or all, of these objects may have been in a degree promoted, the little good thus accomplished has been more than counterbalanced by the evils uniformly attending this species of aid to railroads. What are the evils incident to the general incorporation acts, and local taxation in favor of railroads ?

First. They take from the individual the natural and constitutional right of owning and controlling his own property, and license the agents of a county, city, or town, to incumber his property with a debt, without his consent and against his protest.

Second. The policy engenders a rivalry between different localities, causing reckless extravagance and the creation of an immense indebtedness by public corporations. This indebtedness not unfrequently retards the settlement of the locality expected to be benefitted, and depreciates instead of enhancing the value of property, for the constant and compulsory drain of the resources of the place in payment of the debt thus created can leave nothing but barrenness behind, the rule being, with but few exceptions, that non-residents hold the evidences of the indebtedness, and as a consequence, payment must be made to distant creditors. If one thinks that this is overdrawing the picture, let him examine the condition of those counties and cities that years ago loaned their credit to railroad companies, or subscribed to their capital stock. Localities less favorably situated, with fewer natural advantages, fewer miles of railroad, and with less productive countries tributary to their growth, have far outstripped their bonded neighbors in wealth, improvements, and the increased value of their property. Persons who are seeking locations dread and shun these bond-*cursed* localities, and seek homes elsewhere. New counties far outstrip these old ones in improvement and wealth; new towns and cities spring up and destroy the business of these old bond-ridden ones, and the latter, instead of receiving the anticipated and promised increase of wealth, show a paralyzed industry and depreciated property. Localities that fifteen or twenty years ago gave promise of prosperous future, are less wealthy, less prosperous, and in some instances less populous than when they subscribed stock, and issued bonds to railroads. For years to come, the wealth and industry of these places must suffer from the incubus of enormous taxes levied for the payment of bonds issued under the mistaken idea that great benefit was to result from the indebtedness.

Third. It places the pecuniary interests of all the people of the counties and cities creating this kind of indebtedness in the hands of unscrupulous and relentless non-resident creditors, mainly Wall street stock-jobbers, who obtained it at large discounts, often at one-fourth its par value, and who own not only the county and city bonds, but control the railroads in aid of which they were issued, and so by constantly collecting from the people the oppressive taxes required to pay the interest and principal of these bonds, withdrawing the amounts so collected from circulation and sending it to the east without leaving, or ever having paid any equivalent, they are constantly impoverishing the people with the very means which were to have been sources of prosperity.

Fourth. The aid granted to railroad companies has enabled them to get control of the commerce of the country. As a general rule, all of the railroads receiving subsidies in land, government, state, county, and city bonds, and large gifts in local taxes, have been owned or controlled by the same class of men, and not a few of the roads by the same ring or combination. Then speculators have visited all parts of the country, claiming to be men of " large hearts " who desire to benefit mankind. They talk of their large experience in railroad matters; of the great benefit the particular locality will derive from the construction of a certain line of road; of the great profit to be returned in the shape of dividends if local aid is voted, and after having by fraud, falsehood, and willful deception induced the people to move in the matter, they then turn their attentions to state legislatures and to congress for more aid, and so perfect is their combination, that in almost all their attempts they are successful. Among these rings and combinations are found men to fill every department in the scheme for plundering the people. Some of them become directors in the corporation to which the aid is voted and granted, and they thus get control of the donations, grants, and bonds. Some members of the ring become agents to sell the bonds of the corporation, as well as any others received from the general or local government, and to mortgage the lands granted to the companies. Still another division of the ring become the purchasers of the bonds at their *market* value. They all unite in this way and mortgage their roads, rights, and franchises, and construct the road, taking care that when the road is completed, the liabilities resting upon it shall be sufficient to represent its entire value. By this means they become the creditors of the counties and towns through which the road runs; they own and control the road; and the combination being the same substantially throughout the country, owning and controlling all the roads, holding and using the subsidy bonds, fixing the rates of freight and passenger transportation, they control the whole country and hold the best interests of the people subject to their will. In the prosecution of their ends they bribe local officers, state legislatures, and members of congress. To secure the election of their friends to congress, large gifts are made. In one instance one of these raiders upon the rights of the people bestowed upon a prospective United States senator ten thousand dollars for the purpose, as he stated, of securing friendly legislation for a certain railroad company. The pirates and robbers who prey upon mankind are not more dishonest or unscrupulous than are these rings who make the people their prey. They differ only in the degree of punishment received; the former being executed or sent to prison, while, of the latter, many are elected to congress or to other high and responsible offices, or they are appointed to high places of trust and profit in the government. If the reader will look through the *Railroad Manual*, he will find a long list of names of men, prominent now from the recent raids upon the people and public treasury, who have been engaged in the same business for at least twenty years; men whose names are now as familiar to the western people as "household words," who, like birds of prey, have flitted from one part of the country to another until their blighting influence is felt in the whole land. We are referring of course to the men who have followed the business of "organizing" railroad companies for the purpose of procuring aid in lands, bonds, and taxes, and who have devoted their energies to this class of railroads, and not to those capitalists who, with their own money and credit, have constructed their roads and pursued a legitimate busines. Prominent among the men who have devoted their time and talents to railroad enterprises, will be found the names of Thomas C. Durant, John A. Dix, Henry Farnham and others, whose memory will remain fresh with western men, because of their diligence in procuring local aid to roailroad companies from counties and cities fifteen or twenty years ago, and who, after obtaining such aid, by some means become the owners of city and county bonds, to a large amount, and then to prompt the people to greater diligence in the payment of taxes, levied to liquidate these bonds, applied to the president of the United States for troops to aid in their collection. Slightly varied, the same organization of men which inaugurated the system of constructing railroads through land grants, donations, and subsidies, is still in the same business. With their headquarters in New York and Boston; with Wall street as the principal depot for all railroad stocks and bonds, as well as the bonds of the

United States, and of such states, counties, and cities as have been duped by them, these *raiders* upon the treasury and resources of a people have taken the absolute control of the railroad interests of the country, and "run it" for their own exclusive benefit, to the injury of the country and the absolute destruction of the agricultural interests of the great west. By having placed in their hands the large grants of land and subsidies voted to railroad corporations, they acquired the means of controlling the principal roads throughout the country. Roads in Texas, Louisiana, Alabama, Arkansas, Kansas, Nebraska, Iowa, and in other states and territories, are owned and managed in the exclusive interest of capitalists in eastern cities who have no interest in the communities where these roads are located, save to realize large dividends by extortions and oppressions. All of the roads receiving large grants and subsidies, whether from the general or state government, or as local aid, are in the hands of this class of men, with their fiscal and transfer agencies in the cities above named.

This statement has its illustration in the Kansas City, St. Joseph & Council Bluffs company, which has five directors in Boston, two in New York, one in Michigan, and one in Missouri — Fiscal agency and transfer office, Boston. Peoria & Bureau Valley company has its principal office in New York; Chicago & Northwestern — Financial and transfer office, Wall street, New York; Dubuque & Southwestern — all of the directors, save one, and its financial agency, in New York; Atchinson, Topeka & Sante Fe company — Fiscal agency and transfer office, Boston; Galveston, Harrisburg & San Antonio company — Fiscal and transfer agency, Boston; Leavenworth, Lawrence & Galveston company — Fiscal agency and transfer office, Boston; Kansas City & Sante Fe company — Fiscal and transfer agency, Boston; Cedar Falls & Minnesota company— All of the directors reside in New York; Iowa Falls & Sioux City company — Of the directors, John B. Alley, Oliver Ames, P. S. Crowell, and W. T. Gilden, reside in Massachusetts, J. I. Blair in New Jersey, and W. B. Allison and Horace Williams in Iowa — Fiscal and transfer agency, Boston, Colorado Central company — Of the directors, Oliver Ames, Frederick

L. Ames, and four others reside in Massachusetts, the Fiscal agency is in Boston, and the principal office in California; Cedar Rapids and Missouri River company — John B. Alley, Oliver Ames, and nine others of the directors are in the eastern states, and James F. Wilson, and three others, are of Iowa; Northern Pacific company — Principal office, New York; Hannibal & St. Joseph company—Fiscal and transfer office, New York; Burlington & Missouri River company — Fiscal and transfer office, New York; Union Pacific (central branch)—All but two of the directors in Washington and the east, and the principal office in New York; Union Pacific — Among the directors are Oliver Ames, Oakes Ames, and eleven others in New York and Massachusetts, one in Illinois, and G. M. Dodge in Iowa—Fiscal agency, Boston; transfer offices, Boston and New York; Fremont, Elkhorn & Missouri Valley company—John B. Alley, of Boston, John I. and D. C. Blair, of New Jersey, C. G. Mitchell, of New York, and three Cedar Rapids men, directors (this is a part of the Sioux City & Pacific road); Winona & St. Peters company — Fiscal and transfer office, Wall street, New York; Burlington & Missouri River (in Nebraska) —Principal office, Boston; Sioux City & Pacific company — Directors, Oakes Ames, and six others, in the east, and G. M. Dodge, of Iowa — Fiscal and transfer office, Boston; Missouri River, Fort Scott & Gulf company — Fiscal and transfer office, Boston; Central Pacific company—local offices, San Francisco and New York; *New Orleans, Mobile & Texas company — Oakes Ames and twelve other directors, resident in New York and the east, and two in New Orleans; principal office, New York; Houston & Texas company — Fiscal agency and transfer office, New York; Chicago & Northern Pacific Air Line company — Principal office, New York; Elizabeth, Lexington & Big Sandy company Principal office, New York;

*** Note.—This company has a donation from the state of Louisiana of $3,000,000; a subscription of stock by the same state of $2,500,000; and the same state has indorsed the company's bonds to the amount of $12,500 per mile. This company has also received other large sums in municipal aid and other donations.**

Dubuque & Sioux City company—General offices, Dubuque, Iowa, and New York. *Texas & Pacific company—Principal office, New York.

We might continue the above list indefinitely, but think we have extended it sufficiently to sustain our charges. If the reader is desirous of learning who compose these various companies, the *Railroad Manual* will disclose the same set of leading men, divided into three or four principal squads or companies, who raid from one end of the country to the other; control all the roads that have received aid, and at once place them under the direction of the central railroad combinations in Boston and New York; diverting the grants and donations supposed to have been made for the benefit and in the interest of the people, to their own selfish purposes; making the aid thus granted a means of oppression to the people, rather than an agency for their relief.

*** NOTE.—This company has a grant of 13,440,000 acres of land and other aid.**

CHAPTER XIV.

THE IMPOVERISHING TRANSPORTATION SYSTEM.—THE WAREHOUSE CONSPIRACY.

ONE of the great evils resulting from this bonded subsidy system of building railroads, is that it gives to those who manage them the control of the whole carrying trade of the country, and enables them to impoverish the great agricultural population of the west and south. The wealth of the United States lies in its agricultural products. The greater portion of the people are engaged in agricultural pursuits. Good markets and cheap freights are of the utmost importance to agriculture. However abundant may be the crops, unless a market can be reached without a sacrifice of one-half the product in the shape of freight and commissions the husbandman will be impoverished. If the farmers, the tillers of the soil, do not receive a fair remuneration for their work, all other industrial interests will suffer with them; anything that tends to deprive the producer of the value of his product, tends to the impoverishment of the whole country. Any system of laws, regulations, by government or combinations of men, or corporations, that are oppressive to the producer, oppress the whole people. It matters not whether these oppressions are in taxes, tariffs, or charges for the transportation of the farm product; no matter in what shape it comes, the result is the same. The great oppression now being practiced upon the people is in the enormons charges made by railroad companies for carrying freight. The charters, grants, subsidies, and privileges given to those companies have enabled them to organize a powerful monopoly, through which they demand and receive for transportating meats, grains, and other farm products from the west to the eastern markets, at least one-half the value thereof. The charges of these monopolies are arbitrary, and often fixed by the value of the different kinds of grain carried by them. For instance, they charge one-third more per ton for carrying wheat from the west to the east than for corn and oats; it being worth more in market, they ask a larger dividend from it. It can be carried as cheaply as oats or corn, but because of its value, will bear a greater charge, and still leave one-half of its value for the producer. There is no good reason why a railroad company should charge thirty cents per hundred for carrying wheat from Muscatine (Iowa) to Chicago, when it charges but twenty cents for carrying oats and corn over the same road, the same distance. Yet such is the fact. Those who are in the interest of these monopolists talk about cheap freights; they argue that railroads can transport freights much cheaper than it can be done over ordinary highways. Let us turn again to the *Railroad Manual*, and see how the matter is treated. Says the author: "The cost of transporting Indian corn and wheat over ordinary highways will equal twenty cents per ton per mile. At such a rate, the former will bear transportation only 125 miles to a market where its value is equal to seventy-five cents per bushel; the latter only 250 miles when its value is $1.50 per bushel. With such highways only, our most valuable cereals will have no commercial value outside of a circle having *radii* of 125 and 250 miles, respectively. Upon a railroad the cost of transportation equals one and one-fourth cents per ton per mile. With such a work, consequently, the circle within which corn and wheat at the price named, will have a marketable value, will be drawn upon *radii* of 1,600 and 3,200 miles respectively. The arc of a circle with a *radius* of 125 miles is 49,087 square miles; that of a circle drawn upon a *radius* of 1,600 miles is about 160 times greater, or 8,042,406 square miles. Such a difference, enormous as it is, only measures the value of the new agencies employed in transportation, and the results achieved compared with the old."

Here the fact is acknowledged that freights can be transported over railroads for one and one-fourth cents per ton per mile. At this rate, a ton of freight transported from Muscatine, Iowa, to Chicago, would cost less than $2.50 This is what the advocates of aid to railroad companies publish to the world as a fact, and from it deduce the argument in favor of increased facilities for their construction, with greater privileges to be granted to the companies constructing them. The same rate of charges for transportation from the state of Iowa to the city of New York would not amount to more than from twelve to fifteen dollars per ton, and would allow the producer a fair price for his product. But while it is admitted that the above stated amount will compensate the railroads for transporting freights, the amounts actually charged range from twenty-five to fifty dollars per ton from Iowa to Chicago, with a proportionate increase to New York and other eastern cities. Where commerce is open to competition, a fair remunerative price for carrying freights is all that is demanded or paid. If the railroads of the country were not owned and controlled by the same combinations; if they in any degree answered the ends anticipated by the public when their charters were granted, and privileges were bestowed upon the companies constructing them, these excessive charges would not be made or paid.

We have attempted to show that all the railroads in the country are owned, controlled, and operated in the interest of eastern capitalists, with their headquarters in New York or Boston; and that the only interest these capitalists have in the producer is to extort from him all they can get, even at the risk of ruining the whole country. These monopolists, taking advantage of the great privileges granted them, and of the necessities of the agricultural and producing classes, have combined, and defying all competition, as well as the legal restrictions sought to be placed upon them, are now, and for some time past have been charging such unjust rates for transportation as to render the farm products of the west of little or no value. Corn, worth from sixty to seventy cents in New York, is worth only from fifteen to twenty-five in Iowa — two-thirds of its eastern value being absorbed in charges for transportation, storage, etc. Wheat, worth from $1.50 to $2.00 in New York, is worth but from ninety cents to $1.25 in Iowa, the difference being absorbed in charges for transportation, storage, commissions, and in passing it through elevators. It will be seen that these monopolists who have combined for that purpose are systematically robbing the farmer of about one-half of his crop. After he has labored diligently during the season, and harvested his crops, and prepared them for market, because of the privileges granted to these monopolists he must divide with them, giving them one-half, or let it go to waste, and suffer his family to want for the necessaries of life. The combination against him is so perfect he is without remedy. All other means of transportation have been superseded by railroads, and he is powerless to resist. The banditti who raid upon the country, and levy tribute upon the inhabitants by force, are no greater robbers or oppressors than these monopolists. Indeed, the wrongs practiced by the former are less to be dreaded than those practiced by the latter. The people, supported by natural and common law, as well as by statutes, can rid the country of the bandit; but the monopolist has become so powerful that he defies the people, molds the statutes and decisions of courts to suit himself, and compels the whole country to submit to his extortions. No one would wish those engaged in transporting freights from the west to the east to lose money in the business. On the contrary, the people desire that railroad carriers should receive a fair and liberal compensation in their business, and upon the capital invested. But when it costs but $30,000 per mile to construct and stock the railroads, and when for the purpose of illegitimate gain the persons owning and controlling them water the stock, and add to the actual cost fictitious and imaginary items, that it may appear that these roads have cost fifty or sixty thousand dollars per mile, then issue to themselves or their agents bonds to meet these fictitious amounts, and annually pay to themselves the interest on these bonds, and to increase the value of these bonds declare dividends upon the whole stock, it will readily be seen why the producer does complain of the high rates now charged for transporting his products to market. These companies make it impossible to do an honest business and show dividends, or ever pay the interest upon the bonds they have issued. If it be true that the charges for freights cannot be reduced on railroads, two things are demonstrated: First, that the published statements of the costs of carrying upon railroads are untrue; and second, that railroads have entirely failed to supply the necessities of the country. If we are to depend upon railroads to carry the agricultural products of the country to the seaboard, all hope of competing with other countries in European markets is at an end. If the cost of carrying a bushel of wheat from Iowa to New York is to remain as at present, one of two alternatives is presented. Either the producer must sell at ruinous rates, or a home market must be found for his crop; for the large amount charged for carrying it to the coast, added to the ocean freight, destroys all hope of a foreign market, save in times of failure of crops elsewhere. We now complain of our lack of shipping upon the ocean, and of the fact that the balance of trade is against us. With our large annual products of cereals, meats, cotton, and yield of precious metals, the balance of trade is in favor of England; and American shipping, once the equal of England's, is now classed with only third and fourth rate nations. One of the chief causes of this deplorable state of affairs is the absolute control obtained by these petted monopolists over our inland commerce, and their tyrannical extortions in rates for transportation.

We have spoken of the rates of charges from the west to the east. We need not go into details in this matter, for every farmer knows from experience what proportion of his crop railroads demand as their share. If he does not, let him look at his crib of corn, worth in New York from seventy-five cents to one dollar per bushel, and in Iowa from fifteen to twenty cents. Three-fourths of his crop is what these corporations, *these great blessings to the country*, as they claim to be, demand of him for carrying *his* one-fourth to market, provided he will, at his own proper cost, load his whole crop at the place of shipment, and unload it when it reaches its destination; or, what is worse for him, permit it to go into the company's storehouse. While this state of things lasts it is not a question as to how much the producer is increasing in wealth, but how long will he be able to pay his taxes and keep his family from starving? If he is in debt, he is without hope of paying. No king, emperor, or despotic sultan would dare to extort from his subjects three-fourths of the productions of their toil; yet this oligarchy, composed of men who, from long practice, have come to look upon the people as their vassals, and the fruits of their labor as lawful spoils, demand and receive as their toll from one-half to three-fourths of the entire farm products of the country. The consolidation is now so perfect that these railroad kings can dictate to the people how much they shall receive for their products, and how much they must pay for transporting it to market. Any one of the railroad kings of New York, by a telegraphic dispatch to the west, can depress the price of grain one, five, or ten cents per bushel. The order is made at headquarters, and in one hour from the time it is made the farmer in the west who is about to sell his one thousand dollars worth of wheat must take nine hundred dollars for it, because this railroad king has sent word west that he must have another one hundred dollars added to the already enormous charges for transportation. Unless this combination can be broken up and destroyed, and they who own, manage, and control the carrying trade of the country forced to act honestly, there is no prosperous future for the laboring and producing portion of the people; they must remain bond-servants and vassals of this railroad oligarchy now controlling the country.

Another evil resulting from this railroad system, directly affecting the producer, is the elevator and warehouse system, put in operation, supported by, and prosecuted in the interest of this monopoly. As a necessity in shipping and handling grain and other farm products, there must be at shipping points, as well as at the great grain depots, warehouses, storehouses, and elevators. If these were owned and controlled by individuals, unrestricted by railroad companies, they would be of great benefit to the producer; but such is not the fact. Go to any way station on the roads, or to any of the more prominent points, as well as to the great grain depots, and you will find an arbitrary and oppressive rule adopted, which demands of the producer a further dividend from his products. At unimportant points and way-stations, the warehouses and elevators are built upon the company's depot grounds, and, if not owned by the company, are built under an agreement that there shall be a division of the receipts; and in order to make it mutual, the elevator company, or warehouseman, is to charge certain rates on all grain passing through their hands; and the railroad company is to receive on board their cars no grain that has not paid its duty to the elevator or storehouse. Whether it is stored or not, whether it passes through the elevator or not, this arbitrary toll or levy must be paid before it can be shipped. If the farmer deliver it directly on board the cars of the company, he must pay these charges the same as though he had delivered it to the warehouseman. He cannot avoid this extortion, for the only possible way he has to get his grain to market is to ship it over the road, and this he cannot do unless he pays this charge. But by far the greatest imposition is practiced at the great grain depots at Chicago, New York, and other cities. The immense daily receipts at these great depots demand immense warehouse and elevator facilities. Large numbers of elevators and warehouses were provided and used—formerly by individuals; and while warehousemen dealt individually with the public, there was but little abuse; competition was sufficient to insure reasonable charges. The owner of grain, upon its arrival at its destination, could avail himself of any competition among warehousemen, and select such as his judgment approved or his interest prompted.

But a different rule now obtains. The railroads do not stop half way. Their combination for carrying the product of the country is perfect; but another combination will afford them an opportunity for extorting from the producer an additional portion of his crop in the shape of storage. To effect this object, the different warehouse companies in the principal grain marts have consolidated or "pooled" all their interests, and in combination with the railroad companies have pursued and are pursuing, a course of extortion which is oppressive upon the producer. When his grain reaches its destination, it must go into a warehouse; he is in a worse situation now than when he shipped it; then he had the option to keep it or submit to the first levy in favor of the warehouseman; but he is now entirely helpless in the hands of the *ring* formed to rob him. Without asking his consent, his grain is taken to such warehouse as the railroad agent directs; it is seized by the warehousemen and stored at such ruinous rates as to compel him to sell at once, or have the small portion of the crop which he sowed and harvested, and which thus far the railroad combination has graciously allowed him to retain, absorbed by elevator and warehouse charges. He is obliged to use all these agencies or let the crop go to waste on his hands; and these agencies are all owned and controlled by this vast, this gigantic corporate power, created, enriched, and protected by state and national legislation, and constantly guarded by the decisions of the courts, state and national. Indeed, the old despotic maxim, "The king can do no wrong," that his acts cannot be questioned, seems to have descended to these monopolies. They are protected by government, and, as the case now stands, *their servants, the people,* must be content, because all hope of relief from efficient action on the part of either the legislative or judicial departments of the government is denied them.

CHAPTER XV.

A NEW AND FALSE PRINCIPLE IN HYDRAULICS — WATERED STOCK — ITS UNLAWFUL PROFITS THE SOURCE OF EXTORTIONATE TARIFFS — THE "FAST DISPATCH" SWINDLE.

WE have attempted to show some of the oppressions of the present railroad system upon the agricultural interests of the country, and, at the close of our last chapter, were treating of freights, warehouse charges, etc. Closely connected with these latter charges is another abusive and fraudulent practice, which threatens not only to still further oppress the people, but also to more closely combine the power now so rapidly and surely destroying our republic. I refer to what is known as "Dispatch Companies." To fully understand the object and effect of these companies, it will be necessary to look a little further into the management of railroads, and the method adopted in their balance sheets for showing the cost of their construction, the amounts of paid-up capital, and their total indebtedness. These balance sheets do not present the truth in any instance, and have not that purpose, being only an exhibit that will apparently justify the many extortions and deceptions practiced by these corporations. The actual cost of constructing and stocking the roads is not given; instead we have the cost as represented by the stock and bonds issued and *watered.* For a clear understanding of this book-keeping, let us examine the cost of some of the roads as the same is given to the public, and compare it with the actual cost as shown by other evidence. The "Central Pacific" will do for one illustration.

The Central Pacific is eight hundred and eighty-one miles in length. The cost of the road as given is $120,432,717, or $136,700 per mile. The actual cost per mile, taking the whole length of the road into consideration, was less than one-half the amount reported. This information we get through reliable channels, and is undoubtedly correct. The evidence induces the belief that the cost was less than $50,000 per mile, and less that $50,000,000 for the whole road. The company report a capital stock of $54,283,190, and a funded debt of $82,208,000. They also report the liabilities of the road at $136,491,190, being more than $80,000,000 above the actual cost, and $16,000,000 more than the reported cost. The stock of this company was watered to so great an extent, that to pay the interest on the funded debt, and declare a dividend on the stock, and pay operating expenses, and other contingencies, the road must earn at least fifty per cent. per annum. Or to put in plain language, the company must defraud the public in unjust and extortionate charges.

The "Sioux City & Pacific" is the pet road of Massachusetts and Iowa congressmen. The cost of this road per mile, as shown by the report of the company, is $34,547. This cost is represented by paid-up capital—$2,067,600, and first mortgage bonds—$1,629,000. The road is one hundred and seven miles long. The actual cost of this road was less than $30,000 per mile. This company received $16,000 per mile, government subsidy bonds, amounting in the aggregate to $1,712,000, which does not appear in the report. Aside from these government bonds, the reported cost of the road shows that the stock has been *watered*.

The Chicago, Rock Island & Pacific railroad company has, from Chicago to Davenport, one hundred and eighty-four miles of road, and in Iowa three hundred and sixty miles, making five hundred and forty-four miles in all. The total cost as reported is $28,496,999, or the sum of $52,384 per mile. The actual cost of the Illinois portion, as shown from official reports, did not amount to $30,000 per mile, and the Iowa extension cost still less, but including the bridge at Davenport, the cost will approximate to $30,000 per mile, making the total actual cost $15,320,000, showing that the stock of this road has been watered to the amount of $13,000,000. The Iowa portion of this road received a grant of five hundred and fifty thousand acres of land, and aid by county and city subscriptions amounting at least to $500,000, that do not appear in the published statement.

The Iowa Falls & Sioux City road is under the special care of congressmen. It has one hundred and eighty-four miles of road but no rolling stock. The total cost as given is $7,585,000, or $41,222 per mile, while the actual cost was about $31,000. The stock was watered to the amount of $1,800,000, and this, too, after having received a grant of land to the amount of one million two hundred and twenty-six thousand four hundred and six acres.

We might continue this list, but think we have referred to a sufficient number for our purpose. It will be seen, and is now pretty well understood, that the cost of railroads as reported by the companies, is not their actual cost, but includes large amounts that are pure fictions—an increase of the capital stock, no part of which is used or needed in the construction of the road, stock that is not even paid up, but is distributed among stochholders in proportion to the amount of *bona fide* stock each one holds in the company. The capital stock of the company, and bonds issued by it, are supposed to represent the cost of the company's road, rolling stock, etc. But few roads in this country fail to earn large dividends on this actual cost, and but for the custom of watering stock, would show fair profits after running expenses, repairs, etc., are paid. If these corporations were prohibited by statute from increasing their capital stock above the actual cost of their roads, less money would be required for transportation of freights, and there would be no need of resorting to dispatch companies, or any other ring combinations for the purpose of extorting unjust amounts for transportation. But these combinations do not construct roads simply for the purpose of operating them; this is but a secondary consideration. The main object is to speculate in stock and bonds.

Wall street being the grand center for this kind of speculation, the company, in order to profit by sale of its bonds, must make a showing in this grand mart of receipts sufficient to command public attention, the rule being that stocks and bonds appreciate in value in market in proportion to the dividends declared upon their earnings. They who control these roads have two objects in view: first, to add to their capital stock; and second, to make dividends upon such increase of stock. If a line of road cost $2,000,000, and the company owning it can by any means make it pay dividends on three or four millions, they can issue to themselves stock representing this increase. Having thus increased their stock, under the pretense that they wish to construct more road, or improve or repair what they already have, they issue their bonds to the amount of the increased stock, (sometimes to an amount equal to more than their entire capital,) and put them upon the market. The first object is to get dividends upon whatever stock they have paid up, (if any is paid up,) and next to make their roads earn enough to pay the interest on their bonds, and then, if possible, to force the earnings of their roads to a point where dividends can be paid on the increase of stock. Having increased their capital stock, and issued and sold their bonds, they are in no haste to add to, or improve or repair, their roads; for they have already consummated the object in view, to-wit: made in cash the market value of their bonds. This same operation is repeated as often as their capital stock will bear reducing, and in some instances it has been repeated until the stocks and bonds became almost worthless. This species of speculation does not add one dollar to the wealth of the country, nor aid commerce. It only enriches that class of speculators who prey upon the public.

We have shown that one and one-fourth cents per mile per ton will compensate for transporting freights over railroads, provided the business is conducted fairly and honestly, and we can now begin to understand why such enormous rates are charged. The roads must earn enough to pay the interest upon all the bonds sold and upon the capital stock issued by these companies. The people, the producers, are taxed for this purpose. One-half of the products of every farm in the west goes into the pockets of these Wall street speculators, and the rates for transportation are increased in the same proportion that these stocks and bonds are increased. When more money is demanded in Wall street, telegrams are sent throughout the country by these railroad kings to their agents and employes to advance the rates on transportation. This reduces the price of the farm products, and puts the earnings of the farmer into the pockets of the railroad monopolist, and the stock and bond gambler in Wall street.

It would look as though the combinations of this oligarchy were perfect; that the system of extorting from the people and robbing the producers could not be improved, and that these most unscrupulous oppressors ought to be satisfied. Such is not the case. Either because they wish to have fewer numbers with whom to divide the spoils, or because they have reduced the value of their stocks and bonds until it is necessary that their roads pass under other management, or because they must have still higher rates for transportation, of late a new combination for transportation has been formed, called Dispatch agencies or companies—a kind of "Credit Mobilier" arrangement. These dispatch companies are comparatively new in the west, and we know but little of their organization save that it costs still more to ship with them than with railroad companies. These dispatch agencies are not formed to compete with railroad companies in the transportation of freights, nor are they in any measure rivals or opponents of railroad companies. In the nature of things there must be perfect accord between these two corporations, for the railroad companies could and would at once destroy the dispatch business if the same in any manner conflicted with the interests of railroad managers. The dispatch companies depend entirely upon the railroad companies for cars, locomotives, and railroads for carrying their freight. Enough is known of railroad management to satisfy the most skeptical that the organization of dispatch companies is for purposes other than the more expeditious transportation of freight. These dispatch companies are composed mainly of railroad directors and superinendents, with a few figure heads to represent the outside world. After the formation of the dispatch companies, contracts for the use of cars, locomotives and roads are made upon the same principle and for the same object as in the case of the Union Pacific railroad company and the Credit Mobilier company. The directors of the railway company, representing the company, contract with themselves as a dispatch company, to supply themselves cars, locomotives, and roads for the prosecution of the business of the dispatch company, and for a certain consideration agree to pay themselves, as directors of the railway company, for what is so leased to themselves as a dispatch company; and then, in order to promote the business interests of the dispatch company, and secure to themselves as its directors higher rates for transportation of freight, they make it a point at all times to give the preference to the said dispatch company. As a result of this arrangement the dispatch companies monopolize the principal part of the business. They are in appearance opposition lines to the roads on whose tracks they are carried, and are really so, when the interest of the railroad stockholders not concerned in the dispatch companies are considered. These stockholders get their dividends upon their capital stock and their share of "watered stock" and bonds, but do not participate in the profits of the dispatch business.

Like the Credit Mobilier, it pays large dividends which it extorts from the people, charging even higher rates than the railroad companies; but it only divides among its members, and not with the stockholders of the railroad company, whose track it uses. The interest of these stockholders is not considered. They have built and equipped the road, and selected their directors and managers; but these managers and directors turn the road over to a hostile company, composed of themselves and select friends. To promote the business of the dispatch companies, their trains are transported from one end of the railroad to the other in less than half the time required to transport a train of freight cars belonging to the road. The effect of this course of procedure is obvious. Shippers, finding that these railroad managers discriminate against the cars belonging to the road proper, and that they grant extraordinary favors and facilities to the *opposition* lines, quit patronizing the former, and do business with the dispatch companies. The result is that the dispatch companies now control the freight business, and the railroads have, as a rule, quit providing themselves with freight cars. When applied to for cars, the answer is, "We have none," while at the same time the side tracks are filled with freight cars belonging to these dispatch companies, demanding much higher rates than the regular charges. At the first glance we fail to understand why a course so suicidal to the best interests of the railroad company is pursued by its directors and managers, nor can we readily comprehend why they permit these dispatch companies to monopolize their tracks and destroy the business of their roads. We think we can solve the problem. These managers of the railroads, and such stockholders as are admitted to a participation in the conspiracy, are the proprietors and incorporators of the dispatch companies. After payment of the running and other expenses of the road, and their own salaries (fixed by themselves) the dividends on their railroad stock is small. Their position as stockholders in both the railroad and dispatch companies is the same as was that of the stockholders of the Pacific railroad companies and the Credit Mobilier, who could well afford to sacrifice the interests of the road and its stockholders who had no interest in the Credit Mobilier, provided they received large dividends from their Credit Mobilier stock. So, in organizing the dispatch companies and giving them the preference over the roads, with the absolute control of the freighting business, while the railroad stocks pay no dividends and depreciate in value, and the roads and rolling stock are being worn out, the dispatch business thrives and pays large dividends to this inside *ring*—comparatively small in numbers—which controls the road, and in addition to preying upon the public, so arrange the business as to exclude the stockholders of the road from any share in the profits of the dispatch company. Having oppressed the public by extortionate charges for transportation, increased the stock of the railroad company to an amount that precludes profitable dividends, even from the highest of tariffs, and issued and sold bonds of the company to so large an extent as to make it impossible to pay the interest on them, and at the same time meet the running expenses of the road, including their own salaries as officers and managers, having, in short, loaded the railroad companies with burdens greater than they can bear, as a last master-stroke of financiering they organize themselves into dispatch companies, and while they enrich themselves they reduce the railroad companies in which they are managing directors to absolute bankruptcy. The stockholders who, confiding in the integrity of these men, elected them directors and managers, are swindled out of their legitimate dividends, their stock becomes worthless, debts accumulate against the company, locomotives, tracks, and cars are worn out in transporting freights for the dispatch company, at rates ruinous to the railroad company, and as a grand *finale* the road passes into the hands of these conspirators under the orders or judgments of courts. In the meantime shippers are compelled to pay double prices for freights because the *railroad companies* have not the necessary facilities for shipping; all has passed into the hands and under the control of the dispatch companies. By a mere fiction, the managers of the road contracting with themselves as dispatch companies, a competition is permitted to take the control of the carrying trade over the road, control the track and rolling stock, as well as the officers of the railroad company, destroy their business, and drive them into bankruptcy. Those not in the secret of the orgrnization fail to comprehend its necessity. Why, for example, a train of cars run in the interest of the dispatch companies can travel at double the rate of speed of the trains run in the interest of the railroad company, or why higher rates of transportation should be taxed and paid. The only solution we can give is that it presents additional means for taking from the producer an additional portion of his product in the shape of charges supposed to be paid to a company organized for the purpose of aiding in the transportation of freights, but which is, as a matter of fact, a combination in the interest of the managers of the road with the real purpose of making personal gain to themselves at the sacrifice of the interests of the stockholders.

As a result of this new mode of conducting business, let us see how the price of freights is affected. During the summer and fall of 1872 the price of freights by water from Chicago to New York was $4.25 per ton, and by railroad from $7.00 to

$8.00. With the close of navigation the rates, under the management of the dispatch companies, advanced to from $25.00 to $28.00 per ton. While the railroad companies can carry for $7.00, the dispatch companies charge $25.00. The margin for profit on the stock of these dispatch companies promises to equal the dividends of the Credit Mobilier stock, and from this showing we can have some idea of the robbery being practiced upon the people—particularly the farmers. Well may the producers of the west complain of these swindling monopolies, and band together for mutual protection.

CHAPTER XVI.

A PRIVILEGED CLASS—THE MONOPOLISTS RELIEVED OF THE BURDENS OF TAXATION—AN OUTRAGE UPON REPUBLICAN GOVERNMENT.

ANOTHER evil resulting from the railroad system of the country is the partiality shown railroad companies in the matter of taxation. The constitutions of all the states provide that the levy of taxes shall be uniform; and in contemplation of law each owner of property subject to taxation must bear a proportionate share of the taxes levied for the support of the government. Indeed, it is a part of the compact entered into among all civilized people, that each will contribute a proportionate share towards defraying the expenses of the government under which he lives, and which affords him protection, and secures to him the enjoyment of his rights as a citizen. In a republic where all have, or are supposed to have, equal rights, this contribution to the support of the government is a duty weighing upon all, and to make a discrimination in favor of any man or class of men, or of any companies or corporations, contradicts the fundamental principles of republican government, and recognizes favored or privileged classes. To compel the property of individuals to alone bear the burdens which should be shared by that of corporations violates both the letter and the spirit of the constitution. All public burdens should bear equally upon all people, associations, and corporations. The legislature has as much right to say that the property of one-half of the citizens of a state shall pay the entire expenses of the government, while no taxes shall be imposed upon the property of the other half; or to provide that they who engage in particular branches of business shall supply all the means for defraying the expenses of the government, as to provide for the partial or total exemption from taxation of the property of corporations. Yet as a matter-of-fact railroad corporations are not required to pay their proportionate share of taxes, nor is their property subjected to the same rules of taxation as that of individuals. In almost all the states these corporations are taxed upon their earnings; their own officers keep the books, and once in each year make a showing, and upon this showing a small tax is levied. If they are honest and present a correct statement of the earnings of their road, the amount of tax fixed by the legislature of the state is paid; but if they choose to suppress the truth a less amount must suffice. Take the state of Iowa as an illustration. Prior to 1872 railroad property in this state did not pay more than one-seventh as much tax upon its value as the property of individuals, and under the present law it does not pay more than one-half as much. Yet no property in the state has yielded such large profits on actual cost and value as railroad property. Iowa had in 1872, subject to taxation, 3,160 miles of railroad. Take the value of their roads as fixed by the companies and reported in the *Railroad Manual*, and the average per mile is over, rather than under, $40,000. Then for the pupose of taxation reduce the valuation to about same rates as are fixed upon the property of individuals, and the average would be about $18,000 per mile. This would make the grand aggregate for tax purposes $56,000,000. Now if a two per cent. tax (which is less than the average rate for all purposes) was assessed upon this property, the revenue to the state and counties would amount to the sum of $1,120,000. But if the same rule of taxation were applied alike to all property in the state the rate demanded of individuals would be less than at present, while railroad companies would only be required to do what the constitution exacts of them, to-wit: pay their just proportion of taxes for the support of state government. Is it any wonder that we complain of high rates of taxes when so large a portion of the property in the state is exempt from taxation? In Muscatine county there is at present about eighty-five miles of railroad. At an assessed value of $18,000 per mile the total for taxation would be $1,530,000, which, on a two per cent tax would afford a revenue of $30,600, of which, if divided between the state and county as other taxes are divided, there would be paid into the county treasury about $24,500, which would be a large increase over the amount now paid to the county. The same would be the result in all the other counties in the state where the manner of taxing railroads so changed as to make no discrimination in their favor. The same kind of discrimination is made in most of the states in favor of the railroads and against the people. No good reason has ever been given for this kind of discrimination, nor can it be supported or justified upon principle or upon constitutional grounds. The value of a mile of railroad can be as easily ascertained as that of an acre of ground, or of a house and lot. The depot, and station grounds and buildings can be assessed as readily as any grounds or buildings. The value of their rolling stock is always included by the companies in giving the cost of their roads, and the value of the roads, including rolling stock, can be more easily ascertained by the assessor than the value of many kinds of personal property, yet it has never been considered necessary or permissible under the constitution to discriminate in favor of individuals or classes of individuals when assessing property for the purposes of taxation. But when the property of these gigantic corporations is to be taxed, when they are called upon for their share of taxes to aid in defraying the expenses of the governments that are granting them extraordinary and exclusive privileges, they refuse to submit to the law which prescribes the manner of collecting taxes from the people and ask special legislative enactments in their favor. To secure such enactments they use their great influence in filling the legislative halls with their stockholders, directors, and attorneys. Thus far they have generally succeeded, and in most of the states special statutes, discriminating in their favor, are now in force. Because of this special legislation the people are paying taxes that should be paid by railroad companies, and in return for favors shown, these companies are constantly increasing their extortions, and imposing additional burdens upon the people.

We can more fully realize the extent of the unjust burdens imposed upon the people by ascertaining the amount of capital invested in railroads in the United States, and showing its relative value compared with the taxable property of the country. For this purpose it will not be unfair to take the value of railroad property as given by the different companies and published in the *Railroad Manual*. The reported cost of all but forty-six roads in the United States is $2,070,980,285. If we add to this amount the probable cost of those not reported, among which is the Union Pacific, this large sum will be swollen to nearly $3,000,000,000. The taxable property in the United States, reported in the census of 1870, was $14,178,986,732. If this railroad property was included, these corporations should pay about one-fifth of all the taxes collected in the country. The method of taxing railroad property that has always obtained in Iowa, and some of the other states, relieves it of at least three-fourths of the taxes justly due from it, and requires the people to supply the deficiency created by this exemption. But, as will appear from the census returns, a small portion only of the vast railroad wealth of the country is included in the valuation of property returned; nor is it listed and returned by local assessors as is the case with the property of individuals. In Iowa the census returns show the value of the property in the state to be $302,515,418. The value of railroads in Iowa, as shown by the different companies is $84,067,663. An equal assessment and levy of taxes upon all the property in the state subject to taxation would require this railroad property to pay over one-fourth of all the taxes levied in the state; yet as a matter of fact not one-twentieth of this amount has ever been collected, unless we except the year 1872, when a small increase over old rates was required. While all acknowledge the injustice of this system of discrimination in favor of railroad companies, and while the people are burdened with more than their just proportion of taxes, all efforts to correct the evil seem to have proved abortive. The fact that more than eighty-four millions of dollars, being over one-fourth of the entire wealth of the state, is held and controlled by corporations, possessing under their charters special privileges, who have combined to prevent legislation that would require of them a contribution of their just share for the support of the government, explains the reasons for these discriminations in the collection of taxes. The power of this railroad oligarchy is now so great that it shapes and controls all revenue statutes. In all cases where the interests of the people and those of these corporations conflict, the corporations acting in concert, are triumphant, and the interests of the people are disregarded. Taxes justly due from the corporations, by special legislation, are extorted from the people, because this anti-republican combination, controlling the wealth of the country, demands it.

CHAPTER XVII.

THE STRONG GRASP OF CONSOLIDATED CAPITAL ON AMERICAN LEGISLATION—BEECHER ON "REFORMATION OR REVOLUTION" —"HISTORY OF RAILWAY LEGISLATION IN IOWA."

HOWEVER much we may boast of our purity, patriotism, and political integrity, the history of the legislation of the United States, both state and national, proves that legislators, like other men, are subject to temptation, and that they do not always successfully resist the tempter. It is not a pleasant truth to acknowledge, that the acquisition of money is the controlling motive in the American mind; yet it is a truth. Nor is it pleasing to admit that corporations control the legislation of our nation and state; but the fact is too patent to be denied. Nor will any one who, without prejudice, examines the history of legislation upon the subject of railroads, deny that legislators have been controlled in their acts by the desire, and from the prospect of receiving personal pecuniary benefit by the passage of acts granting special favors to railroad companies. If the instances of corrupt legislation were rare, or if the persons who acted from personal considerations, rather than for the public good, were few in number, we would not feel justified in devoting time to the discussion of the subject. But when this species of legislation becomes the rule, and legislation in favor of the people the exception, as has been the case for years past, we feel fully justified in calling the reader's attention to the matter.

If we were asked what acts passed by the forty-second congress were of benefit to the people, we would be expected to answer that the internal revenue and tariff laws had been modified, and a part of their burdens lifted from the people; but nothing else of benefit to the public. If, however, we were to look through the acts of congress, we would find almost all conceivable acts in favor of corporations, companies, and individuals, granting special privileges, which in almost every instance, might be characterized a "congressional job." Patent right extensions; grants to railroad companies; for the sale of Indian reservations; amendments to railroad charters, bridge charters, and other like interests, have monopolized the time of the national legislature not consumed in investigating alleged irregularities of some of its members. As a rule, lobbyists and rings have shaped and controlled legislation for years, and have constituted themselves one of the established institutions at the national capital. The successful lobbyist demands and receives for his services larger pay than the salary of congressmen. These men never appear at Washington unless they have a congressional job on hand. To them the ear of an average congressman is always open. A measure without any merit, save to advance the interest of a patentee, or contractor, or a railroad company, will become a law, while measures of interest to the whole people are suffered to slumber, and die at the close of the session from sheer neglect. It is known to congressmen that these lobbyists are paid to influence legislation by the parties interested, and that dishonest and corrupt means are resorted to for the accomplishment of the object they have undertaken; that they are a species of brokers whose business it is to beg and buy congressional votes for some pet scheme; to do acts which in former times would have disgraced all parties concerned, but who are now looked upon as a necessary part of the legislative machinery. Of course those interests that can employ the greatest number of these *congressional brokers*, and wield the greatest influence throughout the country, are in the best shape to secure favorable legislation. No one interest in the country, nor all other interests combined, are as powerful as the railroad interest. Railroad corporations, by constantly asking and receiving, have acquired such strength as to control legislation in all cases where their interests are affected. With a net-work of roads throughout the country; with a large capital at command; with an organization perfect in all its parts; controlled by a few leading spirits like Scott, Vanderbilt, Jay Gould,

Tracy, and a dozen others, the whole strength and wealth of this corporate power can be put into operation at any moment, and congressmen are bought and sold by it like any article of merchandise.

We have already shown the value of the railroad property in the United States, and some of the practices of companies, and their abuse of the privileges granted them. We are now treating of their influence upon legislators and legislation, and of the great power their wealth and combination secure for the purpose of controlling legislation. In this connection we must not forget that the vast sums owed by railroad companies in the United States, for which their bonds have been issued and sold, is a powerful persuasion for legislation in their favor.

We look upon the national debt as being enormous, and are apt to complain of the burdens it imposes; but great as it is, these railroad corporations, after showing a paid-up capital equal to the cost of all the roads in the country, less $865,357,-195, show a bonded indebtedness of $2,874,149,667, being two billions over and above the entire cost of all the roads in the United States—showing that the total amount chargeable against the railroads of the country, exclusive of floating debts, is the sum of $5,169,129,664. This vast sum, amounting to more than one-third in value of the entire taxable property of the nation, is concentrated in these corporations, whose interests are at war with the people's. Controlled as it is by a few leading men, who have their partners, agents, and servants every where, it is not strange that the champions of these monopolists should be found in congress. The power of this great monopoly is felt in the nomination and election of congressmen. One-third of the wealth of the nation combined under the control of a few men is a dangerous power in a republic. When the object sought to be accomplished by this power has been to take control of the government, and administer all its departments in the interest of anti-republican institutions, to build up monopolies and trample upon the rights of the people, it has had no trouble to secure the number of congressmen sufficient for its purposes. In proof of this assertion we have only to look at the history of congressional legislation upon the subject of railroads as shown in a former part of this work. We cannot shut our eyes to the fact that the consolidation and combination of wealth and influence of railroad companies have procured the passage of acts of congress under, and by means of which, these corporations have added largely to their wealth, and strengthened themselves for the desperate struggle soon to come between them and the people. Mr. Henry Ward Beecher has had his attention drawn to some of the more alarming phases of our present political condition. In a recent address delivered in St. Louis he used the following language:

"I must, however, make haste to say that among the dangers of the times is one which has developed out of the prodigious rapidity of the accumulation of enormous and consolidated wealth. If I stand in the city of New York and look southward, I see a railroad — the Pennsylvania Central — that runs across the continent with all its connections. Its leases and branches represent a capital of some hundreds of millions of dollars. If I turn my eyes to the north, I see the Erie, where many hundreds of millions dollars lie. If still further to the north, I see the great New York Central, that represents hundreds of millions of dollars. These three roads represent thousands of millions of consolidated capital. Now suppose— in any emergency the railroad interest demands — suppose there were some great national question which demanded that the president of the United States should be a man, and the senate should be composed of men playing into the hands of the great national railroads' concentrated capitalists, what power is there on the continent that could for a moment resist them? It is not a great many years since it would seem almost atrocious to have suggested that thought. But legislatures have been bought and sold, until we think no more about it than of selling so many sheep and cattle. Does any body suppose that if it were a national interest that these vast corporations were seeking to subserve, that there is any legislature on this continent that could not be crushed or bought out by this despot, compared with which even slavery itself were a small danger. One of the greatest humiliations of a nation that is justly proud of so many things is that disaster which has fallen upon our congress. When we see the slimy track of the monster, we may justly ask: 'What are we coming to?' There has got to be a public sentiment created on this subject, or we will be swept away by a common ruin. I tell you that the shadow that is already cast upon the land is prodigious. I do not believe in the scociologists, in the international, nor the communists, but when I see what rich men, as classes, are doing with our legislatures, what laws they have passed, what disregard there is to the great common interest, I fear that the time will come when the workingmen will rise up and say that they have no appeal to the courts, no appeal to the legislatures—that they are bought and owned by consolidated capital—and when that time comes, unless it brings reformation, it will bring revolution. And if any such time does come, I do not hesitate to say I will stand by the common people for the encouragement of the working people, and against the wealth of the consolidated capital of the land."

This great consolidated railroad interest now has its champions in the halls of congress. In the senate is Dorsey, president of the Arkansas Central railroad. Patterson, senator-elect from South Carolina, is a railroad man. Jones, of Nevada, Allison, of Iowa, Mitchell, of Oregon, Carpenter, of Wisconsin, and Windom, of Minnesota, and others are recognized as reliable railroad men. In the house we have Brooks, Kelly, Schofield, and many more who have proved their fealty to this great monopoly on many occasions. In addition to the friends of these corporations in the legislative halls, paid lobbyists throng the capital, supplied with stocks and money, to be used "where it will do the most good." This money is supplied by the railroad companies for purchasing votes for favorite measures, and the recent startling developments show that this fund does not lie idle. All this has resulted in corrupt legislation. Congressmen have aided in procuring grants and special privileges to companies of which they are members, and other congressmen have listened to the *arguments* of lobbyists, and sacrificed the best interests of the people to promote the interests of these monopolies.

The influence of railroad companies over legislation is not confined to the general government. It develops its full strength in state legislatures. There it manifests itself openly. Railroad companies nominate and elect their own men for the avowed purpose of securing the enactment of laws favorable to themselves. Railroad directors, stockholders, and attorneys are elected to the legislature because their interests are adverse to those of the people; they are selected to defeat all legislation tending to protect or relieve the people from the oppression of these corporations. Paid lobbyists are kept in attendance during the legislative session for the same purpose. Free passes are given to legislators as cheap bribes, and money and railroad stock and bonds are placed "where they will do the most good" to the railroad interest. By the use of all these means, majorities in the interest of railroad companies are secured, or such strong minorities as will prevent unfriendly legislation. As a fact, now a part of the history of the country, the legislatures of many of the states are in the interest of, and controlled by, these corporations. They shape all public legislation, and rule the affairs of the state. The people are taxed and robbed by their own legislatures. Immense sums of money, or state bonds, are donated to these corporations, and the people are taxed to pay them, while the railroad property is practically exempt from taxation. The legislature of the state of Louisiana donated to a single railroad company $3,000,000, and guaranteed the bonds of the same company for about as much more. The legislature of the state of Alabama has voted to different railroad companies many millions of dollars. The same is true of Georgia, Texas, North and South Carolina, and many other states. In some of these states men who were elected to represent the people, and who were pledged in their interest, have openly sold themselves to this railroad monopoly. For a consideration paid to them they have assisted in bankrupting their states, and reducing the people who trusted and honored them to a state of servitude scarcely less oppressive than the old system of African slavery. The value of property is destroyed by excessive taxation, and the political and judicial power of the states is handed over to railroad men, who, by combining their interests, have created a great central power, antagonistic to the people and destructive of republican institutions. In the northern states it has been found impossible to procure just legislation where the interests of railroads and of the people conflict. In addition to the license given to railroad companies, by legislative grants and special privileges, to plunder the people, legislators, in violation of constitutional provisions, and of every principle of justice, have persistently refused to require of these corporations their just proportion of taxes, and have just as persistently provided for taxing the people to aid railroad corporations. Take the state of Indiana as an illustration. Counties, cities, and towns have been burdened for years with unjust taxation because of legislation in favor of local aid to railroads. In that state there are now three thousand five hundred and twenty-nine miles of railroads, representing about $100,000,000. For the purposes of taxation all of this railroad property represents but $10,000,000. Some of these roads for the purposes of taxation are appraised at $3,000 per mile, and some as low as $500 and $400. While the property of individuals is appraised at about one-third of its estimated value, this railroad property does not pay taxes upon more than one-tenth part of its estimated value, and when, at a recent session of the legislature, an effort was made to amend the statute so as to make taxation more equal, it was defeated by the railroad men in the legislature, supported as they were by the strong lobby whom they had paid to be in attendance. The history of railroad legislation in the state of Iowa is of the same glaring character. We have the pleasure of laying before our readers the following succinct history of this Iowa legislation, from the pen of Hon. Samuel McNutt, who, for the last ten years, has been a member of the legislature (six years in the house and four in the senate), and who kindly furnishes this communication at our request:

HISTORY OF RAILWAY LEGISLATION IN IOWA.

HON. D. C. CLOUD, Muscatine, Iowa:

DEAR SIR: The progress of the railroad question is remarkable in our own state. As a member of the Iowa legislature for ten consecutive years, I have had occasion to note that progress, and to observe the advancement of that interest from struggling infancy to vigorous growth — from feebleness to a strength that is fearful to contemplate.

The people of Iowa, through their legislature, have always been eminently friendly to the construction of railroads and the promotion of the railway interests. In proof of this, witness the whole history of our legislation; witness our magnificent land grants, subsidies, bonds, subscriptions, and taxes, to the amount of five per cent. of our entire valuation, in one year, as free gifts to railroad corporations. And yet some of these corporations have cheated us as people never were cheated before. We have afforded immunities to capital invested in railroads that are not afforded to any other kind of capital in the state. Witness the hitherto almost entire exemption from taxation of that kind of property. But, more than this, we have laws regulating the charges to be made by those engaged in several of the industrial pursuits, while up to the present time there has been no law upon our statute books interfering with the charges made by railroad corporations; and only *the right* to interfere has been claimed in cases of public necessity, where those corporations are guilty of gross extortion or unjust discrimination.

The first grant of lands to aid in the construction of railroads in our state is known as the "Iowa Land Bill," which passed congress and was approved by the president, May 15th, 1856. Under this act there has been certified to the state, to aid the four original land grant roads, as follows: to the Burlington & Missouri river railroad, two hundred and eighty-seven thousand acres; to the Mississippi & Missouri (now part of the Chicago, Rock Island & Pacific) railroad, four hundred and seventy-four thousand six hundred and seventy-five acres; to the Iowa Central (afterwards the Cedar Rapids & Missouri River) railroad, seven hundred and seventy-five thousand and ninety-five acres; and, to the Dubuque & Sioux City railroad, one million two hundred and twenty-six thousand five hundred and fifty-nine acres. On the 12th of May, 1864, congress passed an act granting lands to aid in the construction of another railroad across the state, from the city of McGregor, westward, on or near the forty-third parallel, to Sioux City. The lands in this grant were supposed to exceed a million of acres, but were found afterwards to be less than half a million. On the 12th of July, 1862, congress authorized the diversion of a portion of the Des Moines River Improvement Company's land grant to the Des Moines Valley Railroad Company, the amount of which I have not before me. It is safe to say that all these railroad land grants, taken together, amount to *over four millions of acres*, or nearly one-eighth of the land of the state; or, more approximately, *one acre out of every eight and a half acres* of the entire area of Iowa has been given away to railroad corporations. In addition to this immense subsidy, the people along the several lines contributed largely toward their construction.

On the 14th of July, 1856, the general assembly, in extra session, passed an act conveying the land of the four first mentioned companies, upon certain conditions. Section 14 of that act (which act is the original "charter" of those corporations), now found as section 1,311 of the Revision of 1860, reads thus: "Said railroad companies accepting the provisions of this act shall at all times be subject to such rules and regulations as may, from time to time, be enacted by the general assembly of Iowa, not inconsistent with the provisions of this act, and the act of congress making the grant."

Under this "charter" the companies went to work, and when some of their roads were extended toward the interior, complaints began to arise that the railroad tariffs were so arranged as to seriously discriminate against the trade and commerce of Iowa towns and in favor of points out of and beyond the state; that these tariff rates were also so arranged as to deprive our people of a choice of markets, rendering the Mississippi river useless as a highway of trade and commerce, and compelling our people either to pay tribute to Chicago or go without a market. The evidence in this matter was of a character that could not be questioned, and although the subject was brought before the general assembly of 1864, we refused to take any action at that time, hoping that the companies which had been so liberally dealt with by our people would, upon remonstrance, deal fairly and justly by them.

When the general assembly met again, in 1866, the matter of railroad discriminations against our people had assumed a still more momentous shape. The greater portion of our time during that session was occupied with that question. Weeks after weeks were spent mainly discussing whether or not the state had the right to prevent unjust discrimination or in any way control railroad corporations as to their charges. The then attorney-general (Hon. F. E. Bissell, now deceased) gave it as his official opinion that the state possessed no such right; but that in the matter of tariff charges, those corporations were above and beyond all legislative control. Whether the fact that he was a "railroad attorney," as well as attorney-general for the state, had anything to do with influencing his "opinion," is not for me to say. We had able lawyers of the very opposite opinion, but the fact of this announcement gave great encouragement to the railroad party, and was calculated to dishearten those of us who believed that the people had some rights which even corporations should respect. It was now openly declared by eminent attorneys, both in the legislature and in the powerful "lobby" that hung around us, that in the original "charter," or grant, the state, while reserving the right to "enact rules and regulations," had either failed or neglected to reserve, in specific and "*express terms*," the particular right to regulate and limit tariff charges, and therefore she could not now exercise that right, and could never regain it.

Listening to these astounding claims, put forth by the attorneys for the corporations, some of us declared that if God and the good people of Iowa ever gave us a chance to reserve, in a railroad charter, the right of control, we would surely do it in such specific and "express terms" as even a railroad attorney could neither mystify nor explain away. The golden opportunity to do this very thing occurred in 1868. A certain state of facts existed regarding the management of the Chicago, Rock Island & Pacific railroad company, which rendered new legislation necessary. The executive committee, headed by

John F. Tracy, had issued and put upon the New York money market nearly *four million dollars'* worth of "watered stock," and realized the cash for it before certain other parties were aware of what had been done. With this money the Tracy party claimed that they intended to build the road from Des Moines to Council Bluffs (the road at this time being completed only to Des Moines). The immediate result of this "stock operation" was a bitter quarrel between the Tracy and the anti-Tracy parties of the stockholders. The Tracy party were said to be in the minority, but they had the money and the executive committee. Suits were commenced against them in the New York courts to forbid their construction of the road west of Des Moines, and to compel them to disgorge the four millions of dollars for distribution among the stockholders. In the meantime the company had forfeited their right to the land grant in consequence of the non-construction of the road beyond Des Moines, according to the terms of the original act. The consolidation of the Chicago, Rock Island & Pacific railroad company's stock (a company organized under the laws of Illinois) with that of the Mississippi & Missouri railroad company (organized under the laws of Iowa), needed legislative sanction by the general assembly of Iowa; and further, the directors of the consolidated company wanted not only a legalizing act covering the above points, but also an extension of their term of office for one year beyond the time for which they had been elected by the stockholders.

Under this state of things, the "Tracy party," legally representing the consolidated company, applied to our legislature for relief and protection; and, accordingly, a bill was introduced covering the desired points, and re-granting the lands to the company under certain conditions and restrictions, which when agreed to by the company, should remain forever *a contract* between the state and the company.

At this juncture, one of the judges of the supreme court of New York issued a solemn injunction upon the general assembly of Iowa, forbidding that body to legislate, in any way, upon the matters I have above recited. Some of us, not having the fear of New York courts nor the majesty of Judge

Cardozo before our eyes, fairly laughed at that judicial functionary's lordly impudence. We thought that the grand opportunity had now arrived when the state could justly step in and pass an act compelling the company to construct the road, for the sake of the extraordinary relief sought, and in that act *reserve, in "express terms,"* as a matter of *contract*, the right to control the tariff rates of at least one powerful corporation, connecting with the Pacific railroad at Council Bluffs, and thereby control the rates of other lines crossing the state with similar connections. This express reservation of right, in the form of what was known as the "Doud Amendment," was inserted in the act in relation to the Chicago, Rock Island & Pacific railroad company, and will be found as the first proviso in the second section of that act (chapter 13, on page 14, Acts of Twelfth General Assembly), and is in the following words: "*Provided*, said railroad company, accepting the provisions of this act, shall at all times be subject to such rules and regulations, and rates for the transportation of freight and passengers, as may from time to time, be enacted by the general assembly of Iowa."

The company, through its proper officers, accepted the terms of this act, and filed that acceptance in the office of the secretary of state, thus closing *a contract* between the state and the company, and setting at rest forever the question of controlling and regulating the charges for freight and passengers in favor of the state. The same proviso was afterwards inserted in the act in relation to the Des Moines Valley railroad company (chapter 57, page 63); also in the act relating to the McGregor Western railroad company (chapter 58, page 67); also, in the act relating to the Dubuque & Sioux City railroad company (chapter 124, page 164); all acts of the twelfth general assembly.

The passage of the last named act aroused unusual commotion along the proposed railroad line from Cedar Falls, via Fort Dodge, to Sioux City, in consequence of the railroad managers declaring that not another mile of that road would ever be built until the proviso for control should be repealed. Work ceased along the line; the laborers were discharged; the people who expected a railroad through their country became alarmed. Meetings were held at Fort Dodge, Sioux City, and other points, and extraordinary efforts were put forth to induce Governor Stone to call an extra session of the legislature for the purpose of repealing the so-called "*Doud Amendment.*" A committee of prominent citizens was appointed to visit, in person, the members of the general assembly, and have them sign a request to the governor in favor of an extra session. This committee, knowing my record on this question, did not do me the honor of a personal visit, but they sent me a letter (still in my possession,) to which I replied through the public press, strongly opposing their movement, and after reciting a portion of the facts herein recapitulated, earnestly requested them to let the Doud Amendment alone; for I believed it to be one of the wisest measures ever enacted by our legislature, and, having been one of its foremost advocates in that body, I would still defend it. The effort to call an extra session failed, and the railroad managers in the north, finding their efforts in that instance vain, after frightening the people nearly a year, concluded to go to work again, and so the building of that road went on to completion.

We had now succeeded in making the question of control a matter of contract between the state and the companies above named; so that, so far as they are concerned, no person or authority can question that *right.* Some of these roads being parallel lines across the state, the limitation of their charges will virtually control the others.

I have always maintained that the state, by virtue of her sovereignty, possesses the right to regulate and limit railroad charges whenever the public necessity, or the public welfare requires such limitation, without any special reservation in any charter or contract. But inasmuch as eminent counsel denied it, I was one of the original prompters and friends of the "Doud Amendment." I was this for the further reason, also, that history teaches me that when the interpretation of constitutions or doubtful laws, in cases where the poor and humble were on one side and wealth and power on the other side, that interpretation has been almost invariably on the side of wealth and power.

During the session of 1870, the question of regulating and taxing railroads came up again; but nothing was done except the passage of a law authorizing the state treasurer to levy a tax on their gross receipts, as follows: On the first $3,000, or part thereof, per mile, one per centum; on receipts over $3,000, and under $6,000, two per centum; and on the excess of $6,000 per mile, three per centum. An act was also passed (which I opposed,) authorizing townships, towns, and cities, to vote a tax, not exceeding five per cent. of their assessed valuation, to aid in the construction of railroads. At this session I succeeded in securing the passage of an act (chapter 90, acts of Thirteenth General Assembly,) providing that taxes levied by order of any court to pay judgments on county or city bonded indebtedness, no penalty but legal interest shall be collected.

At the session of 1872, the question of railroad tariffs, taxation, and control, came up again with increased interest. We passed an act (chapter 12 of public laws,) making the work, etc., of laborers and mechanics a lien upon the road bed, right of way, etc., of railroads, thus securing them in their pay for labor done or materials furnished. The five per cent. tax law was repealed, and an act (chapter 26 of public laws,) was passed, making the census board (now executive council.) a board of assessment of railroad property. Under this act a new plan of assessing this kind of property was adopted, and a much larger revenue derived therefrom than heretofore. A freight and passenger tariff bill (known as the O'Donnel bill,) passed the house but failed in the senate. Those of us in the senate who voted FOR the bill, were remembered by the railroad managers when we met in adjourned session last winter, (January 15th, 1873,) by leaving us out of the list of senators whom they favored with free passes. But they sent passes to all the senators who voted *against* the bill. The passes from the Chicago, Rock Island & Pacific railroad company were accompanied with a private note, stating that free passes were not now given generally, "*but only to their friends.*"

The adjourned session of 1873, was for the special purpose of considering and enacting the new code which the three commissioners had now spent nearly three years upon. Our time was limited by joint resolution to thirty days; and yet, during a considerable portion of our limited time, the railroad question occupied our attention. While we were in session, an extraordinary convention, or gathering of farmers, known as the "State Grange of the Patrons of Husbandry," met in Des Moines. This body was composed of the officers called Masters and Past Masters of the subordinate granges, or lodges, of a new secret society of agriculturists scattered throughout the state. This State Grange, or convention of delegates, numbered over twelve hundred members, representing, it was said, some seventy thousand farmers of Iowa. The meeting of this "Grange" lasted a week, and passed strong resolutions urging the legislature to enact a passenger and freight tariff law, and also presented an official petition to that effect.

The members of the senate in favor of such a law prepared twelve sections, (mainly from the old O'Donnel bill,) to be inserted in chapter 5 of title 10, of the proposed code, and I was chosen to offer them in the senate at the proper time. This I did, and the first section was adopted almost before the railroad men could rally their forces. This section limits the fare for passengers to three and one-half (3½) cents per mile. But the other sections, which fixed a maximum rate for the transportation of all kinds of grain, produce, lumber, manufactures, and commodities, were lost by a tie vote, the president of the senate, Lieutenant Governor Bulis, refusing to vote, which was equivalent to voting against the sections. These sections were afterwards fixed to the chapter by the house, with an additional section, known as the "Keables Amendment," but were again lost in the senate for want of two votes.

The commissioners had omitted from the proposed new code all the so-called "Doud Amendments," and reservations of control by the state over railway corporations, on the ground that they were local or special provisions not to be included in a code of general laws. But some of us thought that those reservations of control, and special contracts, were of too important a character to the people of Iowa to be entirely ignored, and so I prepared an amendment to chapter 5, of title 10, in the following words:

"SEC. 6. All contracts, stipulations, and conditions, regarding the right of controlling and regulating the charges for freight and passengers upon railroads heretofore made, in granting lands or other property, or franchises to railroad corporations, are expressly reserved, continued, and perpetuated, in full force and effect, to be exercised by the general assembly whenever the public good and the public necessity requires such exercise thereof." This was adopted.

I have thus hastily sketched the history of railroad legislation in our state, and yet, perhaps, I have exceeded the space you generously allow me in your valuable work. Time and space would not permit me to detail the skill exercised or the means used to defeat every act of legislation looking toward the control of railway corporations.

To-day both the people and the government of this nation are, to a great degree, under the control of the consolidated money capital of the country, and a few individuals are at the head of this capital. These are men, mainly, who regard republican or democratic institutions as too unstable for the security of wealth, and have no real love for our form of government. It remains to be seen what the people will do in the coming crisis. I have faith in the people.

Yours truly, SAMUEL MCNUTT.

Mr. McNutt tells what he knows, and gives us a correct idea of the means resorted to by these corporations to thwart the will of the people. In view of the vast wealth of these corporations, their combination and consolidation with their absolute control of congress and state legislatures, and the centralization of power in themselves, we may well inquire whether our constitutional guarantees have not been so long disregarded as to be virtually destroyed. The question at issue between the people and these corporations is clearly marked and defined.

This great railroad oligarchy is gradually but surely overturning the principles upon which our government is founded. It is substituting a personal for a constitutional government, and to achieve its purposes it brings to bear its vast wealth and influence; it bribes and buys legislators, and maintains throughout the country a vast army of employes, many of whom occupy high official position under the government. It now boldly proclaims the doctrine, that the interests of this great government and of railroads are one!

On the other side of the question are the people, who begin to realize the oppressions of his oligarchy. They find themselves burdened with taxes; the value of the produce of the country consumed in unjust railroad charges; the halls of congress and of state legislatures cursed by the presence of men who take and give bribes in aid of the people's oppressors; their natural rights denied them; the guarantees of the constitution disregarded; all doubtful points decided in favor of the power that is reducing them to slavery, and making their property and the fruits of their labor of no value. They begin to realize that the final struggle must soon come, and that the question will be whether the people, the sovereign people, or their oppressors are to be the future rulers of the *republic.* The result is not uncertain. Legislatures and courts must restore to the people their constitutional rights. If these are denied, then, other means failing, the people, who are sovereign, *must take their rights by revolution.* The self-evident truth that all men are equal, that they have equal rights to enjoy and possess property, and to the protection of those rights in the courts, and that all should bear their proportionate share of the public burdens, MUST be recognized by all classes as the supreme law of this republic.

CHAPTER XVIII.

THE "TRAIL OF THE SERPENT" IN THE INTERIOR DEPARTMENT.

WE have attempted to show the controlling influence of railroad corporations over the legislative department of the government, and its effect upon the people, without following it through all its various forms, our object being to present what we deemed sufficient evidence to direct the public mind to the great and growing evils resulting from this influence. We now desire to refer to the influence of these corporations over the executive department of the government.

The administration of the laws being confided to the executive department of the government, their impartial and honest administration is of the greatest importance to the people. Congress, without the constitutional right, having granted charters and made large grants of lands and bonds to railroad companies, it became necessary that the executive department should have some kind of supervision over the companies. In the issuing of bonds and certificates for land grants; the transportation of mails, troops, etc.; the appointment of government directors, inspectors, and engineers; the transmission of telegraphic dispatches, and respecting many other matters connected with these corporations, special duties were imposed upon the president and members of his cabinet. The government directors, under the statute, had a place on all business committees of the Union Pacific railroad company. They were government officers, appointed by the president, and were to report from time to time upon the progress of the work and condition of the roads. They were prohibited from holding stock or being personally interested in the roads. Their reports were to be made to the secretary of the interior. If these government directors had faithfully performed the duties laid upon them by the law, the contract of the directors of the railroad company with the Credit Mobilier company could not have taken place without their knowledge, which fact should at once have been communicated to the secretary of the interior. Nor could the directors of the railroad have organized themselves into a Credit Mobilier company and contracted with themselves to rob the government and defraud the people without the knowledge of the government directors. And, unless we concede that they were totally unfit for the discharge of the duties imposed upon them by statute — "more sinned against than sinning"— we must conclude that they had full knowledge of all the abuses being practiced by the railroad companies, and failed to discharge their official duties. The national reputation these government directors had achieved in the halls of congress and elsewhere precludes the idea of their being ignorant of what they should have known, and we are forced to conclude that they had this guilty knowledge of the frauds being perpetrated upon the government and the people. Their action in the premises can only be explained on the ground that they were subject to the same railroad influences which have controlled congress and state legislatures. If their action was not governed by corrupt motives and pecuniary considerations, that persuasive influence which emanates from these corporations blinded their minds and warped their judgments to such an extent as to induce them to wink at the frauds of the companies in the construction of their roads and the prosecution of the business connected therewith. Recent investigations show that some of those directors were controlled in their actions by pecuniary considerations; that these corporations have been able to purchase the influence of the men selected by the president to protect the public interest, and that, by reason of such purchase, the sum of $16,000 per mile, in government bonds, has been duplicated on fifty-eight miles of the Pacific road. Other abuses, such as the defective construction of the roads, unlawful payment by the government of engineering expenses, dishonest returns of the cost of the roads, and other minor but important abuses of the privileges granted to these companies, were permitted by these government directors without objection — showing, beyond all reasonable doubt, that their duties, prescribed by acts of congress, were of secondary importance when the interests of the corporations or of these government directors were to be considered.

While the reckless and dishonest transactions of the company directors were such as to call out a protest from an honest engineer employed on the road, prompting him to resign his position as chief engineer rather than be a party to fraud and scandal, these government directors seem to have remained silent and inactive. A contract had been entered into with a man by the name of Hoxie, who had neither personal means nor position to command any considerable amount of capital, for the construction of a portion of the Union Pacific road. While this contract did not possess all the pecularities of the contract with the Credit Mobilier, it was such an outrage upon right and justice as to elicit from the chief engineer, Peter A. Dey, the following letter, addressed to General John A. Dix, after having tendered his resignation as chief engineer of the Union Pacific road to General Dix, who was then president of the company. Mr. Dey says:

"My views of the Pacific railroad are peculiar. I look upon its managers as trustees of the bounty of congress. I cannot willingly see them take a step in the incipiency of the project that will, I believe, if followed out, swell the cost of construction so much that by the time the work reaches the mountains the representative capital will be accumulated so much that at the very time when the company will have need for all its resources, of capital as well as of credit, its securities will not be negotiable in the market. From my very boyhood I have associated Mr. Cisco and yourself with Mr. Bronson and Mr. Flagg, men whose integrity, purity, and singleness of purpose have made them marked men in the generation in which they lived. Of course my opinion remains unchanged. You are, doubtless, uninformed how disproportionate the amount to be paid is to the work contracted for. I need not expatiate upon the sincerity of my course, when you reflect upon the fact that I have resigned the best position in my profession this country has ever offered to any man.

"With respect, PETER A. DEY."

Mr. Dey protested against the extravagant amount agreed to be paid Hoxie. The cost of the sections of the road contracted to Hoxie was $7,806,181. The amount agreed to be paid Hoxie for the work was $12,974,416. Mr. Dey saw that this man Hoxie was a *straw man*, and that near $5,000,000 were to be divided among the directors as the profit on this contract, and, as engineer, he protested against it. Yet these government directors, whose sole duty it was to look after and protect the interests of the government and the people, failed to discover and report these abuses to the secretary of the interior; or if the same and the Credit Mobilier transactions were so reported, then the influence of these corporations controlled the department of the secretary. The truth is, the position of these government directors was such that without a total disregard of the statutes, and their duties under it, it was not possible to keep all knowledge of these gross abuses from the department. But one conclusion can be drawn from the facts, which is, that the government directors, influenced by these powerful monopolies, were unfaithful to the trust confided to them by the president.

Under the statute, the secretary of the interior has the general control of the issue of bonds, certificates for lands, rights of way, etc. The government directors were bound to report to him. If the duties imposed under the law had been faithfully discharged by him, the great abuses practiced by the Pacific railroad companies would have been prevented. The Hoxie contract, the Ames Credit Mobilier contract, and the Davis contract were all made for about double the cost of building the respective sections of the road covered by these contracts, the actual cost of these respective sections being $50,720,957, and the amounts allowed the contractors being $93,546,387. In this amount is included $1,104,000, which was a duplicate payment allowed Ames for work done, and once paid for under the Hoxie contract. These three jobs put into the pocket of the Credit Mobilier company a net profit of $43,929,337, a large part of which was in subsidy bonds issued by government. These bonds could only issue after the approval by the secretary of the interior of the report of the government directors. If the secretary had discharged his duty, or if the interest of the people, which he was supposed to be protecting, and not the interest of these companies, had controlled his action, *duplicate bonds* would not have been issued at the rate of $16,000 per mile for more than fifty miles of the road. Nor would certificates for land have issued to the companies while they were openly cheating, defrauding, and robbing the government and people. Let the reader look at the laws of congress chartering the roads, with the different amendments, and learn the duties of the secretary of the interior respecting their construction and the issuing of bonds and land certificates, and he will conclude that the secretary was ignorant of what the law made it his duty to know, that he was inexcusably negligent in the discharge of his duty, or what is most probable, that the same potent influences that controlled congress in aiding these companies, found their way successfully to the chief parlor of the interior department. Without the secretary's approval ot the companies' work and accounts, they could not possibly have committed such gross frauds upon the government.

If additional proof of the fact that the secretary of the interior was influenced by, and used his official position to assist the railroad corporations, in the raids upon the treasury, was needed, we have it in his action relative to the homestead and preëmption rights of settlers upon the public lands within the limits fixed by congress for the selection of lands by the different railroad companies. In all cases where lands have been granted to railroad companies, lands to which preëmption rights attached at the time the line of the road was fixed have been saved to the preëmption and homestead claimants. In many instances the railroad companies have not been able to find, within the limits fixed, the amount of lands granted to them belonging to the government. This has caused them to make war upon preëemption and homestead claimants. If these claimants could be forced from their lands, some millions of acres would be thus seized by, and allowed to, the railroad companies. The practice of going upon the public land under the preëmption and homestead acts had become so common, that these claims had been recognized by the public and the government as vesting in the claimant a title which could only be defeated by his failure to comply with the provisions of the law respecting the perfection of his title. No one, save where two or more preëmption claimants were contending for the same tract, could interfere; nor is there any provision of statute by which railroad companies can call in question the preëmption or homestead right. In the absence of any contest between preëmptors, the claimant has only to show a substantial compliance with the law, pay the required amount, and obtain his title. So, also, in regard to homestead rights. Nor did any difficulty arise until railroad companies began to interfere. The acts granting lands to railroad companies made no provision for the selection by them of lands held by preëmption or homestead claimants at the time the lines of their roads were fixed, and subsequently abandoned. The companies applied to the secretary of the interior, and procured from him a construction of the statutes, giving them the right to select as railroad lands all such so abandoned. This was the first decision in their favor, and committed the secretary to their interest.

A war upon preëmption and homestead claimants was begun, and the representation to the department that a claimant had abandoned his claim was sure to pass the title to one hundred and sixty acres to the company. But something more must be done to get hold of the claimed land. The question as to the regularity and validity of the settler's claim is raised by the companies, and then they apply again to the secretary of the interior. While the statute respects and protects the occupancy and rights of the claimant, the secretary, to aid the railroad companies, interpolates the word "valid," and holds that if the claim is invalid, the railroad companies can drive off the claimant and take his land. The action of the department gave the companies an advantage over the claimant which was almost equivalent to the destruction of his claim.

Many claimants became alarmed, and did just what the companies desired — they abandoned their claims to their oppressors, and the companies made large gains. But the claimants were not yet entirely in the power of their oppressors, and resort is again had to the department, and the settlers are placed entirely at the mercy of these monopolists. The interior department issued an order under date of June 22d, 1872, allowing railroad companies to contest the right of preëmption and homestead claimants to their quarter-sections. While the act of congress absolutely prohibited railroad companies from interfering with the rights of these claimants, the interior department, in the interest of these giant monopolies, in violation of the statute, by interpolation and a forced construction of the law, allowed these corporations to appear and dispute the claim of the poor pioneer who had gone in advance of railroads and preëmpted a small tract of land for a home for his family, before the company disputing his right was organized, or had thought of locating a railroad in his vicinity. The preëmption and homestead laws were passed for the benefit of the actual settlers of the country. If they get their lands, they pay the government the price fixed by law; but if the railroad companies get these lands, they aid in building up and strengthening a monopoly already too great for the welfare of the country. The department having lent its powerful aid to this monopoly, and, by unjust rulings, interpolations, and decisions, assisted in turning these poor men adrift, and depriving them of their lands and years of toil, already more than one million of acres— that of right, and under the law, properly interpreted and administered, would have belonged to actual settlers — have become the property of these railroad companies. Claimants are becoming alarmed at the action of the department, and are leaving their lands, choosing to lose their claims and the years of toil expended upon them, rather than defend against these companies, backed by the department.

To still further show the *quasi* collusion between the department and these great corporations, let us look at the circular issued to the different land offices from the department in June, 1872. The circular says:

"A preëmption or homestead claim of record is of course *prima facie* evidence of a valid right; yet it may occur that such a claim has a fraudulent inception. When such is the case, the claim is of course void *ab initio*, and does not defeat the right of the railroad. In view of these rulings the following is communicated for your information and government, to the end that the rights of all parties may be protected, and and the spirit of the *grants* fully complied with:

"1st. In relation to preëmption claims, the preëmption law requires that a person must be over the age of twenty-one years, or the head of a family, a citizen of the United States, or a person who has filed a declaration to become such, and also that a person may file a preëmption claim for such land as he may have settled upon, thus imposing conditions as prerequisite to the initiation of a claim.

"2d. In relation to homestead claims, the law requires that a person must be over twenty-one years of age, or the head of a family, a citizen of the United States, or one who has declared his intention to become such, and under the first and third sections of the amendatory act of March 21, 1864, the persons claiming the benefit of said sections must make settlement upon the tracts before they can obtain the benefit of said sections. Therefore, as the fraudulent character of the preëmption or homestead claim in its inception may be brought in question, it is right that the parties in interest should have an opportunity in all cases to be heard. With this view you are required,

"3d. When application is made by a railroad company to select tracts which are covered by existing preëmption or homestead claims at the date of the right of the road attaching, but subsequently relinquished or abandoned, to allow the company to file such proof as they may have in support of their right to the land, or to have hearings for the purpose, and should the evidence be satisfactory you will permit the selections.

"4th. When any person applies to enter a tract of such lands, claiming the right to do so by reason of such prior abandoned claim, you will order a hearing, notifying the railroad company, as well as the preëmption or homestead claimant, so that they may produce such evidence in support of their right as they may have to furnish. Your inquiry must be directed to the personal qualifications of the original claimant, and his compliance with the law prior to filing an entry; and I desire to enjoin upon you the necessity of excluding all testimony not material to showing the facts upon the subject of inquiry. You will, however, be careful that all such facts are brought out, and if necessary to this end you will yourselves examine and question the witnesses. You will in all cases give the parties interested personal notice of the time and place of hearing, when their whereabouts are known, or they can be reached by such notice. In other cases you will cause the notice of contest to be published at least once a week for four weeks in the newspaper having the largest circulation in the vicinity of the land. Parties initiating a contest must provide for paying the expenses thereof, but when the case comes before you for trial you can apportion the expenses according to the equities of each case. Your particular attention is called to the fact that in some of the earlier railroad grants, lands covered by homestead claims, which may subsequently be cancelled, are not exempted from the operation of the grant. Therefore, in such cases, the tracts revert to the grant, and you will recognize no application for these lands by other parties, but will pay due regard to the rights of the grantees. You will in no case allow preëmption filing, or homestead entry on this class of lands, without instructions from this office."

This circular, in the interest of railroad companies, is signed by Willis Drummond, commissioner, and directed to registers and receivers of district land offices. While the acts of congress exclude from the grants to railroad companies all lands held by preëmption and homestead claims, the secretary of the interior says it means *valid* claims. He then declares all claims invalid or fraudulent when there has not been a literal compliance with the statute. If the preëmptor filed his claim one day or one week before he commenced his occupation, his claim, as against the railroad company, is fraudulent. Or, if for some cause, after having complied with all preliminaries, he should leave his claim for a day or a week, it could be treated as abandoned, and his right would be lost. These rulings, in favor of railroad companies, and adverse to the settlers, having been made, the companies were not slow in taking advantage of them. Men who supposed their claims to be valid, who had invested their all in improving them, have had their validity questioned, or have been charged with abandonment. The first intimation a settler has, is a notice to appear and defend the home of his family against the claim of a powerful corporation that is seeking to take it from him. He must submit to the alternative of losing his home at once, or of protracted, expensive litigation, with the assurance that he is combatting a powerful adversary before a tribunal that has already prejudiced his case in favor of his opponent. All that the railroad companies need do to defraud the settler is to satisfy the register or receiver that, under the rulings of the department we have quoted, the settler's claim is invalid, or that he has abandoned it.

We draw no fancy sketch. The circular speaks for itself, and the large number of men who have been compelled to leave their preëmption and homestead claims, with the constantly increasing quarter-sections of land that are being added to the railroad grants, attest the truth of our statements. We are not aware of any law of the United States recognizing the right of railroad companies to become parties in a contest concerning a homestead or preëmption right. Nor do we believe that the interior department of the government can legally authorize these companies to become claimants for land held by settlers under act of congress. If any question arises between two preëmption claimants, the commissioner of the general land office decides the dispute. If any question is raised as to whether the claimant is entitled to his preëmption, there are, under the acts of congress, but two parties to the controversy—the claimant himself and the interior department. The order allowing railroad companies to appear as parties, and by virtue of numerical strength and immense wealth and influence, to overpower the settler, is doing him injustice, as well as degrading a high official position, and sustains our charge that these railroad companies influence the interior department of the government. We think we have shown that the whole strength of this department is used in favor of these great monopolies, and against the interests of the people. While we do not charge the officers of this department of government with intentional wrong, we do charge that this great corporate power, which has such unlimited influence over the legislative department of the government, has virtually taken control of the department of the interior in cases where its interests can be subserved by the influence of the department.

CHAPTER XIX.

THE MONOPOLISTS AT THE DOOR OF THE WHITE HOUSE.

THE influence of this great corporate power does not spend all its force at the interior department, but it is seen handing in its card at the white house.

While we claim that railroads and other corporations have, to a considerable extent, influenced the distinguished occupants of the presidential chair, we do not wish to be understood as intimating that any of our chief magistrates have acted corruptly. We simply assert that this great corporate interest has secured favorable action from our presidents when they have been appealed to. As will be seen by their perusal, the acts of congress chartering the Pacific railroad and branches, imposed certain duties upon the president in connection with their location and construction. In the discharge of these duties the wishes of the companies were in all cases complied with, and in some instances to the injury and at the cost of the government and the public, and under circumstances leaving no doubt that the president acted wholly upon the representations of the companies.

In the act of July, 1864, the Union Pacific charter was so amended as to permit any company organized under the laws of Iowa, Minnesota, Nebraska, or Dakota, and designated by the president of the United States, to construct a railroad from Sioux City, Iowa, to connect with the Union Pacific road at some point not farther west than the one-hundredth degree of longitude. A company was organized under the laws of Iowa to build a railroad from Sioux City to Missouri Valley in the same state, the latter point being some thirty miles east of Sioux City, and seventy or more miles south. Another company was organized to build a railroad from Missouri Valley to Fremont, in Nebraska, the latter place being a point on the

Union Pacific. These companies were incorporated by a few men, among whom were several members of congress who had aided in the passage of the act of July, 1864. Through the influence of one of the incorporators, then a member of congress, now of the United States senate, the president designated these companies as the companies to build the Sioux City branch of the Union Pacific, and their roads, representing two sides of a triangle, were adopted as a branch road. The road is known as the Sioux City & Pacific. A road running westerly from Sioux City to Fremont would be about seventy-five miles in length. The road, as constructed between these two points, is, as given in the *Railroad Manual*, one hundred and seven miles. The act of congress required the road to be constructed on the most direct and practicable route. This road received the same privileges, subsidies, and grants as the main line, with an addition of eighty sections of land per mile. Now it cannot be presumed that the president, acting on his own judgment, uninfluenced by the railroad company, would have designated these companies, and these roads, as the Sioux City branch of the Union Pacific road, with one hundred sections of land and $16,000 subsidy bonds for every mile of the road. We have given this instance to show the direct influence of this corporate power over the president. This great influence, so dangerous to the welfare of the country, is indirect in its action. Vast mumbers of men have their funds invested in railroad stocks and bonds. They engage in Wall street speculations; they buy and sell stocks and bonds; they operate in gold and values, and have no interest in common with the laboring and producing classes of the country. These corporations own and control property worth billions of dollars; they rule the finances of the country; they have tens of thousands of men in their employ; as they increase in strength and wealth, they are constantly striving for greater powers and privileges. Their lobbyists and retainers surround every department of the government. When public offices are to be filled, they unite in favor of men in their interest; and when decisions are to be made upon questions affecting their rights and obligations, they take care that their friends shall be in position to make or shape these decisions. The president, with his appointing power, if influenced in their favor, becomes an important ally. In his appointments to office, it is not to be expected that he can personally know the qualifications and views of every nominee. He must, of necessity, rely upon others, to a great extent, in making his selections. Next to legislative action in their favor, railroad companies are most deeply interested in the judicial decisions affecting their interests. Judges are apt to be influenced by the same motives that prevail with other men. Years spent by men as railroad attorneys, or as attorneys for any other great interest, will, to a certain extent, control their reasoning and decision upon questions coming before them should they be promoted to the bench. In close relation with, and next in importance to the decisions of courts, on points affecting this great corporate interest, are the rulings and decisions of the attorney general of the United States. If these important offices can be filled by persons whose past pursuits have demonstrated that they entertain views favorable to the interests of these companies, an important gain is made at the start in their favor. To secure such appointments, all and every influence at the command of these corporations are brought to bear upon the president. The services of the most influential men, in congress and out, are engaged; the names of the candidates selected are presented for the consideration of the president, and their appointment urged by the whole railroad and corporate interest of the country. The president, following a long established precedent, usually appoints the persons who are most strongly recommended. This fact is well understood by these corporate interests and hence their vigilance and activity. We do not say that the president, in yielding to this tremendous pressure, acts from improper motives. We simply assert that this pressure is used, and that it is scarcely to be resisted.

The fact that judges of ability and integrity differ in their construction of the constitution and laws, is well understood by the men who lead and control the corporate interests of the country; as also the further fact that the time is not distant when the question whether the people or railroad corporations shall govern, must be determined. To prepare for this issue they use their great influence to have the important positions in the government occupied by their friends. To a considerable extent they have succeeded.

Mr. Ackerman, of North Carolina, was attorney general. He was what might be termed a strict constructionist. His views were conservative. As the legal adviser of the executive department, his opinions were adverse to the interests of the railroad companies on certain questions submitted to him. At the request of the president he resigned, and Judge Williams, of Oregon, was appointed in his stead. No one will question the integrity of the present attorney general; yet is was a well-known fact that at the date of his appointment he was one of the attorneys of the Northern Pacific railroad company; that he was fully committed to the railroad interests, and that his appointment was urged by railroad men in all parts of the country. By his appointment a friend of these corporations became a member of the cabinet, and an important ally is present whenever questions affecting their interests are discussed in executive council.

A question of the greatest importance to these corporations was the construction to be given to the statutes of the United States, and especially the "Legal Tender Act." The first of the legal tender acts was passed July, 1862. This was followed by other acts increasing the amounts of legal tender issues. Prior to the passage of these acts railroad corporations had issued and sold many millions of bonds, and stipulated that both principal and interest should be paid in gold. Soon after the issue of legal tender bills their value depreciated, and from that time to the present there has been, and still is, a wide margin between their value and coin. If these railroad companies could pay their bond indebtedness with legal tender at par, a saving of from ten to fifteen dollars could be effected on every hundred so paid. In the year 1869 the question whether this act was retroactive in its operation or effect was presented to the supreme court. The court was then composed of eight justices. When the case involving this question was presented to and decided by the court, but seven of the justices were on the bench. Of these, four, including the chief justice, were of the opinion that the statute did not affect contracts made before its passage, and decided that these railroad companies must pay their bonds in coin, according to the contract. This decision was not acceptable to this vast corporate power. It was condemned by railroad men throughout the country. The president was approached on the subject, and his great influence was besought in the matter. Four of the justices (one-half of the court) having held adversely to the corporations, a full bench could not reverse their decision. To effect a reversal one of the four must change his opinion, or the number of justices must be increased. The latter alternative was decided to be the more feasible, and the president asked congress to increase their number to *nine*. The reason urged was, that upon important questions, before a full bench, the court might be equally divided, and important questions would remain undetermined. The railroad interest was fully represented in the lobby at Washington, and congress provided for an additional justice. About this time one of the justices retired from the bench, making a vacancy, and rendering it necessary for the president to appoint two new justices. This was a grand opportunity for the railroad interest. If men who were identified with them could be appointed, the decision on the "Legal Tender Act" could be reversed, and they could save from ten to fifteen millions of dollars on every hundred million of dollars due from them. Not only could they save this amount, but in future, as the members of the court are appointed during life or good behavior, they would have no apprehensions of a decision against their interest. At once the president was importuned to appoint William Strong, of Pennsylvania—a man who was fully identified with them by education and employment, he being attorney for the Pennsylvania railroad company—and Joseph P. Bradley, of New Jersey, who was also identified with this interest, he being the attorney of the greatest railroad corporation in that state. Neither of these men had any national reputation; but all at once the city of Washington, as well as the whole country, was enlightened as to their great judicial worth, and railroad men throughout the country were urging their appointment. It was publicly announced, and not contradicted, that they were in favor of reversing the decision of the court on the legal tender act, and their appointment was urged for this reason. This influence controlled the president. These gentlemen were nominated by him, and their appointment was confirmed by the senate in 1870. The decision on the legal tender act was reversed, and railroad men were happy. As we shall attempt to show, when we treat of the controlling influence of these corporations upon the finances of the country, this reversal was most baneful to the country, and detrimental to the best interests of the people. We do not wish to be understood as accusing the president of being governed by improper motives in the appointments of Messrs. Strong and Bradley to the supreme bench; but we do mean that the railroad interests, by concert of action, procured these appointments; it being known, or at least well understood that these appointments would insure a reversal of the decision, as we have recounted, and that by such reversal their interests would be greatly subserved. Nor do we wish to be understood as accusing the persons so appointed of lacking the requisite ability for the honorable stations for which they were selected, or that their decisions were governed by personal considerations, or that they reversed said former decision to specially subserve the interests of railroad corporations. We have long since come to the conclusion that judges of courts, like other men, are influenced by surrounding circumstances; that they are not infallible, and that it is no unusual thing for the most eminent judges to differ upon questions submitted for their decision. While these decisions are honestly made, they are often controlled or dictated by extra-judicial considerations. As we shall have occasion hereafter to examine this subject when treating of the intimate and controlling relations between these corporations and the courts of the country, we are content to leave the case of their influence with the executive department to the proof submitted in these three appointments of Williams, Bradley, and Strong.

CHAPTER XX.

THE UNITED STATES TREASURY THE VASSAL OF WALL STREET—STOCK "OPERATIONS" EXPLAINED.

WE now beg to call the reader's attention to the financial operations of the monopolists, and the course resorted to by them to control the finances of the country.

There are now (January, 1873,) seventy thousand one hundred and seventy-eight miles of railroad completed in the United States and territories. At an expense of $35,000 per mile, the total cost of these roads is $2,456,230,000. The cost, as given by the companies, is $3,436,638,749, or $48,970 per mile. In contemplation of law, and as reported, this cost is represented by stock certificates, and is supposed to be paid up. If the roads cost but $35,000 per mile, then $980,408,749 of the stock certificates (that amount being the excess over actual cost) have only an imaginary value. In addition to the stock certificates representing the above sum of $3,456,230,749, the railroad companies have issued and put upon the market their bonds to the amount of $2,800,000,000, thus making their roads represent the enormous sum of *six billions two hundred and thirty-six millions six hundred and thirty-eight thousand seven hundred and forty-nine dollars, or eighty-eight thousand eight hundred and seventy-two dollars per mile.* The only real value all these bonds and certificates of stock represent is the railroads. These we have put at $35,000 per mile. Of course some lines of road exceed this valuation; but an examination of the actual cost, as reported by the engineers of the respective roads, will show that much the larger portion of the roads has cost less. Now let us look at the amount of the capital represented by a few of these roads, as reported in the *Railroad Manual* and *The Stockholder*. The Chicago, Burlington & Quincy is reputed to be one of the best and most prudently managed roads in the country. This road represents in stock and bonds the sum of $32,845,880, or $43,292 per mile. On the other extreme we will take the Central Pacific, which represents the sum of $182,208,000, or $130,000 per mile. The Atlantic & Great Western (an organization of the New York, Pennsylvania & Ohio) represents the sum of $109,000,000, or about $256,000 per mile. The Cedar Rapids & Missouri River railroad represents the sum of $11,334,000, or $41,000 per mile. The Chicago, Rock Island & Pacific represents the sum of $25,717,000, or $56,667 per mile. The Erie represents the sum of $112,935,710, or $125,750 per mile. The New York Central & Hudson River railroad represents $104,660,049, or $142,656 per mile. The Union Pacific represents $112,911,512, or $109,507 per mile. We give the above as samples of the amounts represented by the different roads. In some other instances the stocks are "watered" more, and in others less than in the roads above named. Taking all the roads in the country, and adding together the stock and bonds issued, they represent $3,800,408,749 more than their actual cost. It will not be out of place here to state that the only resource these railroad companies have for the payment of interest and dividends on their stock and bonds, representing the sum of $6,236,638,749, is the earnings of their roads. While a low rate of charges would pay fair dividends on the actual cost of the roads, yet in order to pay dividends on their "watered" stock, and interest on their bonds, oppressive and extortionate rates must be charged and collected. The men who control these great monopolies, viz.: Col. Scott, who controls roads representing about $700,000,000; Vanderbilt, who controls about as great an interest; Drew, Gould, and some few others of the principal railroad men, care but little about the prosperity of the country, or the profits made by their roads, save as a basis for their Wall street speculations. The roads serve as a basis for financial operations. Like the old "wild cat" banks that issued bills without regard to stock or capital, so the roads controlled by these railroad monarchs are loaded with "watered" stock and bonds, until their value as roads are destroyed, and passengers and shippers are oppressively taxed for the purpose of giving some sort of market value to the bonds and "watered" stock with which Wall street is flooded. The issuing of stock certificates goes on, and will continue as long as dividends can be declared. At the present time the railroads of the country collectively represent about three times their value, or actual cost. If the people were not taxed on "watered" stock and bonds, dishonestly issued, the rates charged for transportation would be but little more than one-third the figures of the present tariff. The vast wealth claimed by railroad corporations is about two-thirds pure fiction, and but for the extortions practiced upon the public, their stocks and bonds, beyond the value of their roads, would not be considered in market; but so long as interest at the rate of six, eight and ten per cent. can be drawn from the public, they are marketable. These stocks and bonds are owned or controlled by the men who not only manage the railroad interests, but also the bond and stock market of the country. Being the leading spirits among Wall street brokers, using their railroads for the purpose of aiding in their stock-jobbing speculations, by compelling them to earn interest on all the worthless stocks and bonds they put upon the market, a fictitious value is given to them. Having their principal place of business in the commercial metropolis of the country, being able whenever their interests demand it to "corner" the money of the country, it could be hardly expected that the treasury department of the government would escape their control. If a conflict should arise between the secretary of the treasury and these vast monopolies, the question of which side would come off victorious could not be doubtful.

The circulating medium of the country is, in legal tender notes, $356,000,000. That of national banks, excluding their reserves, is less than $300,000,000. This currency is scattered over the country—a small portion of it is in foreign countries. No coin is in circulation, most of it being locked up by Wall street brokers, in the interest of these railroad corporations. Many of the national banks of the country are owned by railroad men. In addition to the immense earnings of the railroads, which under the present system are concentrated in the city of New York, almost the entire amount of stock and bonds issued by railroad companies is either owned or represented in Wall street, and as occasion demands is put upon the market. Thus the whole of this corporate influence can be used at any time in a financial conflict with the government. It has been and is still being used against the government. Under the revenue laws of the country, import duties are paid in coin. A part of the sum thus realized is applied in payment of the national debt. There is no good reason why the secretary of the treasury should not apply this sum directly in payment of government bonds. Such a policy would tend toward the resumption of specie payment, making the money of the people of equal value with that used by the government. This would not suit railroad companies. So long as a margin can be preserved between coin and currency (and for their purposes the wider the better) under the decision of the supreme court they can discharge their bond indebtedness, contracted to be paid in gold, with depreciated paper at par, and save the margin. In order that a margin may be continued, instead of making direct payment of government bonds to the direct holders thereof, the secretary of the treasury is required to sell gold in New York, and purchase or liquidate the bonds with the proceeds of these sales. It is noticeable in all cases of the sale of coin, that Wall street brokers are the purchasers, and usually at less than the quoted market value. By this means the interests of these railroad managers are subserved in more than one particular. Their brokers purchase and corner the coin sold, and prevent it going into circulation, and the margin between coin and currency is preserved. The day for the resumption of specie payment is kept in the distant future. The importing merchant must buy gold of the brokers (who are the railroad managers) at its market value, to pay government duties on their imports, and thus the companies make the difference between the price paid and the price obtained. When some favorite railroad stocks are to be forced upon the market, these brokers, who can do so at pleasure, supply the money market, and sell the stocks at a large profit; and when the object is to reduce the value of stocks, they withdraw from circulation a sufficient amount of the currency to cause a stringency in the market, until their end is accomplished. Controlling absolutely the gold market, as well as the secretary of the treasury in his financial operations, they have only to corner a few millions of currency to make the entire commerce of the country subserve their special purposes. With all of their interests united, all their business concentrated in Wall street and controlled by six or eight leading men, they regulate the finances, fix the value of the produce of the country, and hold the producers of the great west in a state of vassalage which has no precedent, even in despotic countries. The secretary of the national treasury, who is supposed to control the financial department of government, is in fact the servant of these men, and whatever policy is beneficial to their interests must be adopted by the government. To the uninitiated it may appear impossible for a few men in New York to exercise a controlling influence over the financial policy of the nation, but if we remember that all the wealth of these corporations, actual and fictitious, is concentrated in that city, or controlled by men doing business there, and that an immense stream of money, received by these corporations from passengers and shippers, is constantly flowing into Wall street from all parts of the country, we can understand their power and appreciate their influence. The fact that it requires more than twice as much money to pay the interest on the bonds issued by these corporations, and dividends on their stock, as would pay the interest on the national debt, is significant. When private corporations combine their interests and become so powerful as to require an annual expenditure of more than twice the amount expended by the United States government, and when their revenues more than quadruple those of the government, they must of necessity exercise a controlling influence over the financial and industrial interests of the country. This fact is now being demonstrated by a combination of the railroad corporations of the country, as the people know to their cost.

It will be proper here to detail the *modus operandi* of these railroad companies at their headquarters in Wall street. We read of large operations in stocks and bonds, as well as in gold, and are apt to conclude that sales and purchases are made by regular transfers in a fair and legitimate manner. Such is not the case. Among the initiated sales are pure fiction in many cases, and in others it is but purchasing or selling the chance of an advance or decline in the price of stocks, bonds, or coin. To call these transactions by their right name—*they are nothing but gambling.* If legitimate sales are made, it is with outside parties, or to the uninitiated. The corporation rings congregated in Wall street, calling themselves bankers and brokers, sell to, or purchase stocks from, each other, without delivery or even payment, all the money passing between the seller and purchaser being the margin between the price agreed to be paid and the market reports at the time fixed for delivery. To illustrate, let us suppose that certain railroad stock is quoted at ninety-three cents, or seven per cent. below par. A, who believes that there will be no further rise in price, but that the same will decline, offers B $10,000 of this stock at ninety-one cents, to be delivered in three days. He has no stock, but believing it will decline to ninety cents or less, within the time fixed for delivery, he expects to buy at a still lower rate than he has agreed to sell, or to borrow it for a consideration if the decline does not meet his anticipations. Or he will settle his contract with B by paying him the difference between the market value at the time of delivery and the price at which he agreed to sell. The same process is gone through if the sale is made with the expectation of the stock advancing in price. A agrees to purchase of B four days after the date, $15,000 in stock at ninety-five cents, being an advance of two per cent. on the market price on the day of sale. The stock does not advance, and at the time for delivery A pays B the margin between two cents on the dollar, and the market price. No stock has passed between them. It was a fight between a "bull" and a "bear" for the margin.

Nearly all of the financial operations of Wall street brokers are of a like character. Some of them involve immense amounts. One man makes a fortune, and another becomes bankrupt in a day. Wall street is the place where men of all creeds and nationalities meet to engage in this kind of gam-

13

bling traffic. Men run about the streets, into the "gold room," the "clearing house," their faces flushed, their whole person excited, their appearance "distorted, hair dishevelled," their voices hoarse—all intent on making money, not in a legitimate way, but by the chance of a rise or fall in gold, bonds, and stock. Let us see some of the terms used by them in their business. The rings operating in stocks are divided into two classes, "bulls" and "bears." They have the advantage of the real bear and bull in this—they can change from one to the other as the occasion serves. Daniel Drew, Colonel Scott, and Commodore Vanderbilt can be bulls to-day, and bears to-morrow, as their interests dictate. The object of the *bulls* is to advance the price of stocks—that of the *bears* to depreciate. They thrive most when the people generally are in want, or when some public calamity unsettles commerce. They oftentimes devise means to bring on a panic that they may break the market, and buy favorite stocks at low rates. They do not care how much the community may suffer, or how many men engaged in legitimate business may be ruined, provided their own interests are served. We take from *Appleton's Journal* a description of some of their terms, and their manner of doing business:

"The terms 'long' and 'short' are of respective application to the 'bull' and 'bear' parties. The bulls are always 'long' of stock, and the bears are always 'short.' The speculator who has stock on hand which he bought with expectation of selling at higher prices, is on the bull side, and, in the parlance of the street, is 'long.' A bear seldom has stock on hand. His business is to sell 'short'—that is, to sell property which he has not got, intending to buy and deliver when prices are lower. Generally, the stock is to be delivered the day after it is sold, but quite often the bear does not buy it for a month, or two, or three months. How, then, can he deliver it in twenty-four hours? By borrowing it from another person. There is in Wall street a regular system of borrowing stock. The borrower, who represents the speculator, procures the stock from another broker, to whom he gives a check as security for the stock borrowed. This transaction is good for one day only, but it may be renewed for the next day, and then the next, and thus several weeks may pass before the stock is really purchased for delivery. Meantime, the seller, if he belongs to a clique, or 'pool,' is trying every day to depress prices, in order that he may buy the stock at a lower figure than that at which he sold it. This is the operation known as 'hammering the market,' and a very exciting one, it sometimes is. But the bears are sometimes badly 'squeezed,' and then they make a rush to 'cover.' When the bulls learn that there is a large 'short' interest in a particular stock, they put their heads together and get up a 'corner.' When a stock is said to be 'cornered,' the meaning is that it is controlled by a clique. The clique hold enough of it to control the market, and exact such terms as may be desired. An upward movement is suddenly developed, and then the bears, who have sold 'short' in expectation of lower prices, become alarmed and begin to buy. In the majority of cases, the men who work the advance are the very ones who bought what the bears sold, and they are now selling it to them at higher figures for delivery back to themselves. 'Twisting' is the process of making the bears pay high prices for what they probably sold at low prices, and 'covering' is the operation of buying stock to 'close' short contracts. Once in a while a stock is so closely 'cornered' that it can only be borrowed at an enormous interest for a day's use—perhaps at a rate that exceeds a thousand per cent. per annum. An operation of this sort is the worst squeeze of all; and it is not to be wondered at that, as the gentlemen of the stock exchange say, the bears generally squeal under it. One shrewd manipulator of stock is known to have cleared $50,000 in one day, by loaning a fancy stock that he had 'cornered.' But the same gentleman sometimes gets into a 'corner' prepared by others. It is commonly understood that he was fleeced to the amount of $2,000,000 during the lively 'Northwest' gale a few weeks since. 'Puts' and 'calls' are terms of more than ordinary difficulty for the uninitiated to understand. A proposes to 'put' to B—that is, to deliver to him—a certain amount of a certain stock at a certain time, at a price agreed upon when the contract is made, and gives B a bonus of one, two, or three per cent., as the case may be, for the privilege. This is a 'put.' If the stock does not decline in value to an amount exceeding the sum given to B, A cannot make anything by the transaction; and, unless he chooses to deliver the stock, he is not obliged to do so. If it falls more than the amount, A makes a good profit, for B, having accepted the bonus, is bound to take it, even though it may be selling five or ten cents below the price at which he agreed to take it. A 'call' is pretty much the same thing—with this difference: A gives B a hundred or a thousand dollars, or whatever sum may be agreed upon, for the privilege of 'calling' from B a certain amount of stock within a given number of days. If it advances, A may 'call' it, and make money. If it declines, he need not 'call' it, but of course the bonus he gave to B is forfeit. There are times when the business in 'puts' and 'calls' is quite large, and a great deal of money is made by it; but, like all other kinds of speculation, it is dangerous to the inexperienced. 'Scoop' is a term less familiar to the public than any of the foregoing. This 'scoop game' is a very common one, and is played in this way: A clique of speculators, let us suppose, wish to get possession of a good deal of some particular stock, which they have reason to believe will soon advance in price; but of course they want to get it cheap, and they accomplish their object by starting a break in the stock. This is done by offering it at low figures. They instruct their brokers to offer small quantities under the market price, and to keep on offering lower and lower, until other holders of the same stock, who are not in their confidence, become alarmed and sell out at the best price they can get. In the meantime, the clique have other brokers buying all the stock that is offered, and thus they get possession of a large amount of stock at low prices, which they can probably sell, a few days later, at a large profit. This 'scoop game' is one of the most profitable that the Wall street gentlemen play. The process of 'washing'—a very good one in its ordinary sense—is often employed in Wall street. 'Washing' is a peculiar operation there, very peculiar indeed, and the outsiders ought to keep as far as possible from the suds. A clique is as necessary to it as it is to the 'scoop' business.

There is a stock on the list, for instance, that the public persist in letting alone, and the holders of it want to stir up some excitement in this stock, and induce the public to buy it. How do they proceed? Their plan is quite simple. Several brokers —let us suppose four—are employed to 'wash' the stagnant stock. No. 1 offers to sell; No. 2 takes what is offered. No. 3 wants to buy; No. 4 sells him all he wants. This is kept up for a few days, the price rising steadily as the 'wash' proceeds; but not one share is actually sold. The innocent outsider, supposing these fictitious transactions to be real, and thinking there is a chance to make a turn in the stock, goes in as a buyer himself. Ten to one he will never get as much for the stock as he paid, for it falls stagnant when the speculators have got it off their hands. 'Coppering' is a term recently introduced, but very well understood in the street. It means operating in a direction contrary to that of another. For example, one buys a particular stock, believing that it will advance; another man, observing that the first has not been lucky in his operations, sells this particular stock, believing it will decline. Or the first may sell a particular stock 'short,' and the second, calculating on the other's ill luck, will buy. This sort of speculation is carried on only among the smaller class of operators, and may be set down as sheer gambling. A 'straddle' is a double privilege, entitling the purchaser to either 'put' or 'call' a stock. The bonus is generally the amount paid for the single privilege of 'put' or 'call.' A 'margin' is the money deposited with the broker through whom the stocks are purchased, as a security against a sudden depreciation. The amount is generally about ten per cent. of the par value of the stock. 'Margins' are the rocks on which many adventurers on the uncertain waters of speculation are utterly wrecked. 'Carrying' means holding stock in anticipation of higher prices. Often a stock is 'carried' for six months, but generally the time is not more than two months, and frequently not more than a week. Quick turns is the rule with a majority of speculators. 'Watering' is the operation of suddenly increasing the capital stock of a company. Wall street was thoroughly familiarized with it by the reckless Erie managers, who earned a notoriety that certainly honorable men would not covet. It is very dangerous to the holders of the stock previously in the market."

The foregoing discloses the manner in which these corporations, through their managers, play the double *role* of operating railroads and operating in Wall street. To outsiders there seems to be but little difference between what is known everywhere as downright gambling, and Wall street operations. The gambler who risks his half-dollar on a game at cards is punished for violating the law; but these Wall street operations, which are but games of chance, are dignified with the name of "speculations." Honorable men, reputed Christian men—Jew and Gentile—all engage in them. While they prey upon the producer in operating their roads, they prey upon the unsuspecting public in their stock operations, and, by way of variety, occasionally devour each other. Controlling, as they do, the means of transporting the products of the country to market, as well as the coin of the country and the stock market in Wall street, they are prepared to get up a "corner" on any marketable commodity—upon the currency of the country, and upon gold. In fact they may have all the coin of the country under their control, save the amount held in the treasury of the government. The monthly reports of the secretary of the treasury show that while there was the amount of about $100,000,000 in the treasury one year ago, there is but about two-thirds of that amount now. The reports of sales show that these Wall street operators have cornered about one-third of the gold held by government within the last year. This cornering process goes on, and is now reduced to a system. Suppose the secretary sells, in the month of January, 1873, in New York, $6,000,000 in coin. It is all bought and cornered by the brokers. The importing merchants require but $3,000,000 during the same month to pay duties. The difference, $3,000,000, is locked up in Wall street. This transaction, in a greater or less degree, is repeated each month, and while the amount of gold in the treasury is decreasing that controlled by railroad brokers is increasing. The treasury weakens, and these gambling rings and combinations strengthen. It is only a question of time, under the present system, when the treasury will be obliged to replenish itself by purchases from the brokers. So completely are the finances of the country under their control, the secretary of the treasury is obliged to keep a large surplus of coin on hand to meet emergencies. In order to prevent a panic, he is obliged to sell coin monthly, and whether the financial condition of the treasury or of the country will warrant it or not, he is obliged to pay some portion of the national debt as an excuse for selling coin. These corporate rings are laboring to control the gold of the country, and thus prevent the resumption of specie payment. To make the resumption impossible, they "bull" gold as well as stock, and thus force gold sales by the secretary. The sooner they can deplete the national treasury, the sooner can they become masters of the situation. They now hold the secretary of the treasury at their mercy, and compel him to serve their selfish purposes. When they achieve their final victory, (and achieve it they will under the present system,) they can, without hindrance, fix the value of gold, and extort from the people and the government just such premiums as they please to ask for it. They can render specie payment impossible, and thus reap the full benefit of the "Legal Tender Decision."

CHAPTER XXI.

HOW WALL STREET BUILDS RAILROADS — A HOT-BED OF CORRUPTION.

WE have attempted to show the controlling influence of these railroad corporations upon the legislative and executive departments of the government, and have placed before the reader the danger to republican institutions and liberties of the people, resulting from this influence. In this connection it remains for us to treat of the influence of these corporations upon the judiciary of the country. Before proceeding to this branch of the subject we desire to direct the reader's attention to some alarming facts respecting these corporations, hitherto only alluded to, and the disastrous results which must follow their present management.

We have already shown that railroads, in stocks and bonds, represent capital to about three times their actual value, and that because of this, the people are compelled to pay rates of transportation ruinous to the agricultural interest of the country. We have shown the relations existing between the men who manage these corporations and the Wall street gamblers, with their manner of issuing and putting upon the market fictitious or "watered" stock. The idea generally prevailing is, that the enormous wealth which these monopolies represent is real. In fact about two-thirds of it is pure fiction. It is *manufactured*, and by reckless and dishonest men, who stop at nothing, and who care not for the prosperity of the nation, or of the government, when their own interests are in view. They drain the country of its wealth, concentrate it in Wall street, and there spend it in stock and gold gambling; and this hot-bed of corruption, which has no counterpart save in the infernal regions, has raised such a combination throughout the country as to control the whole financial policy, and compels even the secretary of the treasury to yield to its demands. The public and private wealth of the country is being rapidly destroyed by these corporations, and all departments of government are compelled to do them homage.

We have shown that the railroads of the country are in the hands of unscrupulous men, whose sole interest in transportation is the money it can extort from the public. This must be so from the manner in which roads are built and controlled. Formerly railroads were paid for from the proceeds of paid-up capital. The men who became stockholders were interested in making good and cheap roads, and in operating them honestly and economically. These men were free from the scandal of watering stock, issuing and selling bonds to an unlimited amount, and were not partners in the iniquitous Wall-street speculations which have become the bane of the country. In Appleton's Railroad and Steamboat Companion, published in 1849, we find a statement of the cost of railroads then constructed. The roads then constructed were supplied with rails that cost less than those now in use; but the road-beds in most cases, in the eastern states, cost much more than those constructed at more recent periods. Some of them were lines of solid masonry, supporting lateral or string timbers throughout the entire length, and the rails were placed upon these timbers. Others were constructed upon the plan now in use, costing less than half the cost of the others. The roads in the eastern states, built upon the plan first named, cost as follows: In Massachusetts and the other New England states, $24,000 per mile; in New York, $26,000; in New Jersey and Pennsylvania, $40,000; in Michigan, Ohio, and Indiana, where the roads were built upon the modern plan, $11,000. Of course, the small cost in these last named states is attributable in part to the nature of the country through which they pass. The facilities for building railroads at the present time more than counterbalance the additional cost of iron, and no good reason can be shown why the actual cost of roads at this time should exceed that of the more substantially constructed roads built thirty or forty years ago. But at the present time the building of railroads from the proceeds of paid-up stock is not generally practiced. A different rule prevails. The general rule now is to get grants of land, government, state, and local subsidies, in amounts sufficient to organize a company and commence the work of construction, then to issue and sell bonds secured by mortgage upon the roads to be constructed, and from the proceeds construct the roads. Then stock certificates representing paid-up capital are issued, when in fact all that has been paid is the local subscriptions obtained by managers from persons located along the line of roads. The roads having been built on borrowed capital, the stock represents nothing but an opportunity for dishonest speculation. A "railroad" now means, to a large majority of those who are engaged in projecting and creating it, nothing but a fraudulent device for extorting money from the public, under cover of developing the country and rendering great public benefit to the nation. After the roads are built, the men who have built the same, and issued and sold the bonds, issue to themselves certificates of stock, no part of which they have paid up, and go into Wall street to unload — that is, to sell their stock. If it be in good demand it will bear "watering." More stock is issued and sold, and by this process men who are worth nothing, but who were so fortunate as to get the control of certain railroad companies without having invested to the amount of a dollar, suddenly become immensely rich. The value of the road to those who have paid up their stock, but are not included in the ring, is destroyed; the road is loaded with a debt that destroys its value. This new method of construction meets with favor among a large class of men in all parts of the country, who have combined to aid each other. All that is lacking on their part to take absolute control of the whole country and government is a consolidation of all the railroads of the country under one management. At this time six or eight great combinations, with a half dozen men at their head, manage the railroad interest of the country. They are extending their power, and it may not be long until all will be consolidated in one, which would give this monopoly absolute control, not only of the markets, but of the whole legislation of the country in matters effecting their interests. "With packed legislatures, state and national, with paid or intimidated judges, and with civil service of several thousand cunning clerks and able-bodied brakemen, conductors and switch-tenders, they would be in that position most to be dreaded by all lovers of liberty — a powerful and enormously rich corporation, surrounded by a weak, timid and helpless public. While we were still engaged in singing pæans over the glorious institutions of our happy country, we would suddenly find that our institutions had disappeared, and that we had, riveted around our necks, a worse despotism than we ever lamented for the down-trodden of other lands. This is really no imaginary picture, as all will see who remember the stronghold, absolutely inaccessible to the law, which Fisk and Gould erected, and for a time maintained, in New York; or the military operations of the employes of the Erie on the Susquehanna road, and who have followed with any attention the helpless struggles of the government of the United States — formerly supposed quite able to take care of itself — in the foul toils of the Union Pacific railroad. These corporations foreshadow what must follow when a perfect consolidation is effected. Now at non-competing points they extort from shippers such enormous rates for transportation as absorb almost the entire value of the farm products, while from points at which there are competing lines of road they will carry at greatly reduced rates. They will charge no more for carrying freight one thousand miles from a point where there is a competing road, than for carrying one-tenth of that distance where there is no competition. When they have the power, and hold the shipper at their mercy, they virtually rob him. What is true of their course where there is no competition will become the universal rule when a perfect consolidation of the whole railroad interest is effected. Add to this the control of the finances of the country (which they are now rapidly securing), and their rule becomes absolute over the whole people and all departments of the government. If the reader has followed us thus far, he will have observed that the corporate interest of the country has assumed a position in antagonism to the people; that it has a secure hold upon the industrial and financial interests, and that, to a great extent, it already controls the action of the legislative and executive departments of the government, state and national.

CHAPTER XXII.

THE SUPREME BENCH INVADED — ITS DECISIONS REVIEWED.

WE are aware that many look upon the final decisions of courts with a degree of awe and respect which is almost reverential. The railroad companies of the country, with all their paid attorneys, are now extremely zealous in their efforts to convince the public that the supreme court of the United States is a body of the greatest jurists the world ever produced; that their decisions are pre-eminently able, and that it is disloyal, if not rank treason, to call them in question, or to even criticize them. While we feel bound to recognize the decisions of courts as binding until they are reversed, we claim that it is not only the right, but the duty, of every citizen of the republic to examine these decisions, and to approve or condemn, as to his judgment shall seem right. We examine, and approve or condemn, acts of congress and state legislatures; we discuss the motives of legislators, and when acts have been passed which are not acceptable, their repeal has been demanded. Not unfrequently repeals have been effected soon after their enactment, either because of patent defects, or because the people condemned them. History has proven that the election of a man to congress, or to the legislature, does not clothe him with wisdom, not always with honesty, but that the frailties of humanity affected him as it did others. The same rule applies to courts and judges. They are made of the same flesh and blood, and are subject to the same infirmities as other men. Their knowledge is not perfect; their judgment is not infallible, nor are their official decisions always pure and free from bias. Instances are not wanting where judges have been impeached and removed for dishonest practices. They have been and still are being influenced by popular feeling, by certain interests, and are always more or less controlled by education and association. Their decisions are often reversed, and they sometimes reverse their own decisions.

If we want examples of a corrupt bench, we can refer to the city of New York, where certain judges have been impeached, and removed from office. Of partisan judges, we find them in Louisiana, Alabama, Arkansas, Kansas, and many other states. Of ambitious judges, those who, while acting in their official capacity, enter into political contests, and use their judicial positions to secure other preferment, we need only to look over the history of any of these states, and to the highest court in the nation. Judges of the supreme court of the United States are found identified with political parties; entering the lists as candidates for higher distinction; and while they are holding high and responsible offices, to which they have been appointed for life, they are seen mixing with politicians as partizans, and seeking nominations. Judges whose judicial decisions have been controlled by public sentiment, can be found in Iowa, Illinois, Indiana and Wisconsin. Judges who have reversed their own decisions, can be found in any state in the Union, and we have recent examples in the supreme court of the United States. Such being the facts, it is not strange that railroads and other great corporations should, to a very considerable extent, influence the actions and decisions of courts We feel warranted in saying, that the decisions of courts, more than everything else combined, have promoted the rapid strides made by railroad corporations toward a complete destruction of republican institutions. The pernicious practice of solving all doubtful points in favor of these corporations by the "judicial construction" of statutes, or what might be called "judicial legislation," has been of vastly more benefit to them than all the grants received from legislative bodies. Legislatures do not possess the power to grant to any individual, company, or corporation, exclusive rights or privileges, unless such power is conferred by the constitution. The rule formerly obtained that, in cases where the rights of the public and that of an individual or corporation came in conflict, an act of the legislature of doubtful authority would be construed in favor of the people. The reason for this rule of construction is obvious. The people are sovereign. All the powers not delegated to the government, or to some department of it, were retained by the people. Hence, when a question was presented involving a doubt of its constitutionality, and a decision in favor of the individual or corporation would deprive the people of any of their reserved rights, it was resolved in favor of the sovereign people. The act was held to be unconstitutional because the legislature could not exceed the scope of the authority conferred upon it. The constitution was a limitation upon legislation.

In a former chapter we have attempted to show the distinction between the power of the states and general government under the constitution; to demonstrate that the power of states was supreme in all matters save in those expressly conferred upon the general government by the constitution, and that for this reason the constitution of the United States should be strictly construed. We are warranted in saying that this rule obtained until questions involving the interests of railroads began to present themselves for the decisions of the supreme court of the United States. When these questions began to arise, a different rule was demanded by the companies, and by a gradual departure the supreme court has reversed this old and just rule, and now the will of that court must be treated as the supreme law of the land. Judicial legislation has usurped the place of judicial investigation, and the people are without remedy unless a return can be had to constitutional rule. There is now a general complaint throughout the whole land, because of the recent interpretation given by the United States courts to the constitution; their disregard of statutes, constitutions, and decisions of state courts, have reached a point which virtually makes the will of the supreme court superior to all constitutional and statute law. During the war, the power and jurisdiction of the United States courts were enlarged, and special powers were conferred upon them to meet the exigencies ot the time. From that period to the present, these courts, by judicial construction of their power under the constitution and new interpretations of that instrument, and by judicial legislation, have gradually extended their jurisdiction, until there seems to be no constitutional or legal barrier to their decisions. Questions connected with railroad companies have increased rapidly. Conflicts have arisen between the public and these corporations; they have multiplied in the federal courts, and, as a general rule, have been decided in favor of the companies. In some instances, upon questions arising exclusively under the constitution and statutes of a state, the judges of the federal courts have disregarded the action of the people of the state, overridden their state constitutions and statutes, and pronounced the decisions of the state courts invalid, and refused to be bound by them, substituting their own conclusions in the interest of these monopolies. To prove this let us compare some of the earlier decisions of these courts with those of more recent date, citing cases where the powers, rights and privileges of corporations were involved, and where conflicts arose between the government of states and of the nation. In the early years of our republic, questions connected with corporate rights were submitted to the supreme court of the United States; they were ably argued by the best constitutional lawyers of the nation, and were carefully considered and decided by the courts. Upon the question as to whether state courts were inferior, the supreme court of the United States decided that they were not. The same court, on a question raised as to the authority of the legislature of a state to grant to private parties exclusive rights to certain property in Georgia, *held*, that the real party in interest was the people, and that it was only when the legislature acted within the power conferred, that their acts were valid; that it was the peculiar province of the legislature to prescribe general rules for the government of society, but not to apply those rules to individuals of society.

The questions as to the rights, powers and privileges of corporations, came before the supreme court of the United States, and was fully examined and decided, in 1819, in what is known as the "Dartmouth College Case." The charter for the college had been granted by the king of England for educational purposes. It was in no sense a corporation for pecuniary profit. Without the consent of the trustees of the college, the legislature of New Hampshire amended the charter in a manner not acceptable to the trustees. They refused to recognize the change made. A suit was instituted, and the case was taken to the supreme court for a decision. The point at issue was whether the college was a public or private corporation; and, also, as to the extent of the power the state legislature possessed over its charter. It is not our purpose to examine all the points raised and decided in that case, but only to notice such as refer to the nature of corporations and the power of the state governments to control them. In deciding these questions, the court seems to have looked at the objects for which corporations were intended. The court says: "A corporation, being a mere creation of law, it possesses only those properties which the charter of its creation confers upon it, either expressly or incidental to its very existence. These are such as are supposed best calculated to affect the object for which it was created. * * *

"The objects for which corporations are created are universally such as the government wishes to promote. They are deemed beneficial to the country, and this benefit constitutes the consideration, and, in most cases, the sole consideration of the grant." * * "From the fact, then, that a charter of incorporation has been granted, nothing can be implied which changes the character of the institution, or transfers to the government any new power over it. The character of civil institutions does not grow out of their incorporation, but out of the manner in which they are founded, and the objects for which they are created. The right to change them is not founded on their being incorporated, but on their being the instruments of government created for its purposes. The same institution, created for the same objects, though not incorporated, would be public institutions, and, of course, controllable by the legislature. The incorporating act neither gives nor prevents this control."

The doctrine above enunciated fixes the line of distinction between public and private corporations. Those created for public or governmental purposes are defined to be "public corporations," and those created for the advancement of private enterprises are "private corporations." Private corporations possess none of the attributes of sovereignty, and hence are to be treated in law as private individuals; the act of incorporation being for the purpose of affording the corporators proper facilities for transacting business. Corporations being the mere creatures of the law, they possess only those properties which the charters of their creation confer upon them. Under the decision to which we have referred, and from which we have quoted, corporations are created by statute, and are subject to the control of the power creating them. A grant from the sovereign power to an individual, or to a company, is not necessarily irrepealable, nor will it in all cases be treated as a contract. Corporations created for public or governmental purposes are binding as contracts only so far as they affect private interests, for the good reason that government cannot contract with itself.

Nor could the legislature confer exclusive privileges upon a corporation, the exercise of which would deprive the people of the rights guaranteed to them in the constitution; for the reason that the attempt to clothe a corporation with such privileges would be an unauthorized act on their part. In the case of "Providence Bank *vs.* Billings & Pittman," decided by the same court, in 1830, it is said that "The great object of an incorporation is to bestow the character and properties of individuality on a collective and changing body of men. This capacity is always given to such a body; any privileges which may exempt it from the burdens common to individuals do not flow necessarily from the charter, but must be expressed in it or they do not exist." The doctrine obtained that corporations can take nothing by implication, and that unless the power to regulate and control them has been surrendered by the legislature, that power remains undiminished. The rule that grants of privileges to corporations are to be strictly construed, when the rights of the public are affected, is recognized in this case. We are warranted in saying that it is only since corporations have become all-powerful in the land that a different rule has obtained. Under the statutes of the United States, and as formerly held by the supreme court, a promissory note given by a citizen of a state to another citizen of the same state, but transferred to a citizen of another state, could not be sued in the United States courts, but the holder was compelled to bring his action in the state courts. This rule obtained until counties, cities, and towns began to issue their bonds to railroad companies, and was then disregarded. Railroad companies had sold and delivered these bonds to parties in Wall street, or elsewhere; they had failed to fulfill their contracts with the parties from whom they had received the bonds, and when suit was brought upon them in the state courts the bondholders were beaten. Suits were then commenced in the federal courts, the plain letter of the statute was disregarded, the established decisions of the supreme courts were overruled, state statutes and constitutions were treated with contempt, the decisions of the supreme court of a state which had been followed for years were called "*oscillations*," and the interests, frauds, and deceits of railroad corporations were fully protected and sustained—not because this course was supported by the statutes or precedents, but because such a course would subserve these harmful interests. This action on the part of the supreme court was not the result of any dishonest or partisan intent, but it was made to prevent what the court was pleased to term "great wrongs about to be inflicted on *innocent* holders of bonds purchased of railroad companies. In many instances the *innocent* bondholders were the same parties who, as railroad men, had cheated the counties and cities, and by fraud and false representation had obtained these bonds, for which no consideration has been paid to the present time. It will not be out of place here, as showing the influence of these corporations over the supreme court of the United States, to refer to the transactions that caused the first departure by the court from the settled rules of decisions on questions arising under the constitutions and statutes of states, and, we may add, initiated a rule of decisions, followed to the present time, which have well nigh destroyed states rights. Under this new rule the whole country is governed by the supreme court and corporations. The people are powerless, and monopolies reign supreme. We refer to the question of aid by counties and municipal corporations to railroads. In many of the states municipal corporations have subscribed stock and issued their bonds to railroad companies, in some instances under express statute authority, and in others without such authority. No one is prepared to admit that compulsory payment by the citizen of a part of his property, or money, to aid a private corporation in building a railroad, is the payment of taxes for the support of government, or that the levy and collection of a tax for that purpose can be supported by any section of the constitution. Yet we all know that such taxes have been and are being levied and collected. Judge Dillon, in his work on municipal corporations, says: "The courts concur, with great unanimity, in holding that there is *no implied authority* in municipal corporations to incur debts or borrow money in order to become subscribers to the stock of railway companies, and that such power must be conferred by *express* grant. To become stockholders in private corporations is manifestly foreign to purposes intended to be subserved by the creation of corporate municipalities, and the practice of bestowing powers of this kind is of recent date and origin; and hence the rule, that in order to exist it must be specially conferred, and cannot be deduced from the ordiary municipal grants."

If the above quotation is good law (and this no one will deny), the recent decisions made by the supreme court cannot be supported. But in order to avoid the force and effect of this principle, and to provide for the collection of bonds illegally issued (by recent decisions), a new doctrine has been promulgated by the court which overturns state statutes, as well as the decisions of state courts. Treating of this class of bonds, Judge Dillon says:

"Respecting negotiable bonds issued under legislative authority, by municipalities for such and kindred purposes, when in the hands of *bona fide* holders, the supreme court of the United States, influenced, doubtless, by a keen sense of the injustice and odium of repudiation, has at all times displayed a strong determination effectually to enforce payment. Accordingly it has refused to follow the subsequent decisions of the state courts against the validity of such bonds, in cases where the prior rulings of the state courts had been in favor of the power to issue them; it has adopted liberal constructions of statutes and charters authorizing the creation of such debts; it has given no favor to defenses based upon mere irregularities in the issue of the bonds, or non-compliance with preliminary requirements, not going to the question of the power to contract; and has held that the circuit courts of the United States were clothed with full power and authority by *mandamus*, or otherwise, to enforce the collection of judgments rendered therein on such bonds, and that this authority could not in the least be interfered with, either by the legislature or the judiciary of the states." It will be seen that for the purpose of relieving railroad companies from their liabilities as guarantors, on bonds issued to them by municipalities (for these bonds were uniformly so guaranteed), the supreme court of the United States has declared the statutes of states, and the decisions of state courts, absolutely null and void. In violation of both the letter and spirit of the constitution, in order to compel the payment of bonds issued without authority, and in violation of every principle known to the law, it has said that these bonds must be paid because they are in the hands of *bona fide* holders.

This same court, as we will hereafter show, when the holders of bonds issued by railroad companies were asking payment, has released the companies from their written agreement to pay in coin, and compelled the holders to take at par depreciated paper. When the bondholders are demanding payment from the people of the bonds issued without authority, the court, in order to compel payment, nullifies state government; but when these same bondholders demand that railroad companies shall live up to their written contracts, have decided that they need not do so. It fears the stigma of repudiation when the people are called upon to pay, but when the call is made upon corporations it decided in favor of repudiation. Our author continues: "It has upheld and protected the rights of such creditors with a firm hand, *disregarding at times, it would seem, principles which it applied in other cases, and asserts the jurisdiction and authority of the federal courts with such striking energy and vigor as apparently, if not actually, to trench upon the lawful rights of states and the acknowledged powers of the state tribunals.*"

Municipal corporations have no right to become stockholders in private corporations; acts of the legislature pretending to confer such authority are void; the officers who control and administer the municipal government are the mere agents of the municipality, and can only act within the scope of the powers conferred upon them by the charter of the municipality they represent. Neither the constitution of a state, nor of the United States, nor the charter of a municipality, can confer upon the nation, state, county, city or town, the authority to compel any citizen against his will to bestow any part of his money or property upon private corporations. And it matters not whether this comes in shape of a tax, an arbitrary appropriation of a fraction or of all his property or possessions to such private corporation, or by a subscription of stock to it. If the national, state, or municipal government can in either of the above methods compel him to aid in building up and supporting private corporations, then private corporations are clothed with attributes of sovereignty, and all private citizens own and possess their property subject to the will of these corporations. If a majority of the qualified voters of a state, or particular locality, are in favor of taxing the state, or local district, to the extent of one-tenth or one-half of the assessed value of all property in the district, and investing the amount in a railroad enterprise, the minority, notwithstanding their protest and remonstrance, must submit to have their property taken from them and applied to the same object. Their constitutional rights are taken from them, and our boasted free government has no real existence. By recent decisions of the supreme court of the United States, the people of the whole country are placed in that position now. Railroad corporations have been, and are now, under the fostering care and protection of this court. Statutes have been so often disregarded by it, when their interests were to be subserved, and in conflicts between the people and these monopolies the decisions have been so uniformly in favor of the latter, that it is now a question whether the government controls corporations, or corporations control the government. If a pernicious law is enacted by congress, or a state legislature, it is soon repealed. The men who compose those bodies are constantly changing, their term of office is short, and the errors committed by them can be speedily corrected. The judges of the supreme court are appointed for life; the people have no control over them; their decisions cannot be reversed by any department of the government. A decision of the supreme court is the supreme law of the land, and cannot be reversed or amended by any other power in the land. It is superior to all statute law, and the power of the court has no limit, save that fixed in the constitution and statutes of the United States, both of which must receive *their* construction and interpretation from the court. We have already said that judges of this court are subject to the infirmities common to all men; that they are liable to be influenced by the same causes that influence others; that no matter how honest and pure they may be in their intentions and actions, their decisions were liable to be controlled by surrounding circumstances, and that the influence of this great corporate power did control them. In proof of this we need only look at their course of decisions on municipal bonds, and on bonds given by railroad companies, before referred to, as well as their decisions upon the nature of railroad corporations. It strikes us as remarkable that the supreme court of the nation should have or entertain any doubts as to the fact that these corporations are private. Upon what principle the court can hold that railroads are public highways is not readily seen. The stock, the roads, and all other property belonging to the different railroad companies, are as much their individual or corporate property as are the furnace, the factory, or the mining interests, the property of the companies owning them. Their ownership is as complete as that of the private person who owns the stage and team used for carrying the mails in certain districts. The same law that governs other common carriers, governs these corporations. Government can only interfere with their business when they abuse the privileges granted in their charters. It cannot compel them to carry the mails, save in pursuance of contracts made with them. They own the ground upon which their roads are built, and no one can travel upon these roads or ship freight over them, save by the permission of the companies. While courts and legislatures have the constitutional right to regulate and control these corporations, and, if need be to prevent abuses and oppressions, to declare their charters forfeited, as in cases of banks, insurance companies, and other corporations,—upon no principle of law can they declare them public corporations. If it is a fact that they are public corporations, then as a resulting consequence they are clothed with the attributes of sovereignty, and are a part of the government. If railroads are public highways for any purpose, they are for all. Until they cease to be owned and controlled by private corporations, it will hardly be claimed by any respectable court that they are public highways, in the same sense as common public roads, nor can they be until they are open to public use. This cannot be until the public becomes the owner of these railroads.

But we are told that the supreme court has decided the question, and declared that they are public highways, no matter whether they are owned by the state or private companies. We have not seen the decision; but if such decision has been made, we are bound to accept it as the law of the land, until the same court reverses it. Yet if the court was to decide that a river was a railroad, or that a steamboat was a train of cars, while we would accept this decision as the law, we would not admit that such was the fact. We are not aware that the question as to whether railroads are public highways has ever been before the supreme court, save in the connection with the right of municipalities to subscribe stock and issue bonds therefor, and upon the question of voting taxes to aid in their construction. When these questions have been presented to the supreme court of the United States it has held that they were public highways. It is noticeable that these decisions have been made only when the interests of these corporations were to be subserved. In a recent case from Wisconsin the supreme court decided that they were public highways, and that it was just as lawful to levy taxes for railroads as *for any other public works.* The same court has decided in a large number of cases when suits were instituted on municipal bonds, that railroad corporations were private companies, and in all of the states where the question has arisen, we believe they have been held to be private corporations. We might cite several recent decisions of the supreme court to the same effect. In the cases of Kansas Pacific Railway Company *vs.* Prescott, Ribon *vs.* Chicago, Rock Island & Pacific Railway Company, Putnam *vs.* New Albany & Sandusky Railway Company, and Chicago & Quincy Railway Company *vs.* The County of Otoe, tried in Washington last winter, the court virtually decided the corporations were private, and not public. The doctrine to be gathered from these decisions is, that when the interests of these corporations demand it they are to be treated as private, but when the question is as to their right to compel the people to contribute of their substance to build railroads, then the roads are public highways. If the corporations are private, and the roads are built and owned by them, the fact that these roads are private still exists, notwithstanding the courts as to the law of the case decide that they are public highways. The fact that such a decision has been made, is strong proof of the correctness of our position, that the corporations have a controlling influence over the judiciary of the country more to be dreaded by the people than all the appliances that can be brought to bear upon the legislative and executive department of the government. But in no other instance has the influence of these corporations over the supreme court of the country been made more manifest than in what is known as the "legal tender" decision. And we might add that no other decision of the court, and no act of any department of the government, has proved so disastrous to the people as this decision. We have already referred to the means used by these corporations to secure a majority of the supreme court favorable to their designs, and of their success in the selection of judges committed to their interests. It only remains for us to review this decision to convince the most skeptical of the fact that corporations have captured the supreme court, as well as the other departments of the government, and the effect of this decision has given to these corporations, and Wall street brokers, and gamblers, the absolute control of the finances of the country. But before coming to the decision, it will not be out of place to remark, that *money* is always the standard of value for all commodities; that the universally adopted idea of money means coin—gold and silver—or, what is called the precious metals. Bank bills, treasury notes, bills of exchange, and all kinds of commercial paper are only valuable as the representatives of money. The fact that they are expected to be converted into money gives them their value in the market. Let it be understood that they cannot at some future day be collected in money, and their commercial value ceases. In proportion to the length of time that must elapse before any bank bills, treasury notes, or other commercial paper can be paid in specie, does its value increase or diminish in commercial transactions. Nothing but money of the standard value can be made a legal tender in contracts between individuals. Congress does not possess the power, under the constitution, to say that A who has contracted to pay B $1,000 in money, can discharge that contract by paying him $1,000 in bank bills or treasury notes, that are worth in money but $800. If such powers exist, then all standard values of property is destroyed, and it fluctuates in value as the price of the paper representing money approaches to, or recedes from, the money standard. The rule that nothing but gold and silver is, or can be, "legal tender" has been uniformly adhered to from the formation of our government, until 1872, when a majority of the supreme court reversed the rule, and decided that what are termed treasury notes are, under the acts of congress, legal tender for all contracts and business intercourse among men.

The question was fully argued in 1869, before a full bench, then composed of a chief justice and seven associates, five of whom concurred in deciding that the act of congress making anything but gold and silver a legal tender was unconstitutional. Before the decision was announced, Justice Grier resigned, leaving but six associates on the bench when the opinion was delivered. Chief Justice Chase delivered the opinion, and, in speaking of the powers of congress, says: "No department of the government has any other powers than those delegated to it by the people. All the legislative power granted by the constitution belongs to congress; but it has no legislative power which is not thus granted. * * Not every act of congress, then, is to be regarded as the supreme law of the land, nor is it by every act of congress the judges are bound. This character, and this force, belongs only to such acts as are made in pursuance of the constitution." The court then decides that there is in the constitution no grant of legislative power to make any description of credit currency a legal tender in payment of debts, and that it does not exist as incidental to any of the granted powers. That the power does exist in congress to issue bills of credit or treasury notes, but not to make them legal tender for debts. The opinion concludes as follows: "We are obliged to conclude that an act making mere promises to pay dollars a legal tender to pay debts previously contracted, is not a means appropriate, plainly adapted, really calculated to carry into effect any express power vested in congress; that such an act is inconsistent with the spirit of the constitution, and that it is prohibited by the constitution." This decision was not acceptable to corporations and railroad managers. It would compel them to live up to the contracts they had made, and destroy their power of controlling, in connection with the Wall street stock jobbers and gold brokers, the entire financial interests of the country. We have already shown how this combination of corporate interests secured an increase in the number of judges, and that Messrs. Strong and Bradley were appointed because of their opposition to the legal tender decision. None of the judges who had concurred in the decision of Judge Chase had changed their opinions; these were then dissenting members of the court. The two new appointees uniting with three dissenting judges, a majority of the court could overrule the long settled decisions of the court, and sustain the act of congress making depreciated paper a legal tender. The law of the land, recognized since the organization of the government, approved by all the eminent jurists and statesmen who have lived in the last century, could be overturned; values could be unsettled; the financial and commercial interests of the country could be made subject to this great corporate power which had obtained such complete control of the different departments of the government.

Soon after the appointment of the two judges above named the legal tender question was again brought before the court, a full bench of nine judges sitting and participating in the decision of the question. Five of the nine concurred in holding the legal tender act constitutional, Justice Strong delivering the opinion of the court. It is a noticable feature of the case that a judge who had just taken his seat should be selected to pronounce the decision; that after a uniform course of decisions, made and upheld by all the great jurists of the country for eighty-five years, two judges who had just been appointed should be found delivering opinions reversing this long settled rule and that both of said judges were appointed because of their avowed friendship for the corporations which were to be so largely benefited by the reversal of this long settled construction of the constitution upon the question of legal tenders, and it seems that even these judges base their decision upon what they deem the necessity for a reversal rather than upon any constitutional grounds. Justice Strong, as preliminary to the opinion of the court, says: "The controlling questions in these cases are the following: Are the acts of congress, known as the legal tender acts, constitutional when applied to contracts made before their passage? and, secondly, Are they valid as applicable to debts contracted since their enactment? These questions have been elaborately argued, and they have received from the court that consideration which their great importance demands. It would be difficult to overestimate the consequences which must follow our decisions. They will affect the entire business of the country, and take hold of the possible continued existence of the government. If it be held by this court that congress has no constitutional power, under any circumstances, or in any emergency, to make treasury notes a legal tender for the payment of all debts, (a power confessedly professed by every independent sovereignty other than the United States,) the government is without those means of self-preservation which, all must admit, may, in certain contingencies, become indispensable, even if they were not when the act of congress now called in question was enacted. It is also clear that if we hold the acts invalid as applicable to debts incurred, or transactions which have occurred since their enactment, our decision must cause, throughout the country, great business derangements, wide-spread distress, and the rankest injustice. The debts which have been contracted since February 25th, 1862, constitute, doubtless, by far the greatest portion of the existing indebtedness of the country. They have been contracted in view of the acts of congress declaring treasury notes a legal tender, and in reliance of that declaration. Men have bought and sold, borrowed and lent, and assumed every variety of obligation, contemplating that payment might be made with such notes. Indeed, legal tender notes have become the universal measure of values. If now, by our decision, it be established that their debts and obligations can be discharged only in gold coin; if, contrary to the expectations of all parties to these contracts, legal tender notes are rendered unavailable, the government has become an instrument of the grossest injustice, and debtors are loaded with an obligation it was never intended they should assume. A large percentage is added to every debt, and such must become the demand for gold to satisfy contracts that ruinous sacrifices, general distress, and bankruptcy may be expected. These consequences are too obvious to admit of question. And there is no well-founded distinction to be made between the constitutional validity of an act of congress declaring treasury notes a legal tender for debts contracted after its passage, and that of an act making them a legal tender for the discharge of all debts, as well those incurred before as those made after its enactment. There may be a difference in the effects produced by the acts and in the hardship of their operation; but in both cases the fundamental question, that which tests the validity of the legislation, is, Can congress constitutionally give to treasury notes the character and qualities of money? Can such notes be constituted a legitimate circulating medium, having a defined legal value? If they can, then such notes must be available to fulfill all contracts, (not expressed by exception,) in money, without reference to the time when the contract was made."

This quotation from the opinion of the court may be taken as a sample of the reasoning in favor of a reversal of former decisions on the question of legal tender. After elaborate argument in the same strain by Justice Strong, and also by Justice Bradley, a majority of the court decide that the legal tender acts are constitutional, while the four judges remaining on the bench, who but a short time before had made a contrary decision, dissent from the opinion of the majority. The argument of the majority in favor of the decision seems to ignore the real question, to wit: the constitutionality of the acts of congress, and to place the decision upon the ground that a contrary holding would be ruinous to the financial interests of the country. The assertion is made that the decision "*will affect the entire business of the country, and take hold of the possible continued existence of the government.*" The decision was made about one year ago, and its effects on the business interests of the country are made manifest. If the court believed that the decision sustaining the legal tender acts would prove beneficial to the people, it was sadly mistaken. But if it believed such a decision would strengthen monopolies and enable a few railroad managers and Wall street brokers to corner and control the finances of the country, then the decision was a success. The effect has been to unsettle the commercial and financial interests of the country, and to show that treasury notes, if they are the standard of values, are a fluctuating standard. The consequence of the decision has taken "*hold of the possible continued existence of the government,*" and has enabled the gold and stock gamblers in Wall street to suck the life-blood of the nation. The decision gives strength to corporations, who, uniting with Wall street brokers, are depleting the treasury of the nation to advance their own private purposes. By the decision two standards of value are fixed: one that is stable, and must ever remain so — the standard of money — gold and silver; the other, the standard of fluctuating paper, of no intrinsic value, liable to be inflated or depressed, as shall best subserve the interests of the parties who, by combining, have got such absolute control of the market as to be able to change the value of this *legal tender* paper at pleasure. The idea advanced in the decision, that to declare that nothing but coin could be a legal tender would cause wide-spread ruin, presents but a partial view of this matter. As a matter of fact, no act of congress prior to 1862 had ever been passed making anything but coin a legal tender; nor was there any decision of the supreme court recognizing or deciding that paper money could be a legel tender until 1872; and yet no such wide-spread ruin had overtaken the financial interests of the country as has manifested itself since that decision was rendered.

Simultaneous with the decision of the court declaring treasury notes legal tender, the quantity of coin in the treasury began to decrease, and one year's experience has sufficed to reduce the amount from one-third to one-half, and in proportion the amount controlled by Wall street has increased. The secretary of the treasury is now obliged to have recourse to the $44,000,000 of treasury notes held as a reserve to prevent panic and disaster. This decision does not benefit the importing merchant, who must pay in coin; it does not benefit the legitimate business of the country; it does not benefit the farmer, or any of the industrial interests of the country, because in buying and selling, if payments are made in paper (*legal tender*), the prices of the articles bought and sold are fixed by a gold or coin standard. Coin is, in all dealings, the measure of values. The decision of the court does not and cannot change these facts. The only parties who derive any real benefit from it are corporations and brokers, who can save large amounts by being released from their contracts. Another argument used by the court in favor of the decision is, that every independent nation possesses the power to make paper a legal tender, and that it must be possessed by our government. The answer to this is, that the constitution does not confer upon congress or the courts, even by implication, any such power; and if we admit that other nations possess it, we conclude it is because the fundamental law recognizes it, or because the government is of unlimited power.

The court decides that "*legal tender notes have become the universal measure of values.*" This is simply untrue. In all quotations of values the measure is fixed by gold, and then legal tender notes are quoted as being worth such per cent. less, or, what amounts to the same thing, gold is quoted as being worth ten, fifteen, twenty or more cents to the dollar more than paper; and while the value of gold is fixed, that of treasury notes is constantly fluctuating. Under this decision railroad companies and their associates, the Wall street gamblers, control the finances, while all the honest and legitimate business of the country languishes. Had the court designed to place the whole interests of the government and the people in the power of these corrupt rings and dishonest brokers, no more effectual means could have been devised or adopted. Justice Bradley, in his opinion concurring with the opinion of Justice Strong, makes use of the following bold and dangerous language: "It is absolutely essential to independent national existence that government should have a firm hold in the two great sovereign instrumentalities of the *Sword* and the *Purse*, and the right to wield them on occasions of national peril." Let this pernicious doctrine be accepted as the law of the land, let the *purse and the sword* be placed in the hands of government officials without restrictions, and what vestige of republican institutions is left? What difference is there between our government and absolute despotism? But more than this: let the highest court of a nation, by a partisan decision, place the *purse* of the nation in the hands of a gigantic monopoly, banded together for the purpose of plundering the public, and what vestige of independence is left the people? Reader, look carefully at the almost unlimited power the corporations of the country have obtained over each department of the government; at the legal tender decision and its effect upon the people of the country, and then ask yourself if we, as a nation, are not nearing the point where we cease to be a republic save in name. This decision impairs the obligation of contracts, in violation of the letter and spirit of the constitution. It compels the creditor to take from the debtor irredeemable paper at par, on a contract payable in money. It says that a mere promise to pay is a legal tender. It makes it absolutely impossible to resume specie payment, because it withdraws all coin from circulation, and does away with the necessity for its use in domestic transactions. The coin of the country is shipped to foreign countries, to meet demands against us in those countries, and to pay for such commodities as we purchase from them. Credit currency, no matter whether it is issued by the general or state government, is not, nor can it, under the constitution, be made a legal tender by act of congress or by a decision of any court in the land, because the laws of trade will control the whole matter, being stronger than legal enactments or judicial decisions. Money is the universal medium or common standard which fixes the value of all other things that can be sold or bartered, and neither the congress of the nation, by the passage of a law declaring that paper shall be a legal tender, nor the supreme court deciding that such law is constitutional, can impart an actual value to such paper, because it is but a promise to pay money. They can no more accomplish this object than can the alchemist convert iron into gold. The only effect of this decision, as we have attempted to demonstrate, is to place the people more completely in the power of corporations. If the reader has followed us he will not fail to perceive that all the departments of the government are virtually controlled by the great anti-republican corporate interests now overshadowing and cursing the land; and that the supreme court of the United States, originally intended to be a check upon unconstitutional legislation, and to guard with jealous care the rights of the people, has become an instrument to aid this great power in its war upon the rights of the citizen; that by judicial construction of statutes involving the rights of corporations and the people, such decisions have been made as leave the people but little to hope for in the future, and induce the belief that the will of the court, and not constitutional law, is to be the "supreme law of the land."

CHAPTER XXIII.

BANK MONOPOLISTS—THEIR CONTROL OF THE CURRENCY.—A BANKRUPT FINANCIAL POLICY.

GOLD and silver are and must remain the standard of values. This being true, any attempt to substitute any other standard unsettles values, and opens avenues for reckless speculation. Bank bills, or other promises to pay, are and always will remain unsafe as a money standard; especially when they cannot be exchanged for specie, save at large discounts. The policy of the government of substituting treasury notes for coin, as legal tender, and then issuing national currency for general circulation by the banks of the country, has been effectual in preventing the circulation of coin, as well as the resumption of specie payment. No good reason can be given for issuing two kinds of currency, or for providing that one kind (treasury notes) shall be legal tender, and the other (national currency) shall be of less value, good in ordinary circumstances, but which no one is obliged to accept in payment of debts.

The present banking law provides that any five or more persons may form a private corporation or banking association, and upon compliance with the provisions of the law, transact all business usually transacted by banking associations. As a condition to the issuing of bank notes, the company, after it has organized according to law, must deposit with the proper officer in Washington, in government bonds, an amount greater by ten per cent. than the amount of bank notes it receives for circulation. If it deposit $100,000 in bonds, it receives from the comptroller of the currency $90,000 in national currency, which it can issue, and, as occasion requires, must redeem in treasury notes. The government bonds are held by the department as security for the redemption of the bank notes received for circulation, and the government pays to the different banking companies semi-annual interest at the rate specified in the bonds deposited by the companies respectively. The amount of tax annually collected from the people to pay this interest to bankers is between $18,000,000 and $20,000,000. All that the people receive in return for this sum is the privilege of borrowing national currency from banks at legal rates of interest. The banking companies receive from government their six per cent. annually in gold on their bonds deposited with the department at Washington, and the lawful rates fixed by the states respectfully upon loans and discounts with such other profits usual among bankers.

The laws of congress creating the national banking system are anti-republican, and at war with the principles of our government. They restrict the currency of the country to a certain fixed amount, and exclude coin from circulation. They clothe the secretary of the treasury with absolute control of the finances — not only of the government, but of the whole people—a power that is unprecedented in republican government, and dangerous to republican institutions. No financial system could be devised that would so completely deprive the people of any control of their finances, or deny to them any knowledge of the solvency of the banking institutions of their own immediate localities. The system is derived from the old world—from monarchical governments where the population is dense, the policy of the ruling powers settled, and where the aristocratic idea prevails that the few should rule, and the many serve; that those who produce the wealth of the country should be subject to the idle classes who rule over them. We have in this country a moneyed aristocracy, composed mainly of men who speculated in their country's misfortunes during the late civil war, who, under the pretence of aiding the government, made their twenty, fifty, and one hundred per cent., and amassed large fortunes by taking advantage of the tide of war as it submerged a nation's hopes. At the time the patriotic men of the nation were in active service—when such were laying down their lives for their country, these men were refusing to aid the government with money unless they had large margins for profit. Clothed with this great moneyed power, they fixed the price of government bonds, as well as the value of all property in the land. As a relief measure, the banking law of 1863 was enacted. At the date of the passage of the act, more than one-half of the wealth of the country was owned and controlled by about four per cent. of the population, who have proceeded to dictate all the financial, revenue, and monetary measures of the government since the breaking out of the rebellion, excepting the measure sustaining the credit of the government—the issue of treasury notes—a measure which alone saved the nation from financial ruin. The banking act, while it was passed as a relief measure, was in fact but a surrender of the finances of the country to an irresponsible class of banking associations. The amount of treasury notes was limited by act of congress, and not being sufficient to supply the wants of the people, about $350,000,000 of currency were issued to these private banking corporations, which they now control in their own interest. One-half of the circulating medium is issued directly in government and treasury notes, and the other half—currency—by these private bankers. These two amounts are all the people can have as a circulating medium. By the creation of these private corporations, congress has placed over the people a moneyed aristocracy who are responsible to the secretary of the treasury, and to whom alone they must account. This banking law deprives the people of coin circulation, and by the assumption of a power at war with Republican institutions, creates a privileged class with the *sovereign power* of controlling the whole moneyed interest of the country.

Was there any necessity for this creation of national banks with currency differing in character and value from treasury notes? The banks were chartered as a war measure. Did government or people gain by this banking system? If banks were desirable as fiscal agents throughout the country, treasury notes were certainly as good a currency as the paper issued to banks, and could have been supplied at less cost to the government and the people. As a circulating medium the whole people have regarded them as the best possible paper *money*. There was no necessity of this banking system for supplying a market for government bonds, inasmuch as the largest amount of bonds was sold after the banking act was passed—not to persons wishing to do a banking business, but to outside parties. Besides, the amount of bonds purchased by bankers, and deposited with the comptroller of the currency, was comparatively small, being less than one-eighth of the national debt. If, instead of selling bonds to bankers, and agreeing to pay them coin interest thereon, treasury notes had been sold to them, the public would have been just as secure, for the faith of the government is pledged to redeem these notes, and, having received value for them, neither the people nor the government would be the losers. On the contrary, a great saving—the interest on the amount of the bonds deposited would have been saved. In fact all the security for the redemption of bank currency is furnished by government. The system is based upon the credit of the United States. If this credit is good as expressed in the bond, it is also good as expressed in the treasury notes. The bankers themselves impart no money value to the bank notes; all this is imparted by government. These bank notes being secured by the credit of the government, and issued by it. They constitute the money of the government, and are a loan to the banks just as much as though government had loaned to them treasury notes; and so far as the bankers are concerned it is a free loan. The banks do not pay interest on the currency loaned to them; on the contrary, government pays them interest on the amount they receive. To illustrate: Let us suppose that government has sold $1,500,000,000 in bonds. These bonds all bear interest at six per cent. payable in coin. That is all the consideration paid by government for the loan. Under the banking act, $350,000,000 of these bonds are purchased and owned by corporations formed for the purpose of doing a banking business. They deposit the amount with the comptroller of the currency, and receive the full amount, less ten per cent., in currency. This currency is issued by the government, and must eventually be redeemed by it. The government, in fact, pays back to the depositors the amount of their bonds, less ten per cent., and at the same time pays interest upon the whole amount.

The bankers have received back ninety per cent. of their deposits, and use the amount received as money; and at the same time government pays six per cent. interest to the bankers on the ninety per cent. delivered to them in currency. Take a single case for a further illustration. A corporation is organized in New York for banking purposes—capital, $1,000,000. It purchases bonds to the full amount of its capital, and deposits them with the comptroller. Upon the whole of this $1,000,000, the corporation receives six per cent. interest in coin, payable semi-annually, while it continues the banking business, and simultaneously with the deposit of its bonds it receives from government $900,000 in currency. On this amount it pays no interest, and no taxes, excepting the one per cent. exacted from all money lenders, brokers, insurance companies, etc. It receives its six per cent. from government on its banking capital, and receives back from government all but ten per cent. of its capital, and loans it to the people at six per cent. or more, thus getting twelve per cent. on the amount it has invested in the banking business. This twelve per cent. has all to be paid by the people in national taxes, besides the interest paid to the banks for loans. If treasury notes had been issued in payment for bonds, or for money paid for them, one-half of this per cent. would have been saved to the people; and the best kind of circulating medium provided by the government would have been furnished to them. Banking, without this government bounty paid to bankers, has always proved to be profitable. Large dividends have been the rule. According to reports made by some of the present banking corporations in favored localities, they are declaring dividends or ten, twenty, forty, and some of them as high as one hundred per cent. per annum. This shows that neither the necessities of the government, nor of the people, required that a bounty should be paid to bankers in order to induce them to take the control of the currency of the country.

It has been said that the banking act was a necessity as a war measure. Is this true? No additional bonds were sold because of the passage of the banking act. The amount of currency issued and distributed over the country did not add to the wealth of the people or the government. The sale of bonds and issue of greenbacks answered all the ends of the government, unless it was supposed that by affording a privileged few among the purchasers of its bonds, the opportunity of making a larger per cent. than was allowed to all other government creditors, would advance its interests. That the object in the passage of the act was not to aid the government, or relieve the people from the burdens then resting upon them is evident by its peculiar provisions. It limits the amount of the circulating medium of the country, and compels the people to pay $20,000,000 annually for a currency inferior to treasury notes, which they could have had without cost. It confers special privileges upon, and pays a bounty to a limited number of the government creditors. The amount of currency is too limited to benefit the government or the people. It gives to the secretary of the treasury, and the banking corporations of the country the control of the *purse*, not only of the government but of the people. It gives to a few capitalists of the country a complete monopoly of the entire business of the nation. It has substituted currency for money and made the resumption of specie payment dependent upon the pleasure of the few men who now control the finances of the country. It is the powerful ally of the brokers and stock-jobbers who are enriching themselves by oppressing the producers of the country. It has fixed an arbitrary limit to the currency of the country, and deprived the people of the power of increasing that amount, or of using coin as a circulating medium. It is anti-republican, and at war with the best interests of the people. It has already cost the people in taxes, to pay interest to banking corporations on their banking capital, the sum of $200,000,000, (which sum is increased $20,000,000 each year,) for which they have recived no consideration save the privilege of borrowing currency from banks. It establishes a moneyed aristocracy who rule over and despoil the wealth-producing classes, reducing labor to a state of vassalage to capital.

We cannot discover the wisdom ot the law which provides that a banking company shall buy an amount of government bonds equal to its capital stock, paying government therefor, and after depositing it with the proper government officials, receive interest on it. If a man pay his note or bond, and gets it in his own possession, he would lack wisdom if he were to continue the payment of semi-annual interest on it after that time. Government is doing this with only this difference: It says to the banking company: "Buy my bonds, pay for them, and then I will hold them in trust, and pay you the interest on them." We can see no good reason for this provision of the law. If the object were to borrow money, it could have been accomplished by receiving it directly from the banking company, and then issuing to such company legal tender notes in payment therefor, and by so doing government would have saved the large amount of interest now being collected from the people. If the object were to furnish a circulating medium, the legal tender treasury notes would have been a preferable currency. The government would have hazarded nothing, because it would have had possession of the full value of the notes or bank bills furnished the company. But if the object were to foster and fatten corporations, then the law, as passed, has fully accomplished its purpose. The law provides for a general system of banking, without requiring the bankers to keep one dollar of coin for the redemption of their issues. It provides for the redemption of *currency* with *currency*, thus making the resumption of specie payment impossible, so long as legal tender notes are in circulation. It locks up from one-tenth to four-tenths of all the capital invested in banking, and compels the people to pay interest on this amount without receiving any equivalent. It fixes arbitrarily the amount of circulating medium for the whole country; the amount being $356,000,000 in legal tender notes, and about the same amount in national currency; and of this last amount the banks are compelled to keep on hand a reserve of from fifteen to twenty-five per cent. on all their bills and deposits, thus leaving for circulation, throughout the entire country, not more than $550,000,000, the whole of which is irredeemable in coin. It places the finances of the whole country under the control of one man—the secretary of the treasury. The amount of currency being fixed by law, and apportioned throughout the country, with no means for its increase, it is not difficult for speculators to withdraw sufficient from circulation to affect injuriously the commerce of the country. The combined corporate interest of the country can, at pleasure, corner such amounts as to create a stringency, and if desired, a panic. We have shown in a former chapter the combination existing between railroad corporations and Wall street brokers, and their control of the finances of the country. We have also shown the effect of the legal tender decision upon the financial interests of the country, and the large benefits the railroad corporations are deriving from it; and that they controlled to a great and dangerous extent all departments of the government. Under the present financial and banking system they hold the whole country at their mercy. They fix prices upon all the farm products of the country. Having full knowledge of the amount of currency in the banks of the great commercial centers, as well as the amounts in the different parts of the country, with the means in their own hands of controlling and expanding these amounts at pleasure, by withdrawing, or as it is termed "cornering" the necessary sum, they fix the price of all articles of commerce, and stocks, and gold. The government, under the present financial policy, cannot prevent this state of things. It has no reserve with which to aid the people. Nor can the banks, if they had the inclination, remedy this evil. The business interests of the country require more money. The government, as well as the banks, are prohibited from issuing more. Because of the lack of quantity required by commerce, the banks are, as a general thing, without any considerable surplus on hand. When these corporations and brokers desire a stringency in the market, they withdraw from the banks a few millions of dollars and lock it up. It is withdrawn from the already insufficient amount in circulation, and legitimate business languishes. Having their vast corporate stock and bond interest to protect, being engaged in constructing railroads, having created large debts upon their roads by reckless and dishonest watering of stock and loose issuing of bonds, they seek to compel all commercial and industrial pursuits to pay tribute to them, and they accomplish this object by controlling the currency of the country. A financial system that can be controlled by one interest, or in the interest of one class of men, is bad. When, as is now the case, that interest is a combination and consolidation of the greatest monopolies that ever cursed a country, the system should be changed.

Under our present system, no matter how evenly the currency was originally distributed over the country, the larger portion of it finds its way to the great commercial centers. The merchant must carry his money to his place of purchase, or what is the same thing, buy an eastern draft from his local bank, which bank, in order to command eastern exchange, must have deposits in eastern banks. The farmer who ships his produce to the east, must pay the charges for transportation, which are usually collected at its place of destination; and these charges being much more than one-half the entire value of the shipment, are retained in the east, or if charges are paid to local agents, they are forwarded to the principal office in the east. Nearly all the great railroad companies having their principal offices in the large eastern cities, their earnings are forwarded to those offices. By these means, the currency of the country is concentrated in the larger commercial cities of the country, mainly in New York, where it is in the absolute custody of these great railroad corporations and brokers; and the financial and banking system of the country, designed to meet the wants of the people, has become, in the hands of these giant monopolies, a principal agency in their oppression. The produce of the farm, and of the entire industrial pursuits of the country, are being swallowed by this huge monopoly, and those others created by our tariff. For this state of things there is no relief without a change of policy on the part of the government. Already there is a wide margin between coin and currency. An increase of the latter would increase that margin, and lessen values. With a fixed amount of increase, the same interest that now controls the finances would, in a short time after its issue, obtain the same control, and this would demand another issue; the same process to be repeated until our currency would be of little or no value, the unlimited increase of irredeemable currency would in the end inflict upon the country absolute ruin. We are now traveling in that direction. Currency is only of value as the representative of money. Now (April, 1873) a dollar in paper represents but eighty-two cents in money. Our government has adopted the Utopian idea of making *small strips of paper*, with certain printed promises thereon, legal tender. This kind of paper has been decided by the supreme court to be *money*, the "measure of values." Notwithstanding the laws of congress and the decision of the supreme court, this measure of values will not become or remain stable; it is gradually shrinking, while gold, the money of the country, is disappearing. Unfortunately for us, our strips of paper will not pass for money, or legal tender, with other nations. For this reason, the coin of the country has to be used in our commerce with foreign nations. Within the last year, the amount of coin in this country has decreased over $38,000,000. The balance against us in our dealings with other countries is the above named amount. Unless some course is adopted that will prevent this large export of gold, it is only a question of time when we shall have no gold in the country, and the only representative of values left us will be paper money without any intrinsic value. Under the present financial policy of the government, and the unlimited control that corporations and rings, with their power all centered in Wall street, have over the finances, we need not hope that the agricultural products of the country can be transported to the seaboard at rates that will enable us to export the same to foreign countries in any considerable amount. We cannot pay inland and ocean transportation, and compete with other grain-producing countries. The markets of the outside world are practically closed against us. With our high protective tariffs, extortionate charges for inland transportation, lack of ocean commerce, and immense foreign debts, public and private, absolute financial ruin must overtake us, unless a different policy is adopted. The amount of currency being fixed by law, the government has in effect declared that the people of this country shall have but this fixed amount for all the purposes for which money is used. The effect of this arbitrary law, followed and supported by the legal tender decision of the supreme court, is to prevent any increase of the currency or money. The control of the currency being placed in the hands of one man, the whole financial interests of the country are dependent upon his will. No matter how great the wants of the country may be, or how inadequate the supply, no departure is allowed from the inflexible rule as to reserves that the banks are required to hold. If the secretary of the treasury conclude to sell gold to ease the market, he does so; if he decide to issue a half million treasury notes, they are allowed to go into the hands of people, and withdrawn, when in his judgment, he deems it advisable. His acts create a feverish excitement in the money market and derange business, carrying loss to everybody, except Wall street brokers. That power, so necessary to a despotism, and so destructive to republican institutions—the control of the purse of the people, and of the government, has fully obtained in this country. The whole people of the land are as completely under the control of the secretary of the treasury (and he in turn ruled by these powerful combinations) as a ward is ruled by his guardian. The system is bad, and should be changed at once. The government should control its own finances, and the people should be permitted to provide for themselves without asking the permission of the government. We subjoin the following expression of views of one of the ablest and most experienced of the bank officers in this country:

"The incompetency of special legislation, when applied to the adjustment and regulation of the paper currency of the country, I presume few sensible men, at all acquainted with the subject, will question; nor is it possible for any man of business, or any possessor of property, in whatever shape, to feel safe while the power to inflate or contract the currency is arrogated by any one man, whether he happens to be some narrow-minded, bigoted, obstinate official, acting on his own volition, or some subordinate clerk, acted upon by others.

"No one should be entrusted or tempted with such a power; for no man, however able and honest, could, by any possibility, justly or accurately exercise it. Foolish as was the experiment, however, we have tried it: and with the ill success that was inevitable.

"The sway to and fro of our currency, controlled by the ebb and flow of our business transactions, consequent upon seed time and harvest, is subject to law as imperious and immutable as any that governs either the physical or moral world; and in just the degree that we understand and conform to its action can we hope for a successful solution of the problem that now so vexes the minds and disturbs the interests of all classes of the community.

"The nearest approximation we have yet made to such an understanding and conformity has been in the New York free banking law, from which the national currency act has borrowed all of any merit it possesses.

"This New York law, free from the vice of monopoly which the national currency act inherits from the necessities of its birth, and open to all men, as any honorable pursuit should be in this republic of ours, is also distinguished by three salient points: perfect security to bill-holders, freedom from arbitrary reserves, and systematic redemption of bills. In this last feature of the law, disagreeable as it is at times to speculation or unwary bankers, lies the key to its success, checking and governing as it does by its conservative action all over-issues, while still leaving the open freedom of the system untouched by any useless restriction; so that, no matter how great the number of those who choose to embark in the business, no more currency can be kept afloat than the wants of the country demand. The national currency act fails because it is a monopoly; because it has only a nominal redemption; and because of its arbitrary reserve clause, which serves only to hamper the means and obstruct the usefulness of our metropolitan banks at the very time when the trade of the country most requires their services, to say nothing of the power for evil which a knowledge of this fixed limit gives to the gamblers and speculators who hang around and within our stock-exchanges; and, lastly, because it has no power of expansion and contraction in response to the varying calls of trade and commerce.

"The substitution of a free banking law for the national currency act — in the mere fact of the release it would give us from constant petitions to Washington officials, leaving the government to attend to its own monetary affairs and strictly mind its own business — would go a great way towards restoring and maintaining the manhood and self-respect we are fast losing, from our constant looking up to and attendance upon the central power, asking to have done for us things which should be self-regulating or which we should do for ourselves. Democrats as we profess to be, we are rapidly aping the follies and acquiring the habits of dependence upon authority characteristic of the older civilizations of monarchial Europe. It is hardly time, I think, for us to take the backward swing of the pendulum of political progress, that is sure eventually to land us where we began."

A careful examination of the financial policy of the government ought to convince us that a change is necessary to prevent ultimate ruin and bankruptcy. With gold driven from circulation — an insufficient amount of depreciated currency for the transaction of the business of the country, and the facilities afforded the monopolies for controlling our whole commerce, the agricultural and industrial interests of the country languish — the farmer receives no reward for his toil — the laborer is poorly paid — and general prostration extends over the land. A return to specie payment, or an increase of sound currency, would relieve all cause of complaint, and enable the industry of the country to receive a fair remuneration for its labor.

CHAPTER XXIV.

OUR TARIFF POLICY—DOES PROTECTION PROTECT?

A DIVERSITY of opinion exists throughout the country upon the question of tariff. Politicians, statesmen, and the people generally, differ as to the policy the government should adopt respecting it. It is generally admitted that the revenue for the support of the government should be derived from duties levied upon imports. The real point upon which a difference exists is, whether the government should levy a tariff for revenue alone, or whether it should be levied for the purpose of affording what is termed a protection to American manufactures and interests. This question is no nearer a solution now than it was forty years ago. Those who favor protection appeal to our national pride; the necessity of encouraging home manufactures, and of competing with the cheap labor of Europe. A tariff for protection has been urged and adopted as the only means of fostering home productions for so long a time that it is deemed one of the necessities of the country by its advocates. They look upon it as a chief means of affording a home market for the farm produce of the country, as well as affording a market for all manufactured articles. While, on the other hand, those who are opposed to a tariff save for revenue, claim that what is termed protection, is, in fact, oppression; that it cripples commerce, taxes the people oppressively and unjustly, and, instead of benefiting the producer by affording him a market, deprives him of it. They insist that the agriculturists of this country need, and must have, the advantage of foreign market in order to make farm pursuits remunerative.

We have been combating monopolies, and shall attempt to show that what is termed a protection tariff affords no protection to the people at large, or to the operatives and laborers in factories and shops, but only to the capitalists of the country. An equitable tax for revenue is one that is levied upon articles of foreign growth or production, that enter into general consumption; and not one that is levied upon articles the main portion of which are of home manufacture. It is only the imported article that pays a duty to the government. The home manufacturer does not sell his fabrics for less price than is paid for the imported articles of like character and value; hence when only a part of any commodity is imported and pays a duty, and the other part is supplied from home manufactures, while the government derives revenue from the imported articles, the manufacturer puts into his own pocket the same per cent. that is paid to the government in shape of import duty. To make it plainer: If a tariff of forty per cent. is paid upon the imported article, when it is sold, the purchaser must re-pay this per cent. to the importer, but the manufacturer can advance the price of his goods so as to realize forty per cent., or the amount of the tariff over his former prices, and still compete with the importer. The tariff protects him at the rate of forty per cent., which must be eventually paid by the consumer. No tariff is paid on home manufactures, and yet, in all cases, the manufacturer adds to the cost of production the amount of the tariff placed on like articles, and collects it from the purchaser or consumer. A tariff for protection gives to the manufacturers a monopoly, in some cases so complete as to drive the foreign article from our ports. In such cases the government receives no revenue, but the manufacturer makes a clean profit of the per cent. fixed by the tariff, all of which is eventually paid by the consumer, and for which he receives no consideration. To illustrate this, let us take the duties on blankets for the year 1871, and the quantity imported. The duties on the four classes of blankets were 87, 88, 100, and 109 per cent., respectively. The whole imports for that year amounted to $19,355, and the tariff duties amounted to $17,316. All of the residue of blankets purchased during that year were home productions. The manufacturer has only to mark up his price to realize about one hundred per cent. over the price at which they would have been sold but for the protection tariff. Take boots and shoes as another illustration: We imported none in 1871, and of course no revenue was received on these articles in that year; yet the manufacturers had the benefit of a tariff of thirty-five per cent. on each pair sold. If a pair of boots was sold at $8.00, the protection the wearer paid the manufacturer was $2.80. The law compels the farmer and laborer to pay that sum as a bounty to the manufacturer. On cotton goods the consumer pays a duty of from thirty-five to sixty-three per cent. For almost every article of clothing worn by man, woman and child a duty must be paid. The average is about forty-five per cent. on the value. Prices are nearly uniform for the same classes of goods, whether of foreign or domestic manufacture. On imported articles the tariff is paid to the government; on domestic manufactures the duty is paid to the manufacturer. This system compels the poor man to contribute more than his fair proportion to protect the already rich manufacturer. To illustrate this, let us suppose that A is worth $500,000, and has a family of four to clothe, while B, who has nothing but his industry, and perhaps a small homestead, has a family of eight dependent upon him (as a general rule the poor man has the larger family). Both families must be clothed and fed; each must contribute to the manufacturer the same rate of protection. The man with his half million in property and family of four will probably purchase as much for his family as the poor man will for his family of eight; each expends for his family, during the year, for clothing, say four hundred dollars. If the duty on the purchase averages forty per cent., each pays for the support of the government and to protect home manufactures the sum of $160.00. The sweat and toil of the poor man contributes just as much as the rich man's half-million. Or, suppose A is a man without family, and has great wealth, and B is dependent upon the product of a small farm for the support of himself and family. A spends for clothing $200.00, while B is obliged to expend $400.00 for clothing his family. Here the labor of the poor man pays twice as much as the capital of the rich man to protect home industry and support the government.

The above illustrations will serve for all articles of general consumption. Let us look at the effect of the tariff upon other articles, taking railroad iron as an illustration. Under a revenue tariff railroad iron was sold for less than two-thirds of its present cost. Manufacturers amassed princely fortunes; laborers were better paid than they are now; the iron interests seemed to be in a prosperous condition; the demand was growing and increasing, and has continued to increase, until the supply is insufficient, and both foreign and domestic markets are depleted, and at times exhausted. With this increasing demand and scant supply there seems to be no good reason for government protection to home manufactures, yet a protective duty of about one-fourth its value is allowed on railroad iron. While the companies constructing the roads pay this duty, the producing classes also pay it in the end, in the shape of appreciated charges for transportation. The protection afforded to manufacturers does not extend to the laborers and operatives. The slight increase on the amount paid them does not meet the increased cost of living resulting from the protection tariff. They must pay more for what they consume, as well as receive the pay for their labor in depreciated currency. The effect of protecting the iron interests is to strengthen a monopoly that is now so rich and powerful that it controls some of the largest states in the union. For this protection it returns no equivalent. The effect is the same in other manufacturing states. The owners of the factories make large profits, but the laborers and operatives, while their wages have advanced, really do not receive as much, over and above the increased cost of what they consume, as they received prior to 1860, under a revenue tariff.

The purchasing power of a dollar before 1860 was as great as that of one and a half dollars now, for the reason that then it was the value of a coin dollar, while at the present time it is the value of an irredeemable paper dollar, at no time worth a dollar in coin, and for the further reason that the present tariff compels labor to pay for its purchases from thirty to eighty per cent. for protection to the manufacturer. Thus, while the actual increase of wages is, as shown by reports made after investigation, but twelve per cent., the cost of living has increased fifty per cent. Under the plea of encouraging home manufactures, the operative and laborer is compelled to work at starvation prices, and it is not strange that they are organizing mutual aid societies.

Another argument in favor of protection, which is often urged, is that we should protect our people from the competing effects of the pauper labor of Europe. If this object were accomplished by a protective tariff, one good purpose would be achieved. But what are the facts? The manufacturers avail themselves of the higher prices warranted under the tariff, and then import their laborers and operatives from Europe; and, instead of finding, as formerly, American factories, furnaces, and machine shops operated by Americans, they are worked mainly by imported laborers and operatives, and those who were to be protected and receive living wages are compelled to seek employment in other pursuits. Instead of protecting our own laborers from the competition of foreign pauper labor, the foreign laborers are imported, and supersede those who were promised protection.

Another argument in favor of a protective tariff is, that it will afford a home market for the agricultural products of the country. Is this true? The vast agricultural resources of the great west and south demand the markets of the world. Illinois and Iowa can produce enough to supply a manufacturing population, who, in turn, could supply all the fabrics and manufactured articles demanded by the entire population of the whole country. If we are to have the balance nicely drawn, so as to have a manufacturing population sufficient to consume the agricultural products of the country, then we could furnish the manufactured articles at rates that will allow us to export to other countries, and compete with them in their own markets, or else the supply will so far exceed the demand that only a limited number could continue manufacturing pursuits, and a protective tariff, no matter how high, could not furnish a market beyond the demand. Let us refer to the returns made to the state department for an illustration of one point: In 1860 the exports of manufactured articles to foreign countries, under a revenue tariff, amounted to $21,351,562. The total amount of like exports in 1871, under the present protective tariff, amounted to $13,038,753, in coin. The exports in 1860 were in excess of those of 1871, under the highest tariff ever known in this country, $8,282,811, showing that under a low or revenue tariff our manufacturers could and did sell in foreign markets more than under the present system of high duties. Again, if we look at the exports of meat and breadstuffs for the years 1860 and 1871, we will find the amount exported in 1860 exceeded and exported in 1871 $2,000,000. We have not the figures before us, but believe they will show a still greater falling off in 1872. Now let us look at the imports during the same period. In 1860 we imported manufactured articles to the amount of $146,177,136, and in 1871 to the amount of $165,463,679, being an excess of the amount for the year 1860 in the sum of $19,286,543. If we add to this the falling off in exports ($2,000,000), the balance of trade against us, on manufactured articles, as between us and other nations, is $21,286,543. The imports for 1872 far exceed those of 1871, and the balance of trade against us for that year was but little less than $40,000,000. But if we take our entire commerce with other nations in account, the balance against us in 1871 was over $100,000,000! In 1872 it was over $140,000,000; and if we add the amount of interest paid annually on bonds held in other countries, payable by railroads and other corporations, and the general government, the balance against us in 1872 was not less than $250,000,000. This balance must be paid with the products of our country or in money. We have not coin with which to pay, and under our *protection* system we cannot pay with our products. A protective tariff makes the farmers, the laborers, and all consumers insurers of a certain profit to the already powerful combination of manufacturers. While the mechanic must depend upon the demand there is for his skill and labor, the laborer must also take his chances in the same way, and be content to accept such wages as his services will command; and the farmer must depend upon the demand and supply for the sale of his farm product, and not unfrequently will sell at ruinous prices, while the manufacturers have a monopoly in their line—they can always sell at a profit; all they need to do is to sell about as cheaply as the same article can be furnished for from a foreign marker, plus the "protection" of the duty. The duty paid on the foreign article is the amount of *royalty* the manufacturer charges for his goods. All other industries are compelled to divide their labor and products with him. The laborer who receives $20.00 per month and buys cloth of domestic manufacture for a suit of clothes, for which he pays $20.00, contributes about $7.35 of that amount to "protect" the manufacturer. The farmer who sells one hundred bushels of wheat for $100.00, and expends the amount in clothing for himself and family, donates about $38.00 to protect the manufacturer. The same is true of all other classes of consumers. Each one pays from thirty to eighty per cent. on his purchases to protect the owners of factories, furnaces, etc.

The protective tariff has destroyed our ocean commerce. It would not be profitable to spend time in reviewing the duty levied upon the materials and in the construction of vessels for ocean commerce. The fact is well known that our carrying has passed into the hands of other nations. That vessels can be built more cheaply in foreign ports is well known, as also that American ship owners build or purchase their ships in Europe, sail under English colors, and use English papers, assigning as a reason therefor their inability to pay the duty upon the materials used in ship building. So oppressive is this duty, and so damaging has it become to our commerce, that congress is being urged to grant subsidies to ship owners. As a necessary result of this system of protective tariff, the American built ships cannot carry freight as cheaply as those built in foreign countries, and the producer must be content to have his produce, already taxed to a half or two-thirds its value for inland transportation, taxed beyond the amounts charged by the vessels of other nations for ocean transportation, or allow the ocean trade to remain as it now is, in the hands of England. American seamen must abandon the ocean, or sail under foreign flags. Protection has destroyed our mercantile navy, and compelled our seamen to seek employment elsewhere, and in other occupations. With our vast agricultural wealth demanding the markets of the world, the protective policy of the government effectually closes our ports to other nations, while the farmer is obliged to accept for his grain the low price that a home market, already glutted, will afford him. The protective tariff is draining the country of coin, and making it impossible to resume specie payment. Taking it in connection with the combination of corporations, and Wall street brokers, the prospect of having coin as a circulating medium is but faint, if it is ever possible.

The products of our mines for the year 1872 were about $62,000,000, and for the last four years have been nearly $200,000,000. The value of petroleum produced in the United States for the year 1872 was not less than $60,000,000, a large portion of which was shipped to and sold in foreign countries, and to that extent should be reckoned as money in our dealing with foreign nations. In 1872 the balance of trade was against us to the amount of about $250,000,000. After absorbing the produce of our mines, and our petroleum, the net balance against us was not less than $120,000,000. This balance had to be paid in coin or in the issue of new bonds. At no time since the enactment of the present tariff has the balance of trade been in our favor. Thus, notwithstanding the high duty paid, and the protection afforded by the tariff, our demands for foreign manufactures increase to such an extent as to threaten the nation with bankruptcy. According to official reports, the amount of coin in the country in 1868 was $350,000,000. The products of the mines since that date amount to $200,000,000. The amount of coin now in the country is reported less than $250,000,000, and most likely will not amount to $200,000,000. Protection to a small band of monopolists has caused an annual decrease in the amount of coin in the country equal to the excess of imports over exports. A few owners of factories and furnaces are being benefited and enriched by protection; the prices of manufactured articles have increased on an average about fifty per cent. The wages of operatives and laborers have increased but twelve per cent; the exports of manufactured articles have decreased;

the value of imports has increased; the ocean commerce of the nation has been destroyed; the prices of the agricultural products of the country are reduced to a point that has blasted the prospects of the farmer, and made it difficult for him to live; the country is being drained of its precious metals, and an irredeemable currency has become the only circulating medium; values are unsettled, and the country is threatened with financial ruin—all to afford protection to home manufacturers and corporations. Protection is but another name for the systematic plunder of the farmer, laborer, and all the industrial interests of the country, by a class of monopolists that should be classed with corporations, stock jobbers, and Wall street brokers, and who are, in part at least, composed of the same men who control the corporate interests of the country.

CHAPTER XXV.

PATENT RIGHTS AND THEIR ABUSES.

CLOSELY allied to the monopolists of which we have been treating is that of patents to inventors. The original idea of granting patents was to protect inventors and discoverers when their inventions and discoveries were *new* and *useful*. It is but just that the person who invents or discovers a new and useful principle in arts or mechanics, or makes a new and useful combination of principles not new, should be protected in his discoveries; that for a limited time he should reap the exclusive benefit of his discovery, in order that he may receive a fair consideration for the benefit his fellow-men are to derive from his studies and enterprise.

To these inventors and discoverers we are indebted for much that is of great value to the public. The arts, sciences, and mechanics, as well as agriculture, have been greatly benefited by discoveries and inventions. The wealth, comfort, and happiness of the nation have been increased, while the inventors, because of the protection afforded them, have received a fair remuneration. The fact that valuable inventions reward the inventor liberally has led to great and growing abuses of the patent right statutes, and to great frauds and impositions. The desire to acquire sudden wealth has caused dishonest adventurers to enter the field of invention and discovery, with the intent of defrauding the people, as well as deceiving the patent office department. The same desire has caused those whose inventions are of value to resort to various schemes and subterfuges to continue their exclusive right to manufacture and sell their inventions long after they have been fully compensated for all they have expended in thought, time, and labor, in arranging and perfecting their discoveries and inventions. Having been granted a monopoly, they contrive to continue it. Lobbyists and congressmen become interested for a consideration, and patents are renewed from time to time by an abuse of the law that was designed to encourage discoveries and inventions, but not to build up and continue oppressions of the people.

No class of the community has suffered as much from these monopolies as the agriculturalists. All improvements in farming implements and machinery are patented. Some of them, patented more than a quarter of a century ago, are still under the exclusive control of the patentees. Reapers that cost the manufacturer but fifty or sixty dollars are sold for from one hundred and seventy-five to two hundred and twenty-five dollars, because the patentee, or his assigns have now, and for nearly a generation have had, an exclusive right to make and sell them. So with seeders, plows, harrows, fanning mills, and almost all farming implements. The farmer is obliged to pay at least one hundred per cent. royalty to the inventor, or his assigns, before he can receive any benefit from a discovery or an invention designed especially for his use. The inventors have already realized princely fortunes from their inventions, and the intent of the law has been fully accomplished; yet the patents are continued, and no one is allowed to make or sell these implements without the permission of the inventor. The law, which gave an exclusive right for fourteen years, has been amended from time to time; the rights have been extended until patentees and their assigns annually claim tribute from the farmer in an amount that is oppressive. Patent right men operate together; they combine for the purpose of extorting from the people of this country, where they have a monopoly, while at the same time they sell their manufactured articles in foreign markets for one-half the price they demand in this country. We might illustrate this by numerous facts, but will content ourselves with reference to sewing machines and reapers. These are all patented, and all have patents for improvements made from time to time, many of which improvements are of little or no value, save as a pretext for the renewal of the patent. A sewing machine that cannot be purchased in the United States for less than seventy dollars costs but twelve or thirteen dollars for work and materials. This same machine (Singer's) is shipped to Europe and sold for $32.00. Here, where the patentee has an exclusive monopoly, we pay $38.00 more for the machine than it costs in England. We could order an American-made sewing machine from Belfast, pay freight and charges twice across the ocean, and get it for one-half it costs to buy it in America. If you purchase a McCormick's reaper in this country it will cost you about $200.00. You can order the same machine from England, pay freights for its passage twice across the Atlantic, and get it for about one-half the money. The manufacturer cannot sell in this country without paying about one hundred per cent. royalty to the inventor, but he can ship to Europe and sell at one-half the price charged in this country, and realize a fair profit on the sale. When a farmer purchases a reaper for himself, and a sewing machine for his wife, paying for the two $270.00, he pays as royalty to the inventor, $135.00. This same rate has been paid for the last twenty-five or thirty years. This large royalty is paid to the inventor and is called protection. Continued beyond a reasonable time, it is nothing but legalized robbery.

The fact that large fortunes have been, and are, made by inventors and pretended inventors, has filled the country with sharpers and swindlers, who are constantly on the lookout for an idea that may lead to some sort of invention upon which they can apply for a patent. The ease with which patents can be obtained encourages them in their undertaking. If we are to judge of the ability and competency of the examiners of models and drafts by the patents issued for almost all conceivable articles, we must conclude that the only qualifications they possess are to receive the fees, and recommend the issuing of letters patent. Principles so old that the date of their discovery is lost, that have been in use so long "that the memory of man runneth not to the contrary," are being monopolized by letters patent, until a mechanic, or farmer, if he puts a handle in a hatchet, a hoe, or rake, or changes the arrangement of a harrow, plow, churn, or washboard, must expect to have a sharp speculator call upon him for royalty for an infringement upon his patent. Or, if a seamstress cuts her thread in a particular way she must pay royalty. If the farmer makes a glove to protect his hands in husking corn, before he has used them a half hour, some vender of patents will call upon him for royalty. If the owner of a house attempts to paint it, or repair the roof, he must pay royalty for the privilege, if his own judgment should prompt him to compound his paints with some article not ordinarily used, or to use for his roof a kind of composition not in general use.

The increase in the business of procuring patents is now so great that it has become a general and common nuisance to the whole country. The following is a list of one week's business in the patent office:

Patents were issued in one week to applicants from the western states for threading nuts; broom corn duster; threshing machine; school desk and seat; station indicator; binding screw; corn sheller; windmill; photograph skylight; corn husking thimble; land pulverizer; manufacture of sweet biscuit; railroad frog; dress pattern; two for plows; thread cutter for sewing machine; corn husking glove; wheel plow; bridle bit; railroad track wrench; cradle; paper file; garden hose holder; sawing machine; saw swage; scythe rifle; butter package; spring hinge; swage for forming horse shoes; automatic grain weigher; fire-place grate; potato digger; automatic gate; faucet; stock for mill-stone picks; piston valve for steam engine; car coupling; motive power; grain basket; dining table; portable fence; fishing torch; extension table; driving gear for hand car; horse collar; harrow; cross-cut saw handle; extension ladder; machine for cutting leather; bee hive; cloth measuring register; cutter for tonguing and grooving lumber; heating stove; rotary steam engine; manufacture of steel; blast furnace; compound for preventing incrustation; fruit press; fire extinguisher; two for cultivators; hub for heavy wheeled vehicles; horse-shoe attachment; egg carrier; hose pipe nozzle; cotton cultivator; shoe pegging and trimming machine; combined seed separator and drill; felloe; filter for corn-juice, oils, etc.; gate hinge; distilling of turpentine; cotton stalk knocker; automatic fan.

The above comprises only a partial list of the patents issued in one week. Followed up for one year, the list of patents would swell to near 4,000, about one in twenty of which are of value, while the residue are of no value save to enable the patentee to defraud the people upon whom he imposes his patent, or to force the timid to pay him royalty. Of the immense number of patents obtained for improved churns and washing machines, but few are of any real value. The same is true of patent bridges, reapers, and mowers, of threshing machines, seeders, and planters, of fences, and almost all farming implements. So of sewing machines.

Many of the patents obtained contained no new principle, discovery, or combination; but, by imposition and fraud, adventurers obtained letters patent for something in general use, for the purpose of levying blackmail in the shape of royalty, upon those who, ignorant of any exclusive right claimed by any one, continue to use an article which has been in general use long before the letters patent were issued. But few farmers or mechanics have escaped the claims of these patent right sharpers. Rather than be at the expense of defending a suit in the United States court, they submit to the demands of the man who presents himself as the agent or assignee of the patentee demanding blackmail, well knowing that the rascal has no legal claim, but preferring to buy peace rather than to be annoyed by vexatious litigation.

No better illustration of the results of granting letters patent for pretended inventions or discoveries, as well as of the careless manner in which letters patent are issued, can be found than is presented by the gate known in the west as "Teel's Patent." This gate in its combination and construction does not contain a single new principle. The same identical gate has been in use for thirty years in various parts of the Union. With the addition of "friction wheels," or "rollers," or "pivot wheels" (as they are indifferently called), this gate was on exhibition and sale in many of the western states in 1863. In fact, the patent for the friction wheels obtained in that year was attached to the gate and publicly exhibited, no claim being made for a patent upon the gate, but only upon the attachment. The gate itself consists of battens nailed upon the ends and near the center of four or five boards, which forms the gate, with the posts so placed that after it is pushed a sufficient distance to make it balance on its center, it can be opened, its center acting as the pivotal point. The balancing principle, for which the patent was obtained, was first discovered by two of the descendants of Father Adam, in their youthful days, when they balanced a pole or board across a log or fence, and, seated one on each end, enjoyed a game of see-saw. The little boy who built a pig-pen years before the great intellect of Teel forged the idea, made the same kind of a balance gate for it. The man or boy of past generations who desired to make a cheap gate, instinctively made a *Teel Gate.* Yet some ten years ago the mighty intellect of Teel forged the idea, produced a model, and forwarded it to the patent office. The *Scientific* (?) *Examiner*, who decides upon the merits of all inventions, who, if he had traveled and observed the common farm gate in many parts of the country, must have seen the gate in actual public use, issued to Teel letters patent, which are safely and securely held until the new western country is settled, and this cheap gate is in general use, when he and his agents and assignees appear and demand *royalty.* He has been given an exclusive monopoly for the making, selling, and using a gate that is not new in any of its principles. By this fraud of the applicant, and the incompetence of the examiner, the farmer is forbidden to use the old invention of a cheap gate until he pays a bounty to a patentee. The law for the protection of discoverers and inventors is prostituted, and the people compelled to pay out their money without consideration.

The same state of facts exists with respect to many other patents. Men travel over the country, examine all machinery and farming implements, not for the purpose of making new or useful discoveries or improvements, but for the purpose of learning whether they cannot so contrive as to collect royalty from others for an invention long in use, but for which the inventor had not asked or received a patent. Add this monopoly of patent rights to the other monopolies now cursing the country, and the need of a speedy reform, or the alternative of poverty and bankruptcy among the producing classes, becomes still more apparent.

This patent right monopoly is, in a great measure, owing to the want of proper care and knowledge in the department of the patent office, where the only pre-requisite for the granting of letters patent for almost anything, where the application is not contested, is a model and the patent office fee. The effect of this free and easy course in the department is to bring into disrepute the really valuable invention and discovery, and to impose upon the people useless burdens.

CONCLUSION.

REFORMATION OR REVOLUTION — A RADICAL CHANGE DEMANDED IN THE ADMINISTRATION OF PUBLIC AFFAIRS — CONCLUSIONS OF THE AUTHOR.

FIRST. We have sought to call the reader's attention to some of the monopolies existing in our land, and to show their power and influence with the government, and their control of the commercial and agricultural interests of the country. It now remains for us to direct his attention to the effect of these monopolies upon the people and prosperity of the country. No country in the world has been as bountifully supplied by the Creator with all the means to make a nation prosperous and happy as ours. It is vast in extent of territory. Its soil is rich, and most of it new. Lying in all latitudes, it produces fruits of every climate. The husbandman is assured of an abundant crop. All agricultural and horticultural pursuits are rewarded with large growths and bounteous harvests. Our shores are washed by oceans, which afford us highways, over which we can avail ourselves of the markets of the world; while flowing through the agricultural portions of our common country are our great rivers, upon whose waters the produce and manufactures of the land are transported to market. Our great lakes furnish us an outlet for the surplus product of the great west. Our sixty or seventy thousand miles of railroad traverse our country in all directions, reaching from the Atlantic to the Pacific, and spreading like a net-work from the lakes to the gulf. Our mines produce immense yields of the precious metals, while our hills and mountains are full of iron, coal, and lead. Petroleum flows in quantities which should add largely to the wealth of our common country. Our timber is not excelled by that of any growth in the world. Our lands are rich in fertility, and poor only in price. The Creator has done for us all that could be desired to make us prosperous and contented. Our government is, or was intended to be, based upon the will of the people. Our constitution recognizes no royal rulers, no lords, no titled gentry. Under it we are all equal. They who administer the laws are selected by the people. In contemplation of law, all are equal—all are free and independent. With all these blessings and advantages we ought to be the happiest and most prosperous people on the earth. Peace, plenty, and contentment should reign supreme throughout the land. What are the facts?

Throughout the entire length and breadth of our land, mutterings and complainings are heard. From the farmers, the mechanics, and laborers alike, the complaint is heard, "We cannot pay our taxes and support our families." "Our wages will not enable us to buy the necessaries of life, because of the large duties laid upon them." "Our farm products will not pay taxes, charges for transportation, and other burdens imposed upon us, and leave us any margin." "We had better let our lands lie idle than to attempt to cultivate them." These and like complaints are heard from the laboring and producing classes. Nor are their complaints without cause. Another interest has arisen in the land—it has become all-powerful. This interest penetrates the remotest portions of the country. It calls upon the laborer, the operative, the mechanic, the farmer, and all private citizens, for a division of the products of their labor. It enters the halls of legislatures and of congress, and demands, and not unfrequently purchases, special privileges and powers. It visits the executive department of the government, and there secures special favors. It stalks boldly into the courts of the country, and *there* procures unjust decisions in its interest. It indeed places its own men upon these *seats of justice*, that the judiciary of the country may not fail to support its aims. It has already obtained complete control of the finances of the country. It has corrupted legislatures and congressmen, until the law-making power has become a party to schemes of robbery and plunder. By corrupt legislation and *ex parte* judicial decisions, it has destroyed all the old republican landmarks, overriden the provisions of the constitution, and substituted for the government prepared for us by our forefathers an oligarchy that rules the land and holds the people at its mercy, and their property as its lawful booty. This great oppressor of the people is the railroad corporations and their associates, of which we have been treating. Railroad and other corporations, brokers, and stock-jobbers, have obtained such complete control over the government, the people, and the financial and commercial interests of the country, that they who depend upon agricultural pursuits, or upon their labor for a support, are deprived of those God-given rights which formed the base of our political superstructure.

Formerly, the people, through the ballot box, governed the country; they were sovereign. In this republic no rival power existed, and it was our boast that our people were free and independent. Our fundamental law is still the same. In theory, our people are still sovereign; in fact, most of their sovereignty has been legislated from them. Statutes are enacted compelling the people to divide their hard-earned substance with private corporations without any consideration; and the highest courts of the country have affirmed the constitutionality of these laws. The freedom and equality which was our national boast, have disappeared, and instead thereof the people are ruled by cruel and oppressive task-masters, who are fostered and supported by legislatures and courts in their united purpose of controlling the country. These oppressions have been endured by the people with but feeble efforts to regain their rights, until the alternative is presented of organized resistance or absolute ruin. Throughout the length and breadth of our common country, the laboring and producing classes are struggling for the necessaries of life, whilst those who own and manage the corporations of the country have firmly grasped and now control the financial and commercial interests of the country, and are amassing princely fortunes and rolling in wealth. To stay the course of their oppressors, and get back some of their rights, the laboring classes are organizing, and demanding of their employers such compensation as will enable them to supply the common necessaries of life. They demand that their wages shall be increased in proportion to the increased cost of living, occasioned by special grants and privileges bestowed upon corporations and monopolies; that instead of being treated as vassals of the despots who now rule the country and control the government, that their rights as freemen shall be recognized.

The operatives and mechanics are banding together for the same purpose. They are all seeking, in the same degree, to counteract the evil effects of the grants and privileges conferred upon monopolies. The farmers, who, as a class, have always been deemed the most independent in the country, are so impoverished by these monopolies that they have been compelled to band together for mutual protection. No choice was left them. The bestowal of such great powers and special privileges upon corporations presented the alternative of utter financial ruin, or united and combined efforts on the part of the people to check the great and growing power which now is fattening upon their toil and industry. While under ordinary circumstances, all class organizations are attended with some bad results, yet when any interest becomes so powerful as to oppress all others, when it has such strength that it can defy all ordinary attempts at reform, then any and all organizations having for their object the correction of abuses, the restortion of the rights of the people, the destruction of an oligarchy that has already obtained such power in the land as to subvert the very nature of free institutions, is not only right, but its objects are patriotic. Though the organization may have for its object the protection of a single interest, the correction of a single abuse, the restoration of a single right, it benefits all classes who suffer like oppressions. It is fortunate that while the grants of great bounties and special privileges to corporations have resulted in great wrongs and oppressions to the people generally, they have also been the means of effecting organizations that will eventually restore to the people those rights which in our government are considered as inalienable. When the agriculturists of the whole country become united in their demands for redress, neither the state legislatures, the congress of the nation, or the courts, will dare to disregard their demands. Numbering more than all who are engaged in other pursuits, being a majority of the whole people, when their united voice is heard it will not be an "uncertain sound." It will command obedience. Grants of bounties and privileges to corporations have depressed and sometimes destroyed other great interests to the injury of the people, and divided the people into classes, one class representing the capital and corporate interests of the country, and the other comprised of the laboring and producing classes; but this special legislation has also resulted in bringing to the front the great agricultural population, who possess the power, by united action, of restoring to the people their lost rights, while corporations shall enjoy equal rights with other interests, shorn of their power granted to them by corrupt and interested legislation and partial decisions of courts. This legislation and these decisions we have reviewed in preceding pages. It now remains for us to present our views upon the policy rendered necessary by the grave situation of the country.

SECOND. — *The Constitutional Right and Duty Resting upon the People to Repeal all Class Legislation.* — While we do not claim to possess more knowledge than other men, and while our views as to the means to be employed for remedying the evils under which we now suffer may be erroneous, we shall venture to present them with the hope of aiding the efforts now being made to arrest the rapid concentration of the whole political, commercial, and financial interests of the country in corporations and other monopolies. We must not lose sight of the fact that under our constitution the people are sovereign, that the will of the majority expressed as provided by the fundamental law is supreme; that all the rights, privileges, and powers possessed by a man in his normal state are retained by the people, save such as they have transferred to the different departments of the government, state and national; that these rights, not so transferred, can be asserted and enforced as occasion requires; that when those entrusted with the administration of the government transcend or abuse the powers delegated to them, and by so doing deprive the people of the rights they possess under the constitution, the people are fully justified in resorting to whatever means may be necessary for the restoration and protection of those rights. In pursuing these necessary measures of relief, no injury is done to a minority, or to any individual, for the foundation on which our republic rests is equal and exact justice to all men, and the equality of all men before the law. All acts of legislatures, and all decisions of courts which deny to the citizen, or to any class of citizens, or to a particular trade, occupation, business, or profession, the same privileges and protection granted to others, or which grant to any class of citizens or to corporations, privileges which infringe upon the rights of others, are abuses of power and assumptions of authority not delegated by the people to the government, or to any department of it. It follows that any attempts of congress or legislatures to confer upon any corporations grants of power which enable them to override the rights reserved by the people, transcend the authority with which such legislatures are clothed, and are not binding upon the public. As agents they have exceeded their power, and their acts do not bind their principals. If an agent acts under special authority, his acts, within the scope of his authority, are binding upon his principal; but if he violates his instructions, and attempts to make a contract not warranted by his letter of attorney, his acts have no binding force upon his principal. The same is true of those men who are elected and appointed to fill the different offices in the government. The constitution is their letter of attorney. They are bound by it. When they act outside of their instructions, as contained in that instrument, their acts are void. This will be conceded. Even members of railroad companies will not controvert this proposition. The real point is, Who is to decide when an act is in conflict with the constitution? The answer is, the courts, for such is the law. When complaint is made of usurpations of corporations, we are told that they are only exercising the privileges conferred upon them by law; that the courts have decided in their favor, and that from these decisions there is no appeal; nor can any redress be obtained, because the question has been settled in their favor by the highest power in the land — the supreme court of the United States.

To this general rule of determining controverted questions there must be some exceptions, unless we concede that supreme power is vested in the courts, and that the constitution clothes them with all the attributes of despotic governments. We have shown that judges of courts are governed and controlled by the same influences which influence other men; that they are not infallible; that their decisions are influenced by surrounding circumstances; that education, association, and habits of life, have an important bearing upon their minds, and not unfrequently warp their judgments, and it is not treason to say that decisions of state and federal courts prove that they are as liable to change their views as are the majority of the people. The supreme power must have a permanent lodgment somewhere. If it remains with the people, it does not vest in the supreme court, and that court is but the agent of the people, and acts for them when it decides upon the validity of a statute, or defines the rights and duties of the people. Under our form of government, certain rights and powers are conferred upon the general government; these are all such as are necessary for our existence as a nation; they are limited, and should be strictly construed, because all powers and rights not expressly conferred upon the general government, "are reserved to the states or to the people." The states being sovereign, their power is superior to that of the general government, save in those matters surrendered to it. Hence the state governments have a general, expressed, and implied jurisdiction in all matters not surrendered, and state constitutions are to be liberally construed.

But over and above the powers vested in the general and state governments, that God-given right of self-protection remains with the people. This right they have never surrendered to legislatures or to courts. If by the action of the legislature, or of congress, or of the courts, the rights reserved to the people can be abridged, denied, or destroyed, then we do not live under a republican, but are the subjects of a despotic, government. If congress were to enact a law providing that one-tenth of the annual income of each inhabitant in the land should be paid to railroad corporations, and the supreme court of the United States should decide the act to be constitutional, if it be true that there is no appeal from these decisions, and that as good citizens of the government we are obliged to accept them as valid and binding, there could be no redress. This doctrine of submission we do not endorse. Such a decision would cause the people to resort to the powers and rights retained by them, and to make use of whatever means they possessed to reverse or destroy the force and effect of such a decision. They would be justified in resorting to nature's first law to rid themselves of so unjust a decision. While no such law has been passed, and no such decision has been made, laws have been enacted, and their validity affirmed by the courts, which are paving the way for the destruction of the civil and political rights of the people, and the centralization of all power in the general government. By a series of legislative enactments and decisions of courts, special privileges have been conferred upon railroad companies antagonistic to, and destructive of, the rights of the people. How are these rights to be restored? These questions will now claim our attention.

All laws granting to railroads or other corporations organized for pecuniary profit, special and exclusive privileges, which encroach upon the rights of the public, should be repealed. The most prominent argument againt repeal exists in the doctrine that railroads are public highways, and that a charter granted to a railroad corporation by the legislature is in the nature of a contract, and is therefore irrepealable. By the constant and persistent assertion of these propositions, and by frequent adjudication of the questions, candor compels us to admit that the current of judicial decisions supports this doctrine. Yet as the ancient dogma of tyrants, "The king can do no wrong," does not obtain in this country, we beg leave to call in question the soundness of this doctrine. If railroads are public highways, there can be no question as to the right of legislatures to exercise the same control over them that they assert in regard to common public roads. If they are public, private parties cannot have the exclusive control of them;

nor can the legislature grant away the rights of the public by exclusive charters to private parties, for the reason that the legislature (the department of government which enacts all statutes) cannot, by the enactment of a statute, take from the whole people one of the rights belonging to them and confer it upon a private corporation. The legislature has no power to enact a statute declaring a foundry, or a mill, built by an individual or a company with private capital (the absolute title vesting in such party) to be a public foundry or mill. If such a statute were enacted, it would not change the title to the property, nor would it prevent the owner from using and enjoying it as his own, exclusively. Whether it be called public or private would not change the nature of the ownership or convert the interest into public property. No matter by what name it might be called, it is still private property. The same is true of railroads. They are built and owned by private corporations; they are under the control of their owners, who retain for their own use the earnings of their roads. If these roads are public highways, then the legislature, acting for the public good, occupies the anomalous position of granting charters to private parties to construct public highways, and to own them after their construction. The supreme court of the United States, and the courts of some of the states, have decided that they are public highways, and, according to the usual custom, these decisions are to be received as final.

The courts having declared them public corporations does not change the facts in the case. The facts still remain. The roads are owned and controlled by private corporations. The title cannot be taken from them arbitrarily. The companies receive the earnings of the roads, and every fact contradicts the decision of the courts. If the courts were to decide that a crow was white and *not* black, we would acknowledge the binding force of the decision, and admit, that by virtue of the decision, the crow *is* white. But when we look at the *fact*, we would still insist that, notwithstanding the decisions of the courts, the crow is as black as it was before the decision was made. If the courts were to decide that common highways were railroads, as a matter of law we would accept the decision as final; but as a matter of fact we would know that they were common highways. Railroads, owned and controlled by private parties, are not public highways. If railroads are public highways, then the other position, that the charters granted to railroad companies are irrepealable, is not tenable—for the reason that the legislature possesses full power to alter, amend, or repeal all laws enacted for the benefit of the public. Public highways are public property as much as public buildings, court houses, school houses, asylums, and other institutions created for the use and benefit of the public. The legislature does not possess the power to vest in a company the exclusive right to build and own any of these public buildings. If a charter were granted for any such purpose, it could not be claimed that it was in the nature of a contract between the state and the company, absolutely binding upon all future legislation; that the company had acquired, by virtue of its charter, rights that neither courts nor future legislatures could disturb. Or suppose that a private company should obtain a charter for constructing and owning all the highways within a certain township or county, would it be contended that future legislatures could not alter or repeal the charter? If railroads are public highways, the companies constructing them must be subject to the same laws and decisions that apply to all other matters of like public character. Their charters are at all times under the control of the legislative authority, and subject to be altered, amended, or repealed. Being the component part of the government, of a public nature, the doctrine that private parties can acquire rights in the nature of a contract that cannot be disturbed without their consent is not tenable. Whether railroads are to be considered as private property, or as public highways, they are subject to the control of the legislature—because, under the constitution, the power to create corporations by charter, with absolute powers, does not exist. If the converse of this is true, then legislatures could, by conferring special privileges upon individuals and corporations, deprive the public of all attributes of sovereignty, and place the entire government in the hands of individuals and companies. The constitution has conferred no such power upon any department of the government. If such power is conferred, the constitution, instead of being the paramount law as intended—establishing the rights of the people, controlling legislative enactments, defining the powers of the different departments of the government, and guaranteeing protection from unjust and oppressive laws, and decisions of courts—is intead but an instrument to be used for the enslavement of the people. The power to grant to private parties a monopoly of any of the rights belonging to the whole people, or to confer upon these private parties such exclusive privileges as will infringe upon or take from the public, the rights that naturally attach or belong to the whole people, was never conferred upon the legislature of the state or nation. If legislatures have entered into contracts with corporations, under which the rights belonging to the people are transferred to such corporations, they have exceeded the power vested in them, and the charters granted, so far as they infringe upon the rights of the public, are null and void. The plea that a repeal or amendment of such charters would destroy vested rights, has no force, because the power to make such grants or contracts is wanting. Nor does the plea that innocent third parties would suffer, add any strength to the position. The corporations are the parties with whom these innocent parties contract, and to whom they must look for the fulfillment of their contracts. All acts of legislatures, granting to railroads or other corporations, rights belonging to the whole people, are subject to the control of future legislatures, and are repealable. The only purpose for which a railroad charter should be granted is to subserve the public interest. For this purpose the legislatures possess the power to confer upon corporations such rights and privileges as are necessary to enable them to have continued being, and to transact business, but reserving at all times the right to control them and reform abuses. Good faith on the part of railroad companies requires of them fair and honest dealing with the people. Adopting the idea that the public was to receive great benefit from the construction of railroads, large grants of land, subsidy bonds, local municipal subscriptions, donations of money, and direct taxation in different localities, have been afforded the different companies for the purpose of aiding in the construction of their roads. The benefit the public was to receive, and which the companies agreed to afford, was the only consideration expected by the people. This consideration the public has never received. We have shown the course pursued by railroad companies in constructing their roads — watering their stock and selling their bonds, and the oppressions practiced by them to force from the people the means for declaring dividends on fictitious stock, and to pay the interest on the immense amounts of bonds issued and sold to the different corporations. Assuming that their charters are contracts between themselves and the states, they defy all efforts made by the people to arrest their extortions. Our government being instituted for the protection and benefit of the whole people, they possess the power, and it is their right, to amend or appeal all laws that deny or abridge their own rights. Railroad companies should be compelled to reduce their stock to the actual cost of constructing their roads, and the rates of charges for the transportation of freights and passengers should be fixed by statute at such rates as would afford a fair dividend upon the capital actually invested. The public should not be compelled to pay interest or dividends on stock or bonds issued in excess of the actual cost of the roads. The property of railroad companies should be taxed by the same rules, and at the same rate, as the property of individuals. A general supervision of all railroad corporations throughout the country should be exercised by the respective state authorities. It may be said: "All this is proper, but how will you accomplish it? All efforts heretofore made in that direction have been defeated in the different legislative bodies, or by the decisions of the courts." We are compelled to admit that if future attempts at reform are to be measured by past efforts, the prospect is not flattering. When relief bills have been introduced into legislative bodies they have generally failed. Railroad men have been able to defeat almost every attempt at reform. The idea seems to have obtained in all legislative bodies that the men who built railroads were self-denying; that they were philanthropists ; that for the purpose of developing the country, of affording speedy and cheap transportation to the eastern markets of the products of the west, they were sacrificing their personal comfort and wealth, and that the least the people could do was to extend to them a helping hand — to grant them local aid, to exempt them from taxes, to assist them in procuring the right of way, and, instead of enacting laws to protect the people from the abuses of railroad corporations, statutes should be enacted to prevent any interference with the corporations, and allowing them extraordinary privileges. Men who were elected to the legislature under pledges to favor the passage of statutes for the protection of the people against the encroachments of corporations were found enlisted in their favor, and these monopolies, instead of being restricted in their powers, have continually received additional favors and privileges.

When the people have appealed to the courts for redress, they have met with defeat. Lengthy decisions have been written and published, setting forth the great benefit of railroads, instructing the people that railroad charters are contracts, and that unless courts decide in favor of railroad companies, "innocent third parties," who have purchased railroad bonds, will sustain loss. Thus, through the legislative and judicial departments of the government the people are reduced to a state of vassalage, with railroad corporations as their masters and rulers.

Notwithstanding this gloomy outlook, the people still retain sufficient power to correct the evil and to recover their constitutional rights. The country is now divided into two parties. One party is composed of the people, strong in nothing but numbers and the determination to battle for their rights; the other side is composed of corporations, stock-jobbers, brokers and capitalists, whose strength consists in the organization and consolidation of their interests, their control of the finances of the country, and of the different departments of the government. The lines dividing these parties are clearly and distinctly marked. Their interests are conflicting. The people now demand such legal enactments as will restrict extortionate charges by railroad companies, and compel them to pay their just share of taxes for the support of the government. Legislators being elected for short terms, being frequently called upon to render an account of their official acts to their constituents, if the people are united and persistent, it will not be difficult to procure the passage of such statutes as will compel railroad companies to deal fairly and honestly with the public. To effect reform and obtain redress, the aid of another department of the government must be obtained, to wit: the courts of the country.

THIRD.—*The People have a Precedent for a Pledged Judiciary.*—In treating of the courts and their decisions we are venturing upon grounds that will subject us to criticism. The decision of a court of last resort upon controverted questions is generally received as final. In questions of constitutional law, or when the rights of the public or of private parties are involved, the final decisions of our highest tribunal are accepted by general consent as the supreme law of the land.

We look upon the judges of courts as men possessing superior legal sagacity, and upon their decisions as embodying the highest wisdom. The congress of the nation, or the legislatures of states—composed in part, at least, of men of extensive legal knowledge, who have made the science of government a life-long study, who have carefully and critically examined the provisions of the constitution, who have full knowledge of the mischief to be remedied or the rights to be enforced—carefully digest, prepare, and after full discussion in their respective bodies enact a law which they believe will accomplish the intended purpose, and at the same time contravene no provision of the constitution. An attempt is made to enforce the law, and a question arises as to its constitutionality, or its meaning and effects. The court is appealed to. On this bench are sitting three, five, seven or more judges. After argument this court, by a majority of one, decides the law unconstitutional, giving to it an interpretation which defeats the object for which it was enacted. The minority of the court dissent from the opinion of the majority, and set forth at length the reasons for such dissent. The fact that five judges concur in the majority opinion and four dissent makes the decision of one man the supreme law of the land. It annuls acts of congress and state legislatures, and makes the opinions and decisions of four members of the court concurring with a majority of congress of no avail. One man's opinion is the law for the whole people. This we have shown in the action of the supreme court in the legal tender cases. Now it is not considered out of place to criticise the acts of congress or of legislatures, or the motives and influences that govern and control those bodies in the enactment of laws; yet it is looked upon as almost treasonable to refuse to accept the decisions of courts as good law, or to discuss the motives and influences leading to these decisions. In 1869 the supreme court of the United States, by a majority of one judge, decided that treasury notes were not legal tender for pre-existing debts. In 1871 the same court, by a majority of one, decided they were a legal tender for all debts, public or private, save when there were special exceptions. So in other questions in the United States courts, and in the courts of the states, it has sometimes happened that the law of the land has been changed by the change of one or two judges. In Iowa this is demonstrated in the decisions of the supreme court upon the questions whether the legislature could authorize the levy and collection of a special tax to aid in the construction of railroads. We refer to these matters to show that judges are not infallible, and that sitting as courts, they are apt to differ as to the law and facts of the case. Instances are not wanting when judges have been appointed and elected because of their views upon certain questions, and when with the changes of the *personnel* of the court, its final decisions have been reversed, thus making the supreme law of the land depend upon the election or appointment of one man to the bench. The argument to be drawn from this is, that no such sanctity surrounds the court or judges as forbids a scrutiny of their decisions or the motives prompting them. But it is said, if you discuss the motives underlying judicial decisions, you will debase the judiciary of the country; that candidates for the bench, like those for legislative or executive offices, will be selected because of their views respecting certain interests and questions that may come before them for judicial determination, and, like legislators they will be appointed or elected because these views harmonize with those of certain classes or interests. The answer to this is, that as a general rule judges are now appointed or elected because of their political views. In almost every instance the man who is elected or appointed accords in his political views with the majority, and indeed, men have been nominated and elected, or appointed, as judges of courts because of their publicly expressed opinions on some particular subject. The decisions of courts upon constitutional and other questions change frequently. The most important interests and rights of the people under the constitution and laws of the country have been differently decided by the same court of last resort in both national and state tribunals. The constitution has been declared to mean one thing at one time, and a directly opposite meaning has been given to the same clause at another term of the same court, with but a few months intervening. An elasticity has been given this instrument neither contemplated by its framers, nor calculated to increase respect for it, or for the judiciary of the country. While we would not advocate the policy of candidates for judicial offices pledging themselves upon any questions that may come before them for a decision, we claim that the people should exact from every candidate a pledge to "support, protect, and defend the constitution," to abstain from the dangerous practice which now obtains of construing the fundamental law of the land in favor of particular interests, and to abstain from judicial legislation. More danger to the liberties of the people is to be apprehended from the courts, than from any other source. The constitution is inelastic, unchangeable, save by amendment in the manner provided. No court should disregard it, nor warp its meaning. If the rules of construction practiced of late are to be continued, its sanctity is destroyed, and its provisions are no more binding than those of a statute. It is the duty of the courts to interpret the constitution, but not to supply its (to them) seeming defects, or to override its plain provisions. We all feel a deep interest in the election of legislators, for the reason that all are to be affected by the laws enacted, but we seem not to realize to its full importance the fact that all laws passed by congress or a state legislature are liable to be declared null and void by the courts; that the interpretation and construction of statutes belong exclusively to the courts; that the men elected to judicial positions, under the constitution, are clothed with a power superior to that of the legislative and executive departments of the government; that by a single decision the supreme court of the state, or of the nation, can suspend or annul a statute which has been in force for years, or that an interpretation of the constitution, long acquiesced in, can be reversed and a new meaning given to it. Yet these are facts, and from these decisions there is no appeal. The courts may change their opinions upon constitutional questions at every term, and the nation must receive their decisions as the supreme law.

We have said that the constitution is inelastic. It must remain so for the protection of the rights of the people. If courts can change its meaning as occasion requires, the will of the court and not the constitution, is the supreme law of the land. The decisions of courts, in the recent conflicts between railroad corporations and the people, and upon the legal tender question, demonstrate that the will of the court is already the supreme law of the land. One of the questions in the determination of which the courts have substituted their will for constitutional law, relates to the authority of state governments to aid in the construction of railroads. The constitution of Iowa prohibits the state from participating in or becoming a stockholder in any private corporation or any corporation created for profit. Counties are, necessarily, a part of the government; their creation and organization are a necessity in the administration of the state government. While the state is prohibited from aiding in the construction of railroads, the courts have said that the constitution does not prohibit counties from subscribing stock to railroad corporations and creating onerous debts in payment therefor. In other words, while the constitution forbids any participation on the part of the state, as a state, in the construction of railroads, it is no violation of the fundamental law for the inferior branches of the state government to become stockholders in the same corporations. Though the whole state is forbidden to aid in the construction of railroads, by dividing the state into counties, it is no violation of the fundamental law for these counties to aid in their construction. No one doubts that it was the intention of the framers of the constitution to protect the people against the evils of oppressive burdens always resulting from a participation of the public authorities in the construction of railroads. The question of the authority of counties to subscribe stock to railroads, in Iowa, has often been before the courts. The decisions have been numerous, but not unanimous or uniform. At no time has the supreme court of the state by unanimous decision held that the power existed; but on several occasions the court has united in deciding that the power did not exist, the constitutionality of such right depending entirely upon who were elected judges. Thus the fundamental law, which can only be changed by amendment in the manner provided, has been held to permit or forbid public aid in building railroads, as suited the peculiar views of the men who had been elected judges. What was constitutional one day was unconstitutional the next. The decision of the men who happened to occupy seats upon the supreme bench, has been the supreme law, and not the constitution. On the question of voting local aid to railroads the supreme court decided that the act of the legislature authorizing such aid was unconstitutional. In one year from that time the same supreme court, three judges concurring, decided that the law was constitutional, the reason of this variance being that in the interim two judges had retired from the bench and two new ones elected in their place. Here, again, the will of the men who happened to be elected changed the meaning of the constitution. The same curious history has been enacted in many other states. When men who are interested in railroads, or who desire that the public should aid in their construction, occupy seats on the bench of the supreme court, the constitution is construed to allow such aid, and where the judges are opposed to the allowance of such aid, they decide the constitution does not authorize, but forbids it. In each case the fundamental law is interpreted to suit the peculiar views of the judges who occupy the bench, until it has ceased to have any binding effect. With this state of facts, known to all men, it is not strange that the people now demand pledges from men who aspire to judicial station. When state constitutions are made to mean anything or nothing, as suits the men whose duty it is to interpet them, and when laws are pronounced constitutional or unconstitutional, as caprice or the interests of corporations may prompt, "nature's first law, self-preservation," demands that those who aspire to become judges of courts should be controlled by the constitution rather than by their personal views as to what it should be; and that they should be fully committed and pledged to abstain from judicial constructions of the constitution which abridge the rights of the people and increase the power of corporations. While the decisions of the state courts have tended to abridge the rights of the people and increase the already too great power of corporations; while they have, in fact, decided that, under the constitution, a citizen can be compelled to bestow a part of what he possesses upon railroad corporations without an equivalent, the greatest danger to the liberties of the people and the perpetuity of republican government is to be apprehended from the supreme court of the United States. It possesses, under the constitution, unlimited jurisdiction upon all matters arising under the constitution and laws of the United States, but not the same general jurisdiction that appertains to state tribunals. Yet, as under the constitution it is a court of last resort, and its members hold their offices for life, it is independent of the people. Not only so, but it cannot be called to an account by any department of the government, state or national. It possesses powers superior to all other departments of the government; it rises above all law, and becomes a law in itself. Its decisions being final, the whole people must accept them as the supreme law of the land. No matter how oppressive, or unjust, or absurd, the whole government and people must accept these decisions as the highest law and authority in the land. These facts, taken

18

into consideration with some of its recent decisions in favor of railroad corporations and other monopolies, raise the question whether we are governed by constitutional law or by the edicts of the supreme court, promulgated in the guise of judicial decisions.

Let us look at a few of these decisions, now in full force as the law of the land. In the construction of railroads, counties, cities, and towns have assisted by subscribing stock and levying taxes to pay such subscription. State courts have decided that under the constitution and laws of the states such subscription was unconstitutional, illegal, and void. The power to afford such aid to railroad companies was derived from state statutes, passed by virtue of the power presumed to be conferred by the constitution. Following precedents which had been established and recognized from the organization of our government, the decisions of the state courts should have been final and binding upon the courts of the nation. Yet the supreme court of the United States, by a bare majority of one, in violation of all precedent, assumed power not conferred upon it by the constitution of the United States, annulled state constitutions, disregarded state laws, and reversed and refused to be bound by the decisions of state courts. The will of one man, who happened to occupy a seat upon the supreme bench, is made the supreme law of the land, not by virtue of any provision of the constitution, but by trampling upon the rights of states and the people. When it is remembered that these decisions were made in favor of corporations, and that their effect was to compel the people to contribute a part of their substance to help build up and strengthen monopolies, which have proved to be oppressive task-masters, we are justified in saying that the fundamental law of the land has been misinterpreted and the rights of the people sacrificed. We assert that no provision of the constitution can be shown that even indirectly authorizes taxation to aid in the construction of railroads owned by private corporations. The idea is at war with every principle of right and justice. When the supreme court of the nation assumed to decide in favor of such authority, it occupied the position and assumed the prerogative of an absolute monarch. The supreme court of the United States was as much bound by the decision of the state courts upon questions arising under state constitutions and laws as were the courts of the states by the decisions of the federal courts upon questions arising under the constitution and statutes of the United States. The adoption of a different rule will subvert the principles of our government, and, as a necessary result, the will of the supreme court will become the supreme law of the land.

We might give other instances wherein the federal courts have overridden state tribunals without warrant of law and in disregard of state rights; but we pass to another question which is now engrossing public attention, and upon which the supreme court has recently made a decision. The question whether railroad corporations are public or private has been before the supreme court. The court has passed upon it, and decided that railroads are public highways; but it has not yet decided that railroad corporations are public. No question connected with railroads is of more importance to the people. If they are public highways, then the legislatures of the states have full control of them, and the roads are as much a part of the public or common property of all the people, to be used as occasion requires, as are common highways. Then the right to levy and collect taxes to aid in their construction, or to wholly construct them, cannot be questioned. The supreme court of the United States, in a very recent case appealed from the state of Wisconsin, has decided that for the purposes of taxation, railroads are public highways. The opinion was delivered by Justice Strong, and is ingenious as well as unique. We desire to call the reader's attention to some portions of it, for the purpose of showing how the rights of the people are protected by the judiciary of the United States. The opinion pronounced by Justice Strong fully illustrates the fact that association and education will influence the decisions of judges as well as those of other men; and while we impute no improper motives to the judiciary of the nation, we say that this decision disposes of some of the rights of the people, supposed to be fully protected by the fundamental law, with as little hesitation as would be manifested by an inferior court in a case involving only the plainest legal points. The court says:

"The legislature cannot create a public debt, or levy a tax, or authorize a municipal corporation to do so, in order to raise funds for a mere private purpose. It cannot, in the form of a tax, take the money of a citizen and give it to an individual, the public interest or welfare being in no way connected with the transaction. The objects for which money is raised by taxation must be public, and such as subserve the common interest and well-being of the community required to contribute."

That this is good law, all will admit; but what shall we say of the following, copied from the same opinion:

"To justify the court in arresting the proceedings and declaring the tax void, the absence of all *possible public interest* in the purpose for which the funds are raised must be clear and palpable—so clear and palpable as to be perceptible by every mind at the first blush."

It is decided by the supreme court of the United States that if there is any "possible public interest" in the purposes for which a tax is levied, then such levy of tax is constitutional, and this decision is to be received as the supreme law of the land. Is this good law? The public has an interest in toll-bridges, plank roads, ferries, manufacturing companies, and many other enterprises prosecuted and controlled by private corporations and individuals—are these all so connected with the administration of the government as to be proper objects of compulsory contributions for their support? The man who crosses the bridge pays toll; the party driving over the plank road does the same; the ferryman exacts fare—and all receive it, not for the benefit of the public, but for their own private uses. Yet the public have an interest in them. Are they public corporations? Suppose the legislature of the state should, by statute, declare them public corporations, under what provision of the constitution is found the power to tax the people for their construction while they are owned and controlled by private parties? Stage coaches and steamboats are owned by private parties; they are common carriers, sub ject to be regulated and controlled by law; the public have an interest in them; the legislature can prescribe rules and regulations to be observed by them in the prosecution of their business as common carriers. Can the people be compelled to pay taxes for their support? No distinction exists between common carriers by water or by land over ordinary highways and railroad companies as to their rights and duties when the public are concerned, except that railroads cannot be built until the companies building them have procured the right of way. Private companies own the roads; they sell and mortgage them; they receive all the profits, and control them in their own interest. If a tax can be levied to aid in building railroads owned by private parties, then taxes can be levied in amount sufficient to build the entire road. If the decision is sound, its results will prove most disastrous.

The people will be compelled to build the roads for private corporations, and, after they are built, pay toll or fare for the privilege of using them. The people pay for the roads, yet they do not own them, and have no interest in them, or right to use them, except upon payment of such sums as the private corporations owning them may choose to demand. We insist that no such power is vested in the legislatures or in congress. If the power does exist—if the people can be compelled to build railroads for private corporations — in the language of a distinguished judge of the state of New York, "It is legal robbery, less respectable than highway robbery, in this: that the perpetrator of the latter assumes the danger and infamy of the act, while this act has the shield of legislative responsibility." The effect of this decision is to make railroad companies a component part of the government, to draw more clearly the line between the people and the combination of monopolies that now control the country. When the court of last resort in the nation comes boldly to the front, and, by an edict (for it cannot be treated as a judicial decision), declares that unless there is an "absence of all possible public interest, so clear and palpable as to be perceptible by every mind at first blush," the power to levy and collect taxes in aid of railroads owned and controlled by private corporations exists, the people have reason to fear that the interests of railroads and not the constitution of the country is the paramount law. But says the court, "That railways, though constructed by private corporations, and owned by them, are public highways has been the doctrine of nearly all the courts ever since such conveniences for passage and transportation have had an existence. Very early the question arose whether a state's right of eminent domain could be exercised by a private corporation created for the purpose of constructing a railway. Clearly it could not, unless taking land for such a purpose was taking land for public use. The right of eminent domain nowhere justifies the taking of property for private use. Yet it is a doctrine universally accepted that a state legislature may authorize a private corporation to take land for the construction of such road, making compensation to the owner. What else does the doctrine mean if not that building a railway, though it be built by a private corporation, is an act done for a public use. And the reason why the use has always been held a public one is that such a road is a public highway, whether made by the government itself, or by the agency of corporate bodies, or even by individuals, when they obtain their power to construct it from legislative grant." If the court had been employed as the attorneys of the parties seeking to collect the tax, no more ingenious or partisan argument could have been for the claimants than is presented in this opinion. As a finishing argument in favor of the taxing power, the court says: "Whether the use of a railway is a public or a private one depends in no measure upon the question who constructed it or who owns it." The court decides that railroads are used for public purposes; that the right of eminent domain attaches to them; that, being used for public purposes, and having the right of eminent domain, they are public highways; and, being public highways, taxes may be levied upon the people to private parties in constructing them. We have quoted enough of this decision to give the reader an idea of the train of reasoning resorted to by the court to support the theory that railroads owned and controlled absolutely by private parties are public highways, and that the people may be taxed to build and maintain them.

If the supreme court of the United States possessed the power under the constitution to pass upon the constitutionality of the law of the state of Wisconsin, we would be compelled to accept this decision as the law of the case; to acknowledge that as a question of law private railroads were public highways; yet, as a matter of fact, we would still have to insist that they remained private roads, over which the public could ride or ship freight, upon making compensation to the owners, just as they could ride or ship freight upon a steamboat or common road wagon upon paying the required amount to the owner or master. While legislatures grant to railroad companies the right to appropriate the lands of others in procuring the right of way, upon making compensation therefor, no part of the price for this right of way is paid by the government, or the public. It is paid by the companies building the roads. We are not prepared to admit that the grant of this privilege to railroad companies makes them a part of the government, or that it clothes them with any of the attributes of sovereignty. Taxes can only be levied for public purposes, for the support of the government, and for the benefit of the public. The compulsory payment of taxes to private corporations cannot be supported upon any other basis than of our government being a despotism, and not a constitutional republic. We have before referred to the action and decisions of the supreme court on questions arising between the people and corporations, and only refer to it here for the purpose of showing the necessity of reform. The action of the courts shows that, whatever may have been their intention, they have departed from old constructions of the constitution; that judicial legislation has superseded constitutional restrictions and limitations, and that the personal views of the judges constituting a majority of the court have become the supreme law of the land.

Another noticeable fact is that the recently appointed judges are the most prominent in this new departure. We make the assertion that the supreme court of the United States does not possess the power under the constitution to overrule or disregard the decision of a state court upon questions arising under state laws and constitutions. No paragraph, line, or syllable of the constitution of the United States confers this power upon the supreme court, save when the state law or constitution contravenes some provision of the constitution of the United States, or some statute passed in aid of constitutional provisions. If the reader will examine the decisions from which we have been quoting he will find that the rights of the states and of the people, expressly guaranteed by the constitution, have been, by a bold and unwarranted assumption by the United States supreme court, obliterated. The decision of the supreme court of a state, whose decision was final and binding upon the supreme court of the United States, has been overruled and declared null and void—not by virtue of any constitutional right vested in the United States court, but by an assumption of power making the will of that court the supreme law, and placing corporations beyond the control of the states granting them their charters. The fact that the reason upon which the decision is based appears in the nature of an apology for the decision, while constitutional rights are lost sight of, proves the truth of our assertion, that judges of courts are subject to influences that control other men, and that the interest of monopolies, and not the constitutional rights of the people, has a controlling influence in the highest court in the nation. It also demonstrates the fact, that no thorough reform can be effected until the constitution of our common country shall control the decisions of the courts.

In proof of the facts that the decisions of the supreme court of the United States are not always controlled by the constitution, let us again refer to the legal tender decisions. Here again the opinion of a bare majority of the court (five of the judges concurring and four dissenting) establishes the law for forty millions of people, and does violence to both the letter and spirit of the constitution. Under the constitution the power to coin money and regulate its value is vested in congress. The states are prohibited from coining money, and from making anything but gold and silver coin a legal tender in payment of debts. The letter of the constitution does not deny to congress the power to issue paper money and make it a legal tender; but when we take into consideration that the power is denied to the states, the conclusion is irresistible that the power was intended to be denied to the general as well as to the state governments. While as a war measure the power might be exercised, it certainly could not be in time of peace. Being one of the extraordinary powers vested in congress in time of war, rising above the constitutional restriction, if we may use the expression, governed by the law of necessity, the power should not be enlarged by judicial interpretation, nor should the plain letter of the acts of congress passed as war measures be made to extend beyond its express provisions. When the highest court in the nation decided that the legal tender act was retroactive in its operations, that court decided, in effect, that under the constitution congress possessed the power to annul contracts made between private citizens, that one might legally take from another a part of his property without compensation. While that court has uniformly decided that bonds obtained from counties, cities and towns, fraudulently and without consideration, must be paid, it decides that a retroactive statute may be passed which takes a man's property without consideration; and that congress, without any such power being conferred by the constitution, can substitute a new standard of values. Not only that congress can do this, but that the legal tender act extended beyond its plain reading, and made paper money, a thing that is of no intrinsic value, a legal tender for debts generally; that this paper was the standard of values, and that coin, gold and silver, were but articles of commerce, the value of which was fixed by this new paper standard. If one not learned in the law had been called upon to interpret the constitution, he would have arrived at a different conclusion. If ten years ago one learned in the law had been called upon to interpret the meaning of the constitutional provision above referred to, he would, without hesitation, have decided that such an act was unconstitutional. If the eminent jurists who graced the supreme bench at any time since the organization of our government had been required to decide as to the validity of the statute, or to construe its terms, or declare its meaning, a realizing sense of the obligation resting upon them, and of the danger of violating the provisions of the constitution, would have deterred them from making such a decision. When, in the winter of 1869, the question was before the court, upon careful examination, Chief Justice Chase, who was the author of the statute under which the question arose, and four other judges, decided that it only applied to contracts made after its passage, and then only as a war measure. The supreme court of the United States declared that the legal tender act had no retroactive operation, and that, under the constitution, it could not be extended beyond its terms; that to extend it further would be a violation of the fundamental laws. Here the matter should have ended. This decision was, and should have remained, final. But it did not meet the approval of corporation rings and Wall street gamblers. They demanded a different decision, and their demand was gratified. To obtain a reversal without a reconstruction of the court was not expected. It was suddenly discovered that there was a necessity for an additional judge. The reason given was, that an even number of judges might divide, and no decision could be rendered; hence the necessity for one more. It was known to them that one judge was about to resign, and that one had concurred in the decision which they desired reversed. Two judges were to be appointed. If both were in favor of reversal, then five of the nine would favor a reversal. (We have referred to this matter before, and do it now for a purpose that will soon appear.) Two railroad attorneys, Strong and Bradley, were recommended and appointed before the close of the term of the court at which the legal tender decision had been rendered. Notice was at once given that the legal tender case would again be presented to the court for a decision. It was announced, both before and after the appointment of Messrs. Strong and Bradley, that they were committed to a reversal of the legal tender decision. Soon after these *fresh-caught railroad attorneys* had taken their seats upon the supreme bench, we find them redeeming the pledges the friends of a reversal claimed had been made, and writing long arguments in favor of a reversal of the opinion of Chief Justice Chase and the four other eminent judges, in which argument they seem to disregard constitutional restrictions, and to apologize for the opinions they pronounced, declaring that treasury notes are a legal tender for all debts, save those that are excepted in favor of the government. Thus, by the appointment of two judges, understood to be pledged to the railroad interests, the supreme law of the United States makes paper "promises to pay" a legal tender when contracts call for money, fixes this kind of paper as the standard of values, and makes gold and silver coin articles of commerce, while at the same time the constitution makes coin a legal tender and the standard of values, and prohibits the states from making anything but coin a legal tender. To serve a particular *interest* and benefit railroad corporations, the personal views of these two judges, approved by three others, became the supreme law of the land, in disregard of the plain letter of the constitution, as well as the decisions of the same court upon the same statutes made but a few months before.

We have been thus particular in referring to this decision, and the means used to procure it, for the purpose of showing that the idea of exacting pledges of men who are candidates for judicial position is not new, and that those who apparently look with alarm at what they are pleased to term an innovation upon long-established precedents, as well as an attempt to destroy the independence of the courts of the country, have themselves been successfully practicing the same thing, and securing the election and appointment of judges whose views accorded with their own.

FOURTH.—*Judicial and Partisan Legislation Reviewed, and a Remedy Suggested.*—The consequence of special legislation in favor of railroad corporations, the granting of subsidies of land and bonds, is not what is claimed by the advocates of such legislation. It has placed the whole producing interests of the country at the mercy of soulless corporations. It has given railroad corporations title to, and absolute control of, enough of the public land to make an empire of vast extent. Lands that of right belong to the people are owned by these corporations, and instead of the nominal price fixed by the government upon them, our pioneers, who settle and develop the country, must pay whatever sum is demanded by these corporations, or content themselves with such lands as they can find in less desirable localities.

It has given to railroad corporations the absolute control of the coal lands of the country, so that in the future, as well as at the present time, at all points where there is a scarcity of timber, the people are compelled to pay such prices as are, and in the future will be, demanded of them or perish with cold.

It has established an unequal and unjust system of taxation, by means of which corporations are relieved from the payment of their just proportion of the public taxes. It sanctions and supports base frauds upon the public, in permitting corporations to add to their capital stock at pleasure, making the apparent cost of these roads much greater than they really are, and permitting them to extort from the people for transportation of freights sufficient amounts to pay the interest and dividends on this "watered stock." It has taken from the people the rights guaranteed to them by the constitution, and transferred their rights to railroad companies. These are a part of the evil consequences of partial and special legislation in favor of corporations; and they could be speedily remedied, but for the decisions of the courts.

These decisions we have noticed, and have shown that whatever may have been the intention of the courts rendering them, their tendency has been to strengthen and uphold the mighty power asserted by corporations. Where conflicts have arisen between counties and municipalities on the one side, and these corporations on the other, the courts have treated these railroad companies as private corporations, and have decided in their favor. When the majority of a legislature, believing that corporations were subject to legislative control, have attempted to restrict their powers and correct their abuses, the courts have said their charters were in the nature of contracts, which the legislature could not alter or amend, and the people have been compelled to submit. When the question of the right to levy taxes for the purpose of building railroads is to be decided, another phase of the question is presented. All the courts agree that taxes cannot be levied for a private purpose. The difficulty is met and overcome in this way.

First.—It is announced that railroad corporations have the right of eminent domain, that this right is an attribute of sovereignty; and for this reason they must be considered public corporations. We have referred to this already, but refer to it again for the purpose of showing that the argument is not sound. The right of public domain is possessed by the supreme power of the nation. It belongs to all governments. Of right it is not inherent in, nor can it be acquired by, any private person or corporation. If the right is ever exercised by any corporation, company, or individval, it must be by the permission of the governing power; in this country by legislative grant. If it belonged to corporations they could exercise it without any consent of the legislature. They could themselves decide how, when, and where they would exercise it. They could prescribe the mode of condemning the property of others to their own use, and no power in government could question their acts. It will not be contended that without special legislative enactment, railroad companies could appropriate the property of others for the purpose of building their roads upon it. All will agree that before they can do this, the legislature must confer the right upon them. Does the act of granting to corporations the right to build their roads through the property of others confer upon them any of the attributes of sovereignty? If so, the legislature possesses the power of granting its attributes to corporations or to any private person. It would be immaterial whether a single person, a company, or a corporation, desired to build a railroad. To make such person, company, or corporation a part of the government, the legislature need but delegate to the party desiring to build a railroad the right of eminent domain; and from that moment the individual or corporation becomes a part of the government. A moment's reflection will convince the reader that the position is untenable. If one of the attributes of sovereignty can be *farmed out* to railroad corporations, another can be to some other interest, and in process of time the government itself would become a mere skeleton, having delegated all its powers to private parties, remaining only a government in name. From time immemorial, the legislature has granted to various parties the same kinds of privileges that are granted to railroad companies; yet it never was, and is not now claimed, that because of such grants, the parties obtaining them become public corporations, or that they were clothed with any of the attributes of sovereignty. Ferry companies, plank-road companies, and turnpike road companies, have been chartered with power to take the property of others, and place their ferries, buildings, and roads upon the property so taken, upon payment of the appraised value. In many of the states laws have been enacted under which private parties have been granted the same privilege. Persons building mills are permitted to construct dams across streams and appropriate such portions of the overflowed lands of adjoining owners to their own use, upon payment of its value as found by appraisers. A and B, and their associates, desire to build a mill; in the construction of their dam they cause the backwater to flood the land of C. Under the provisions of the statute a jury is called, who assess the value of the land of C so overflowed and appropriated by A and B. The mill is built for the accommodation of the public. All who desire to do so can take their grain to this mill and have it ground upon payment of the required toll. The owners have, under the statute, the same right of eminent domain that is conferred upon railroad companies; and their mill is used expressly for grinding for all who patronize it and pay the required toll. The owners of the railroad, and the owners of the mill alike, serve the public. Both do it for pecuniary consideration. Both have the same right of appropriating the property of others. Yet the railroad, under the decision of the courts, is a public corporation' while the mill is a private one. The railroad corporation is clothed with one of the attributes of sovereignty, while the owners of the mill retain their character as a private corporation. No good reason appears for this distinction. While we admit that the supreme court of the United States has decided that because of the fact of legislatures having granted to railroad companies the right to appropriate the lands of other persons to be used as road-beds, they become public corporations, and that until reversed we must accept it as the law, we contend that as long as the railroads are owned and controlled by private parties, and their earnings are appropriated and used exclusively for private purposes, the facts are in direct conflict with the law as declared by the supreme court, and that either the facts or the law must be changed before they harmonize.

Second.—It has also been decided by the courts that railroads are public highways (an absurdity on its face, that under the law railroads are public highways, while they are owned and controlled by private companies, who become public corporations because of one of the attributes of sovereignty having been conferred upon them), and that, because they are public highways, taxes can be levied upon the people for building and repairing them. The fact being admitted that private parties own and control railroads; that the government receives no part of their earnings, and that neither the government nor private persons can ride upon them without paying for the privilege, or procuring a pass, and that no freights can be shipped over them without payment of the amounts demanded, seems to conflict with the decisions of the courts. Under the decisions of the supreme court, the property of the citizen is taken from him without compensation, and bestowed upon a private corporation and, the plain provision of the constitution has received a new interpretation which compels the property owners to bestow a part of it on corporations without any consideration whatever. The situation is about as follows: When a conflict arises between the people and railroad corporations, or when the legislature attempts to reform abuses practiced by them, the courts hold that railroad charters are in the nature of contracts, and that the legislature can neither alter, amend, or repeal them. The companies are then treated as private corporations. In proof of this look at the following decision, of recent date :

"SUPREME COURT OF THE UNITED STATES.

"*The Wilmington & Weldon Railroad Company, Plaintiff in error vs. John A. Reid, Sheriff, etc. In error to the Supreme Court of the State of North Carolina.*

"Mr. Justice Davis delivered the opinion of the court:

"This is a writ of error to the supreme court of the state of North Carolina, and brings up the question whether the recent legislation of the state, concerning the collection of taxes, is, as it affects the plaintiff in error, in violation of that provision of the constitution of the United States which declares that no state shall pass any law impairing the obligation of contracts. As early as 1833, the general assembly of North Carolina incorporated the Wilmington & Weldon railroad company, for the purpose of constructing a railroad in the state, and inserted a provision in the charter 'that the property of said company, and the shares therein, shall be exempted from any public charge or tax whatsoever.' It has been so often decided by this court that a charter of incorporation granted by a state creates a contract between the state and the corporators which the state cannot violate, that it would be a work of supererogation to repeat the reasons on which the argument is founded. It is true that when a corporation claims an exemption from taxation, it must show that the power to tax has been clearly relinquished by the state, and if there be a reasonable doubt about this having been done, that doubt must be solved in favor of the state. (The Binghampton Bridge Case, 3 Wallace.) If, however, the contract is plain and unambiguous, and the meaning of the parties to it can be clearly ascertained, it is the duty of the court to give effect to it, the same as if it were a contract between private persons, without regard to its supposed injurious effects upon the public interests.

"It may be conceded that it were better for the interests of the state that the tax-paying power, which is one of the highest and most important attributes of sovereignty, should on no occasion be surrendered. In the nature of things, the necessities of the government cannot always be foreseen, and in the changes of time the ability to raise revenue from every species of property may be of vital importance to the state, but the courts of the country are not the proper tribunals to apply the corrective to improvident legislation of this character. If there be no constitutional restraint on the action of the legislature on this subject, there is no remedy except through the influence of a wise public sentiment, reaching and controlling the conduct of the law-making power.

"There is no difficulty whatever in this case. The general assembly of North Carolina told the Wilmington & Weldon railroad company, in language which no one can misunderstand, that if they would complete the work of internal improvement for which they were incorporated, their property and the shares of their stockholders should be forever exempt from taxation. This is not denied, but it is contended that the subsequent legislation does not impair the obligation of the contract, and this presents the only question in the case. The taxes imposed are upon the franchise and rolling stock of the company, and upon lots of land appurtenant to and forming part of the property of the company, and necessary to be used in the successful operation of its business. It certainly requires no argument to show that a railroad corporation cannot perform the functions for which it was created without owning rolling stock and a limited quantity of real estate, and that these are embraced in the general term property. Property is a word of large import, and, in its application to this company, included all the real and personal estate required by it for the successful prosecution of its business. If it had appeared that the company had acquired either real or personal estate beyond its legitimate wants, it is very clear that such acquisitions would not be within the protection of the contract. But no such case has arisen, and we are only called upon to decide upon the case made by the record, which shows plainly enough that the company has not undertaken to abuse the favor of the legislature.

"It is insisted, however, that the tax on the franchise is something entirely distinct from the property of the corporation, and that the legislature, therefore, was not inhibited from taxing it. This position is equally unsound with the others taken in this case. Nothing is better settled than that the franchise of a private corporation — which, in its application to a railroad, is the privilege of running it and taking fare and freight — is property, and of the most valuable kind, as it cannot be taken for public use even, without compensation. (Redfield on Railways, p. 129, Sec. 70.) It is true it is not the same sort of property as the rolling stock, road-bed, and depot grounds, but it is equally with them covered by the general term, 'the property of the company,' and, therefore, equally within the protection of the charter.

"It is needless to argue the question further. It is clear that the legislation in controversy did impair the obligation of the contract which the general assembly of North Carolina made with the plaintiff in error, and it follows that the judgment of the supreme court must be reversed. It is so ordered, and the cause is remanded for further proceedings, in conformity with this opinion.

"D. W. Middleton,
"C. S. C. U. S."

When the question of the right to levy taxes upon the people for the purpose of building railroads, is before the courts, they decide that such right exists: First, because the right of eminent domain has been conferred upon the company; and, second, because the railroads are public highways; so, that in every phase the question assumes, the decisions of the courts are in favor of these corporations, and adverse to the people.

Notwithstanding the fact that the decisions of the courts fix the status of the railroad corporations as public in their nature, the real fact remains that railroads are owned and controlled by private parties, and it is a mere fiction of law to call them public; and while we accept the decisions as law, the facts are unchanged. The effect of the legislation to which we have referred is apparent to all. It has strengthened corporations, enlarged their powers, and constantly encroaches upon the rights of the people. So great has this evil become that almost the entire population of the country, not under the control of or interested in railroad corporations, are demanding a change of legislation, and relief from the oppressions heaped upon them by these monopolies.

But the injuries inflicted upon the people by the decisions of the courts are far greater than those resulting from legislation. By the decisions of the supreme court of the United States, the distinction between public and private rights has been obliterated; the constitution of the country has become of no more binding force than statute laws. State statutes and the decisions of state courts have been overridden and annulled where the interests of corporations were to be subserved; the settled decisions of the same court have been overruled, and a new doctrine, in conflict with the settled interpretation of the fundamental law of the land, has been announced, which makes the people the vassals of railroad corporations. The rights of the people and the states have been disregarded, and the edicts of the supreme court have been substituted for constitutional law. By the decree of that court, railroad corporations are clothed with the attributes of sovereignty, and the people are compelled to pay taxes to aid in the construction of their roads. That court has engaged in judicial legislation, and fastened upon the people a despotic government, with railroad corporations as their rulers. If it be true that railroad corporations are public and not private, they are not subject to the control of state courts or state legislatures. They are not by their charters, or the powers derived from legislative grants, made public corporations, and if they are public, they are made so by the decisions of the supreme court, or by some assumed power not visible to the public eye. It is contended by some, that if it is fully established that they are public corporations, the state legislatures and the state courts can regulate and control them. Is this so? Will not that fact take from the states all jurisdiction over them? The decision making railroad corporations public, also makes their roads public highways extending throughout the country. It is claimed that the general government, having power to regulate commerce between the states, can take control of all the railroads in the United States. No power is conferred upon state legislatures, in many of the states, to grant charters to railroad companies, conferring upon them any sovereign powers. And by the constitutions of some of the states they are deprived of the power of aiding in any works of internal improvement. As a consequence, there could not be uniform legislation among the states in relation to railroads. Being public highways, and the corporations being also public, the power of regulating and controlling them, and preventing discrimination among the states, would belong to the general government, and these powerful corporations, chartered by the state in which they are located, could defy state authority. With a congress composed of their friends, and a supreme court already committed to their interests, the people would be powerless. But on the other hand, if (as we insist is the fact) railroad companies are private corporations, then they are within the jurisdiction, and subject to the control of, the authorities of the states in which they are located. This we insist is the true status of railroad corporations, and the courts, by their decisions, cannot change this character. The decisions of the courts of the different states and of the nation have not been of a character to command the respect of the people, and unless we accept the last edict of the supreme court of the nation, as the supreme law of the land, and admit that it supersedes the constitutions and statutes of the states, as well as the decisions of the state courts, it is difficult to determine the character of railroad corporations and their relations to the people. Accepting that decision as final, the constitution of the United States is but of small value, and state governments are of but little benefit to the people. Upon the various questions that have arisen in connection with the construction of railroads, and the rights of the people, and railroad corporations respectively, there has been such confusion in the decisions of the courts, as well as contradiction, reversals, and overrulings that there now exists a necessity for the regular issue of a judicial bulletin, like the market reports, that the people may know what is the latest interpretation of the constitution. By the supreme court of the state of Iowa, it was decided to be constitutional for counties and cities to subscribe stock to railroad companies, and that there was a statute authorizing such subscriptions. By the same court it was decided, overruling the above named decision, that the constitution did not confer the power to subscribe stock to railroad companies, and that there was no law of the state authorizing such subscription. The whole matter arose under the constitution and laws of the state. The supreme court of the United States overruled this last decision of the state courts, and decided that such subscription was constitutional and was authorized by the laws of the state. The courts of the states of Pennsylvania, Illinois, Indiana, Wisconsin, Missouri, and others, made like decisions, and the supreme court of the United States overruled them. The legislatures of some of the states—Iowa, Wisconsin, and Michigan included—passed statutes authorizing local aid in shape of tax to be voted to railroad companies. The supreme courts of these states decided that the statutes were unconstitutional, and within fifteen months thereafter the supreme court of Iowa decided that the Iowa act was constitutional. Like decisions were made in some of the other states. In Wisconsin the state courts decided the act was unconstitutional, and the supreme court of the United States overruled that decision and decided the act was constitutional. Some of the state courts hold that railroad corporations are private, whilst others decide that they are public. The supreme court of the United States, by its decisions, clothes them with one of the attributes of sovereignty, and declares that under the law they are public corporations, and that their roads are public highways. The same court, upon the legal tender issues, decided that treasury notes were not legal tender for debts contracted before the enactment of the statute providing for their issue. In a few months after that decision was made, and after the friends of railroad corporations had so reconstructed the court as to have a majority of the court in favor of a re-hearing of the question, the same *high court* decided that treasury notes were not legal tender for all debts (save those excepted by the statutes,) but that they were the standard of values. In all of the above decisions made by the supreme court of the nation, either reversing the decisions of the state courts, or reversing and overruling its own decisions, such reversals and overrulings were in favor of the corporations and against the people. When courts, whose duty it is to declare the law and interpret the constitution, differ so widely and change so often, it is not strange that the people should begin to look with suspicion upon, and doubt the binding force of, these decisions; and when it is received as a truth, that in the appointment of judges care was taken to select men who were pledged to decide important issues then pending, in accordance with the interests and expressed wishes of railroad companies, it will not appear strange that the people, before voting for a judge, should demand of him a pledge in favor of measures advocated by them, or that he at least should pledge himself to abstain from judicial legislation and from twisting the meaning of the constitution to suit the views of the monopolists who are already clothed with too much power. If it is important that men elected to congress and state legislatures should be in sympathy with the people in their struggle to regain their rights, now usurped by the different monopolies of the country; and if it is necessary that the executive departments of the state and national government should be filled with men who are friends of the people and in favor of restricting corporations within proper and legitimate bounds,—it is of vastly more importance that the seats of justice, the courts of the country, should be filled and controlled by men who, instead of deciding cases according to their own personal views of what the constitution ought to be, will accept in letter and spirit as it is, and decide accordingly. An inordinate desire to interpret the fundamental law, to give it a new meaning, or, as it is commonly expressed, for amending the constitution by judicial legislation, seems to have seized the courts, and has been followed to such length as to make it almost impossible for even the courts themselves to decide when an act is constitutional and when it is not. A new decision is made as often as a new judge is appointed, not unfrequently overruling the long settled decisions of the courts. These decisions, no matter how absurd or unjust, must be accepted by the whole country as the supreme law of the land. Of late years, by accident or design, most of the decisions on questions of a general nature have been adverse to the interests of the people, and in favor of monopolies. Newly appointed judges, scarcely warm in their seats, have not hesitated to overrule the decisions of "Marshall," of "Story," and "Chase;" to disregard the views of "Webster," of "Adams," of "Jefferson," of "Washington," and "Hamilton," on constitutional questions. Their own personal views have been substituted for constitutional law, until the protection that instrument is supposed to afford the private citizen is entirely destroyed, and the absolute control of the government is transferred to the few monopolists, who, under the sanction of the courts, oppress the whole people. Whatever reform may be effected in the legislative and executive departments of the government, no real reform can obtain without a reformation of the courts.

FIFTH.—*The effect of the Legal Tender Decision, and its Antidote.*—The power of congress to issue treasury notes and government paper as a war measure, is not denied. The authority or the right, under the constitution, to make government promises to pay (treasury notes) legal tender, is not admitted. We have already treated of the legal tender decisions; of the reconstruction of the court, and the means used to secure the appointment of judges to insure a majority in favor of the validity of the legal tender act, and its general application to all debts save those excepted in the act, no matter at what time they were contracted. We recur to this subject again for the purpose of showing its effect upon the financial interests of the country. Whatever may have been the views of congress in passing the act, or of the court in declaring it constitutional, it has proved destructive of the interests of the people, and of great benefit to the corporate oligarchy that now rules the country. Whatever may have been the views of a majority of the court, or the motives that prompted and controlled that majority in rendering the legal tender decisions, these decisions have proved disastrous to the interests of the people, and added greatly to the already great power of corporations and Wall street speculators. In our commerce with foreign nations we are obliged to use *money* or its equivalent. While the acts of congress and the decisions of the courts may make treasury notes legal tender for all domestic debts, and all foreign debts payable in this country, neither the acts of congress nor the decision of courts can have any power or controlling influence over other nations. Debts due from us payable in foreign countries must be paid in coin or its equivalent. Our governmental promises to pay will not pass current as money in foreign countries, even though accompanied and supported by the decision of the supreme court, deciding that they are to be received by us as legal tender in all of our transactions. No one will claim that treasury notes are money, or that they are of intrinsic value. It is because the government is pledged to redeem this class of paper with coin that it has a market value. All other nations recognize coin—gold and silver—as the measure of values. It is the standard for all other articles of barter or sale. It is *money*. All other issues are but the representatives of money. Debts due from us, payable in foreign countries, must be paid in money; legal tender will not answer. But if debts due us from persons residing in other countries are to be paid here, the debtors can take their money, buy our legal tenders at a discount of fifteen or twenty dollars to the hundred, and discharge their debts, saving for themselves the difference between coin and paper. The confidence we have in the promises of the government to redeem in coin is all that makes treasury notes pass current, or gives them a market value.

The hope of an early resumption of specie payment is blasted by the legal tender decision. Its effect is to drain the United States of coin in our commerce with foreign nations, thus making it impossible to resume. Our coin grows less from day to day, and the secretary of the treasury is obliged to sell gold in New York at short intervals and in large amounts, in order to prevent the Wall street brokers making a margin of twenty-five per cent. or more between coin and government paper. While stock-jobbers and gold brokers make large profits in the appreciated price of gold; and railroad companies, in paying their bonds, make a net gain to the amount of the difference in value between gold and legal tender currency, the farmers and producers suffer loss to the amount of this difference in disposing of their products. When wheat is sold for one dollar per bushel, the seller gets but eighty-four cents, or just the value of treasury notes, and not one dollar in money, as he imagines, because the dollar he gets has no intrinsic value, but sells at its market worth, coin being the standard of values.

Another result of the legal tender decision is to make the value of farm products dependent upon the operations of Wall street sharpers. Legal tenders are the standard of values, says the court; coin and all marketable articles have their values measured by treasury notes. The price of treasury notes fluctuates. This fluctuation is not caused by any real change in the relative value of coin and treasury notes, but results from the dealings and operations in Wall street. If the "bull" corner gold, its value rises, or, more properly speaking, treasury notes depreciate in value. When the "bears" control the market, the price of treasury notes advances. This legal measure of values is constantly changing, and with its rise and fall the prices of western products also rise or fall. Railroads, railroad stocks and bonds, and the currency of the country, as well as the coin are all under the control of Wall street operators, and as long as treasury notes are treated as legal tender, these same operators will control the markets of the whole country.

The legal tender acts and decisions in effect, provide an irredeemable paper currency for the people, and coin for the government. Duties on imports must be paid in coin. Wall street brokers have the coin of the country cornered; the importer must buy it of them; he pays it to the government; government sells it to the broker, and he again sells it to the importer. It cannot get into general use, because the brokers preserve so great a margin between gold and paper as to drive all coin from circulation. They monopolize the gold market; and, under the legal tender decision, control the money market of the whole country. This state of things must continue until the legal tender act is repealed, or the decisions of the supreme court are reversed.

It is contended that gold and silver have no property value, beyond their utility as material for plate and ornament; that their money value is not inherent in the metal, but depends upon the custom and law of nations; that the money power of coin is *law*, and that it can be just as forcibly imparted to paper as to the precious metals; that the ignorance of the people and the selfishness of financiers alone prevent this money value being imparted to paper; that this value has been imparted to treasury notes by act of congress, and decisions of the supreme court. Is all this true? We admit that congress has attempted to stamp paper with an intrinsic value, but we say that this effort has proved a failure. So far from it having a money value, it has only a marketable value, measured by the money standard—the standard of all values, to-wit: the precious metals. Gold and silver have an intrinsic value, the same as all other metals, the difference being that their value is greater than that of any other metal, because of their scarcity. For this reason coin has been accepted by all civilized nations as the measure of all values. It is the universal standard. The attempt to make *paper promises to pay* a legal standard of values is Utopian. The theory of imparting to it an actual, stable, money value is fallacious. No decision of any court in the world can make paper currency of the same uniform value as coin, or prevent its fluctuation in price. It will rise and fall in market the same as wheat, cotton, iron, and all other articles of trade, sale, or barter. While coin retains its uniform value, which can only be changed by act of the government, its price neither increases nor diminishes in the market, but remains the standard by which all other values are measured.

The government cannot control the value of paper. The laws of trade—of demand and supply—fix its value the same as they fix the value of any other marketable commodity. If government possesses the power to make its paper legal tender for all purposes, it has also the power to fix the amount of this legal tender, or *paper money* used by the people for the transacting of all the business of the country. Having made it impossible to return to specie payments, and forced the people to use as money a currency which all other nations refuse to accept as money, the amount of this depreciated paper—this *legal tender*—can be arbitrarily increased until ten dollars of it would not purchase one coin dollar. Or it could reduce the volume of this legal tender until the people would be virtually without money or its representative. The whole business of the country would be dependent on the views of the majority of the congressmen — of congressmen, be it remembered, too often influenced by the different monopolies of which we have been treating. The majority of congress at one session may favor a large issue of legal tender paper, and the majority in the next congress may favor a limited issue—thus destroying stability and confidence in business, and giving the "bulls" and "bears" the absolute control of the trade and finances of the whole country. The arbitrary power of fixing the amount of money graciously allowed to the people by their rulers is as unalterably vested in congress, as it is in any of the rulers of the old world. The legal tender decisions say in substance: You shall not have coin as a circulating medium, nor shall you have legal tender or government currency save in such amounts as your rulers shall see proper to vote to you. When it is remembered that giant corporations and Wall street brokers can at their pleasure withhold from the business men and producers just such portions of the paper money of the country as suits their purposes of speculation and extortion, and can corner all the coin in the land, and dictate to the secretary of the national treasury the financial policy of the government, as they have done for the last few years, we can, to some extent, at least, appreciate the bad results of the legal tender decisions. The present banking system of the country is anti-republican; it tends to a centralization of the finances of the country in corporations; but the legal tender decisions, because of the undisputed control they give to combined and concentrated capital in the hands of railroad corporations, and other combinations whose interests are at war with those of the people, have done more to reduce the people to a state of servitude than all the acts of congress and legislatures united. With the amount of currency limited; specie payment rendered impossible; the control of the finances of the country vested by law in one man—the secretary of the treasury; the immense wealth and power of railroad companies, brokers, and stock-jobbers, recognized and feared by him—while they control the commerce of the country, and fix the value of its products; the people oppressed with unjust and unequal burdens imposed upon them by bad and unconstitutional legislation—the supreme court of the nation, with all these facts in view, has, by its decisions, made it possible for these oppressors of the people to control the destinies of the nation, and to despoil and rob them, not only of their property, but of all the republican features of their government.

We have argued that these decisions were unconstitutional. In support of this position, we refer the reader to the appendix to this work. If the power of the monopolists is now so great as to rule the country, shape legislation, reform the courts in their interests, and secure unconstitutional decisions in their favor from the supreme court of the nation, overruling the long-settled policy of the country, and substituting treasury notes for money, that the sellers of bonds, stocks, and corporate shares may repudiate their money contracts, and make large gains by so doing; while the same courts, with a dread of the disgrace which follows repudiation, destroy state constitutions and state statutes, and disregard the decisions of state courts, to compel the people to pay these giant monopolies money claimed by them on contracts obtained by fraud, and which the people did not owe—with this frighful aspect before us, we have reason to be alarmed for the safety of our rights, as well as to fear for the perpetuity of our republican government.

The imagination cannot devise a more perfect system for the subjection of the best interests of the people to the control of railroad and moneyed corporations and companies, and Wall street brokers and gamblers. It needed but the legal tender decision to make it perfect; to subject the whole country to the rule of rings and combinations of unscrupulous and dishonest men; to reduce the people to a state of vassalage more degrading than that of the Russian serfs. In name we are a free people, protected by the constitution of our country; in fact we are the servants of these giant monopolies. We retain of the proceeds of our labor such portion as they graciously permit us to keep. With the congress of the United States, and the legislatures of most of the states, committed to their interests, and the supreme court of the nation issuing its edicts in their favor, they can defy the people and continue their oppressions.

Sixth. — *Popular Measure of Relief Discussed — The Nature of the Reform Needed.*—We recognize no higher human power than the will of the people. When the servants of the people, elected and appointed to represent their interests in legislative bodies, or to decide upon questions affecting public interests, prove recreant to the trusts and interests confided to them, the people— the sovereign power — can remove them in the method provided by the fundamental law, or, if this cannot be effected, then the people have the right, the God-given right, to resort to nature's first law for self-preservation. If by legislation the rights of the people are taken from them, then that power, retained by the whole people to be exercised when their rights are refused them—that power which is inherent in the supreme rulers of our country — can be exercised. Under our system of government it should not be asserted save in the last extremity. When all other means fail — when redress can be obtained in no other way — then the people, as supreme rulers, should arise in their majesty, and, by the exercise of their reserved rights, *take* what their servants have denied them. As a people we have not yet reached the point which would justify extreme measures. While the different monopolies of which we have been treating, by their shrewd management, by the use of their money, and by concert of action, have obtained almost unlimited control of all the departments of the government, numerically they comprise but a small part of the population of the country. Their success is to be attributed to two causes : their systematic organization, and their unlimited control of the finances of the country. We might add, as a further cause of their success, the inattention of a large majority of the people to the political affairs of the country, and their willingness to follow a few political leaders, to whom they seem to have intrusted the entire control of the politics of the country. As a rule, we submit to wrongs in the administration of the affairs of state, as well as the national government, until we individually suffer from their mal-administration; then what has been termed the "sober second thought of the people" manifests itself, and reforms are effected. The situation of the affairs of the nation, and the great power that the monopolists have obtained in the land, have aroused that "sober second thought," and never in the history of our government has there been more urgent need of action on the part of the people. Never were issues presented that demanded more earnestly the united efforts of all who love and prize constitutional liberty. The evils of which we have been treating can be remedied by demanding of all who fill official positions a recognition of the superior binding force of the constitution. It is not to be expected that those men filling official places in the legislative and judicial departments of the government, who, from interest and custom, have become addicted to the habit of giving new meanings and interpretations to the constitution, will reform the abuses that have been rapidly accumulating, or that they will manifest any zeal or alacrity in stripping the railroad corporations and other monopolies of the great powers conferred upon them, or that any real reformation can be effected without a thorough change of public servants. No matter what political party has control of the government, or to what party the men selected to fill the different offices belong, or with what political organizations they affiliate, unless they acknowledge the superior binding force of the fundamental law, they should be requested to vacate their official positions, and their places should be filled by men who are willing to acknowledge the binding force of the constitution, and will pledge themselves to abstain from judicial legislation. Men elected to congress and state legislatures are the servants of the people, elected to protect their interests; hence their will should control the action of members of congress and state legislatures. Being elected to serve the people, and not to promote selfish interests or support class legislation, the people, before supporting any candidate for a legislative office, should demand of him a pledge to labor for and support only such measures as will tend to a restoration of the rights that have been taken from and denied to them, and by special charters and grants conferred upon corporations and other monopolies. Railroad corporations being created by legislative grants, their business being that of common carriers for hire, the legislature possesses full power to enact such laws as will limit and restrict their charges for transportation to a reasonable tariff, prohibit and punish extortions and unjust discriminations, and provide for the swift infliction of penalties whenever the laws are violated. Before the people elect any man to a legislative office he should pledge himself to support and obey the requirements of the constitution, and to abstain from that bane of a republican government—special class legislation. By supporting only such men as would, in good faith, pledge themselves as above suggested, and who, as legislators, would abide by their pledges, unjust discriminations would cease, and some of the rights of the people would be restored. But reforms must extend beyond the points named. Railroad companies being chartered and railroads constructed for the prosecution of the business of common carriers, having received aid in lands and bonds from the general government, and from states, counties, cities and towns, bonds and taxes, as well as special privileges not granted to any other corporations, in contemplation of law, these companies are bound to act honestly. It was never the intent of the legislatures (if they acted in good faith) to create these powerful corporations, to grant them extraordinary aid and privileges, and then allow them, by false and fictitious reports as to the cost of their roads, to charge unjust prices for carrying freights and passengers. By the watering process to which we have referred, the pretended cost of the roads, as shown from their reports, is often two or three times the actual cost, and the rates that are charged for transportation are such as to pay dividends not only on the cost of the road, but on the fictitious or added stock. Indeed, in many cases the stock reported as paid up is not paid in a legitimate manner; but when the company is organized, by selling bonds it builds its road from the proceeds, and from the earning of the road pays not only the interest on its bonds but accumulates a surplus. This surplus is divided among the stockholders — not as dividends on their paid-up stock, but is capitalized and stock issued to subscribers. The road is made to pay the interest, and eventually the principal, of the capital borrowed to build it, and also to earn money enough to show a paid-up capital to the amount of the actual cost of the road. This species of financiering on the part of the company is robbing the people and abusing the privileges conferred by the charter. No thorough reform of the abuses practices by railroad companies can be effected until the legislatures, by statutes, compel each and every company to purge its stock of every spurious dollar, so that the stock of each company shall not appear to be in excess of the cost of its road. If the legislature does not possess the power to do this, then it has the power to create a corporation that, by arbitrarily increasing its stock to any amount it may choose, can extort from the people sufficient to pay the interest upon such amount, and defy the power of its creator. The position is not sound. Any and all abuses practiced by railroad corporations can be corrected by legislative enactment, unless we admit that the creature is greater than the creator.

But it is claimed that if the legislature should by statute compel railroad companies to reduce their stock to the cost of constructing their roads, or to their actual value, and then limit their tariff of charges to reasonable rates, great injustice would be done the innocent holders of their bonds; that such reduction would render it impossible for them to pay either the interest or principal of these bonds; that such statutes would impair the obligations of contracts; that many of the bonds are held by widows and orphans, who would be ruined. This may or may not be true. If true, who is responsible for it? Certainly not the states or the people. Originally the bonds were purchased of the railroad companies. If these companies by false representations have obtained credit on their roads to two or three times their actual value, the companies are the responsible parties, and not the public. While innocent persons may suffer, their suffering results from their own imprudence, or it is a misfortune occasioned by the fraud of the railroad company. There is no justice in allowing these companies to extort from the people money sufficient to relieve themselves from the consequences of their frauds. A owns a farm worth $2,000; he represents it to be worth $6,000, and by reason of this false representation obtains from B a loan of $4,000, secured by a mortgage on this farm. He fails to pay the money borrowed, and B forecloses his mortgage, and sells the farm. It pays but one-half his judgment or decree. Would B have any claim upon the public for the balance of his debt ? He made his own contract, and expected a profit on his investment, but was disappointed. Under the law A had full authority to mortgage his land, and B had the option of loaning his money to A and taking a mortgage. He acted in good faith, and believed his security was ample, but was mistaken. Is there any difference in principle between the case of A and B and the purchasers of railroad bonds ? Both parties will suffer loss because of the fraud of the party with whom they dealt. Neither have any claim upon the public in law or in equity, and both must look to the parties with whom they contracted. The charters to railroad companies empowered them to transact business, but did not empower them to commit frauds, by mortgaging their roads for three times their actual value. To require railroad companies to act honestly and charge reasonable rates for carrying freights, does not impair the obligations of any contract. Nor does it, to compel them to reduce their stock to what it actually should be, measured by the value of their roads. The legislature should be composed of men who are not embarrassed by personal interest, and who have not received bribes. We do not claim that because of the fact that men are stockholders or directors in railroad companies they are disqualified for seats in the legislatures of states, or of congress. But do insist that when men are elected for the express purpose of advocating the increase of the already too great powers and privileges conferred upon corporations, they prostitute their offices to base and illegitimate purposes. When the sole aim of men elected to represent the people is demonstrated to be to defeat every measure designed to relieve them from the effect of unjust laws and to correct abuses practiced by the combined influence of corporations, they dishonor the place they fill. The rights of the people can be neither restored or preserved, until legislatures are purged of this class of men. Men who receive any remuneration from any man, class of men, or corporations, paid or bestowed for the purpose of securing friendly legislation, are unfit to represent the people. It makes no difference whether the consideration is paid in money, or in *passes over the railroads*—it is given as a *bribe*. Passes are called complimentary; they are accepted as complimentary, yet it is a fact that these complimentary passes are placed where they "will do the most good." They are given to congressmen, legislators, judges of courts, and executive officers. If it were necessary to offer proof that these passes were intended as bribes, we need only look at the manner of their distribution to the members of the last Iowa legislature. They were distributed among those friendly to legislation in favor of railroads, and withheld from those opposed to such legislation. If passes are purely complimentary, this was wrong; but if they are given as *bribes* it was the proper distribution of them. The legislator who accepts a pass, and the party giving it, should be punished under the provisions of the statutes against "bribery and corruption in office." And the provisions of the same statutes ought to be enforced against all persons holding official positions in the states, and in the general government. If officers cannot afford to pay for travel over railroads on their present salaries, increase them so as to make them independent of railroad companies, who estimate official integrity as being equal in value to a pass over their respective roads. History demonstrates that in some cases these passes have been received as full consideration for official influence. Legislatures possess the power to regulate and control railroad companies, and should exercise that power in every case of abuse of their privileges by the railroad companies. Some deny the power of legislatures to compel railroad companies to reduce their stock to the actual cost of their roads. This power is lodged in some department of government. We are not prepared to admit that these corporations are supreme; that they can openly, and in defiance of law, and the rights of the governing power, practice frauds, which, if practiced by an individual, would consign him to prison. If the legislature does not possess it, the courts certainly do, as we will hereafter demonstrate. We have shown that by the manner of building roads with borrowed capital obtained by sale of bonds, and by extortionate charges for transportation, making their roads earn sufficient to pay dividends on stock which had not been paid, as well as on the watered stock, the railroad companies in the United States whose roads cost $2,456,230,000, yet in fact representing the enormous sum of $6,236,638,749, in what purports to be paid-up capital stock, and bonds, were robbing the people.

The question we are now discussing is, How to remedy these evils. Our attempt thus far has been to demonstrate the fact that the remedy is exclusively within the state authorities, and not in those of the United States, and that railroad companies are private, and not public. Adhering to these views, we contend that railroad companies are subject to taxation at the same rate on the assessed value of their property as an individual; and the legislature cannot adopt a different rule for taxing railroad property without disregarding the letter and spirit of the constitution. The chartering, regulating, and controlling of railroad companies, and all corporations created for pecuniary profit, must remain with the states. To concede the exercise of this power to the national administration is to overturn republican government and take from the people the rights and powers reserved to them and the states; create a great central power without constitutional limit or restitution, but governed by the personal views of those in office. We have treated of this subject in the preceding pages, and refer to it here in considering the remedies for the evils endured by the people. We know that congress has granted charters to corporations organized for pecuniary profit, and that United States courts have taken jurisdiction of cases arising under state statutes, and disregarded the action of state legislatures and state courts on questions affecting the interests of railroad corporations, and have also decided that congress possesses the power to charter railroad companies. But we do not recognize the decisions as right, nor do we believe they will remain long unreversed. The opinion generally prevails that railroad corporations have abused, and are abusing, their charters; that they are oppressing the people; that there must be a reform of the abuses practiced by them. But differences of opinion exist as to the means to be applied. If we recognize the people as the source of power, and that they retain all the power they have not delegated to the government, the more nearly the interests of the people and the companies approach each other, the more closely they can be blended and united, and the more readily can abuses be corrected. To divide their rights and interests; to provide different governments, and rules of decisions for them; to make the people amenable to state authority, while the United States authority takes control of corporations, will create rival interests, and render railroad companies independent of the people. If the congress of the United States, claiming to have the constitutional right, should provide by statute for transferring the exclusive control of railroad corporations to the United States, an entire change of the relation between the states and the general government would be the result. The states would not have the power to redress any abuses of the charter privileges granted to these companies, either by legislative enactment or by judicial decisions. Railroad companies created by state legislatures, and hitherto subject to the jurisdiction of state courts, would be released from all obligations to state government, and from the control of state legislatures and courts. The congress of the United States and the federal courts would have exclusive control and jurisdiction over them, and constant confusion and conflicts of jurisdiction would naturally follow. Such a course would confer upon railroad companies still greater power, and place in their hands more efficient means for oppressing the people. Another evil resulting from such a course would be, that the whole corporate interest of the country could combine and concentrate their whole influence for the purpose of accomplishing any desired object. Now both congress and state legislatures must be bought over to their support; but if the United States government should take the whole control of corporations and railroad companies, the whole railroad force of the country, from the men who own, manage, and control this great interest, to the most menial employés, could be directed to a single purpose—that of securing congressional favor.

Now, state legislatures must be approached, and *persuaded.* as well as congress; then a single legislative body, and that one the farthest removed from the people, would be the only body to claim the attention of this great corporate interest. When grants were once made to railroad companies, and privileges conferred upon them, it would be simply impossible to effect any change, no matter how oppressive they might be upon the people. The idea that railroads are public highways, and that railroad companies are public corporations, already obtains among congressmen and in the supreme court of the United States. This is well understood among railroad men, as well as the fact that there is an increasing demand on the part of the people for the reform of the many abuses that are now practiced by them. Hence their anxiety to have the United States government assume control of railroad corporations. They desire it for another reason: Most of the special favors and grants they have received have been the result of bargain and sale. The same means will be used in the future unless a thorough reform is effected, and it will cost the corporate interests of the country less to deal with one body representing all the states than it would to deal with the legislatures of all the states. Another reason for this desire on the part of railroad companies is, that the supreme court, as now formed, is in full sympathy with them upon the points at issue between corporations and the people.

One of the reasons urged by railroad companies and their supporters in favor of the general government taking control of all the railroads in the country is, that unless government does so, our local discriminating statutes will preclude the possibility of inter-state commerce over these roads; that such statutes would, in effect, place embargos on the commerce of the west with the east; and that if congress fails to assume such control, the day is near when not a bushel of grain will be shipped over the railroads from the west to the sea-board. These apprehensions are urged with apparent seriousness, and so persistently that many citizens really believe that danger is to be feared from the action of state legislatures in the premises, and that congressional control alone would provide a certain and lasting relief. This kind of reasoning rests upon the presumption that the people are too ignorant to understand their best interests; or that for the purpose of injuring others, they will destroy the value of their own property.

The great want of the people is lower rates of transportation, and greater facilities for reaching markets. The state legislatures are supposed to represent the people; in all their enactments, the protection and not the destruction of the best interests of their constituents will presumably govern their action. It is also fair to presume that they will be controlled by the constitution of the nation, as well as of their own state. Should statutes be enacted in any state, discriminating between its own citizens and those of other states, such statutes would contravene the provisions of the constitution, and would be without effect. The more free and unrestricted the intercourse between different states the greater the benefits to the people. The farm products of the eastern and middle states are not important in quantity, and their people cannot afford to see an embargo placed upon their commerce with the west. The prosperity of the south and west depends largely upon commerce with the eastern and middle states. No state in the union could be prosperous if it should adopt the selfish and unconstitutional policy of non-intercourse with other states. The only conclusion deducible from these facts, is that the people of no state or section will be guilty of legislation so suicidal as to deprive its citizens of a free commerce with other portions of the country. Their own interest and prosperity forbid such a course. The plea of the necessity of interference on the part of the general government for the purpose of preventing such a state of things, is used by the friends of railroad corporations to prepare the public mind to accept as a necessity what is in fact but a scheme, planned and concocted by these corporations themselves for withdrawing all control of railroads and railroad coporations from the state governments, and placing them under the jurisdiction of one great body or government, which at the present time is more intent upon extending its jurisdiction and strength, than interested in the observance of constitutional restrictions, or the preservation of the rights and liberties of the people.

The plea of the necessity of government interference is bad for another reason. It is well to judge of the future by the past. When a line of conduct has been followed for years, and has become settled, and understood by all; when it has proved itself successful in accomplishing its ends, it is not apt to be changed unless some latent defect should be discovered, or some new cause should arise demanding new provisions. Real, not imaginary, necessity must be shown to justify a change. If, as a matter of fact, state legislatures and courts were framing and administering our laws, to prevent or retard inter-state commerce, there might be some ground for a transfer of jurisdiction from the states to the national government. But it should require more than mere assertion to justify such a change. A measure so radical, proposing such great changes—stripping the states of the power to control corporations chartered by, and existing only in the states from which they received their charters, and permitting a great central power to take control of them, should not be adopted when it rests upon the declarations of interested parties for its only support—while the facts negative the declarations.

Railroads have been built and operated in the United States for more than a generation. During the last decade they have multiplied all over the west. They can be found in every state in the union. All, or nearly all of these roads have been constructed by companies chartered by state legislatures; these companies and their roads have been almost exclusively under the control of state legislatures and courts, each state acting independently. No instance can be shown where any state legislature has passed a statute attempting to restrict commerce between different states, or to discriminate between citizens of different states, nor of unfriendly or restrictive legislation by any state on the subject of commerce over railroads passing from one state into another. No complaints have been made on account of any alleged discrimination. Then what is the necessity for the interference of congress and the general government. If the desire and design are to place railroad corporations beyond the reach and control of the people and the states; to render it impossible for the people or the states to correct abuses practiced by these corporations; to give the combined railroad corporate interest a position that will enable it to command the whole country—then there is necessity for speedy action on the part of the general government. But if, as is claimed, the object is to protect the people from oppressions and unjust discriminations, and to regulate and control these corporations, then there is no good reason for the general government attempting the bold, dangerous and unconstitutional experiment of withdrawing from the states the power vested in them of regulating corporations of their own creation. The plea made in behalf of congressional interference in order to protect inter-state commerce is without any real foundation. It is manufactured and urged by those who are opposed to state sovereignty; who are in favor of a strong and supreme central government, and who are willing to sacrifice the best interests and liberties of the people, that the great corporate interests of the country, already controlling the finances and commerce of the whole nation, may be released from all responsibility and accountability to the people and the states from which they received their charters. The advocates of this measure seem to forget that there is no power conferred upon the general government by any part of the constitution, to take from the states the management of their own internal affairs:—that railroad companies, being chartered by the states in which their roads are located, are and must remain subject to the exclusive control of the power creating them until there is a change in the fundamental law.

Careful consideration and examination of this question will satisfy the people that their only hope for the restoration and preservation of their rights in the conflict now existing between themselves and the railroad companies is in states retaining exclusive jurisdiction and control of all the railroad corporations and railroads within their respective borders. Another remedy suggested is, for the general government to purchase and own all the railroads in the country, and control them in the future. If this plan were feasible it is of doubtful wisdom. The purchase could not be made without the consent of the owners of the roads. This consent could only be obtained upon payment of the prices demanded, because railroad stock is not such property as can be condemned for public use. It is not to be expected that the companies owning the stocks and roads would sell for less than cost; and this cost would be the amount of money represented by the roads. This we have shown is over $6,000,000,000. To pay less than this amount, (being nearly three times their actual cost,) would be aiding the companies to defraud their creditors, for the reason that the roads are the only security the bondholders have. The purchase of the roads would increase the national debt to the amount paid for them, and impose additional burdens in the shape of taxes upon the people. It would add to the list of government officers and employés at least two hundred thousand men, whose influence could be relied upon when the interests of the people and those persons in office conflicted.

It may be said that the government would not operate the roads, but would lease them. Would this afford relief? It would require two parties to make the contract. The contractor would agree to pay a certain stipulated amount for the use of the road. He would then fix his own rate of charges for transportation, and being only a lessee, would be virtually irresponsible. Government could not fix the price to be paid for the use of the road, and also the tariff of charges. But the lessee would demand the right to fix his own tariff in order that he might have sufficient to make repairs, pay for the use of the road, and make his profit. This system would be subject to the abuses of which the shippers now complain. Irresponsible persons would often have control of these roads, or a part of them, and a wide field would be open for fraud and irregular practices. The wants of the people demand some other and cheaper mode of transportation; either a cheaper system of building and operating railroads, so that the tariffs can be reduced, or some new method. The present roads may be superseded and another kind adopted. In that case, the present railroad system would become of little value, and would prove a loss to the government. Last of all, the general government cannot go into the railroad business without contravening the provisions of the constitution. In addition to the above reasons why the government should not become the owner of the railroads, is this one, which outweighs all others: It would place them entirely beyond the control of the people. If the control of corporations is left to the states, they are in the hands of the people; each county, town, and neighborhood can bring its influence to bear upon the questions at issue. In the election of congressmen and other United States officers, local issues are lost sight of. National questions engage the public mind, while in the election of members of the state legislatures and other state officers, local questions enter largely in the canvass. Numerically, the monopolists are but a small fraction of the people; their great strength lies in the control they have obtained over the business and finances of the country. The people, united against the monopolists, can elect whom they choose to any state office, and can secure a majority in their favor. The remedy is in their own hands, and by united action they cannot fail of success. If a reform is ever effected, if the people ever regain their lost rights, they must commence at the *ballot box*. The producers throughout the west and south are largely in the majority; they can elect their own men. If they fail to do so, if they do not themselves apply the remedy, they ought not to complain of others because they do not apply it for them. There need be no difficulty or delay in effecting reforms dependent upon legislative action, provided the people are true to their own interests. They elect their agents to act for them. If they do not elect men who are with them in principle, sympathy, and feeling, they ought not to complain.

But, says the reader, admitting that legislative reform can be accomplished, how can the decisions of the courts be changed? This question presents more difficulty. It has been the custom from time immemorial for courts to be governed and controlled by precedents. This is adopted in order that the law may be settled and certain. When questions arise under statutes, the meaning of which is ambiguous, resort is had to former decisions under like statutes, for a rule of construction, and thus the law is *settled*. We accept the decision as the law of the land, and to criticise it is seemed discourteous to the court making it. To call in question the motives of the courts, or to doubt their wisdom, is deemed rank "treason." The rule governing them may be of ancient date; the reason for its adoption may have long since ceased; the rule itself may be obsolete. Yet, to find a precedent for a decision that outrages justice and is at war with the best interests of the people, but in favor of the corporate interests of the country, this old rule is dragged from its long repose and made the basis of new decisions. Most of these old precedents originated in monarchical countries, where all doubtful questions were construed in favor of the crown, and where the rights of the people always yielded to kingly prerogative. While precedents should have their true weight in determining between private parties, when none of the great questions arise affecting the national welfare, and while interpretations of the constitution, acquiesced in for many years, should remain as the settled law of the land, and be observed by the courts, the practice of solving constitutional problems by resort to old monarchical precedents, and the adoption of the reasoning of the high courts of the king's *exchequer*, should not be tolerated in a republic. Our form of government is new. Our courts should be the courts of the people, and not a *star chamber* for the protection and perpetration of the monarchical dogma, that "it is absolutely essential to independent national existence that government should have a firm hold of the two great sovereign instrumentalities of the *sword* and the *purse*," as was declared by the supreme court of the United States, in December, 1871. Such declarations are at war with our ideas of republican government. It has no support save in despotic governments and decisions emanating from them; yet it is the doctrine that must obtain, if the recent decisions of the supreme court are to remain as the settled law of the nation. To accept this doctrine as a final exposition of the relative rights of the people and the government, is to acknowledge that the agents and servants of the people elected and appointed to office, become their masters, clothed with imperial powers.

It is not only in the adoption of old precedents that the rights of the people have been denied in courts, but by wresting the meaning of the earlier decisions made by the distinguished men who graced the bench of the supreme court in its earlier and purer days. The "Dartmouth College" case was the first in which the rights of states or the people to interfere with charter privileges was determined. We have given the history of this case in the preceding pages. It in no sense justifies or supports the recent decisions of the court, as to the rights and privileges of corporations organized for pecuniary profit. Yet, taking the decision in that case as a precedent, the supreme court has gradually encroached upon the rights of the people, until, under its latest decisions, railroad corporations are public corporations, their roads are public highways, and the property of all the tax-payers can be taxed, and the taxes thus collected can be used by these private corporations to pay for building and repairing their roads. This is the latest new departure, and with the "Legal Tender" decision, makes the interest of the whole people, as well as the value of their property, depend upon the action of corporations.

No good reason can be shown why the decisions of courts should not be subjected to criticism the same as the acts of legislative bodies. The courts are a coördinate branch of the government, but with a power greater than that of the legislative and executive branches combined. The decisions of courts render nugatory the acts of the other departments of the government. To admit that the decisions of the judiciary cannot be questioned, is to concede to it all the prerogatives possessed by absolute tyrants. Not only have the people the right to question the decisions of the courts, and if need be to examine the motives which prompted them, but also to know the views of the men who aspire to judicial positions upon all questions of a general and public nature. No candidate for judicial position should be expected to form an opinion upon, or decide a question affecting the rights of parties until it had been finally submitted. But, upon the great questions that frequently arise affecting the public welfare, his views should be publicly known. Let the people understand the views of the men seeking for a seat on the bench before his election, and judicial legislation and partisan decisions will soon disappear. The judges of the supreme court of the United States hold their offices for life, by appointment, that court is further removed from the people than state courts. Reforms are not easily effected. Judges recently appointed received their appointment because of their understood views upon certain public questions. The course of decisions of this court demonstrates that the rights of the people are considered of less importance than the demands of corporations, in cases of conflict. While the present system of selecting these judges continues, with their life terms, it will be hard for the people to regain their rights. There are times when, because of oppressions, the people have the right to demand changes in the fundamental law. At the present time they are demanding redress; they are asking to be relieved from the unjust burdens imposed upon them by companies and corporations, who are petted and supported by the supreme court. But one certain means is left them, and that is an amendment to the constitution restricting their term to a certain number of years and providing for their election by the people. We could then free ourselves from the burdens imposed upon us by this anti-republican department of our national government, and take from corporations some of their oppressive powers and privileges now assured to them by the decisions of the supreme court. If any relief is afforded the people from the oppressions under which they now suffer they must obtain it through their own efforts. No other channel is now open. All of the departments of the government, state and national, are more or less controlled by the monopolies against which the farmers are now preparing to fight. The silent ballot is the weapon to use; when used by a united people victory is assured. It is more potent than all the appliances of an army; more thorough in its execution than the bullet. It is the dread of the unfaithful legislator, dishonest office-holder, and the unjust judge. It strikes terror into the hearts of the unscrupulous men, who are willing to sacrifice honor, country, and future happiness for the purpose of amassing wealth, by extortions practiced upon the sweating, toiling millions who till the ground. While partial relief may be obtained through other channels, real, genuine and lasting redress can only be obtained by organized action at the polls.

How can the abuses of the transportation system be corrected? This question is now having a practical test in Illinois, and is being discussed throughout the country. It is being demonstrated that a *pro rata* tariff will not afford relief; and that some other means must be adopted. What that may be, time will develop. No uniform *pro rata* tariff would be just to either the companies or the people. The shipping of way freights is always attended with more proportionate expense and delay than at prominent and terminal points. The extensive shipper, who loads a large number of cars for a single train, should be allowed more favorable rates than the one who ships at some way station but one car of freight at long intervals. The real cause of complaint is the uniformly exorbitant rates charged for carrying freights in connection with the present warehouse and elevator system. The legislatures and the courts are clothed with full power to prevent oppressive or unjust charges for carrying freight. They care not how much per cent. the companies shall make upon their investments; but when their charges amount to an abuse of their charter privileges the legislatures and the courts can correct them. The rule established by railroad companies to force from shippers such rates as will pay interest or dividends upon an amount of imaginary stock is unjust. The process by which they increase their stock to two or three times the amount invested is fraudulent. The legislatures and the courts possess the power to compel railroad companies to make a return of the actual amounts of money invested in their respective roads, in order to determine whether their charges are excessive and oppressive. Railroad companies being dependent upon state legislatures for such grants as will enable them to construct their roads, and being common carriers, the legislature can, by statute, restrict the capital stock to the amount invested. If this course had been adopted years ago many of the abuses now endured by the people would have been prevented. Not only has the law-making power the right to restrict the stock to the actual cost of the road, but it has also the power to fix the maximum rates for transportation. Competition will always have a controlling influence upon the price of any commodity, as well as fixing the price of any species of services or labor. The legislature has the power to enact statutes to prohibit the consolidation of the busines of railroad companies, or a combination on their part to charge excessive tariffs; and the courts possess the power to enforce the observance of such statutes by the infliction of suitable penalties. In this connection the abuses practiced by the dispatch companies may be considered. The railroad companies receive their charters with the understanding and implied agreement on their part, that, as common carriers, they will deal honestly with the public, and that they will furnish the necessary locomotives, cars, etc., for the purpose of supplying the ordinary wants of the people. This they are bound to furnish, and also to do the ordinary carrying of freights for a reasonable compensation.

We have already given a history of the dispatch lines, and told who composed the companies, and how they do the business the railroad companies agreed to transact when they obtained their charters. These dispatch lines are a fraud upon the public, for which the companies should be held responsible. Every dollar paid to them, in excess of the regular rates of the railroad companies' regular tariff, can be recovered from the companies. The fiction of hiring their roads and locomoctives to another company, and giving such company a monopoly of the trade over their road, in order that higher rates may be charged, is an abuse that the legislature can correct and the courts can punish. Of the same nature are the "warehouse" and "elevator" combinations. Of these we know what is open and visible; but of the internal workings and divisions of the "pools," or, more properly speaking, the "spoils," we know but little. We know that it is a means of oppression, and that it compels farmers to sell to *inside* men, or sacrifice the moiety of the crop the railroad companies allow them to retain. In law, railroad companies are bound to ship for all who pay the regular rates without bestowing a bounty upon elevator and warehouse men; and they are also bound to deliver the freight at such warehouses as the shippers direct. For a refusal to do so, they are liable to the shipper for damages to the amount of the loss suffered, and sums extorted. Shippers can compel the companies to receive their freights on board their cars at regular stations, and to deliver their freights at the place designated, irrespective of any and all combinations to prevent it. To conclude this whole matter, the people have the power to reform all the abuses they suffer at the hands of these monopolies by the election of men to legislative offices whose hands will not touch bribes, and by filling the seats of justice with judges who are not so wedded to ancient precedents as to do injustice rather than make a new departure; by men whose chief object shall be to do equal and exact justice to all, and not resort to judicial legislation and new interpretations of the constitution in order to uphold and strengthen the power and advance the interests of corporations already too powerful in the land.

In order to restore to the people the rights now denied them, and to abridge the combined power of the monopolies who now rule the country, the control of the finances must be taken from them. The financial policy of the government, adopted during the late civil war as a war measure, is still adhered to. The internal commerce of the whole country is controlled by a few men—the same who own and operate the railroads and rule the *business* in "Wall street." The peculiar financial policy of the government tends to concentrate the money of the country

—to gather it together, rather than to scatter it abroad. New York City being the great commercial center, and the internal commerce of the country being under the control of a few men who make this metropolis their principal place of business, with their vast lines of railroads extending over the whole country, bringing to them a never-ceasing stream of money, they are able to regulate the market value of almost all articles of commerce, and to limit the supply of the circulating medium as occasion serves. We have already shown the bad results of the system upon the interests of the people, and do not intend to repeat it here. Ordinarily, the laws of trade, of demand and supply, will regulate and equalize the distribution of the circulating medium over the country. Such will always be the case if no special causes exist to prevent it. But with the railroad interest of the country controlled by the same combination of men who "corner" all the coin in the country; with the established policy of the government making depreciated paper the only circulating medium, and the "legal tender" decision making this depreciated currency the standard of values; with the constant fluctuation of prices resulting from the above named causes—it is not strange that these corporations and Wall street brokers control the finances of the country. Until this control is taken from them, the wrongs of the people cannot be redressed.

Money is said to be "power," and when a certain interest or locality has the absolute control of this "power" all others must suffer. One means of stripping railroad magnates and Wall street gamblers of this power would be the resumption of "specie payment." As we have shown, under the present financial and tariff policy of this country, this is out of the question. With our legal tender decisions, our depreciated currency, and our tariff system, the balance of trade is largely against us; our coin is being shipped to other countries, not leaving us sufficient for the purposes of resumption, or for circulation. Add to this the fact that the Wall street brokers own or control most of what is in the country, and the truth is patent that resumption cannot be effected until the whole financial policy of the government is remodeled. Will an increase of the banking facilities of the country under the present system accomplish this object? We answer, No. An increase of banks and of the currency, would only afford temporary relief. Suppose $100,000,000 should be added to the present amount of currency, and that it should all be distributed in the west and south. Wall street operators would only have to increase their operations to gather the whole of it under their control. They now, in their various ramifications, own and control capital more than sufficient to pay the whole of the national debt and leave them a large surplus. While the distribution of additional currency through the country might afford them temporary relief, under the combined management of railroad corporations and Wall street brokers, and without any change in their present system, they could and would soon absorb this surplus of currency, and resume the absolute control of the finances of the country. The people would again be in their power, with an additional burden imposed upon them, "to-wit:"—the payment of the interest on an additional $100,000,000 of government bonds. Would a change in the banking system of the country take from these monopolists the control of the finances of the country? This would depend upon the character of the change. If the secretary of the treasury or his department, should retain the entire management of the system, no real relief could be expected. While the general government has the exclusive right to regulate the coinage and value of coin (money), it is the assumption of power not delegated to vest in one man or department the exclusive management of the finances of the entire country —not only of the government, but of all private persons. We do not comprehend the wisdom of fixing and limiting the amount of currency the country may have for a circulating medium, and empowering one man to decide how, when, and where it shall be distributed. Conceding to the general government the power to charter banks, and issue treasury notes, the power is not exclusive. There is no limit to the volume of gold and silver, and if government should attempt to limit the amount of coin, it could not do it. The laws of trade, the demand and supply, would fix the amount. Under our present banking system, coin is driven from circulation, and a definitely fixed amount of treasury notes and government paper is all that the country is permitted to have for the transaction of its whole business—and this amount must be placed just where the comptroller of the currency shall determine.

The legal tender decisions have made the resumption of specie payment impossible. The present banking system prevents an increase of currency or treasury notes, and gives concentrated capital absolute and unlimited control of the business of the country. Any other banking system, if left under the same control, would be subject to the same objections. No one department of the government, nor the whole government combined, can determine the amount of currency necessary for transacting the business of the country. Fixing the amount in the present banking act has afforded the means to Wall street operators for "cornering" such amounts of currency as would derange the market and depress prices. No valid objection can be offered to what is known as the "free banking system." Such a system, if generally adopted, would strip railroad corporations, Wall street jobbers, and all other rings and combinations of men, of the power to control the finances of the country. Another advantage would result to the people: It would free them from the annual payment of from $18,000,000 to $20,000,000 interest on government bonds purchased by bankers, and deposited with the treasury department. Such a system of banking would reduce the margin between coin and currency, and promote the resumption of specie payment, and, instead of having only depreciated paper as a circulating medium, we would have a currency convertible into coin. The giant corporations and other monopolies that now rule would be shorn of much of their strength, and the people would be freed from their relentless grasp.

SEVENTH.—*Free Trade and Direct Taxation.*—Our conclusion would not be complete were we to omit a reference to the subject of tariff. Indeed, it so interlaces the question of transportation and the construction of railroads as to become an integral part of our discussion. Disclaiming any partisan views of the question, we shall try to demonstrate that all tariffs are unjust and oppressive. In a former chapter we have shown the operations of our tariff, and some of its results. We now proceed to demonstrate that the true rule in all our dealings and commercial transactions is, *to sell where we can obtain the best prices, and to purchase where we can obtain the desired article for the least money.* Demand and supply should regulate the prices in our dealings, and protective tariffs should be repealed. A "protection" that taxes three-fourths or four-fifths of the whole people, in order that the remaining fraction may amass riches, is an oppression that ought not to be tolerated. No class is more oppressed by protective tariffs than the farmers and producers of the country. They do not ask, nor do they receive any protection.

With high or protective tariffs, farmers and producers pay much more than their just proportion to the support of the government. The consumer simply pays tariff duties on what he consumes, while the producer not only pays on what be consumes, but his product must pay a large part of the duty upon what is consumed by others. The products of the country are its wealth. No matter who is obliged to pay the duty in the first instance, ultimately the producer must pay it. To illustrate this proposition, let us take any given article produced, manufactured, or constructed in the United States. There is a duty on some of the material used in the manufacture of the reaper. The manufacturer pays this duty, and adds it to the cost of the machine purchased by the farmer. In the erection of factories, machine shops, furnaces and foundries dutiable articles are used; all of which, in the end, must be paid for from the products of the country. In the construction of railroads, locomotives, cars, etc., iron and other articles are used upon which there are high tariff rates. These duties are paid by the companies in the first instance; the amounts paid are included in the cost of the roads, and must be returned in shape of increased rates for transportation over the roads. In the end these duties are paid by the producer. Every bushel of wheat, corn, or other grain shipped over a railroad pays part. Protective tariffs are so interwoven with the construction of railroads and the internal commerce of the country that they cannot be separated from the questions we have been discussing. All tariff duties are direct charges upon the productions of this country, and not on any other. Import duties are not paid by the people of the country from whence the goods are imported, but by our own people. It matters not who pays the tax in the first instance; in the end it must be paid from the product of the country. The main product of our country, especially of the west and south, being from the soil, it follows that the farmer must pay by far the greatest portion of tariff duties. The burdens imposed on him are more than his just share. In the first place, he pays directly the duty charged upon what he consumes, and then pays indirectly much the larger part of the duties paid in the first instance by others. He is charged with the cost of shipping his grain to market, whether that market is in the United States or Europe, and his product must pay the cost of shipping the return cargo from Europe to America, with the addition of such protective duty as congress may fix by statute. His product must bear the whole burden. "In other words, the question of transportation is part and parcel of the tariff question, and cannot be dealt with apart from it. Transportation is made dear by the dearness of supplies; that is to say, the railroads are taxed enormously, and, through the railroads, the farmers, for the benefit of special industries. There can be no cheap transportation without cheap iron, cheap cars, cheap stations; and, what is more, there can be no market for American produce abroad so long as the sale of all foreign commodities, except gold, is made as difficult as high duties and vexatious custom-house regulations can make it. Agricultural produce at the west is now a glut; it must become more and more of a glut if either more railroads are opened or the cost of transportation on the present roads is diminished, as long as new markets are not provided, or, in other words, as long as access to the crowded regions of the Old World is artificially impeded. Of course, there may come a time when there will be population enough in the west to eat up all its corn and pork; but, at the present rate of agricultural and railroad development, this will not be witnessed by either the present generation or the next, and the cry of the 'Granges' ought to be for a clearing of the outlets to the Old World in all ways. To secure this it is not enough to cheapen transportation; we have to offer a market to the foreigner for his commodities, in order to get him to take ours."

As we have before remarked, the settled plan for raising revenue for the support of the general government is by import duties. By common consent this plan has been accepted as the most feasible. While we have been following this method from the organization of our government, by legislation we have been making war upon foreign commerce, by imposing tariffs for the protection and government of domestic manufactures. By congressional enactment we determine that we will support the government by the collection of duties levied upon foreign imports; and then we levy high rates of duties for the purpose of prohibiting these foreign imports, and for building up and protecting home manufactures. Under the present tariff, but for the fact that our own manufacturers take advantage of the high rate of duties, and advance the price of their own products to the extent of the duty, foreign importations would cease, and some other means would have to be adopted to supply the revenue needed by the government.

The only benefit thus far resulting from our present high tariff is the enriching of a few men by the imposition of unjust and unequal burdens upon the farming and producing classes. It might be pertinent to inquire whether there is any justice in any kind of tariff. All are bound to contribute their *pro rata* share for the support of the government. In theory the property of the country is taxed for this purpose. Such a system of taxation is just and equitable, because it is uniform; the property of each individual pays its *pro rata* share, and the burden is equally divided. As we have already shown, revenue derived from tariffs is a tax upon the labor of the citizen, and not on the wealth or property of the country. The poor man—the man who depends entirely upon his daily labor for the support of himself and family—pays as much for the support of the government as the man of immense wealth. His daily toil, considered in the light of its value to the government, is taken as equivalent to the $500,000 of the rich man. The industry, and not the wealth, of the country is made to support the government when the revenue is derived from import duties. No one will deny the right of the general government to provide for its own support, nor its right to provide means to this end by the levy of import duties; yet the wisdom of these duties does not so clearly appear. The reader will have noticed that this method of raising revenue operates unequally; that it gives to American manufacturers an absolute monopoly of business; that the only reason why imports do not cease is because the prices of American fabrics have been arbitrarily raised to the highest point allowable without permitting the importer to undersell the home-made article. The manufacturers, under the statute, having a complete monopoly, are not slow in availing themselves of it, and, as a natural result, the whole country is compelled to contribute to their support. It may be asked: How would you provide for the support of the government? We answer: By direct taxation; because this is a just and equitable manner of raising revenue, compelling the wealth and property of the country, and not the labor of the toiling millions, to support the government. Because it will prove less expensive, and will do away with custom houses and custom-house officers — with the frauds, swindling and robbery that now afflict the country. Because it will open to us the markets of the world, and give us an outlet and market for our agricultural products. Now the balance of trade is against us; our country is being drained of its coin and its wealth; all productive industries languish, because of our selfish policy of attempting to become exclusive in our commerce.

We are content to trammel all dealings with foreign nations in the way of barter, sale, and exchange, and send our coin to Europe, while we use, as the representative of money, an irredeemable paper currency. Free trade would enable us to increase our commerce and shipping on the ocean; to arrest the stream of coin that is flowing from us to Europe; to sell where we could obtain the best prices, and buy where we could make the best bargains. We are in favor of direct taxation for the support of the government, because it will simplify our revenue system, and consequently require less revenue than is now needed. It will compel more rigid economy in the administration of the government, and place within the reach of the people the means of ascertaining how much is annually expended by those in power. It will destroy one branch of the system of monopolies that is robbing the agricultural and producing classes of their substance. Let us not become alarmed at the thought of this direct taxation. We accept it as the best method for raising revenue for the support of state and municipal government; and no good reason can be shown why the same method would not be best for the general government. The amount to be paid by the men of wealth would be in excess of what they now pay, because their property, and not what they consume, would be the basis of taxation. But to the laborer with a family, the mechanic, the farmer with small means, and to a majority of men who now pay in shape of duties from $100 to $200 annually, the amount required would be but a tithe of the sum now demanded. To learn something of the rate per cent. necessary to support the government, let us look at the valuation of the property in the United States, as returned with the census in 1870. The actual amount as returned was $14,178,486,732 — call it in round numbers $15,000,000,000; a tax of one per cent. on this amount would produce a revenue of $150,000,000. The above valuation is taken mainly from the returns made by assessors, and is but little more than one-third of the real value. Let us double the amount, then the value of the property in the United States will be $30,000,000,000. By an examination of the returns it will be seen that little railroad property is included in the valuation. If this property is added, the above amount will be largely increased. By supposing the real value of the assessable property to be $30,000,000,000; then a tax of one-half per cent. would raise a revenue of $150,000,000, a sum sufficient to pay all the necessary current expenses of the government and leave something to apply on the national debt. A tax of three-fourth per cent. would raise a revenue of $225,000,000, enough to support the government and pay the interest on the whole of the national debt. Should the special tax be continued on spirits and tobacco, then a tax of four mills would raise a sufficient revenue for all legitimate governmental purposes. Now, a laboring man must pay from the proceeds of his labor from thirty per cent. upwards for almost all his purchases of clothing for his family, and the same on many other articles of consumption. If, in the course of a year, he purchases to the amount of $150, of this sum $50 is paid, indirectly, it is true, but nevertheless it is paid, and is a tax. With direct taxation, if his homestead should be worth $1,000, instead of paying $50 as he now does, he would pay five for the support of the government, and the other forty-five dollars now paid by him from the proceeds of his labor would be charged against the property of his rich neighbor. There is no injustice in this method of raising revenue for the support of the government, and its adoption would relieve the people from the oppressions of a ring of wealthy monopolists who now control the entire manufacturing industries of the country, and would allow the laws of trade, of demand and supply, to fix the prices of manufactured articles. No reason now exists for the continuance of a law that assures to the manufacturer large dividends on his investments, while the farm products must be sold and bartered for a nominal price. The producer asks no protection save access to the market and the privilege of keeping for his family and himself the net proceeds of his crops, without being compelled to bestow one-third of it as a gratuity upon the already rich and lordly manufacturer. This right the agriculturists will never enjoy until the old anti-republican theory of protective and revenue tariffs is exploded, and the equal rights of all are vindicated. When this tariff embargo on commerce is removed, when this blockade is raised, and the producer can send his grain to Europe, and in return receive such manufactured articles as he needs, without paying *royalty* to some American lord, in shape of tariff (ironically called "protection") the producing classes will ask no other aid of government. Then will appear the dawn of that universal brotherhood of man, which sooner or later will illuminate the whole civilized world. With "free trade" and direct taxation, a death blow will be given to monopolists, and the burden so long borne by the laboring .and producing classes will be lifted from them, and they will be permitted to enjoy the fruits of their own labor.

EIGHTH.—*Patent Rights—Cash Payments Recommended in Place of Long Standing Mortgages on the Genius of American Industry.*—We have shown some of the abuses connected with the patent system of the country, and their effect upon the people. While the monopoly of inventions is not of as great magnitude as some others of which we have treated, the oppressions resulting from it are more annoying than many that engage general attention. Inventions are patented because they are expected to be of public benefit, and because it is but just that the inventor should be rewarded for a discovery or invention that will advantage the public generally, or individuals who may make use of the invention or discovery. The monopoly given to the inventor, or discoverer, is to enable him to compensate himself for the time, labor, and skill, as well as the talent or genius bestowed upon the invention, and also to encourage others to enter the list as inventors or discoverers of new and useful articles and principles. But our patent system was never designed for giving a monopoly to any one who happened to shape a plow handle different from those now in use, or who cut a thread used in operating a sewing machine in a peculiar manner, or for the many hundreds of trifling alterations made in many articles in general use, or in the manner of using them. An examination of the list of patents issued will demonstrate that not one in ten contains any new principle, or is of any value to any one, save the patentee. The apparent ease with which patents are obtained, and the indiscriminate manner of their issue, is a great and growing evil that should be remedied. No patent should be issued until a test had demonstrated its perfection and usefulness. An examination of many articles on which letters patent have been issued, coupled with the attempt to use them, discloses the fact that the invention, if it ever could be of any particular value, required further improvement to make it of such value, and that letters patent had been issued for an undeveloped theory. If the invention had been submitted to a practical test, this state of things would not have occurred, and the public would not have been defrauded. Patented articles enter so largely in the prosecution of all industrial pursuits that it is of the utmost importance that they should be perfect in their plans and construction, and that the governernment should assume some kind of responsibility in all cases when letters patent are issued. Such letters say in substance, that the patented article is new and useful, and that it is reasonably fit for the work in the view of the inventor. These letters patent are a letter of credit to the patentee; as a license permitting him to sell his invention, and forbidding all persons to sell or use the invention without his consent. Under the present law it is simply a special favor, in shape of an exclusive right, granted to an individual to defraud the persons with whom he deals. The law should be so modified as to make the government or the examining officer responsible in all cases when patents issued for pretended discoveries or inventions prove to be neither new or useful. If such were now the law, there would be less complaint of frauds practiced by pretended inventors, and the utter failure of patented articles to answer the purposes for which they were intended. The law should be so amended as to prevent oppressions and extortions in the sale and use of articles of real merit, for which the inventor should be rewarded, and should have an exclusive right to use and sell his invention. There should be some limit to the price of the article. Government has given him an exclusive right; he should be restricted to such prices as would fairly compensate him for his discovery. His case is not like that of other men, who in their dealings come in competition, and where this competion and the laws of demand and supply fix the prices of the commodities in which they deal. He has the whole business in his own hands, and any attempt on the part of others to interfere with his exclusive right is forbidden and punished. We have already stated that

machines sold in this country for $75 could be bought in England for less than half that sum. Most of the articles and machines of different kinds patented in this country, and used in Europe, are sold by the patentees, their agents and assigns, at less than half the sums demanded here at home. In Europe, where they have no monopoly, no exclusive right, they come in competition with others; hence they sell at fair prices. But in this country, where they have an exclusive right, they extort from the purchaser from one hundred to five hundred per cent. on the cost of the article. This, government should prevent. But a better way to adjust the whole matter between the public and the inventor would be for the government to pay a premium according to merit, for all new and useful inventions, and remove all restrictions. Let all be free to make, use, and sell, not the invention, but the thing invented. This course would require careful and thorough examination and experiment before the principle was indorsed by the government, and the premium paid. Or, if his invention proved to be new and useful, let government pay to the inventor such sum as would fairly and liberally compensate him, and give the invention to the public. Government has bestowed immense grants of land upon railroad companies, for the avowed purpose of assisting in the development of the country; with greater justice could it bestow upon the whole people all useful discoveries and inventions. Such a course, adopted and executed in good faith, would make it impossible for adventurers, sharpers, and swindlers to impose worthless inventions and pretended discoveries upon the government, and then palm them off upon the people. Under the present system of obtaining letters patent, the people are wronged and often cheated, and for their wrongs the government is mainly responsible. Some other plan should be adopted, which in its operations would liberally compensate the inventor, and at the same time protect the people from extortions practiced by the owners of valuable inventions, and also from the thousands of adventurers who have been so fortunate as to obtain letters patent upon pretended discoveries of principles neither new nor

useful, using their letters of credit for the purpose of defrauding the public.

Conclusion.—We now approach the end of our labors. We have sought to present to the reader a candid statement of the different questions we have discussed; to lay before him evidence of the great and growing power of the men who are surely and swiftly getting control of the departments of the government, and monopolizing the finances and commerce of the whole country. In doing this we have endeavored to direct attention to the exclusive and munificent grants made to railroad companies, and to their abuse of these grants; to the means used by them to get control of the legislative and judicial departments of the government, and their apparent success in that direction; to the abridgement of the rights of the people incident thereto; to the dishonest and fraudulent practices of the men constructing, owning, and operating railroads; to the disgraceful Credit Mobilier swindle, and its influence upon the country; to the questionable position of some of the men representing the people in congress; to the destruction of the rights of the states and of the people; to the disregard of the constitutional restrictions and safeguards when the interests of these corporations were to be subserved; the purposes for which taxes should be levied; to the nature of railroad corporations—that they are private in their organization, and subject to the control of the people; to the effect of the policy of affording local aid to railroad companies by taxation, etc.; to the blighting influence attending municipal subscriptions to railroad companies; to the impositions practiced in transporting freights, and the warehouse and elevator abuses; to the fraudulent increase of capital stock by railroad companies through the watering process, and the extortions necessary to this dishonest practice; to their relative immunity from the burdens imposed for the support of government; to the strong grasp of consolidated capital upon the legislation of the country; to the special privileges granted to corporations by state legislatures; to the influence of these corporations on the executive department of the government; to the absolute control of the treasury and the finances enjoyed by corporations and Wall street brokers, with the manner of doing business in Wall street; to the influence of corporations in the selection of judges of the supreme court, with the decisions following the reconstruction of that court; to the banking and financial policy of the government, and its bad results; to the tariff policy and its effect upon the agricultural and producing classes; to the patent system and its abuses; and finally to the fact demonstrated, that unless the many abuses that have obtained in the land can be corrected, the people will be justified in calling into action their inherent rights for regaining those privileges refused to them, but conferred upon the corporations, rings, and combinations which have obtained such great power in the government. We do nót claim that our work is free from errors. We have sought to state the facts correctly. If they are inaccurate, the errors are unintentional. It was not with the wish or intention of doing injustice to any man, class of men, corporations, or officers of the government, that we undertook this work; but with the firm belief and strong conviction that the liberties of the people were being taken from them, while a gigantic oligarchy was obtaining control of the government. We believe the remedy is yet with the people; but to save themselves prompt, speedy, and united action is imperative. We have watched with increasing interest the growing power of corporations, for years, hoping that the time would come when the people would awake to the necessity of asserting their latent powers for the restoration of their rights. The civil war and other great political questions have engaged the public attention, while selfish and ambitious men have combined and consolidated their wealth and corporate power for the purpose of controlling the government and commerce of the country. Their success has been such as to alarm the agricultural, the producing, and laboring classes. The indications now are that active and aggressive war will be waged against these oppressors of the people until they are shorn of their great power and the rights of the people are restored. Desiring to aid in this great reform, we have deemed the present a favorable time to present this work to the public. While the combination the people are now combatting is powerful—possessing a dangerous influence over the legislative and judicial branches of the government, well organized and vigorous, controlling the finances of the country and holding our commerce in its grasp—strong in wealth, and in the extent of its organization —notwithstanding these fearful facts, that old republican truth still obtains, that "the people are the source of all power." That power is now being aroused. The watchword now heard, is "Equal and exact justice to all." That potent, though silent weapon, the ballot, is a sure correction of all the abuses when intelligently used. The signs of the times are hopeful from the fact that, for the first time in many years, the people, especially the agricultural, producing, and laboring classes are taking the lead. They are reading, thinking and acting independently of old political and partisan leaders; they are exercising their rights as freemen. They have declared that "old things shall be done away, and all things shall become new;" that the government shall be taken out of the old political grooves in which it has been running; that it shall assume new life, with the rights of the people fully recognized. That when the rights of the people and of free government on the one hand, and the privileges claimed by the combined corporate interests of the country on the other, are at issue, these rights shall not be made to yield to old precedents originating in monarchial and despotic governments, in order that the privileges claimed by corporations may be upheld.

The organization of the Patrons of Husbandry forms a nucleus around which all reformers can rally. The reforms they seek will effect the liberation of the whole people from the oppressions under which they now suffer. Our aim is to aid in this work. We feel assured that there is an irreconcilable conflict between the monopolies and the people; that the powers and privileges assured to corporations are at war with republican institutions, and hostile to the constitution of our country. To effect reforms will require time. Some relief can be speedily obtained, but to accomplish thorough reform, and bring the administration of the government under the control of the people, will require that the offices shall be filled by men whose education and pursuits have been such as to place them in full sysmpathy with the people—men who will not spend their time as legislators and judges in discussing federal prerogatives, and classing our republican government with old time despotisms. The doctrine that corporations are subject to legislative control must be fully established as the fixed and settled policy of our government. When this point is reached, the farmer will not be obliged to divide his crops with railroad companies—and so with all other abuses. The power to correct all abuses must remain with the people. The prosperity of the people, the perpetuity of our form of government, the rights of the states and the public can only be preserved by guarding against all encroachments made upon free institutions, whether they originate in congress or out of it—whether they are enunciated from the bench of the supreme court, or from the stump. In these days when the tendency is to a strong centralized government—when a few men control the finance of the country—when the whole commerce of the country is controlled by Wall street gamblers—when special grants and privileges are bestowed upon companies and indi viduals, and when the property of each individual is insecure and liable to be assessed for the building of railroads—at this time, there came from Justice Bradley of the supreme court of the United States, these ominous words: "It is absolutely essential to the independent national existence that *government* should have a firm hold on the two great sovereign instruments of the *sword* and the *purse*." This announcement is made from the bench of the supreme court of the United States, on the fifteenth day of January, 1872. The government must have a firm hold on the purse and sword. This is the declaration of the court made but a few months before it decided that railroad corporations were public, and that the property of private third parties of the whole people could be taxed to build them. We claim that under our form of government the people are the power to retain the control of the purse and sword; that to place them together in the hands of those persons who fill, for the time being, the government offices, is to take from the governing power its rights. But when the people's purse and the government finances are subject to the action of corporations and rings, the special favorites of the courts, the people are imperatively called upon to arise and assert their rights as freemen—to throw off this oppressive yoke—to stamp with the seal of condemnation, not only the enunciation of such anti-republican sentiment, but the judge who uttered it. The real question at issue between the people and monopolies fostered and protected by government is, whether the people shall rule, or remain the servants and vassals of the monopolists. The final determination of this question will decide whether we are to live under the republic planned and formed for us by our revolutionary ancestors, or are to submit to the oligarchy shaped for us by recent enactments and decisions in favor of a class of men, who, for the sake of private gain, are overturning and destroying our free institutions. The issue is fairly presented; the lines distinctly drawn. The corporate hosts are marshaling their forces; the people, under the lead of the tillers of the soil, are preparing for battle.

When the Union was threatened with disruption, and the armies were about to engage in conflict, they armed themselves with the death-dealing sword and gun. Hundreds of thousands of brave and patriotic men proved their devotion to their country by the sacrifice of their lives for its preservation. No such sacrifices are now demanded. In a legal, constitutional manner, these corporations, rings, and combinations, can be routed, "horse, foot, and dragoons;" their friends "at court" can be displaced; their paid agents and attorneys can be driven from the halls of congress and the state legislatures; their judges can be invited to vacate their seats that others, elected by the votes of the people, may fill them; and the standard of "equal rights" can be again reared aloft without the use of bullets or the shedding of blood.

But after all these errors and abuses shall have been corrected, other questions will arise. The farmer of the west and south must have cheap transportation to the seaboard. It may be demonstrated that our present system of building railroads will not answer the purpose because of the great expense of constructing and operating them, and that other means must be adopted. Under the constitution, the general government has exclusive maritime jurisdiction, and can make canals and slack-water navigation. History demonstrates that water transportation is always cheapest. The government should provide for water transportation from the great agricultural centers to the seaboard.

The general government possessing, under the consitution, the exclusive jurisdiction over all the navigable waters of the United States; having full authority to improve these national highways by deepening and widening their channels; removing obstructions; building locks, dams, and lighthouses, and establishing harbors; it has also the right—by making new channels, canals, and outlets for rivers and lakes—to connect inland navigable waters with the seaboard, and thus make these great national channels available for commercial purposes. By this means, the people would be freed from the oppressions and extortions of railroad companies, which at present have the undisputed and absolute control of the commerce of the country.

It may be asked upon what principle we advocate the making of canals, and the provision of slack-water navigation, and at the same time oppose the construction or control of railroads by the general government. The answer is obvious. The title to the navigable waters of the country cannot pass to or vest in private companies or individuals. The government itself has not the authority to divest the interest and rights of the public in and to the waters of the United States; they must remain free and open to use by any and all the people of the country. The general government has jurisdiction over them, not for taking their use from the whole people, and conferring the right to navigate them upon certain classes or corporations, but for the purpose of keeping them free for the uses of navigation as well as to remove and prevent obstructions. Navigable waters being natural public highways, and the constitution wisely placing their absolute control in the hands of the general government, the duty of making them available for public use is a necessary adjunct to the power and jurisdiction already conferred. The compact, or contract, entered into between the states, being for the benefit of all the people of all the states, and the control of these navigable streams having been surrendered by the states to the general government, it follows that the creation of slack-water navigation and the making of canals by the national government is the legitimate exercise of a constitutional power. And when the power thus vested shall have been exercised, and continuous channels or water highways shall have been opened from the great agricultural districts of the south and west to the east, the monopoly now enjoyed by the railroads will cease. Corn, shipped from Iowa to Boston, instead of allowing the owner a margin of thirteen cents per bushel over the cost of transportation will net him from forty to fifty cents per bushel.

The advantage of these water highways cannot be over-estimated. They are not subject to the control of any company, class, or combination of men, but are open to all. The right to place boats and vessels upon them, and to navigate them, is as unrestricted as the right to use the public roads of the country. Competition would be unlimited, and cheap transportation the result. At the present time, with limited water communication during the navigable season, when the water routes come in competition with railroads, freights are carried over railroads for less than one-half the rates charged when winter has closed the competition.

The question of the cost of furnishing water communication to the seaboard markets is of but little moment when we remember the princely donations made by the government to railroad companies. Less would be required to relieve the whole people from the oppression of railroad companies than has been bestowed upon these monopolies and used by them to oppress and rob the producing portions of the country. The sums demanded to furnish water communications would be expended for the benefit of the whole people, and if they were taxed for the means to prosecute the work, it would be for their own direct interest, and not for the purpose of enriching private corporations.

It may be objected that water transportation would not be practicable in all parts of the country at all seasons. True;

but it could be used to move most of the grain from the west to the east during the navigable season, and it would have the effect to destroy the monopoly now impoverishing the farmers of the west, and which entails upon the east a cost of living far out of proportion to the real necessities of the case. The reduced price of transportation would allow a fair profit to the producer on less prices than now obtain in the east. To illustrate: Take the instance of five car loads of corn recently shipped from Iowa to New York. It was shipped to Chicago over the Northwestern railroad; thence to New York over the North Shore and Erie lines, and there sold for fifty-six and a half cents per bushel. The charges for transportation amounted to forty-eight and a half cents per bushel. The shipper got *eight cents per bushel for his corn!* Another instance: A lot of corn was bought in Iowa for thirteen cents per bushel, and sold in Springfield, Massachusetts, for sixty-nine cents. The charges for transportation, etc., were fifty-five cents per bushel. The man who purchased in Iowa for thirteen cents had left *one cent per bushel* over cost, all but fourteen of the sixty-nine cents being absorbed by the railroad companies. If we take as authority the published statements of railroad companies, they could have made a fair profit on these shipments at ten or twelve cents per bushel. If only a fair rate had been charged, the farmer in Iowa could have sold his corn for thirty, instead of thirteen cents, the consumer in the east could have bought for less, and the shipper would have made a reasonable profit on his investment. The same state of facts apply to other products. Indeed the rule is to charge higher rates for wheat, because it will bear a greater pressure. If we had water communication from the west to the east, this wholesale extortion would cease. Competition would compel railroad companies to reduce their rates to an honest standard.

It is believed by many that if the general government were to take the control of the railroads, the evils of which we have been treating would be corrected. We have already expressed our views upon this proposition. If it were practicable, still it would not afford relief. No matter who owns the roads —

whether government or private corporations—relief cannot be fully afforded without greatly increased capacity; and were that capacity ample for the carrying trade of the whole country, the main *desideratum*—cheap transportation—would still be wanting. The cost of the roads—the expense of operating them — the rapid wear, requiring great outlay for repairs — their perishable character, and the necessity of their being under the exclusive care and control of private parties, and not open for the free use of all who might choose to engage in the business of common carriers, negative the idea that transportation by rail can ever be as cheap as by water.

With proper facilities for commerce throughout the whole country, and such as will enable the great agricultural centers to ship at such rates as to allow their products to reach the seaboard without their value being destroyed or seriously impaired by charges for transportation, our producers, who are now scarcely able to make current expenses, would, with the markets of the east and of the world thrown open to them, receive a fair return for their investments and constant toil. We cannot expect to reach these desirable ends without water transportation. When the people become fully alive to the importance of this great measure its accomplishment will not be long delayed.

This kind of improvement the general government can lawfully make, and an expenditure of a small part of the wealth bestowed upon private railroad corporations would open up water channels, affording cheap transportation from the west to the east and south. Grain and meats could then be shipped to the seaboard at such rates at would warrant their transportation to foreign markets, which, with the abolition of protective duties, would furnish the farmer a good sale for his products, and an opportunity of purchasing his supplies free from the bounty he now pays the eastern manufacturer. With such means for shipping the farm products of the west and south, with protective tariffs abolished, and the financial policy of the nation so changed as to furnish to the people the same kind of money used by the government, with "specie payment" resumed, and the large margin between coin and paper removed, prosperity would again attend farming pursuits, and contentment would fill the land.

With all the advantages Providence has given us in this great country, with the pure and simple republic bequeathed to us by the heroes and statesmen of Seventy-Six, we ought to be a prosperous and happy people. But, with the blighting curse of oppressive monopolies fastened upon us, upheld by bought legislation and strengthened by the decisions of judges and courts, who, from education, occupation, and sympathy with the oppressors of the people, or from baser motives, have become the special guardians of the monopolists, the laboring and producing classes find it difficult to live, and in many instances are being reduced to absolute want. The farmer has abundant harvests, but their value is absorbed in oppressive charges for transportation to market, and he is bound down with onerous and unequal taxes until his labor has ceased to be remunerative. While this is true of most industrial pursuits, the manufacturer, protected by the government, the moneyed men in Wall street, who operate in gold and stocks, and the railroad men who are protected by the decisions of the courts of the country, all amass princely fortunes—the result of special privileges bestowed upon them. As a necessary consequence the interests of the country are being divided. A moneyed "nobility" are arrayed against the laboring and producing classes. Special privileges, at war with republican institutions, are granted them; their wealth is virtually exempted from taxation, and they are fast becoming the governing power, while those who produce the wealth of the country are compelled to spend their strength and devote their lives to the business of adding to the wealth of their oppressors. It may be asked why this state of things exists. There are two reasons for it. First, the indifference manifested by the people to the affairs of the government; their willingness to allow others to direct and control the affairs of the nation, while they devote their time to their own personal interests, seemingly forgetful that they have any interest in national affairs, or in the administration of their own state government, and permitting those who now oppress them to shape legislation, and to obtain those grants and privileges which have now become the means of their oppression. The second cause is the disposition of those in power to override and disregard constitutional restrictions. During the civil war the constitution possessed no restrictive force. The law of necessity governed; the personal will of those in office was the supreme law. Acts of congress were passed with direct reference to a state of war, and decisions of courts were controlled by the same causes. With the return of peace these laws remained unrepealed; the decisions of courts remained unreversed; constitutional restrictions were deemed irksome and of little moment. Laws remained on our statute book which contravened the plain provisions of the constitution, and the decisions of courts have continued in the same channel, until the great charter of our civil liberty has become obsolete, and the personal opinions of courts, like the edicts of a monarch, have become the supreme law. Under this species of legislation, and this class of decisions, these great oppressions of the country have grown up until their power is superior to that of all other interests, and not unfrequently defies the law. The first great reform to be effected is to reëstablish the supremacy of the constitution, and to demand of courts and legislators a strict observance of its provisions. When this is effected, the rights of the states and the people will be protected. The courts of the United States, and all other departments of the government, must remember that in our republican system the federal government is limited and restricted to the exercise of such powers as are expressly delegated to it, and that all attempts to confer special charters and privileges upon private companies are usurpations. They must remember that we have no government with kingly prerogatives; that in a republic the people retain control of the *purse* and *sword*, and that the liberties of the people, the equality of all before the law, as well of the perpetuation of republican institutions, are in the care and keeping of the sovereign people.

That there should be some means adopted to arrest this great and growing power of corporations is now forcibly demonstrated. Since writing the preceding pages, still another fatal stab has been given to the republic. Vanderbilt, the leader in the raid made by corporations upon the liberties of the people, and also an operator in Wall street gambling, has added to the other roads under his control the Lake Shore & Michigan Southern railway, and now controls the commerce of the west with the seaboard, and can fix the price of a barrel of flour, or bushel of wheat or corn, and from his decision there is no appeal. Extending these monopolies still further, Vanderbilt and his co-conspiritors are about to take control of all the telegraph lines in the country, and dictate to the whole people the price to be paid for dispatches. Thus these enemies of republican government are surely getting control of all the business and commerce of the country. The finances, the carrying trade, the produce market, the price and sale of manufactured articles, and the means of communication between the different portions of the country, are all passing into the hands of the enemies of the people. At the present time if any railroad company attempts to act independently and honestly, this combination of sharpers and swindlers make war upon it and force it to surrender, or drive it into bankruptcy.

No wonder that the people are becoming alarmed, and are preparing for the conflict. The attempt made to dissolve the Union was an open and bold one. The people met the issue and triumphed. The attempt made to divide the country aroused the national patriotism. The attempt of this great combination of monopolists to obtain absolute control of the government, the finances, and commerce of the country, presents more serious cause for alarm than did the attempt to dissolve the Union. Our institutions cease to be of any value when they are perverted to means of oppression. When men in high official positions trifle with the liberties of the people and encourage their oppressors, an indignant constituency should hurl them from power. If, knowing the wrongs that are committed against us, the encroachments being made on our liberties, the threatened and partially accomplished destruction of republican institutions, we silently acquiesce, we are not freemen, and we deserve to be held as the bond-servants of our oppressors for all time to come. But while the people are long-suffering and patient under adversity, there is a point beyond which their oppressors cannot venture without arousing them to action. That point is now reached; the fiat of the sovereign power in this land has gone forth; the voice of the people is heard from all portions of our common country demanding redress, and that the government shall be brought back to constitutional limits; that the power of their oppressors shall be destroyed; that their rights as freemen shall be restored to them; that the halls of legislation and the courts of justice shall be filled by men who do not legislate for bribes, and who administer justice without respect to persons or interests, and prize constitutional restrictions and the liberties of the people above the interests of corporations and rings formed to oppress them. If redress cannot be obtained at the ballot-box; if the influences which now control the government and business of the country cannot be overcome; if redress is denied in legislative halls and in the courts — then the people have the right, the "God-given right," to arise in their sovereign power and take what their servants have refused to give them. If reform cannot be obtained, or the wrongs of the people redressed in any other method, a resort should be had to *revolution* — peaceable, if possible, but such as will bring the country back to the days of its purity, and compel all to acknowledge the *sacred* binding force of the constitution.

In closing, we desire to remind the reader of the binding form of the constitution, which seems to be entirely disregarded by legislators and courts, in their efforts to strengthen the power that now curses the nation. Our ideas of the inviolable nature of constitutional provisions may be considered antiquated, and our belief that its provisions have been disregarded may be deemed mere fancy; yet we cannot shut our eyes to the fact that special favors have been granted to classes, by the legislation of states and the nation; that this kind of legislation has deprived the people of rights guaranteed by the constitution; nor are we ignorant of the fact that this special class legislation has received the sanction of the courts. If the binding force of the fundamental law is disregarded, the people are left without any legal means for recovery of their rights.

A government based upon a constitution is, and must be unchangeable, save by alteration of, or amendment to *its* constitution. Any attempt to arrest its meaning or destroy its force by legislation or by judicial decision, because it may be deemed expedient to do so, or because an emergency may demand it, is incipient revolution, persisted in, it will eventually destroy constitutional government and supply in its stead, one that has no basis, other than the will of those in power. We have attempted to show that in the legislation of congress, as well as in that of some of the states, in favor of monopolies that now oppress the country, and also by the decisions of courts sustaining such legislation, we, as a nation had arrived at the point where the personal views of those in power were the sole rule of action, and that in fact the binding force of the fundamental law had ceased to have any control over them. The continuance of our republic as well as the prosperity and security of the people, demands a return to constitutional government.

We say that the legislative power conferred upon congress is limited. Article one, section one, of the constitution, says: "All the legislative powers herein granted shall be vested in a congress of the United States, which shall consist of a senate and house of representatives." No general power of legislation is vested in congress. Its legislation is restricted.

No where in the powers granted to congress can be found the power to charter railroads or other private corporations, nor can it be implied from any power that is vested in congress, nor in the granting of such charters necessary to the execution of any granted power. As a nation we have long admitted that congress had the power to enact laws for the protection of manufacturers known as "protective tariff acts," yet it may well be questioned whether such a power is vested in it. No one will doubt its power to levy and collect tariff duties for revenue purposes, but the question of a tariff for protection is another thing, and the right to provide by law for a tariff for protection alone cannot be found in any part of the constitution. We refer to this for the purpose of showing how ready we are to accept as constitutional any and all acts of congress. For the purpose of making our point let us see what is the power conferred upon congress. Article one, section eight, "Congress shall have power to lay and collect taxes, duties, imports and excises to pay the *debt* and *provide* for the *common defence* and *general welfare* of the United States; but all duties, ~~imports~~ and excises shall be uniform throughout the United States." If a power to provide a tariff by statute for protection is given to congress, it is contained in the paragraph above quoted. Revenue can only be collected for governmental purposes under this provision. The fact that statutes have been passed for the protection of certain classes of citizens by discriminating in their favor; that without any provisions of the constitution conferring the power to pass such statutes upon congress and that the people have not questioned their constitutionality demonstrates the ease with which constitutional provisions can be disregarded and the rights of the people taken from them. Again the constitution vests in congress authority to regulate commerce with foreign nations and among the several states, and also "To establish post offices and post roads." If any power is conferred upon congress to charter private corporations or joint stock companies, other than banking and financial institutions, such power is derived from the provisions last quoted. Let us not forget that the congress of the nation is not clothed with general powers like the legislature of a state, but that its powers are special and specified in the constitution, and we will better understand the extent of its usurpations of power in chartering and endowing private corporations with the people's lands and money. It does not require a vast amount of legal knowledge to decide that congress in granting charters to private corporations organized for pecuniary profit has disregarded both the letter and spirit of the constitution. That it has done when the plea of necessity could not be urged in favor of the act; when nothing but a desire to aid private parties in their efforts to enrich themselves by appropriations of the public moneys and land could have influenced its action. Congress has the power "To coin money, regulate the value thereof and of foreign coin and to fix the standard of weights and measures:" "To borrow money on the credit of the United States." These are the only provisions of the constitution touching upon the question of *money* and indebtedness of the United States.

If the constitution confers upon congress the power to make anything but *coin* "money or legal tender," that power is derived from the above quoted provisions. Can such a power be fairly deduced from these provisions? No act of congress has tended so greatly to centralize the wealth of the country and place all the money of the nation in the hands of the few as the act known as the legal tender act. Yet the power to pass it cannot be derived from any provisions of the constitution without *perverting* and *destroying* its meaning. The constitution vests in congress the power to coin money, and congress assumed the power to pass an act declaring that *past due, dishonored treasury notes* shall be accepted as coin in payment of debts. It has declared that an irredeemable currency, an unmitigated cheating device threatening the gravest injury to all persons, excepting the favored class of subsidied private corporations, stock jobbers and speculators shall be the best money the people shall be permitted to own or use, and pretend that this species of legislation is authorized by the constitution. We have quoted the provisions of the constitution, controlling legislation on some of the subjects we have been discussing for the purpose of showing how entirely this great charter of our liberty is disregarded by our law-makers when some favorite object is to be achieved. On the question of protective tariff, the creation of private corporations and the legal tender act, congress seems to have lost sight of the country at large and in aid of the "favored few" trampled upon the fundamental law, and reduced the people to a state of vassalage to a class of oppressors, whose creation dates from the destruction of constitutional restrictions. Is it strange that a people taxed oppressively to supply money to parties receiving special favors from the general government;

with from one-half to three-fourths of the proceeds of their daily toil taken from them to enrich private corporations, lordly manufacturers and rings of stock jobbers and Wall street gamblers, should be alarmed at the encroachments that are being made upon their liberties? The perpetuity of our government, as well as the preservation of the rights of the people, demand that all the departments of the national administration should abstain from further assumptions of powers, not granted to them.

Not all the oppressions and abuses practiced by railroad corporations, and other parties receiving special favors from congress, or the immense influence they now wield in the affairs of the nation, are fraught with consequences as fatal to the rights of the people as the seeming disregard of constitutional guarantees and restrictions by the congress of the United States.

The constitution is being changed and its provisions amended —not in the manner provided, but by congressional usurpation. A dangerous precedent has been established. The letter and spirit of the great charter of our liberty have been obliterated. A privileged class, with extraordinary powers, has been placed over the people, by acts of congress at war with republican principles, and in violation of the plain letter of the fundamental law of the land. Under the fostering care of a congress presumed to act for the whole people, and for the protection of their interest, giant corporations have been created which now own and control more wealth and money than all the other interests of the people combined. Their influence in the affairs of the nation, and on the commerce of the country is more powerful than that of all the departments of the government, backed by the whole American people.

We do not mean to say that these corporations actually own more than one-half of the wealth of the nation, but that their power is so great that they fix the value upon the property or wealth of more than one-half of the whole country, and that because of the special favors shown them they now control the affairs of the nation. Not only so, but they defy the power of the general government. Suits are being commenced against the Credit Mobilier company by the general government. Does any one familiar with the matter believe it can be prosecuted to a successful termination? The unrestricted powers and privileges conferred upon the Pacific Rail Road companies, and their close connection with the Credit Mobilier company, will enable them to defy and defeat the government. All the great powers and privileges conferred upon the private corporations of the country by congress were conferred in violation of the great charter of our liberty, and we now are compelled to witness the spectacle of the creature defying the power of its creator; oppressing the people; controlling the commerce of the country, and managing its finances because congress ventured upon the dangerous experiment of giving to the constitution an interpretation not warranted by its letter and spirit. By this kind of legislation the basis of our political system has been destroyed. The people respect and observe the charter of their liberties, and no innovation has been made upon it in their interest or for their benefit. It is noticeable that all the encroachments made upon it have been in the interest of the corporations, companies, and classes whose interests are at war with those of the people. That not only acts of congress but decisions of the courts sustaining those acts have all been in favor of the classes, corporations, and rings of stock-jobbers and Wall street gamblers, who are united in making war upon the people and the government. We have not heeded the admonitions of Washington in his farewell address, and the disastrous consequences of our reckless course predicted by him are now upon us. In his farewell address, Washington said: "The basis of our political system is the right of the people to make and alter their constitutions of government, but the constitution which at any time exists, till changed by an explicit and authentic act of the whole people, is sacredly obligatory upon all. The very idea of the power and the right of the people to establish government pre-supposes the duty of every individual to obey the established government." He further says: "Towards the preservation of your government, and the permanency of your present happy state, it is requisite that you steadily discountenance irregular opposition to its acknowledged authority, but also that you resist with care the *spirit of innovation upon its principles, however specious the pretext.*" Further on, in the same address, he says: "It is important likewise that the habit of thinking in a free country should inspire caution in those intrusted with its administration to confine themselves within their respective constitutional spheres, avoiding in the exercise of one department to encroach upon another. The spirit of encroachment tends to consolidate all the departments in one, and thus to create, whatever the form of government, a real despotism."

We have shown, in treating of courts, that they have assumed the province of the legislative department of government, and have, by judicial legislation, become absolute rulers of the whole country. The supreme court has disregarded the admonition of Washington, and, by assumption of power, it is converting our republic into a despotism. But the evil most to be dreaded, and against which the immortal Washington warned us, has overtaken us, and we now realize its disastrous consequences — that is, constitutional change by usurpation. He warns us of this danger in the following language: "If, in the opinion of the people, the distribution or modification of the constitutional powers be, in any particular, wrong, let it be corrected by an amendment in the way the constitution designates. *But let there be no change by usurpation*, for though this in one instance may be the instrument of good, it is the *customary weapon by which governments are destroyed.* The precedent must always greatly overbalance, in permanent evil, any partial or transient benefit which the use can at any time yield."

It will be recollected that the courts of the United States are not courts of general jurisdiction, but that their jurisdiction is defined and limited by the constitution. Of course, within the prescribed limits their jurisdiction is superior. We have shown the encroachments made by congress and the supreme court upon the fundamental law, and have referred to some of the influences that have promoted those encroachments. Their effect is seen and known by all. In no way can the rights of the people and of the government in its purity be preserved and perpetuated save by the restoration and preservation of the safeguards contained in the constitution. We may effect a thorough charge of the persons who fill the executive, legislative, and judicial departments of the government; we may fill all the offices in the whole nation with men pledged to reform; we may secure legislative and congressional enactments in favor of, and may succeed in effecting temporary reform; the people may be relieved from present oppressions and extortions; statutes may be passed designed to prevent future abuses; but unless we awake to the necessity of a full and complete restoration of all the constitutional guaranties and restrictions, which, by legislative and judiciary usurpations, have been overridden, and for the time being destroyed, no lasting or permanent reform can be effected.

We witness the vast and constantly increasing power of railroad corporations; we see them strengthening and combining their forces; we witness the fact that a few master spirits, like generals-in-chief, command, manage, and direct the whole railroad force of the country; we hear these great generals of this force issue their edicts to the farming and producing industries of the country, commanding them to increase their contributions to their task-masters, and we know that as the matters are now shaped, the people must submit. We know that these same generals of the corporate forces of the country are in league with Wall street gamblers and speculators for the purpose of controlling the finances of the country. We know that utter and financial ruin is stayed by the secretary of the treasury, who is compelled to fight the bulls in Wall street. We see the effect of the legal tender decisions in the large exportations of gold to Europe, and its absence from our midst. We know that this same combination, under the lead of the same commanders, have almost the entire control of the banks at the great commercial centres. We know that these enemies of the people, by fraud, corruption, and deceit, have obtained untold amounts of money and land, enough to make vast empires, from the people. We all feel assured that if the truth has been told, that this same corrupt body of men have bought legislative grants, and in some instances have bought the decisions of courts. This same corporate power has been practically exempt from taxes, while the people have been compelled to make larger contributions to supply the deficit. We see these corporations defying the government and the people, overriding laws, and refusing to obey the orders of courts. We know that they have taxed the people in charges for transportation until labor ceases to be remunerative, while the proceeds of the laborer's toil go to fill the coffers of Wall street speculators. We know that honesty and morality have departed from these men; that being possessed of vast wealth and unlimited credit to-day, they venture it all in a simple gambling operation, and on to-morrow they are bankrupt, and their creditors are ruined. We see this struggling, gambling, battling mass of men in Wall street, striving for the supremacy in financial circles, alternating from vast wealth to abject poverty, intent on sudden riches, while the people of the whole country are subsidized to supply immoral, polluted Wall street gamblers with the money with which to ply their vocation. This giant of oppression and corruption has developed itself within the last few years. It is anti-republican, and threatens the existence of the government. Its vise-like grasp has siezed the vitals of the nation. It had its origin in unconstitutional legislation; it has been supported from the same fountain. All attempts at reformation will be of no avail unless we strike at the fountain head. The watchword of all who are battling for their rights should be, "The repeal of all unconstitutional acts of congress, and a strict interpretation of the constitution by the courts." With constitutional liberty restored to the people, the abuses practised by corporations reformed, their assumed power taken from them, and all their rights and privileges defined and preserved, prosperity will again attend us, and our country will again own a happy and contented people.

Having an abiding confidence that the reform being inaugurated by the farmers of the country will advance to a triumphant issue, we present this volume to the public as a humble but honest champion of the cause, acknowledging its imperfections, expecting criticisms and condemnations from the monopolists and their dependents, but asking a careful perusal and earnest consideration of the doctrine advocated.

APPENDIX.

APPENDIX.

CHAPTER I.

AS our position on the "Legal Tender" decisions and their effect upon the finances and commerce of the country have been controverted by some of the *legal men* to whom we have shown our manuscript, at the risk of wearying the reader, we quote the dissenting opinions of the late Chief Justice Chase and his associates, on the points at issue in those cases, feeling assured that these opinions fully sustain us. If our views are correct as to the effect of these decisions upon the best interests of the country, and their tendency to increase the power of the combinations that now have such control over the different departments of the government, as well as the financial and commercial interests of the country, it follows that no real relief from the oppressions under which the people are suffering can be obtained until the legal tender statutes are repealed and the latest decisions of the supreme court as to their constitutionality and scope are reversed.

We have claimed that those decisions were in conflict with the provisions of the constitution. Our position is supported by the opinions quoted. We have said that the supreme court of the United States was reorganized in the interests of railroad corporations and other monopolies, before the legal tender questions were re-argued and reversed. The opinions quoted sustain us in this particular. But we desire the reader to examine these opinions and determine for himself.

CHAPTER II.

DISSENTING OPINION OF CHIEF JUSTICE CHASE.

WE dissent from the argument and conclusion in the opinion just announced.

The rule by which the constitutionality of an act of congress passed in the alleged exercise of an implied power is to be tried, is no longer, in this court, open to question. It was laid down in the case of *McCulloch* v. *Maryland*, by Chief Justice Marshall, in these words: "Let the end be legitimate, let it be within the scope of the constitution, and all means which are appropriate, which are plainly adapted to that end, which are not prohibited, but consistent with the letter and spirit of the constitution, are constitutional."

And it is the plain duty of the court to pronounce acts of congress not made in the exercise of an express power, nor coming within the reasonable scope of this rule, if made in virtue of an implied power, unwarranted by the constitution. Acts of congress not made in pursuance of the constitution are not laws.

Neither of these propositions was questioned in the case of *Hepburn* v. *Griswold*. The judges who dissented in that case maintained that the clause in the act of February 25th, 1862, making the United States notes a legal tender in payment of debts, was an appropriate, plainly adapted means to a constitutional end, not prohibited, but consistent with the letter and spirit of the constitution. The majority of the court as then constituted, five judges out of eight, felt "obliged to conclude that an act making mere promises to pay dollars a legal tender in payments of debts previously contracted is not a means appropriate, plainly adapted, really calculated to carry into effect any express power vested in congress, is inconsistent with the spirit of the constitution, and is prohibited by the constitution."

In the case of *The United States* v. *De Witt*, we held unanimously that a provision of the internal revenue law prohibiting the sale of certain illuminating oil in the states was unconstitutional, though it might increase the production and sale of other oils, and consequently the revenue derived from them, because this consequence was too remote and uncertain to warrant the court in saying that the prohibition was an appropriate and plainly adapted means for carrying into execution the power to levy and collect taxes.

We agree, then, that the question whether a law is a necessary and proper means to execution of an express power within the meaning of these words, as defined by the rule—that is to say, a means appropriate, plainly adapted, not prohibited, but consistent with the letter and spirit of the constitution — is a judicial question. Congress may not adopt any means for the execution of an express power that congress may see fit to adopt. It must be a necessary and proper means within the fair meaning of the rule. If not such it cannot be employed consistently with the constitution. Whether the means actually employed in a given case are such or not the court must decide. The court must judge of the fact — congress of the degree of necessity.

A majority of the court, five to four, in the opinion which has just been read, reverses the judgment rendered by the former majority of five to three, in pursuance of an opinion formed after repeated arguments, at successive terms, and careful consideration, and declares the legal tender clause to be constitutional; that is to say, that an act of congress making promises to pay dollars legal tender as coined dollars in payment of preëxisting debts is a means appropriate and plainly adapted to the exercise of powers expressly granted by the constitution, and not prohibited itself by the constitution, but consistent with its letter and spirit. And this reversal, unprecedented in the history of the court, has been produced by no change in the opinions of those who concurred in the former judgment. One closed an honorable judicial career by resignation after the case had been decided, after the opinion had been read and agreed to in conference, and after the day when it would have been delivered in court, had not the delivery been postponed for a week, to give time for the preparation of the dissenting opinion. The court was then full, but the vacancy caused by the resignation of Mr. Justice Grier having been subsequently filled, and an additional justice having been appointed under the act increasing the number of judges to nine, which took effect on the first Monday of December, 1869, the then majority find themselves in a minority of the court, as now constituted, upon the question.

Their convictions, however, remain unchanged. We adhere to the opinion pronounced in *Hepburn* v. *Griswold*. Reflection has only wrought a firmer belief in the soundness of the constitutional doctrines maintained, and in the importance of them to the country.

We agree that much of what was said in the dissenting opinion in that case, which has become the opinion of a majority of the court as now constituted, was correctly said. We fully agree in all that was quoted from Chief Justice Marshall. We had indeed accepted, without reserve, the definition of implied powers in which that great judge summed up his argument, of which the language quoted formed a part. But if it was intended to ascribe to us "the doctrine than when an act of congress is brought to the test of this clause of the constitution," namely, the clause granting the power of ancillary legislation, "its necessity must be absolute, and its adaptation to the conceded purpose unquestionable," we must be permitted not only to disclaim it, but to say that there is nothing in the opinion of the then majority which approaches the assertion of any such doctrine. We did indeed venture to cite, with approval, the language of Judge Story in his great work on the constitution, that the words necessary and proper were intended to have "a sense at once admonitory and directory," and to require that the means used in the execution of an express power "should be *bona fide*, appropriate to the end," and also ventured to say that the tenth amendment, reserving to the states or the people all power not delegated to the United

States by the constitution, nor prohibited by it to the states, "was intended to have a like admonitory and directory sense," and to restrain the limited government established by the constitution from the exercise of powers not clearly delegated or derived by just inference from powers so delegated. In thus quoting Judge Story, and in this expression of our own opinion, we certainly did not suppose it possible that we could be understood as asserting that the clause in question "was designed as a restriction upon the ancillary power incidental to every grant of power in express terms." It was this proposition which "was stated and refuted" in *McCulloch* v. *Maryland*. That refutation touches nothing said by us. We assert only that the words of the constitution as much as admonish congress that implied powers are not to be rashly or lightly assumed, and that they are not to be exercised at all unless, in the words of Judge Story, they are "*bona fide* appropriate to the end," or, in the words of Chief Justice Marshall, "appropriate, plainly adapted" to a constitutional and legitimate end, and "not prohibited, but consistent with the letter and spirit of the constitution."

There appears, therefore, to have been no real difference of opinion in the court as to the rule by which the existence of an implied power is to be tested, when *Hepburn* v. *Griswold* was decided, though the then minority seemed to have supposed there was. The difference had reference to the application of the rule rather than to the rule itself.

The then minority admitted that in the powers relating to coinage, standing alone, there is not "a sufficient warrant for the exercise of the power" to make notes a legal tender, but thought them "not without decided weight, when we come to consider the question of the existence of this power as one necessary and proper for carrying into execution other admitted powers of the government." This weight they found in the fact that an "express power over the lawful money of the country was confided to congress and forbidden to the states." It seemed to them not an "unreasonable inference" that, in a certain contingency, "making the securities of the government perform the office of money in the payment of debts would be in harmony with the power expressly granted to coin money." We perceive no connection between the express power to coin money and the inference that the government may, in any contingency, make its securities perform the functions of coined money, as a legal tender in payment of debts. We have supposed that the power to exclude from circulation notes not authorized by the national government might, perhaps, be deduced from the power to regulate the value of coin; but that the power of the government to emit bills of credit was an exercise of the power to borrow money, and that its power over the currency was incidental to that power and to the power to regulate commerce. This was the doctrine of the *Veazie Bank* v. *Fenno*, although not fully elaborated in that case. The question whether the quality of legal tender can be imparted to these bills depends upon distinct considerations.

Was, then, the power to make these notes of the government—these bills of credit—a legal tender in payments an appropriate, plainly adapted means to a legitimate and constitutional end? or, to state the question as the opinion of the then minority stated it, "Does there exist any power in congress, or in the government, by express grant, in execution of which this legal tender act was necessary and proper in the sense here defined and under the circumstances of its passage?"

The opinion of the then minority affirmed the power on the ground that it was a necessary and proper means, within the definition of the court, in the case of *McCulloch* v. *Maryland*, to carry on war, and that it was not prohibited by the spirit or letter of the constitution, though it was admitted to be a law impairing the obligation of contracts, and notwithstanding the objection that it deprived many persons of their property without compensation and without due process of law.

We shall not add much to what was said in the opinion of the then majority on these points.

The reference made in the opinion just read, as well as in the argument at the bar, to the opinion of the chief justice, when secretary of the treasury, seems to warrant, if it does not require some observations before proceeding further in the discussion.

It was his fortune at the time the legal tender clause was inserted in the bill to authorize the issue of United States notes and receive the sanction of congress, to be charged with the anxious and responsible duty of providing funds for the prosecution of the war. In no report made by him to congress was the expedient of making the notes of the United States a legal tender suggested. He urged the issue of notes payable on demand in coin or received as coin in payment of duties. When the state banks had suspended specie payments, he recommended the issue of United States notes receivable for all loans to the United States and all government dues except duties on imports. In this report of December, 1862, he said that "United States notes receivable for bonds bearing a secure specie interest are next best to notes convertible into coin," and after stating the financial measures which in his judgment were advisable, he added: "The secretary recommends, therefore, no mere paper money scheme, but on the contrary a series of measures looking to a safe and gradual return to gold and silver as the only permanent basis, standard, and measure of value recognized by the constitution." At the session of congress before this report was made, the bill containing the legal tender clause had become a law. He was extremely and avowedly averse to this clause, but was very solicitous for the passage of the bill to authorize the issue of United States notes then pending. He thought it indispensably necessary that the authority to issue these notes should be granted by congress. The passage of the bill was delayed, if not jeoparded, by the difference of opinion which prevailed on the question of making them a legal tender. It was under these circumstances that he expressed the opinion, when called upon by the committee of ways and means, that it was necessary; and he was not sorry to find it sustained by the decisions of respected courts, not unanimous indeed, nor without contrary decisions of state courts equally respectable. Examination and reflection under more propitious circumstances have satisfied him that this opinion was erroneous, and he does not hesitate to declare it. He would do so just as unhesitatingly if his favor to the legal tender clause had been at that time decided, and his opinion as to the constitutionality of the measure clear.

Was the making of the notes a legal tender necessary to the carrying on the war? In other words, was it necessary to the execution of the power to borrow money? It is not the question whether the issue of notes was necessary, nor whether any of the financial measures of the government were necessary. The issuing of the circulation commonly known as greenbacks was necessary, and was constitutional. They were necessary to the payment of the army and the navy and to all the purposes for which the government uses money. The banks had suspended specie payment, and the government was reduced to the alternative of using their paper or issuing its own.

Now it is a common error, and in our judgment it was the error of the opinion of the minority in *Hepburn* v. *Griswold*, and is the error of the opinion just read, that considerations pertinent to the issue of United States notes have been urged in justification of making them a legal tender. The real question is, Was the making them a legal tender a necessary means to the execution of the power to borrow money? If the notes would circulate as well without as with this quality it is idle to urge the plea of such necessity. But the circulation of the notes was amply provided for by making them receivable for all national taxes, all dues to the government, and all loans. This was the provision relied upon for the purpose by the secretary when the bill was first prepared, and his reflections since have convinced him that it was sufficient. Nobody could pay a tax, or any debt, or buy a bond without using these notes. As the notes, not being immediately redeemable, would undoubtedly be cheaper than coin, they would be preferred by debtors and purchasers. They would thus, by the universal law of trade, pass into general circulation. As long as they were maintained by the government at or near par value of specie they would be accepted in payment of all dues, private as well as public. Debtors, as a general rule, would pay in nothing else unless compelled by suit, and creditors would accept them as long as they would lose less by acceptance than by suit. In new transactions, sellers would demand and purchasers would pay the premium for specie in the prices of commodities. The difference to them, in the currency, whether of coin or of paper, would be in the fluctuations to which the latter is subject. So long as notes should not sink so low as to induce creditors to refuse to receive them because they could not be said to be in any just sense payments of debts due, a provision for making them a legal tender would be without effect except to discredit the currency to which it was applied. The real support of note circulation not convertible on demand into coin, is receivability for debts due the government, including specie loans, and limitation of amount. If the amount is smaller than is needed for the transactions of the country, and the law allows the use in these transactions of but one description of currency, the demand for that description will prevent its depreciation. But history shows no instance of paper issues so restricted. An approximation in limitation is all that is possible, and this was attempted when the issues of United States notes were restricted to one hundred and fifty millions. But this limit was soon extended to four hundred and fifty millions, and even this was soon practically removed by the provision for the issue of notes by the national banking associations without any provision for corresponding reduction in the circulation of United States notes; and still further by the laws authorizing the issue of interest-bearing securities, made a tender for their amount, excluding interest.

The best support for note circulation is not limitation, but receivability, especially for loans bearing coin interest. This support was given until the fall of 1864, when a loan bearing increased currency interest, payable in three years and convertible into a loan bearing less coin interest, was substituted for the six per cent. and five per cent. loans bearing specie interest, for which the notes had been previously received.

It is plain that a currency so supported cannot depreciate more than the loans; in other words, below the general credit of the country. It will rise or fall with it. At the present moment, if the notes were received for five per cent. bonds, they would be at par. In other words, specie payments would be resumed.

Now, does making the notes a legal tender increase their value? It is said that it does, by giving them a new use. The best political economists say that it does not. When the government compels the people to receive its notes, it virtually declares that it does not expect them to be received without compulsion. It practically represents itself insolvent. This certainly does not improve the value of its notes. It is an element of depreciation. In addition, it creates a powerful interest in the debtor class and in the purchasers of bonds to depress to the lowest point the credit of the notes. The cheaper these become, the easier the payment of debts, and the more profitable the investments in bonds bearing coin interest.

On the other hand, the higher prices become, for everything the government needs to buy, and the greater the accumulation of public as well as private debt. It is true that such a state of things is acceptable to debtors, investors in bonds, and speculators. It is their opportunity of relief or wealth. And many are persuaded by their representations that the forced circulation is not only a necessity but a benefit. But the apparent benefit is a delusion and the necessity imaginary. In their legitimate use, the notes are hurt not helped by being made a legal tender. The legal tender quality is only valuable for the purposes of dishonesty. Every honest purpose is answered as well and better without it.

We have no hesitation, therefore, in declaring our conviction that the making of these notes a legal tender was not a necessary or proper means to the carrying on of war or to the exercise of any express power of the government.

But the absence of necessity is not our only, or our weightiest objection to this legal tender clause. We still think, notwithstanding the argument adduced to the contrary, that it does violate an express provision of the constitution, and the spirit, if not the letter, of the whole instrument. It cannot be maintained that legislation justly obnoxious to such objections can be maintained as the exercise of an implied power. There can be no implication against the constitution. Legislation to be warranted as the exercise of implied powers must not be "prohibited, but consistent with the letter and spirit of the constitution."

The fifth amendment provides that no person shall be deprived of life, liberty, or property without compensation or due process of law. The opinion of the former minority says that the argument against the validity of the legal tender clause, founded on this constitutional provision, is "too vague for their perception." It says that a "declaration of war would be thus unconstitutional," because it might depreciate the value of property; and "the abolition of tariff on sugar, or iron," because it might destroy the capital employed in those manufactures; and "the successive issues of government bonds," because they might make those already in private hands less valuable. But it seems to have escaped the attention of the then minority that to declare war, to levy and repeal taxes, and to borrow money, are all express powers, and that the then majority were opposing the prohibition of the constitution to the claim of an implied power. Besides, what resemblance is there between the effect of the exercise of these express powers and the operation of the legal tender clause upon preëxisting debts? The former are indirect effects of the exercise of undisputed powers. The latter acts directly upon the relations of debtor and creditor. It violates that fundamental principle of all just legislation that the legislature shall not take the property of A and give it to B. It says that B, who has purchased a farm of A for a certain price, may keep the farm without paying for it, if he will only tender certain notes which may bear some proportion to the price, or be even worthless. It seems to us that this is a manifest violation of this clause of the constitution.

We think also that it is inconsistent with the spirit of the constitution in that it impairs the obligation of contracts. In the opinion of the then minority it is frankly said: "Undoubtedly it is a law impairing the obligation of contracts made before its passage," but it is immediatly added: "While the constitution forbids the states to pass such laws, it does not forbid congress," and this opinion, as well as the opinion just read, refers to the express authority to establish a uniform system of bankruptcy as a proof that it was not the intention of the constitution to withhold that power. It is true that the constitution grants authority to pass a bankrupt law, but our inference is, that in this way only can congress discharge the obligation of contracts. It may provide for ascertaining the inability of debtors to perform their contracts, and, upon the surrender of all their property may provide for their discharge. But this is a very different thing from providing that they may satisfy contracts without payment, without pretence of inability, and without any judicial proceeding.

That congress possesses the general power to impair the obligation of contracts is a proposition which, to use the language of Chief Justice Marshall, "must find its vindication in a train of reasoning not often heard in courts of justice." "It may well be added," said the same great judge, "whether the nature of society and of government does not prescribe some limits to legislative power; and, if any be prescribed, where they are to be found, if the property of an individual, fairly and honestly acquired, can be seized without compensation? To the legislature all legislative power is granted, but the question whether the act of transferring the property of an individual to the public is in the nature of a legislative power is well worthy of serious reflection."

And if the property of an individual cannot be transferred to the public, how much less to another individual?

These remarks of Chief Justice Marshall were made in a case in which it became necessary to determine whether a certain act of the legislature of Georgia was within the constitutional prohibition against impairing the obligation of contracts. And they assert fundamental principles of society and government in which that prohibition had its origin. They apply with great force to the construction of the constitution of the United States. In like manner and spirit Mr. Justice Chase had previously declared that "an act of the legislature contrary to the great first principles of the social compact cannot be considered a rightful exercise of legislative authority." Among such acts he instances "a law that destroys or impairs the lawful private contracts of citizens." Can we be mistaken in saying that such a law is contrary to the spirit of a constitution ordained to establish justice? Can we be mistaken in thinking that if Marshall and Story were here to pronounce judgment in this case they would declare the legal tender clause now in question to be prohibited by and inconsistent with the letter and spirit of the constitution?

It is unnecessary to say that we reject wholly the doctrine, advanced for the first time, we believe in this court, by the present majority, that the legislature has any "powers under the constitution which grow out of the aggregate of powers conferred upon the government, or out of the sovereignty instituted by it." If this proposition be admitted, and it be also admitted that the legislature is the sole judge of the necessity for the exercise of such powers, the government becomes practically absolute and unlimited.

Our observations thus far have been directed to the question of the constitutionality of the legal tender clause and its operation upon contracts made before the passage of the law. We shall now consider whether it be constitutional in its application to contracts made after its passage. In other words, whether congress has power to make anything but coin a legal tender.

And here it is well enough again to say that we do not question the authority to issue notes or to fit them for a circulating medium, or to promote their circulation by providing for their receipt in payment of debts to the government, and for redemption either in coin or in bonds; in short to adapt them to use as currency Nor do we question the lawfulness of contracts stipulating for payment in such notes, or the propriety of enforcing the performance of such contracts by holding the tender of such currency, according to their terms, sufficient. The question is, has congress power to make the notes of the government, redeemable or irredeemable, a legal tender without contract and against the will of the person to whom they are tendered? In considering this question we assume as a fundamental proposition that it is the duty of every government to establish a standard of value. The necessity of such a standard is indeed universally acknowledged. Without it the transactions of society would become impossible. All measures, whether of extent, or weight, or value, must have certain proportions of that which they are intended to measure. The unit of extent must have certain definite length, the unit of weight certain definite gravity, and the unit of value certain definite value. These units, multiplied or subdivided, supply the standards by which all measures are properly made. The selection, therefore, by the common consent of all nations, of gold and silver as a standard of value was natural, or, more correctly speaking, inevitable. For whatever definitions of value political economists may have given, they all agree that gold and silver have more value in proportion to weight and size, and are less subject to loss by wear or abrasion than any other material capable of easy subdivision and impression, and that their value changes less and by slower degrees, through considerable periods of time, than that of any other substance which could be used for the same purpose. And these are qualities indispensable to the convenient use of the standard required. In the construction of the constitutional grant of power to establish a standard of value, *every presumption* is, therefore, against that which would authorize the adoption of any other materials than those sanctioned by universal consent.

But the terms of the only express grant in the constitution of power to establish such a standard leave little room for presumptions. The power conferred is the power to coin money, and these words must be understood as they were used at the time the constitution was adopted. And we have been referred to no authority which at that time defined coining otherwise than as minting or stamping metals for money; or money otherwise than as metal coined for the purposes of commerce. These are the words of Johnson, whose great dictionary contains no reference to money of paper.

It is true that notes issued by banks, both in England and

America, were then in circulation, and were used in exchanges, and in common speech called money, and that bills of credit, issued both by congress and by the states, had been recently in circulation under the same general name; but these notes and bills were never regarded as real money, but were always treated as its representatives only, and were described as currency. The legal tender notes themselves do not purport to be anything else than promises to pay money. They have been held to be securities, and therefore exempt from state taxation; and the idea that it was ever designed to make such notes a standard of value by the framers of the constitution is wholly new. It seems to us impossible that it could have been entertained. Its assertion seems to us to ascribe folly to the framers of our fundamental law, and to contradict the most conspicuous facts in our public history.

The power to coin money was a power to determine the fineness, weight, and denominations of the metallic pieces by which values were to be measured; and we do not perceive how this meaning can be extended without doing violence to the very words of the constitution by imposing on them a sense they were never intended to bear. This construction is supported by contemporaneous and all subsequent action of the legislature; by all the recorded utterances of statesmen and jurists, and the unbroken tenor of judicial opinion until a very recent period, when the excitement of the civil war led to the adoption, by many, of different views.

The sense of the convention which framed the constitution is clear, from the account given by Mr. Madison of what took place when the power to emit bills of credit was stricken from the reported draft. He says distinctly that he acquiesced in the motion to strike out, because the government would not be disabled thereby from the use of public notes, so far as they would be safe and proper, while it cut off the pretext for a paper currency, and particularly for making the bills a tender either for public or private debts. The whole discussion upon bills of credit proves, beyond all possible question, that the convention regarded the power to make notes a legal tender as absolutely excluded from the constitution.

The papers of the Federalist, widely circulated, in favor of the ratification of the constitution, discuss briefly the power to coin money, as a power to fabricate metallic money, without a hint that any power to fabricate money of any other description was given to congress; and the views which it promulgated may be fairly regarded as the views of those who voted for adoption.

Acting upon the same views, congress took measures for the establishment of a mint, exercising thereby the power to coin money, and has continued to exercise the same power, in the same way, until the present day. It established the dollar as the money unit, determined the quantity and quality of gold and silver of which each coin should consist, and prescribed the denominations and forms of all coins to be issued. Until recently no one in congress ever suggested that that body possessed power to make anything else a standard of value.

Statesmen who have disagreed widely on other points have agreed in the opinion that the only constitutional measures of value are metallic coins, struck as regulated by the authority of congress. Mr. Webster expressed not only his opinion but the universal and settled conviction of the country when he said: "Most unquestionably there is no legal tender, and there can be no legal tender in this country, under the authority of this government or any other, but gold and silver, either the coinage of our mints or foreign coin at rates regulated by congress. This is a constitutional principle, perfectly plain and of the very highest importance. The states are prohibited from making anything but gold and silver a tender in payment of debts, and although no such express prohibition is applied to congress, *yet as congress has no power granted to it in this respect but to coin money and regulate the value of foreign coin*, it clearly has no power to substitute paper or anything else for coin as a tender in payment of debts and in discharge of contracts."

And this court, in *Gwin* v. *Breedlove*, said: "*By the constitution of the United States gold and silver coin* made current by law *can only be tendered* in payment of debts." And in *The United States* v. *Marigold*, this court speaking of the trust and duty of maintaining a uniform and pure metallic standard of uniform value throughout the Union, said: "The power of coining money and regulating its value *was delegated to congress by the constitution for the very purpose*, as assigned by the framers of that instrument, *of creating and preserving the uniformity and purity of such a standard of value.*"

The present majority of the court say that legal tender notes "have become the universal measure of values," and they hold that the legislation of congress, substituting such measures for coin by making the notes a legal tender in payment, is warranted by the constitution.

But if the plain sense of words, if the contemporaneous exposition of parties, if common consent in understanding, if the opinions of courts avail anything in determining the meaning of the constitution, it seems impossible to doubt that the power to coin money is a power to establish a uniform standard of value, and that no other power to establish such a standard, by making notes a legal tender, is conferred upon congress by the constitution.

My brothers Clifford and Field concur in these views, but in consideration of the importance of the principles involved will deliver their separate opinions. My brother Nelson also dissents.

CHAPTER III.

DISSENTING OPINION OF JUSTICE CLIFFORD.

MONEY, in the constitutional sense, means coins of gold and silver fabricated and stamped by authority of law, as a measure of value, pursuant to the power vested in congress by the constitution.

Coins of copper may also be minted for small fractional circulation, as authorized by law and the usage of the government for eighty years, but it is not necessary to discuss that topic at large in this investigation.

Even the authority of congress upon the general subject does not extend beyond the power to coin money, regulate the value thereof and of foreign coin.

Express power is also conferred upon congress to fix the standard of weights and measures, and of course that standard, as applied to future transactions, may be varied or changed to promote the public interest, but the grant of power in respect to the standard of value is expressed in more guarded language, and the grant is much more restricted.

Power to fix the standard of weights and measures is evidently a power of comparatively wide discretion, but the power to regulate the value of the money authorized by the constitution to be coined is a definite and precise grant of power, admitting of very little discretion in its exercise, and is not equivalent, except to a very limited extent, to the power to fix the standard of weights and measures, as the money authorized by that clause of the constitution is coined money, and, as a necessary consequence, must be money of actual value, fabricated from the precious metals generally used for that purpose at the period when the constitution was framed.

Coined money, such as is authorized by that clause of the instrument, consists only of the coins of the United States, fabricated and stamped by authority of law, and is the same money as that described in the next clause of the same section as the current coins of the United States, and is the same money also as "the gold and silver coins" described in the tenth section of the same article which prohibits the states from coining money, emitting bills of credit, or making "anything but gold and silver coin a tender in payment of debts."

Intrinsic value exists in gold and silver, as well before as after it is fabricated and stamped as coin, which shows conclusively that the principal discretion vested in congress under that clause of the constitution consists in the power to determine the denomination, fineness, or value and description of the coins to be struck, and the relative proportion of gold or silver, whether standard or pure, and the proportion of alloy to be used in minting the coins, and to prescribe the mode in which the intended object of the grant shall be accomplished and carried into practical effect.

Discretion, to some extent, in prescribing the value of the coins minted is beyond doubt vested in congress; but the plain intent of the constitution is that congress, in determining that matter, shall be governed chiefly by the weight and intrinsic value of the coins, as it is clear that if the stamped value of the same should much exceed the real value of gold and silver not coined, the minted coins would immediately cease to be either current coins or a standard of value, as contemplated by the constitution. Commercial transactions imperiously require a standard of value; and the commercial world, at a very early period in civilization, adopted gold and silver as the true standard for that purpose, and the standard originally adopted has ever since continued to be so regarded by universal consent to the present time.

Paper emissions have, at one time or another, been authorized and employed as currency by most commercial nations, and by no government, past or present, more extensively than by the United States; and yet it is safe to affirm that all experience in its use as a circulating medium has demonstrated the proposition that it cannot by any legislation, however stringent, be made a standard of value or the just equivalent of gold and silver. Attempts of the kind have always failed, and no body of men, whether in public or private stations, ever had more instructive teachings of the truth of that remark than the patriotic men who framed the federal constitution, as they had seen the power to emit bills of credit freely exercised during the war of the Revolution, not only by the confederation, but also by the states, and knew from bitter experience its calamitous effects and the utter worthlessness of such a circulating medium as a standard of value. Such men, so instructed, could not have done otherwise than they did do, which was to provide an irrepealable standard of value, to be coined from gold and silver, leaving as little upon the subject to the discretion of congress as was consistent with a wise forecast and an invincible determination that the essential principles of the constitution should be perpetual as the means to secure the blessings of liberty to themselves and their posterity.

Associated as the grant to coin money and regulate the value thereof is with the grant to fix the standard of weights and measures, the conclusion, when that fact is properly weighed in connection with the words of the grant, is irresistible that the purpose of the framers of the constitution was to provide a permanent standard of value, which should, at all times and under all circumstances, consist of coin fabricated and stamped, from gold and silver, by authority of law, and that they intended at the same time to withhold from congress, as well as from the states, the power to substitute any other money as a standard of value in matters of finance, business, trade or commerce.

Support to that view may also be drawn from the last words of the clause giving congress the unrestricted power to regulate the value of foreign coin, as it would be difficult, if not impossible, to give full effect to the standard of value prescribed by the constitution, in times of fluctuation, if the circulating medium could be supplied by foreign coins not subject to any congressional regulation as to their value.

Exclusive power to regulate the alloy and value of the coin

struck by their own authority, or by the authority of the states, was vested in congress under the confederation, but the congress was prohibited from enacting any regulation as to the value of the coins unless nine states assented to the proposed regulation.

Subject to the power of congress to pass such regulations it is unquestionably true that the states, under the confederation as well as the United States, possessed the power to coin money, but the constitution, when it was adopted, denied to the states all authority upon the subject, and also ordained that they should not make anything but gold and silver coin a tender in payment of debts.

Beyond all doubt the framers of the constitution intended that the money unit of the United States, for measuring values, should be one dollar, as the word dollar in the plural form is employed in the body of the constitution, and also in the seventh amendment, recommended by congress at its first session after the constitution was adopted. Two years before that, to-wit: July 6, 1785, the congress of the confederation enacted that the money unit of the United States should "be one dollar," and one year later, to-wit: August 8, 1786, they established the standard for gold and silver, and also provided that the money of account of the United States should correspond with the coins established by law.

On the 4th of March, 1789, congress first assembled under the constitution, and proceeded without unnecessary delay to enact such laws as were necessary to put the government in operation which the constitution had ordained and established. Ordinances had been passed during the confederation to organize the executive departments, and for the establishment of a mint, but the new constitution did not perpetuate any of those laws, and yet congress continued to legislate for a period of three years before any new law was passed prescribing the money unit or the money of account, either for "the public offices" or for the courts. Throughout that period it must have been understood that those matters were impliedly regulated by the constitution, as tariffs were enacted, tonnage duties imposed, laws passed for the collection of duties, the several executive departments created, and the judiciary of the United States organized and empowered to exercise full jurisdiction under the constitution.

Duties of tonnage and import duties were required, by the act of the 31st of July, 1789, to be paid "in gold and silver coin," and congress, in the same act, adopted comprehensive regulations as to the value of foreign coin, but no provision was made for coining money or for a standard of value, except so far as that subject is involved in the regulation as to the value of foreign coin, or for a money unit, nor was any regulation prescribed as to the money of account. Revenue for the support of the government, under those regulations, was to be derived solely from duties of tonnage and import duties, and the express provision was that those duties should be collected in gold and silver coin.

Legislation under the constitution had proceeded thus far before the treasury department was created. Treasury regulations for the collection, safe-keeping, and disbursement of the public moneys became indispensable, and congress, on the 2d September, 1789, passed the act to establish the treasury department, which has ever since remained in force. By that act, the secretary of the treasury is declared to be the head of the department, and it is made his duty, among other things, to digest and prepare plans for the improvement and management of the public finances and for the support of the public credit; to prepare and report estimates of the public revenue and of the public expenditures; to superintend the collection of the revenue; to prescribe forms of keeping and stating accounts and for making returns; to grant all warrants for moneys to be issued from the treasury, in pursuance of appropriations by law, and to perform all such services relative to the finances as he shall be directed to perform.

Moneys collected from duties of tonnage and from import duties constituted at that period the entire resources of the national treasury, and the antecedent act of congress, providing for the collection of those duties, imperatively required that all such duties should be paid in gold and silver coin, from which it follows that the moneys mentioned in the act creating the treasury department were moneys of gold and silver coin which were collected as public revenue from the duties of tonnage and import duties imposed by the before-mentioned prior acts of congress. Appropriations made by congress were understood as appropriations of moneys in the treasury, and all warrants issued by the secretary of the treasury were understood to be warrants for the payment of gold and silver coin. Forms for keeping and stating accounts, and for making returns, and for warrants for moneys to be issued from the treasury were prescribed, and in all those forms the secretary of the treasury adopted the money unit recognized in the constitution, and which had been ordained four years before by the congress of the confederation.

Argument to show that the national treasury was organized on the basis that the gold and silver coins of the United States were to be the standard of value is unnecessary, as it is a historical fact which no man or body of men can ever successfully contradict. Public attention had been directed to the necessity of establishing a mint for the coinage of gold and silver, several years before the convention met to frame the constitution, and a committee was appointed by the congress of the confederation to consider and report upon the subject. They reported on the 21st February, 1782, more than a year before the treaty of peace, in favor of creating such an establishment, and on the 16th of October, 1786, the congress adopted an ordinance providing that a mint should be established for the coingage of gold, silver, and copper, agreeable to the resolves of congress previously mentioned, which prescribed the standard of gold and silver, and recognized the money unit established by the resolves passed in the preceding year.

Congressional legislation organizing the new government had now progressed to the point where it became necessary to re-examine that subject and to make provision for the exercise of the power to coin money, as authorized by the constitution. Pursuant to that power, congress, on April 2d, 1792, passed the act establishing a mint for the purpose of a national coinage, and made provisions, among other things, that coins of gold and silver, of certain fineness and weight, and of certain denominations, value, and descriptions, should be from time to time struck and coined at the same mint. Specific provision is there made for coining gold and silver coins, as follows: First, gold coins, to-wit: Eagles of the value of ten dollars or units; half-eagles of the value of five dollars; quarter-eagles of the value of two and a half dollars, the act specifying in each case the number of grains and fractions of a grain the coin shall contain, whether fabricated from pure or standard gold. Second, silver coins, to-wit: "DOLLARS OR UNITS," each to contain 371 grains and $\frac{4}{16}$ths parts of a grain of pure silver, or 416 grains of standard silver. Like provision is also made for the coinage of half-dollars, quarter-dollars, dimes, and half-dimes, and also for the coinage of certain copper coins, but it is not necessary to enter much into those details in this case.

Provision, it must be conceded, is not there made, in express terms, that the money unit of the United States shall be one dollar, as in the ordinance passed during the confederation, but the act under consideration assumes throughout that the coin called dollar is the coin employed for that purpose, as is obvious from the fact that the words dollars and units are treated as synonomous, and that all the gold coins previously described in the same section are measured by that word as the acknowledged money unit of the constitution. Very strong doubts are entertained whether an act of congress is absolutely necessary to constitute the gold and silver coins of the United States, fabricated and stamped as such by the proper executive officers of the mint, a legal tender in payment of debts. Constituted, as such coins are, by the constitution, the standard of value, the better opinion would seem to be that they become legal tender for that purpose, if minted of the required weight and fineness, as soon as they are coined and put in circulation by lawful authority, but it is unnecessary to decide that question in this case, as the congress, by the sixteenth section of the act establishing a mint, provided that all the gold and silver coins which shall have been struck at, and issued from, the said mint shall be a lawful tender in all payments whatsoever—those of full weight "according to the respective values herein declared, and those of less than full weight at values proportioned to their respective weights." Such a regulation is at all events highly expedient, as all experience shows that even gold and silver coins are liable to be diminished in weight by wear and abrasion, even if it is not absolutely necessary in order to constitute the coins, if of full weight, a legal tender.

Enough has already been remarked to show that the money unit of the United States is the coined dollar, described in the act establishing the mint, but if more be wanted it will be found in the twentieth section of that act which provides that the money of account of the United States shall be expressed in dollars or units, dimes or tenths, etc., and that all accounts in the public offices, and all proceedings in the federal courts, shall be kept and had in conformity to that regulation.

Completed, as the circle of measures adopted by congress were, to put the new government into successful operation, by the passage of that act, it will be instructive to take a brief review of the important events which occurred within the period of ten years next preceding its passage, or of the ten years next following the time when that measure was first proposed in the congress of the confederation. Two reasons suggest the 21st of February, 1782, as the time to commence the review, in addition to the fact that it was on that day that the committee of congress made their report approving of the project to establish a national mint. They are as follows: (1) Because that date just precedes the close of the war of the Revolution; and (2) because the date at the same time extends back to a period when all America had come to the conclusion that all the paper currency in circulation was utterly worthless, and that nothing was fit for a standard of value but gold and silver coin, fabricated and stamped by the national authority. Discussion upon the subject was continued, and the ordinance was passed; but the measure was not put in operation, as the convention met the next year, and the constitution was framed, adopted, and ratified, the president and the members of congress were elected, laws were passed, the judicial system was organized, the executive departments were created, the revenue system established, and provision was made to execute the power vested in congress to coin money and provide a standard of value, as ordained by the constitution.

Perfect consistency characterizes the measures of that entire period in respect to the matter in question, and it would be strange if it had been otherwise, as the whole series of measures were to a very large extent the doings of the same class of men, whether the remark is applied to the old congress, or the convention which framed the constitution, or to the first and second sessions of the new congress which passed the laws referred to, and put the new system of government under the constitution into full operation. Wise and complete as those laws were, still some difficulties arose, as the several states had not adopted the money unit of the United States, nor the money of account prescribed by the twentieth section of the act establishing the mint. Such embarrassments, however, were chiefly felt in the federal courts, and they were not of long continuance, as the several states, one after another, in pretty rapid succession, adopted the new system established by congress, both as to the money unit and the money of account. Virginia, December 19th, 1792, reënacted that section in the act of congress without any material alteration, and New Hampshire, on the 20th of February, 1794, passed a similar law. Massachusetts adopted the same provision the next year, and so did Rhode Island and South Carolina. Georgia concurred on the 22d of February, 1796, and New York on the 27th of January, 1797, and all the other states adopted the same regulation in the course of a few years. State concurrence was essential in those particulars to the proper working of the new system, and it was cheerfully accorded by the state legislatures without unnecessary delay.

Congress established as the money unit the coin mentioned in the constitution, and the one which had been adopted as such seven years before in the resolve passed by the congress of the confederation. Dollars, and decimals of dollars, were adopted as the money of account by universal consent, as may be inferred from the unanimity exhibited by the states in following the example of congress. Nothing remained for congress to do to perfect the new system but to execute the power to coin money, and regulate the value thereof, as it is clear that the constitution makes no provision for a standard of value, unless the power to establish it is conferred by that grant.

Power to fix the standard of weights and measures is vested in congress by the constitution in plain and unambiguous terms, and it was never doubted—certainly not until within a recent period—that the power conferred to coin money, or to fabricate and stamp coins from gold and silver, which, in the constitutional sense is the same thing, together with the power to determine the fineness, weight, and denomination of the moneys coined, was intended to accomplish the same purpose as to values. Indubitably it was so understood by congress in prescribing the various regulations contained in the act establishing the national mint, and it continued to be so understood by all branches of the government—executive, legislative, and judicial—and by the whole people of the United States, for the period of seventy years from the passage of that act.

New regulations became necessary, and were passed in the meantime, increasing slightly the proportion of alloy used in fabricating the gold coins, but if those enactments are carefully examined, it will be found that no one of them contains anything inconsistent in principle with the views here expressed. Gold, at the time the act establishing the mint became a law, was valued fifteen to one as compared with silver, but the disparity in value gradually increased, and to such an extent that the gold coins began to disappear from circulation, and, to remedy that evil, congress found it necessary to augment the *relative* proportion of alloy by diminishing the required amount of gold, whether pure or standard. Eagles coined under that act were required to contain each two hundred and thirty-two grains of pure gold, or two hundred and fifty-eight grains of standard. Three years later congress enacted that the standard for both gold and silver coins should thereafter be such that, of one thousand parts by weight, nine hundred should be of pure metal and one hundred of alloy, by which the gross weight of the dollar was reduced to four hundred and twelve and a half grains, but the fineness of the coins was correspondingly increased, so that the money unit remained of the same intrinsic value as under the original act. Apply that rule to the eagle, and it will be seen that its gross weight would be increased, as it was in fact by that act, but it continued to contain, as under the preceding act, two hundred and thirty grains of pure gold and no more, showing conclusively that no change was made in the value of the coins.

Double eagles and gold dollars were authorized to be "struck and coined" at the mint, by the act of March 3d, 1849, but the standard established for other gold coins was not changed, and the provision was that the new coins should also be legal tender for their coined value.

Fractional silver coins were somewhat reduced in value by the act of February 21st, 1853, but the same act provided to the effect that the silver coins issued in conformity thereto should not be a legal tender for any sum exceeding five dollars, showing that the purpose of the enactment was to prevent the fractional coins, so essential for daily use, from being hoarded or otherwise withdrawn from circulation.

Suppose it be conceded, however, that the effect of that act was slightly to debase the fractional silver coins struck and coined under it, still it is quite clear that the amount was too inconsiderable to furnish any solid argument against the proposition that the standard of value in the United States was fixed by the constitution, and that such was the understanding, both of the government, and of the people of the United States, for a period of more than seventy years from the time the constitution was adopted and put in successful operation under the laws of congress. Throughout that period the value of the money unit was never diminished, and it remains to-day, in respect to value, what it was when it was defined in the act establishing the mint, and it is safe to affirm that no one of the changes made in the other coins, except, perhaps, the fractional silver coins, ever extended one whit beyond the appropriate limit of constitutional regulation.

Treasury notes, called United States notes, were authorized to be issued by the act of February 25th, 1862, to the amount of $150,000,000, on the credit of the United States, but they were not to bear interest, and were to be made payable to bearer at the treasury. They were to be issued by the secretary of the treasury, and the further provision was that the notes so issued should be lawful money and legal tender in payment of all debts, public and private, within the United States, except duties on imports, and interest upon bonds and notes of the United States, which the act provides "shall be paid in coin." Subsequent acts passed for a similar purpose also except "ce tificates of indebtedness and of deposit," but it will not be necessary to refer specially to the other acts, as the history of that legislation is fully given in the prior decision of this court upon the same subject.

Strictly examined it is doubtful whether either of the cases before the court present any such questions as those which have been discussed in the opinion of a majority of the court just read; but suppose they do, which is not admitted, it then becomes necessary to inquire in the first place whether those questions are not closed by the recorded decisions of this court. Two questions are examined in the opinion of a majority of the court: (1) Whether the legal tender acts are constitutional as to contracts made before the acts were passed. (2) Whether they are valid if applied to contracts made since their passage.

Assume that the views here expressed are correct, and it matters not whether the contract was made before or after the act of congress was passed, as it necessarily follows that congress cannot, under any circumstances, make paper promises of any kind a legal tender in payment of debts. Prior to the decision just pronounced, it is conceded that the second question presented in the record was never determined by this court, except as it is involved in the first question, but it is admitted by the majority of the court that the first question, that is the question whether the acts under consideration are constitutional as to contracts made before their passage, was fully presented in the case of *Hepburn* v. *Griswold*, and that the court decided that an act of congress making mere paper promises to pay dollars a legal tender in payment of debts previously contracted is unconstitutional and void.

Admitted or not, it is as clear as anything in legal decision can be that the judgment of the court in that case controls the first question presented in the cases before the court, unless it be held that the judgment in that case was given for the wrong party and that the opinion given by the chief justice ought to be overruled.

Attempt is made to show that the second question is an open one, but the two, in my judgment, involve the same considerations, as congress possesses no other power upon the subject than that which is derived from the grant to coin money, regulate the value thereof, and of foreign coin. By that remark it is not meant to deny the proposition that congress, in executing the express grants, may not pass all laws which shall be necessary and proper for carrying the same into execution, as provided in another clause of the same section of the constitution. Much consideration of that topic is not required, as the discussion was pretty nearly exhausted by the chief justice in the case of *Hepburn* v. *Griswold*, which arose under the same act, and in which he gave the opinion. In that case the contract bore date prior to the passage of the law, and he showed conclusively that it could never be necessary and proper within the meaning of the constitution, that congress, in executing any of these express powers, should pass laws to compel a creditor to accept paper promises as fulfilling a contract for the payment of money expressed in dollars. Obviously the decision was confined to the case before the court, but I am of the opinion that the same rule must be applied whether the contract was made before or after the passage of the law, as the contract for the payment of money, expressed in dollars, is a contract to make the payment in such money as the constitution recognizes and establishes as a standard of value. Money values can no more be measured without a standard of value than distances without a standard of extent, or quantities without a standard of weights or measures, and it is as necessary that there should be a money unit as that there should be a unit of extent, or of weight, or quantity.

Credit currency, whether issued by the states or the United States, or by private corporations or individuals, is not recognized by the constitution as the standard of value, nor can it be made such by any law which congress or the states can pass, as the laws of trade are stronger than any legislative enactment. Commerce requires a standard of value, and all experience warrants the prediction that commerce will have it, whether the United States agree or disagree, as the laws of commerce in that respect are stronger than the laws of any single nation of the commercial world. Values cannot be measured without a standard any more than time or duration, or length, surface, or solidity, or weight, gravity, or quantity. Something in every such case must be adopted as a unit which bears a known relation to that which is to be measured, as the dollar for values, the hour for time or duration, the foot of twelve inches for length, the yard for cloth measure, the square foot or yard for surface, the cubic foot for solidity, the gallon for liquids, and the pound for weights; the pound avoirdupois being used in most commercial transactions, and the pound troy "for weighing gold and silver, and precious stones, except diamonds."

Unrestricted power "to fix the standard of weights and measures," is vested in congress, but until recently congress had not enacted any general regulations in execution of that power. Regulations upon the subject existed in the states at the adoption of the constitution, the same as those which prevailed at that time in the parent country, and Judge Story says that the understanding was that those regulations remained in full force, and that the states, until congress should legislate, possessed the power to fix their own weights and measures.

Power to coin money and regulate the value of domestic and foreign coin was vested in the national government to produce uniformity of value and to prevent the embarrassments of a perpetually fluctuating and variable currency.

Money, says the same commentator, is the universal medium *or common standard* by a comparison with which the value of all merchandise may be ascertained; and he also speaks of it as "a sign which represents the respective values of all other commodities." Such a power, that is the power to coin money, he adds, is one of the ordinary prerogatives of sovereignty, and is almost universally exercised in order to preserve a proper circulation of good coin, of a known value, in the home market.

Interests of such magnitude and pervading importance as those involved in providing for a uniform standard of value throughout the Union were manifestly entitled to the protection of the national authority, and in view of the evils experienced for the want of such a standard during the war of the revolution, when the country was inundated with floods of depreciated paper, the members of the convention who framed the constitution did not hesitate to confide the power to congress, not only to coin money and regulate the value thereof, but also the power to regulate the value of foreign coin, which was denied to the congress of the confederation.

Influenced by these considerations and others expressed in the opinion of the chief justice, this court decided in the case referred to, that the act of congress making the notes in question "lawful money and a legal tender in payment of debts," could not be vindicated as necessary and proper means for carrying into effect the power vested in congress to coin money and regulate the value thereof, or any other express power vested in congress under the constitution. Unless that case, therefore, is overruled, it is clear, in my judgment, that both the cases before the court are controlled by that decision. Controversies determined by the supreme court are finally and conclusively settled, as the decisions are numerous that the court cannot review and reverse their own judgments.

But where the parties are different, it is said the court, in a subsequent case, may overrule a former decision, and it must be admitted that the proposition, in a technical point of view, is correct. Such examples are to be found in the reported decisions of the court, but they are not numerous, and it seems clear that the number ought never to be increased, especially in a matter of so much importance, unless the error is plain and upon the clearest convictions of judicial duty.

Judgment was rendered for the plaintiff in that case on the 17th of September, 1864, in the highest court of the state, and on the 23d of June, in the succeeding year, the defendants sued out a writ of error, and removed the cause into this court for reëxamination. Under the regular call of the docket the case was first argued at the December term, 1867, but at the suggestion of the attorney general an order was passed that it be re-argued, and the case was accordingly continued for that purpose. Able counsel appeared at the next term, and it was again elaborately argued on both sides. Four or five other cases were also on the calendar, supposed at that time to involve the same constitutional questions, and those cases were also argued, bringing to the aid of the court an unusual array of counsel of great learning and eminent abilities. Investigation and deliberation followed, authorities were examined, and oft-repeated consultations among the justices ensued, and the case was held under advisement as long as necessary to the fullest examination by all the justices of the court, before the opinion of the court was delivered. By law, the supreme court at that time consisted of the chief justice and seven associate justices, the act of congress having provided that no vacancy in the office of associate justice should be filled until the number should be reduced to six. Five of the number, including the chief justice, concurred in the opinion in that case, and the judgment of the state court was affirmed, three of the associate justices dissenting. Since that time one of the justices who concurred in that opinion of the court has resigned, and congress having increased the number of associate justices to eight, the two cases before the court have been argued, and the result is that the opinion delivered in the former case is overruled, five justices concurring in the present opinion and four dissenting. Five justices concurred in the first opinion, and five have overruled it. Persuaded that the first opinion was right, for the reasons already assigned, it is not possible that I should concur in the second, even if it were true that no other reasons of any weight could be given in support of the judgment in the first case, and that the conclusion there reached must stand or fall without any other support. Many other reasons, however, may be invoked to fortify that conclusion, equally persuasive and convincing with those to which reference has been made.

All writers upon political economy agree that money is the universal standard of value, and the measure of exchange, foreign and domestic, and that the power to coin and regulate the value of money is an essential attribute of national sovereignty. Goods and chattels were directly bartered one for another when the division of labor was first introduced, but gold and silver were adopted to serve the purpose of exchange by the tacit concurrence of all nations at a very early period in the history of commercial transactions. Commodities of various kinds were used as money at different periods in different countries, but experience soon showed the commercial nations that gold and silver embodied the qualities desirable in money in a much greater degree than any other known commodity or substance. Daily experience shows the truth of that proposition, and supersedes the necessity of any remarks to enforce it, as all admit that a commodity to serve as a standard of value and a medium of exchange must be easily divisible into small portions; that it must admit of being kept for an indefinite period without deteriorating; that it must possess great value in small bulk, and be capable of being easily transported from place to place; that a given denomination in money should always be equal in weight and quality, or fineness, to other pieces of money of the same denomination, and that its value should be the same, or as little subject to variation as possible. Such qualities, all agree, are united in a much greater degree in gold and silver than in any other known commodity, which was as well known to the members of the convention who framed the constitution as to any body of men since assembled and intrusted to any extent with the public affairs. They not only knew that the money of the commercial world was gold and silver, but they also knew, from bitter experience, that paper promises, whether issued by the states or the United States, were utterly worthless as a standard of value for any practical purpose.

Evidence of the truth of these remarks, of the most convincing character, is to be found in the published proceedings of that convention. Debate upon the subject first arose when an amendment was proposed to prohibit the states from emitting bills of credit or making anything but gold and silver coin a tender in payment of debts, and from the character of that debate, and the vote on the amendment, it became apparent that paper money had but few, if any, friends in the convention. Article seven of the draft of the constitution, as reported to the convention, contained the clause, "and emit bills on the credit of the United States," appended to the grant of power vested in congress to borrow money, and it was on the motion to strike out that clause that the principal discussion in respect to paper money took place. Mr. Madison inquired if it would not be sufficient to prohibit the making such bills a tender, as that would remove the temptation to emit them with unjust views. Promissory notes, he said, in that shape—that is, when not a tender — "may in some emergencies be best." Some were willing to acquiesce in the modification suggested by Mr. Madison, but Mr. Morris, who submitted the motion, objected, insisting that if the motion prevailed there would still be room left for the notes of a responsible minister, which, as he said, "would do all the good without the mischief." Decided objections were advanced by Mr. Ellsworth, who said he thought the moment a favorable one "to shut and bar the door against paper money;" and others expressed their opposition to the clause in equally decisive language, even saying that they would sooner see the whole plan rejected than retain the three words, "and emit bills." Suffice it to say, without reproducing the discussion, that the motion prevailed—nine states to two—and the clause was stricken out, and no attempt was ever made to restore it. Paper money, as legal tender, had few or no advocates in the convention, and it never had more than one open advocate throughout the period the constitution was under discussion, either in the convention which framed it, or in the conventions of the states, where it was ratified. Virginia voted in the affirmative on the motion to strike out that clause, Mr. Madison being satisfied that if the motion prevailed it would not have the effect to disable the government from the use of treasury notes, and being himself in favor of cutting "*off the pretext for a paper currency, and particularly for making the bills a tender, either for public or private debts.*" When the draft for the constitution was reported, the clause prohibiting the states from making anything but gold and silver a tender in payment of debts, contained an exception, "in case congress consented," but the convention struck out the exception and made the prohibition absolute, one of the members remarking that it was a favorable moment to crush out paper money, and all or nearly all of the convention seemed to concur in the sentiment.

Contemporaneous acts are certainly evidence of intention; and if so, it is difficult to see what more is needed to show that the members of that convention intended to withhold from the states, and from the United States, all power to make anything but gold and silver a standard of value or a tender in payment of debts. Equally decisive proof to the same effect is found in the debates which subsequently occurred in the conventions of the several states, to which the constitution, as adopted, was submitted for ratification. Mr. Martin thought that the states ought not to be totally deprived of the right to emit bills of credit, but he says "that the convention was so smitten with the paper money dread that they insisted that the prohibition should be absolute."

Currency is a word much more comprehensive than the word money, as it may include bank bills and even bills of exchange, as well as coins of gold and silver; but the word money, as employed in the grant of power under consideration, means the coins of gold and silver fabricated and stamped as required by law, which, by virtue of their intrinsic value, as universally acknowledged, and their official origin, become the medium of exchange and the standard by which all other values are expressed and discharged. Support to the proposition that the word money, as employed in that clause, was intended to be used in the sense here supposed, is also derived from the language employed in certain numbers of the Federalist, which, as is well known, were written and published during the period the question whether the states would ratify the constitution was pending in their several conventions. Such men as the writers of those essays never could have employed such language if they had entertained the remotest idea that congress possessed the power to make paper promises a legal tender.

Like support is also derived from the language of Mr. Hamilton in his celebrated report recommending the incorporation of a national bank. He first states the objection to the proposed measure, that banks tend to banish the gold and silver of the country; and, secondly, he gives the answer to that objection made by the advocates of the bank, that it is immaterial what serves the purpose of money, and then says that the answer is not entirely satisfactory, as the permanent increase or decrease of the precious metals in a country can hardly ever be a matter of indifference. "As the commodity taken in lieu of every other, it (coin) is a species of the most effective wealth, and as the money of the world it is of great concern to the state that it possesses a sufficiency of it to face any demands which the protection of its external interests may create." He favors the incorporation of a national bank, with power to issue bills and notes *payable on demaad in gold and silver*, but he expresses himself as utterly opposed to paper emissions by the United States, characterizing them as so liable to abuse and even so certain of being abused that the government ought never to trust itself "with the use of so seducing and dangerous an element." Opposed as he was to paper emissions by the United States, under any circumstances, it is past belief that he could ever have concurred in the proposition to make such emissions a tender in payment of debts, either as a member of the convention which framed the constitution or as the head of the treasury department. Treasury notes, however, have repeatedly been authorized by congress, commencing with the act of 30th of June, 1812, but it was never supposed before the time when the several acts in question were passed that congress could make snch notes a legal tender in payment of debts. Such notes, it was enacted, should be received in payment of all duties and taxes laid, and in payment for public lands sold by the federal authority. Provision was also made in most or all of the acts that the secretary of the treasury, with the approbation of the president, might cause treasury notes to be issued, at the par value thereof, in payment of services, of supplies, or of debts for which the United States were or might be answerable by law, to such person or persons as should be *willing to accept the same* in payment; but it never occurred to the legislators of that day that such notes could be made a legal tender in discharge of such indebtedness, or that the public creditor could be compelled to accept them in payment of his just demands.

Financial embarrassments, second only in their disastrous consequences to those which preceded the adoption of the constitution, arose towards the close of the last war with Great Britain, and it is a matter of history that those embarrassments were too great and pervading to be overcome by the use of treasury notes or any other paper emissions without a specie basis. Expedients of various kinds were suggested, but it never occurred either to the executive or to congress that a remedy could be found by making treasury notes, as then authorized, a legal tender, and the result was that the second bank of the United States was incorporated. Paper currency, it may be said, was authorized by that act, which is undoubtedly true; and it is also true that the bills or notes of the bank were made receivable in all payments to the United States, if the same were at the time payable on demand, but the act provided that the corporation should not refuse, under a heavy penalty, the payment in gold and silver, of any of its notes, bills, or obligations, nor of any moneys received upon deposit in the bank or in any of its offices of discount and deposit.

Serious attempt is made, strange to say, to fortify the proposition that the acts in question are constitutional from the fact that congress, in providing for the use of treasury notes, and in granting the charters to the respective national banks, made the notes and bills receivable in payment of duties and taxes, but the answer to the suggestion is so obvious that it is hardly necessary to pause to suggest its refutation. Creditors may exact gold and silver or they may waive the right to require such money, and accept credit currency, or commodities, other than gold and silver, and the United States, as creditors, or in the exercise of their express power to levy and collect taxes, duties, imposts, and excises, may, if they see fit, accept the treasury notes or bank bills in such payments as substitutes for the constitutional currency. Further discussion of the proposition is unnecessary, as it is plainly destitute of any merit whatever.

Resort was also had to treasury notes in the revulsion of 1837, and during the war with Mexico, and also in the great revulsion of 1857, but the new theory that congress could make treasury notes a legal tender was not even suggested, either by the president or by any member of congress.

Seventy years are included in this review, even if the computation is only carried back to the passage of the act establishing the mint, and it is clear that there is no trace of any act, executive or legislative, within that period, which affords the slightest support to the new constitutional theory that congress can by law constitute paper emissions a tender in payment of debts. Even Washington, the father of our country, refused to accept paper money in payment of debts contracted before the war of independence, and the proof is full to the point that Hamilton, as well as Jefferson and Madison, was opposed to paper emissions by the national authority.

Sufficient also is recorded in the reports of the decisions of this court to show that the court, from the organization of the judicial system to the day when the judgments in the cases before the court were announced, held opinions utterly opposed to such a construction of the constitution as would authorize congress to make paper promises a legal tender as between debtor and creditor. Throughout that period the doctrine of the court has been, and still is, unless the opinion of the court just read constitutes an exception, that the government of the United States, as ordained and established by the constitution, is a government of enumerated powers; that all the powers not delegated to the United States by the constitution, nor prohibited by it to the states, are reserved to the states respectively or to the people; that every power vested in the Federal government under the constitution is in its nature sovereign, and that congress may pass all laws necessary and proper to carry the same into execution, or, in other words, that the power being sovereign includes, by force of the term, the requisite means, fairly applicable to the attainment of the contemplated end, which are not precluded by restrictions or exceptions expressed or necessarily implied, and not contrary to the essential ends of political society.

Definitions slightly different have been given by different jurists to the words "necessary and proper," employed in the clause of the constitution conferring upon congress the power to pass laws for carrying the express grants of power into execution, but no one ever pretended that a construction or definition could be sustained that the general clause would authorize the employment of such means in the execution of one express grant as would practically nullify another or render another utterly nugatory. Circumstances made it necessary that Mr. Hamilton should examine that phrase at a very early period after the constitution was adopted, and the definition he gave to it is as follows: "All the means requisite and fairly applicable to the attainment of the end of such power which are not precluded by restrictions and exceptions specified in the constitution, and not contrary to the essential ends of political society." Twenty-five years later the question was examined by the supreme court and authoritatively settled, the chief justice giving the opinion. His words were: "Let the end be legitimate, let it be within the scope of the constitution, and all means which are appropriate, which are plainly adapted to that end, and which are not prohibited but consistent with the letter and spirit of the constitution, are constitutional."

Substantially the same definition was adopted by the present chief justice in the former case, in which he gave the opinion of the court, and there is nothing contained in the Federal reports giving the slightest sanction to any broader definition of those words. Take the definition given by Mr. Hamilton, which, perhaps, is the broadest, if there is any difference, and still it is obvious that it would give no countenance whatever to the theory that congress, in passing a law to execute one express grant of the constitution, could authorize means which would nullify another express grant, or render it nugatory for the attainment of the end which the framers of the constitution intended it should accomplish.

Authority to coin money was vested in congress to provide a permanent national standard of value, everywhere the same, and subject to no variation except what congress shall make under the power to regulate the value thereof, and it is not possible to affirm, with any hope that the utterance will avail in the argument, that the power to coin money is not an express power, and if those premises are conceded it cannot be shown that congress can so expand any other express power by implication as to nullify or defeat the great purposes which the power to coin money and establish a standard of value was intended to accomplish.

Government notes, it is conceded, may be issued as a means of borrowing money, because the act of issuing the notes may be, and often is, a requisite means to execute the granted power, and being fairly applicable to the attainment of the end, the notes, as a means, may be employed, as they are not precluded by any restrictions or exceptions, and not repugnant to any other express grant contained in the constitution. Lighthouses, buoys, and beacons may be erected under the power to regulate commerce, but congress cannot authorize an officer of the government to take private property for such a purpose without just compensation, as the exercise of such a power would be repugnant to the fifth amendment. Power to levy and collect taxes is conferred upon congress, but the congress cannot tax the salaries of the state judges, as the exercise of such a power is incompatible with the admitted power of the states to create courts, appoint judges, and provide for their compensation.

Congress may also impose duties, imposts, and excises to pay the debts and provide for the common defense and general welfare, but the congress cannot levy any tax or duty on articles exported from any state, nor can congress give any preference by any regulation of commerce or revenue to the ports of one state over those of another, as the exercise of any such power is prohibited by the constitution. Exclusive power is vested in congress to declare war, to raise and support armies, to provide and maintain a navy, and to make rules for the government and regulation of the land and naval forces. Appropriations to execute those powers may be made by congress, but no appropriations of money to that use can be made for a longer term than two years, as an appropriation for a longer term is expressly prohibited by the same clause which confers the power to raise and support armies. By virtue of those grants of power congress may erect forts and magazines, may construct navy-yards and dock-yards, manufacture arms and munitions of war, and may establish depots and other needful buildings for their preservation, but the congress cannot take private property for that purpose without making compensation to the owner, as the constitution provides that private property shall not be taken for public use without just compensation.

Legislative power under the constitution can never be rightfully extended to the exercise of a power not granted nor to that which is prohibited, and it makes no difference whether the prohibition is express or implied, as an implied prohibition, when once ascertained, is as effectual to negative the right to legislate as one that is expressed; the rule being that congress, in passing laws to carry the express powers granted into execution, cannot select any means as requisite for that purpose or as fairly applicable to the attainment of the end, which are precluded by restrictions or exceptions contained in the constitution, or which are contrary to the essential ends of political society.

Concede these premises, and it follows that the acts of congress in question cannot be regarded as valid unless it can be held that the power to make paper emissions a legal tender in payment of debts can properly be implied from the power to coin money, and that such emissions, when enforced by such a provision, become the legal standard of value under the constitution. Extended discussion of the first branch of the proposition would seem to be unnecessary, as the dissenting justices in the former case abandoned that point and frankly stated in the dissenting opinion delivered that they were not able to see in those clauses, "standing alone, a sufficient warrant for the exercise of this power." Through their organ on the occasion they referred to the power to declare war, to suppress insurrection, to raise and support armies, to provide and maintain a navy, to borrow money, to pay the debts of the Union, and to provide for the common defense and general welfare, as grants of power conferred in separate clauses of the constitution. Reference was then made in very appropriate terms to the exigencies of the treasury during that period and the conclusion reached, though expressed interrogatively, appears to be that the provision making the notes a legal tender was a necessary and proper one as conducing "towards the purpose of borrowing money, of paying debts, of raising armies, of suppressing insurrection," or, as expressed in another part of the same opinion, the provision was regarded as "necessary and proper to enable the government to borrow money to carry on the war."

Suggestions or intimations are made in one or more of the opinions given in the state courts that the power assumed by congress may be vindicated as properly implied from the power to coin money, but inasmuch as that assumption was not the ground of the dissent in the former case, and as the court is not referred to any case where a court affirming the validity of the acts of congress in question has ventured to rest their decision upon that theory, it does not appear to be necessary to protract the discussion upon that point.

Such notes are not declared in the acts of congress to be a standard of value, and if they were the provision would be as powerless to impart that quality to the notes as were the processes of the alchemist to convert chalk into gold, or the contrivances of the mechanic to organize a machine and to give it perpetual motion. Gold and silver were adopted as the standard of value, even before civil governments were organized, and they have always been regarded as such to the present time, and it is safe to affirm that they will continue to be such by universal consent, in spite of legislative enactments and of judicial decisions. Treasury notes, or the notes in question, called by what name they may be, never performed that office, even for a day, and it may be added that neither legislative enactments nor judicial decisions can compel the commercial world to accept paper emissions of any kind as the standard of value by which all other values are to be measured. Nothing but money will in fact perform that office, and it is clear that neither legislasive enactments nor judicial decisions can perform commercial impossibilities. Commodities undoubtedly may be exchanged as matter of barter, or the seller may accept paper promises instead of money, but it is nevertheless true, as stated by Mr. Huskisson, that money is not only the *common measure* and *common representative* of all other commodities, but also the common and universal equivalent. Whoever buys, gives, whoever sells, receives such a quantity of pure gold or silver as is equivalent to the article bought or sold; or if he gives or receives paper instead of money, he gives and receives that which is valuable only as it stipulates the paynent of a given quantity of gold or silver.

"Most unquestionably," said Mr. Webster, "there is no legal tender, and there can be no legal tender, in this country, under the authority of this government, or any other, but gold and silver. * * This is a constitutional principle, perfectly plain and of the very highest importance." He admitted that no such express prohibition was contained in the constitution, and then proceeded to say: "As congress has no power granted to it in this respect but to coin money and to regulate the value of foreign coins, *it clearly has no power to substitute paper* or anything else for coin as a tender in payment of debts and in discharge of contracts," adding that "congress has exercised the power fully in both of its branches. It has coined money and still coins it, it has regulated the value of foreign coins and still regulates their value. The legal tender, therefore, THE CONSTITUTIONAL STANDARD OF VALUE, IS ESTABLISHED AND CANNOT BE OVERTHROWN." Beyond peradventure he was of the opinion that gold and silver, at rates fixed by congress, constituted the legal standard of value, and that neither congress nor the states had authority to establish any other standard in its place.

Views equally decisive have been expressed by this court in a case where the remarks were pertinent to the question presented for decision. Certain questions were certified here which arose in the circuit court in the trial of an indictment in which the defendant was charged with having brought into the United States from a foreign place, with intent to pass, utter, publish, and sell certain false, forged, and couterfeit coins, made, forged, and counterfeited in the resemblance and similitude of the coins struck at the mint. Doubts were raised at the trial whether congress had the power to pass the law on which the indictment was founded. Objection was made that the acts charged were only a fraud in traffic, and, as such, were punishable, if at all, under the state law. Responsive to that suggestion the court say that the provisions of the section "appertain rather to the execution of an important trust invested by the constitution, and to the obligation to fulfill that trust on the part of the government, namely, the trust and the duty of creating and maintaining *a uniform and pure metallic standard of value throughout the Union;* that the power of coining money and of regulating its value was delegated to congress by the constitution for the very purpose of *creating and preserving the uniformity and purity of such a standard of value*, and on account of the impossibility which was foreseen of otherwise preventing the inequalities and the confusion necessarily incident to the different views of policy which in different communities would be brought to bear on this subject. The power to coin money being thus given to congress, founded on public necessity, it must carry with it the correlative power of protecting the creature and object of that power." Appropriate suggestions follow as to the right of the government to adopt measures to exclude counterfeits and prevent the true coin from being substituted by others of no intrinsic value, and the justice delivering the opinion then proceeds to say, that congress "having emitted a circulating medium, *a standard of value indispensable for the purposes of the community* and for the action of the government itself, the congress is accordingly authorized and bound in duty to prevent its debasement and expulsion and the destruction of the general confidence and convenience by the influx and substitution of a spurious coin in lieu of the constitutional currency."

Equally decisive views were expressed by the court six years earlier, in the case of *Gwin* v. *Breedlove*, in which the opinion of the court was delivered by the late Mr. Justice Catron, than whom no justice who ever sat in the court was more opposed to the expression of an opinion on a point not involved in the record.

No state shall coin money, emit bills of credit, or make anything but gold and silver a tender in payment of debts. These prohibitions, said Mr. Justice Washington, associated with the powers granted to congress to coin money and regulate the value thereof and foreign coin, most obviously constitute members of the same family, being upon the same subject and governed by the same policy. This policy, said the learned justice, was to provide and fix a uniform standard of value throughout the United States, by which the commercial and other dealings between the citizens thereof, or between them and foreigners, as well as the moneyed transactions of the government should be regulated. Language so well chosen and so explicit cannot be misunderstood, and the views expressed by Mr. Justice Johnson, in the same case, are even more decisive. He said the prohibition in the constitution to make anything but gold or silver coin a tender in payment of debts is *express and universal.* The framers of the constitution regarded it as an evil to be repelled without modification, and that they have therefore left nothing to be inferred or deduced from construction on the subject.

Recorded as those opinions have been for forty-five years, and never questioned, they are certainly entitled to much weight, especially as the principles which are there laid down were subsequently affirmed in two cases by the unanimous opinion of this court.

Strong support to the view here taken is also derived from the case of *Craig* v. *Missouri*, last cited, in which the opinion was given by the chief justice. Loan certificates issued by the state were the consideration of the note in suit in that case, and the defense was that the certificates were bills of credit, and that the consideration of the note was illegal. Responsive to that defense the plaintiff insisted that the certificates were not bills of credit, because they had not been made a legal tender, to which the court replied, that the emission of bills of credit and the enactment of tender laws were distinct operations, independent of each other; that both were forbidden by the constitution; that the evils of paper money did not result solely from the quality of its being made a tender in payment of debts; that that quality might be the *most pernicious* one, but that it was not an essential quality of bills of credit nor the only mischief resulting from such emissions.

Remarks of the chief justice in the case of *Sturges* v. *Crowninshield*, may also be referred to as even more explicit and decisive to the same conclusion than anything embodied in the other cases. He first describes, in vivid colors, the general distress which followed the war in which our independence was established. Paper money, he said, was issued, worthless lands and other property of no use to the creditor were made a tender in payment of debts, and the time of payment stipulated in the contract was extended by law. Mischief to such an extent was done, and so much more was apprehended, that general distrust prevailed, and all confidence between man and man was destroyed. Special reference was made to those grievances by the chief justice, because it was insisted that the prohibition to pass laws impairing the obligation of contracts ought to be confined by the court to matters of that description, but the court was of a different opinion, and held that the convention intended to establish a great principle, that contracts should be inviolable, that the provision was intended "to prohibit the use of any means by which the same mischief might be produced." He admitted that that provision was not intended to prevent the issue of paper money, as that evil was remedied and the practice prohibited by the clause forbidding the states to "emit bills of credit," inserted in the constitution expressly for that purpose, and he also admitted that the prohibition to emit bills of credit was not intended to restrain the states from enabling debtors to discharge their debts by the tender of property of no real value to the creditor, "because for that subject also particular provision is made" in the constitution; but he added, "NOTHING BUT GOLD AND SILVER COIN CAN BE MADE A TENDER IN PAYMENT OF DEBTS."

Utterances of the kind are found throughout the reported decisions of this court, but there is not a sentence or word to be found within those volumes, from the organization of the court to the passage of the acts of congress in question, to support the opposite theory.

Power, as before remarked, was vested in the congress under the confederation to borrow money and emit bills of credit, and history shows that the power to emit such bills had been exercised before the convention which framed the constitution assembled, to an amount exceeding $350,000,000. Still the draft of the constitution, as reported, contained the words, "and to emit bills," appended to the clause authorizing congress to borrow money. When that clause was reached, says Mr. Martin, a motion was made to strike out the words, "to emit *bills of credit;*" and his account of what followed affords the most persuasive and convincing evidence that the convention, and nearly every member of it, intended to put an end to the exercise of such a power. Against the motion, he says, we urged that it would be improper to deprive the congress of that power; that it would be a novelty unprecedented to establish a government which should not have such authority; that it was impossible to look forward into futurity so far as to decide that events might not happen that would render the exercise of such a power absolutely necessary, etc. But a majority of the convention, he said, being wise beyond every event, and being willing to risk any political evil rather than admit the idea of a paper emission *in any possible case*, refused to trust the authority to a government to which they were lavishing the most unlimited powers of taxation, and to the mercy of which they were willing blindly to trust the liberty and property of the citizen of every state in the Union, *and* "*they erased that clause from the system.*"

More forcible vindication of the action of the convention

could hardly be made than is expressed in the language of the Federalist, and the authority of Judge Story warrants the statement that the language there employed is "justified by almost every contemporary writer," and is "attested in its truth by facts" beyond the influence of every attempt at contradiction. Having adverted to those facts, the commentator proceeds to say, "that the same reasons which show the necessity of denying to the states the power of regulating coin, prove with equal force that they ought not to be at liberty to substitute a paper medium instead of coin."

Emissions of the kind were not declared by the Continental congress to be a legal tender, but congress passed a resolution declaring that they ought to be a tender in payment of all private and public debts, and that a refusal to receive the tender ought to be an extinguishment of the debt, and recommended the states to pass such laws. They even went further, and declared that whoever should refuse to receive the paper as gold or silver should be deemed an enemy to the public liberty; but our commentator says that these measures of violence and terror, so far from aiding the circulation of the paper, led on to still further depreciation. New emissions followed and new measures were adopted to give the paper credit by pledging the public faith for its redemption. Effort followed effort in that direction, until the idea of redemption at par was abandoned. Forty for one was offered, and the states were required to report the bills under that regulation, but few of the old bills were ever reported, and of course few only of the contemplated new notes were issued, and the bills in a brief period ceased to circulate, and in the course of that year quietly died in the hands of their possessors.

Bills of credit were made a tender by the states, but all such, as well as those issued by the congress, were dead in the hands of their possessors before the convention assembled to frame the constitution. Intelligent and impartial belief in the theory that such men, so instructed, in framing a government for their posterity as well as for themselves, would deliberately vest such a power, either in congress or the states, as a part of their perpetual system, can never, in my judgment, be secured in the face of the recorded evidences to the contrary which the political and judicial history of our country affords. Such evidence, so persuasive and convincing as it is, must ultimately bring all to the conclusion that neither the congress nor the states can make anything but gold or silver coin a tender in payment of debts.

Exclusive power to coin money is certainly vested in congress, but "no amount of reasoning can show that executing a promissory note, and ordering it to be taken in payment of public and private debts is a species of coining money."

Complete refutation of such theory is also found in the dissenting opinion in the former case, in which the justice who delivered the opinion states that he is not able to deduce the power to pass the laws in question from that clause of the constitution, and in which he admits without qualification that the provision making such notes a legal tender does undoubtedly impair the "obligation of contracts made before its passage." Extended argument, therefore, to show that the acts in question impair the obligation of contracts made before their passage is unnecessary, but the admission stops short of the whole truth, as it leaves the implication to be drawn that the obligation of subsequent contracts is not impaired by such legislation. Contracts for the payment of money, whether made before or after the passage of such a provision, are contracts, if the promise is expressed in dollars, to pay the specified amount in the money recognized and established by the constitution as the standard of value, and any act of congress which in theory compels the creditor to accept paper emissions, instead of the money so recognized and established, impairs the obligation of such a contract, no matter whether the contract was made before or after the act compelling the creditor to accept such payment, as the constitution in that respect is a part of the contract, and by its terms entitles the creditor to demand payment in the medium which the constitution recognizes and establishes as the standard of value.

Evidently the word dollar, as employed in the constitution, means the money recognized and established in the express power vested in congress to coin money, regulate the value thereof, and of foreign coin, the framers of the constitution having borrowed and adopted the word as used by the Continental congress in the ordinance of the 6th of July, 1785, and of the 8th August, 1786, in which it was enacted that the money unit of the United States should be "one dollar," and that the money of account should be dollars and fractions of dollars, as subsequently provided in the ordinance establishing a mint.

Repeated decisions of this court, of recent date, have established the rule that contracts to pay coined dollars can only be satisfied by the payment of such money, which is precisely equivalent to a decision that such notes as those described in the acts of congress in question are not the money recognized and established by the constitution as the standard of value, as the money so recognized and established, if the contract is expressed in dollars, will satisfy any and every contract between party and party. Beyond all question the cases cited recognize "the fact accepted by all men throughout the world, that value is inherent in the precious metals; that gold and silver are in themselves values, and being such, and being in other respects best adapted to the purpose, are *the only proper measures of value;* that these values are determined by weight and purity, and that form and impress are simply certificates of value, worthy of absolute reliance only because of the known integrity and good faith of the government which" put them in circulation.

When the intent of the parties as to the medium of payment is clearly expressed in a contract, the court decide in *Butler* v. *Horwitz*, above cited, that damages for the breach of it, whether made before or since the enactment of these laws, may be properly assessed so as to give effect to that intent, and no doubt is entertained that that rule is correct. Parties may contract to accept payment in treasury notes, or specific articles, or in bank bills, and if they do so they are bound to accept the medium for which they contracted, provided the notes, specific articles, or bills, are tendered on the day the payment under the contract becomes due, and it is clear that such a tender, if seasonable and sufficient in amount, is a good defense to the action. Decided cases also carry the doctrine much further, and hold, even where the contract is payable in money, and the promise is expressed in dollars, that a tender of bank bills is a good tender if the party to whom it was made placed his objections to receiving it wholly upon the ground that the amount was not sufficient.

Grant all that, and still it is clear that where the contract is for the payment of a certain sum of money, and the promise is expressed in dollars, or in coined dollars, the promisee, if he sees fit, may lawfully refuse to accept payment in any other medium than gold and silver, made a legal tender by act of congress passed in pursuance of that provision of the constitution which vests in congress the power to coin money, regulate the value thereof, and of foreign coin.

Foreign coin of gold and silver may be made a legal tender, as the power to regulate the value thereof is vested in congress as well as the power to regulate the value of the coins fabricated and stamped at the mint.

Opposed, as the new theory is, by such a body of evidence, covering the whole period of our constitutional history, all tending to the opposite conclusion, and unsupported as the theory is by a single historical fact, entitled to any weight, it would seem that the advocates of the theory ought to be able to give it a fixed domicil in the constitution, or else be willing to abandon it as a theory without any solid constitutional foundation. Vagrancy in that behalf, if conceded, is certainly a very strong argument at this day, that the power does not reside in the constitution at all, as if the fact were otherwise, the period of eighty-five years which has elapsed since the constitution was adopted is surely long enough to have enabled its advocates to discover its locality, and to be able to point out its home to those whose researches have been less successful and whose conscientious convictions lead them to the conclusion that, as applied to the constitution, it is a myth without a habitation or a name.

Unless the power to enact such a provision can be referred to some one or more of the express grants of power to congress, as the requisite means, or as necessary and proper for carrying such express power or powers into execution, it is usually conceded that the provision must be regarded as unconstitutional, as it is not pretended that the constitution contains any express grant of power authorizing such legislation. Powers not granted cannot be exercised by congress, and certainly all must agree that no powers are granted except what are expressed or such as are fairly applicable as requisite means to attain the end of a power which is granted, or, in other words, are necessary and proper to carry those which are expressed into execution.

Pressed by these irrepealable rules of construction, as applied to the constitution, those who maintain the affirmative of the question under discussion are forced to submit a specification. Courts, in one or more cases, have intimated that the power in question may be implied from the express power to coin money, but inasmuch as no decided case is referred to where the judgment of the court rests upon that ground, the suggestion will be dismissed without further consideration, as one involving a proposition too latitudinous to require refutation. Most of the cases referred to attempt to deduce the power to make such paper emissions a legal tender from the express power to borrow money, or from the power to declare war, or from the two combined, as in the dissenting opinion in the case which is now overruled.

Authority, it is conceded, exists in congress to pass laws providing for the issue of treasury notes, based on the national credit, as necessary and proper means for fulfilling the end of the express power to borrow money, nor can it be doubted at this day, that such notes, when issued by the proper authority, may lawfully circulate as credit currency, and that they may, in that conventional character, be lawfully employed, if the act authorizing their issue so provides, to pay duties, taxes, and all the public exactions required to be paid into the national treasury. Public creditors may also be paid in such currency by their own consent, and they may be used in all other cases, where the payment of such notes comports with the terms of the contract. Established usage, founded upon the practice of the government, often repeated, has sanctioned these rules, until it may now be said that they are not open to controversy, but the question in the cases before the court is whether the congress may declare such notes to be lawful money, make them a legal tender, and impart to such a currency the quality of being a standard of value, and compel creditors to accept the payment of their debts in such a currency as the equivalent of the money recognized and established by the constitution as the standard of value by which the value of all other commodities is to be measured. Financial measures, of various kinds, for borrowing money to supply the wants of the treasury, beyond the receipts from taxation, and the sales of the public lands, have been adopted by the government since the United States became an independent nation. Subscriptions for a loan of twelve millions of dollars were, on the 4th of August, 1790, directed to be opened at the treasury, to be made payable in certificates issued for the debt according to their specie value. Measures of this kind were repeated in rapid succession for several years, and laws providing for loans in one form or another appear to have been the preferred mode of borrowing money, until the 30th of June, 1812, when the first act was passed "to authorize the issue of treasury notes."

Loans had been previously authorized in repeated instances, as will be seen by the following references, to which many more might be added.

Earnest opposition was made to the passage of the first act of congress authorizing the issue of treasury notes, but the measure prevailed, and it may be remarked that the vote on the occasion was ever after regarded as having settled the question as to the constitutionality of such an act. Five millions of dollars were directed to be issued by that act, and the secretary of the treasury, with the approbation of the president, was empowered to cause such portions of the notes as he might deem expedient to be issued at par "to such public creditors *or other persons as may choose to receive such notes in payment*," it never having occurred to any one that even a public creditor could be compelled to receive such notes in payment except by his own consent. Twenty other issues of such notes were authorized by congress in the course of the fifty years next after the passage of that act and before the passage of the acts making such notes a legal tender, and every one of such prior acts, being twenty in all, contains either in express words or by necessary implication, an equally decisive negation to the new constitutional theory that congress can make paper emissions either a standard of value or a legal tender. Superadded to the conceded fact that the constitution contains no express words to support such a theory, this long and unbroken usage, that treasury notes shall not be constituted a standard of value nor be made a tender in payment of debts, is entitled to great weight, and when taken in connection with the persuasive and convincing evidences, derived from the published proceedings of the convention, that the framers of the constitution never intended to grant any such power, and from the recorded sentiments of the great men who have arguments in favor of the reported draft procured its ratification, and supported as that view is by the repeated decisions of this court, and by the infallible rule of interpretation that the language of one express power shall not be so expanded as to nullify the force and effect of another express power in the same instrument, it seems to me that it ought to be deemed final and conclusive that congress cannot constitute such notes or any other paper emissions a constitutional standard of value, or make them a legal tender in payment of debts—especially as it covers the period of two foreign wars, the creation of the second national bank, and the greatest financial revulsions through which our country has ever passed.

Guided by the views expressed in the dissenting opinion in the former case, it must be taken for granted that the legal tender feature in the acts in question was placed emphatically, by those who enacted the provision, upon the necessity of the measure to the further borrowing of money and maintaining the army and navy, and such appears to be the principal ground assumed in the present opinion of the court. Enough also appears in some of the interrogative sentences of the dissenting opinion to show that the learned justice who delivered it intended to place the dissent very largely upon the same ground.

Nothing need be added, it would seem, to show that the power to make such notes a standard of value and a legal tender cannot be derived from the power to borrow money, without so expanding it by implication as to nullify the power to coin money and regulate its value, nor without extending the scope and operation of the power to borrow money to an object never contemplated by the framers of the constitution; and if so, then it only remains to inquire whether it may be implied from the power to declare war, to raise and support armies, or to provide and maintain a navy, or "to enable the government to borrow money to carry on the war," as the phrase is in the dissenting opinion in the former case.

Money is undoubtedly the sinews of war, but the power to raise money to carry on war, under the constitution, is not an implied power, and whoever adopts that theory commits a great constitutional error. Congress may declare war and congress may appropriate all moneys in the treasury to carry on the war, or congress may coin money for that purpose, or borrow money to any amount for the same purpose, or congress may levy and collect taxes, duties, imposts, and excises to replenish the treasury, or may dispose of the public lands or other property belonging to the United States, and may in fact, by the exercise of the express powers of the constitution, command the whole wealth and substance of the people to sustain the public credit and prosecute the war to a successful termination. Two foreign wars were successfully conducted by means derived from those sources, and it is not doubted that those express powers will always enable congress to maintain the national credit and defray the public expenses in every emergency which may arise, even though the national independence should be assailed by the combined forces of all the rest of the civilized world. All remarks, therefore, in the nature of entreaty or appeal, in favor of an implied power to fulfill the great purpose of national defense or to raise money to prosecute a war, are a mere waste of words, as the most powerful and comprehensive means to accomplish the purpose for which the appeal is made are found in the express powers vested in congress to levy and collect taxes, duties, imposts, and exercise without limitation as to amount, to borrow money also without limitation, and to coin money, dispose of the public lands, and to appropriate all moneys in the public treasury to that purpose.

Weighed in the light of these suggestions, as the question under discussion should be, it is plain, not only that the exercise of such an implied power is unnecessary to supply the sinews of war, but that the framers or the constitution never intended to trust a matter of such great and vital importance as that of raising means for the national defense or for the prosecution of a war to any implication whatever, as they had learned from bitter experience that the great weakness of the confederation during the war for independence consisted in the want of such express powers. Influenced by those considerations the framers of the constitution not only authorized congress to levy and collect taxes, duties, imposts, and excises to any and every extent, but also to coin money and to borrow money without any limitation as to amount, showing that the argument that to deny the implied power to make paper emissions a legal tender will be to cripple the government, is a mere chimera, without any solid constitutional foundation for its support.

Comprehensive, however, as the power of federal taxation is, being without limitation as to amount, still there are some restrictions as to the manner of its exercise, and some exceptions as to the objects to which it may be applied. Bills for raising revenue must originate in the house of representatives; duties, imposts, and excises must be uniform throughout the United States; direct taxes must be apportioned according to numbers; regulations of commerce and revenue shall not give any preference to the ports of one state over those of another; nor shall vessels bound to or from one state be obliged to enter, clear, or pay duties in another; nor shall any tax or duty be laid on articles exported from any state.

Preparation for war may be made in peace, but neither the necessity for such preparation nor the actual existence of war can have the effect to abrogate or supersede those restrictions, or to empower congress to tax the articles excepted from taxation by the constitution. Implied exceptions also exist, limiting the power of federal taxation as well as that of the states, and when an exception of that character is ascertained the objects falling within it are as effectually shielded from taxation as those falling within an express exception, for the plain reason that the "government of the United States is acknowledged by all to be one of enumerated powers," from which it necessarily follows that powers not granted cannot be exercised.

Moneys may be raised by taxes, duties, imposts, and excises to carry on war as well as to pay the public debt or to provide for the common defense and general welfare, but no appropriation of money to that use can be made for a period longer than two years, nor can congress, in exercising the power to levy taxes for that purpose, or any other, abrogate or supersede those restrictions, exceptions, and limitations, as they are a part of the constitution, and as such are as obligatory in war as in peace, as any other rule would subvert, in time of war, every restriction, exception, limitation, and prohibition in the constitution, and invest congress with unlimited power, even surpassing that possessed by the British parliament.

Congress may also borrow money to carry on war, without limitation, and in exercising that express power may issue treasury notes as the requisite means for carrying the express power into execution; but congress cannot constitute such notes a standard of value, nor make them a legal tender, neither in time of war nor in time of peace, for at least two reasons, either of which is conclusive that the exercise of such a power is not warranted by the constitution: (1.) Because the published proceedings of the convention which adopted the constitution, and of the state conventions which ratified it, show that those who participated in those deliberations never intended to confer any such power. (2.) Because such a power, if admitted to exist, would nullify the effect and operation of the express power to coin money, regulate the value thereof and of foreign coin, as it would substitute a paper medium in the place of gold and silver coin, which, in itself, as compared with coin, possesses no value, is not money, either in the constitutional or commercial sense, but only a promise to pay money, is never worth par, and often much less, even as domestic exchange, and is always fluctuating and never acknowledged either as a medium of exchange or a standard of value in any foreign market known to American commerce.

Power to issue such notes, it is conceded, exists without limitation; but the question is, whether the framers of the constitution intended that congress, in the exercise of that power or the power to borrow money, whether in peace or war, should be empowered to constitute paper emissions of any kind a standard of value, and make the same a legal tender in payment of debts. Mere convenience, or even a financial necessity in a single case, cannot be the test; but the question is, what did the framers of the constitution intend at the time the instrument was adopted and ratified?

Constitutional powers of the kind last mentioned — that is, the power to ordain a standard of value and to provide a circulating medium for a legal tender — are subject to no mutations of any kind; they are the same in peace and in war. What the grants of power meant when the constitution was adopted and ratified they mean still, and their meaning can never be changed except as described in the fifth article providing for amendments, as the constitution "is a law for rulers and people, equally in war and in peace, and covers with the shield of its protection all classes of men, and under all circumstances."

Delegated power ought never to be enlarged beyond the fair scope of its terms, and that rule is emphatically applicable in the construction of the constitution. Restrictions may at times be inconvenient, or even embarrassing; but the power to remove the difficulty by amendment is vested in the people, and if they do not exercise it, the presumption is that the inconvenience is a less evil than the mischief to be apprehended if the restriction should be removed and the power extended, or that the existing inconvenience is the lesser of the two evils; and it should never be forgotten that the government ordained and established by the constitution is a government "of limited and enumerated powers," and that to depart from the true import and meaning of those powers is to establish a new constitution or to do for the people what they have not chosen to do for themselves, and to usurp the functions of a legislator and desert those of an expounder of the law. Arguments drawn from impolicy or inconvenience, says Judge Story, ought here to be of no weight, as "the only sound principle is to declare *ita lex scripta est*, to follow and to obey."

For these reasons I am of the opinion that the judgment in each of the cases before the court should be reversed.

CHAPTER IV.

DISSENTING OPINION OF JUSTICE FIELD.

WHILST I agree with the chief justice in the views expressed in his opinion in these cases, the great importance which I attach to the question of legal tender induces me to present some further considerations on the subject.

Nothing has been heard from counsel in these cases, and nothing from the present majority of the court, which has created a doubt in my mind of the correctness of the judgment rendered in the case of *Hepburn* v. *Griswold*, or of the conclusions expressed in the opinion of the majority of the court as then constituted. That judgment was reached only after repeated arguments were heard from able and eminent counsel, and after every point raised on either side had been the subject of extended deliberation.

The questions presented in that case were also involved in several other cases, and had been elaborately argued in them. It is not extravagant to say that no case has ever been decided by this court, since its organization, in which the questions presented were more fully argued or more maturely considered. It was hoped that a judgment thus reached would not be lightly disturbed. It was hoped that it had settled forever, that under a constitution ordained, among other things, "to establish justice," legislation giving to one person the right to discharge his obligations to another by nominal instead of actual fulfillment could never be justified.

I shall not comment upon the causes which have led to a reversal of that judgment; they are patent to every one. I will simply observe, that the chief justice and the associate justices who constituted the majority of the court when that judgment was rendered, still adhere to their former convictions. To them the reasons for the original decision are as cogent and convincing now as they were when that decision was pronounced; and to them its justice, as applies to past contracts, is as clear to-day as it was then.

In the cases now before us the questions stated by order of the court, for the argument of counsel, do not present with entire accuracy the questions actually argued and decided. As stated the questions are: 1st. Is the act of congress known as the legal tender act constitutional as to contracts made before its passage? 2d. Is it valid as applicable to transactions since its passage?

The act thus designated as the legal tender act is the act of congress of February 25th, 1862, authorizing the issue of United States notes, and providing for their redemption or funding, and for funding the floating debt of the United States, and the question as stated would seem to draw into discussion the validity of the entire act, whereas the only questions intended for argument, and actually argued and decided, relate—1st, to the validity of that provision of the act which declares that these notes shall be a legal tender in payment of debts, as applied to private debts and debts of the government contracted previous to the passage of the act; and, 2d, to the validity of the provision as applied to similar contracts subsequently made. The case of *Parker* v. *Davis* involves the consideration of the first question; and the case of *Knox* v. *Lee* is supposed by a majority of the court to present the second question.

No question was raised as to the validity of the provisions of the act authorizing the issue of the notes, and making them receivable for dues to the United States; nor do I perceive that any objection could justly be made at this day to these provisions. The issue of the notes was a proper exercise of the power to borrow money, which is granted to congress without limitation. The extent to which the power may be exercised depends in all cases upon the judgment of that body as to the necessities of the government. The power to borrow includes the power to give evidences of indebtedness and obligations of repayment. Instruments of this character are among the securities of the United States mentioned in the constitution. These securities are sometimes in the form of certificates of indebtedness, but they may be issued in any other form, and in such form and in such amounts as will fit them for general circulation, and to that end may be made payable to the bearer and transferable by delivery. The form of notes varying in amounts to suit the convenience or ability of the lender, has been found by experience a convenient form, and the one best calculated to secure the readiest acceptance and the largest loan. It has been the practice of the government to use notes of this character in raising loans and obtaining supplies from an early period in its history, their receipt by third parties being in all cases optional.

In June, 1812, congress passed an act which provided for the issue of treasury notes, and authorized the secretary of the treasury, with the approbation of the president, "to borrow from time to time, not under par, such sums" as the president might think expedient, "on the credit of such notes."

In February, 1813, congress passed another act for the issue of treasury notes, declaring "that the amount of money borrowed or obtained by virtue of the notes" issued under its second section should be a part of the money authorized to be borrowed under a previous act of the same session. There are numerous other acts of a similar character on our statute books. More than twenty, I believe, were passed previous to the legal tender act.

In all of them the issue of the notes was authorized as a means of borrowing money, or of obtaining supplies, or paying the debts of the United States, and in all of them the receipt of the notes by third parties was purely voluntary. Thus, in the first act, of June, 1812, the secretary of the treasury was authorized not only to borrow on the notes, but to issue such notes as the president might think expedient "in payment of supplies or debts due by the United States to such public creditors or other persons" as might "*choose to receive such notes in payment at par.*" Similar provisions are found in all the acts except where the notes are authorized simply to take up previous loans.

The issue of the notes for supplies purchased or services rendered at the request of the United States, is only giving their obligations for an indebtedness thus incurred; and the same power which authorizes the issue of notes for money must also authorize their issue for whatever is received as an equivalent for money. The result to the United States is the same as if the money was actually received for the notes and then paid out for the supplies or services.

The notes issued under the act of Congress of February 25th, 1862, differ from the treasury notes authorized by the previous acts to which I have referred in the fact that they do not bear interest and do not designate on their face a period at which they shall be paid, features which may affect their value in the market but do not change their essential character. There cannot be, therefore, as already stated, any just objection at this day to the issue of the notes, nor to their adaptation in form for general circulation.

Nor can their be any objection to their being made receivable for dues to the United States. Their receivability in this respect is only the application to the demands of the government, and demands against it, of the just principle which is applied to the demands of individuals against each other, that cross-demands shall offset and satisfy each other to the extent of their respective amounts. No rights of third parties are in any respect affected by the application of the rule here, and the purchasing and borrowing powers of the notes are greatly increased by making them thus receivable for the public dues. The objection to the act does not lie in these features; it lies in the provision which declares that the notes shall be "a legal tender in payment of all debts, public and private," so far as that provision applies to private debts, and debts owing by the United States.

In considering the validity and constitutionality of this provision, I shall in the first place confine myself to the provision in its application to private debts. Afterwards I shall have something to say of the provision in its application to debts owing by the government.

In the discussions upon the subject of legal tender the

advocates of the measure do not agree as to the power in the constitution to which it shall be referred; some placing it upon the power to borrow money, some on the coining power, and some on what is termed a resulting power from the general purposes of the government; and these discussions have been accompanied by statements as to the effect of the measure, and the consequences which must have followed had it been rejected, and which will now occur if its validity be not sustained, which rests upon no solid foundation, and are not calculated to aid the judgment in coming to a just conclusion.

In what I have to say I shall endeavor to avoid any such general and loose statements, and shall direct myself to an inquiry into the nature of these powers to which the measure is referred, and the relation of the measure to them.

Now if congress can, by its legislative declaration, make the notes of the Uuited States a legal tender in payment of private debts—that is, can make them receivable against the will of the creditor in satisfaction of debts due to him by third parties —its power in this respect is not derived from its power to borrow money, under which the notes were issued. That power is not different in its nature or essential incidents from the power to borrow possessed by individuals, and is not to receive a larger definition. Nor is it different from the power often granted to public and private corporations. The grant, it is true, is usually accompanied in these latter cases with limitations as to the amount to be borrowed, and a designation of the objects to which the money shall be applied—limitations which in no respect affect the nature of the power. The terms "power to borrow money" have the same meaning in all these cases, and not one meaning when used by individuals, another when granted to corporations, and still a different one when possessed by congress. They mean only a power to contract for a loan of money upon considerations to be agreed between the parties. The amount of the loan, the time of repayment, the interest it shall bear, and the form in which the obligation shall be expressed are simply matters of arrangement between the parties. They concern no one else. It is no part or incident of a contract of this character that the rights or interests of third parties, strangers to the matter, shall be in any respect affected. The transaction is completed when the lender has parted with his money, and the borrower has given his promise of repayment at the time, and in the manner, and with the securities stipulated between them.

As an inducement to the loan, and security for its repayment, the borrower may of course pledge such property or revenues, and annex to his promises such rights and privileges as he may possess. His stipulations in this respect are necessarily limited to his own property, rights, and privileges, and cannot extend to those of other persons.

Now, whether a borrower—be the borrower an individual, a corporation, or the government—can annex to the bonds, notes, or other evidences of debt given for the money borrowed, any quality by which they will serve as a means of satisfying the contracts of other parties, must necessarily depend upon the question whether the borrower possesses any right to interfere with such contracts, and determine how they shall be satisfied. The right of the borrower in this respect rests upon no different foundation than the right to interfere with any other property of third parties. And if it will not be contended, as I think I may assume that it will not be, that the borrower possesses any right, in order to make a loan, to interfere with the tangible and visible property of third parties, I do not perceive how it can be contended that he has any right to interfere with their property when it exists in the form of contracts. A large part of the property of every commercial people exists in that form, and the principle which excludes a stranger from meddling with another's property which is visible and tangible, equally excludes him from meddling with it when existing in the form of contracts.

That an individual or corporation borrowing, possesses no power to annex to his evidences of indebtedness any quality by which the holder will be enabled to change his contracts with third parties, strangers to the loan, is admitted; but it is contended that congress possesses such power, because, in addition to the express power to borrow money, there is a clause in the constitution which authorizes congress to made all laws "necessary and proper" for the execution of the powers enumerated. This clause neither augments nor diminishes the expressly designated powers. It only states in terms what congress would equally have had the right to do without its insertion in the constitution. It is a general principle that a power to do a particular act includes the power to adopt all the ordinary and appropriate means for its execution. "Had the constitution," says Hamilton, in the Federalist, speaking of this clause, "been silent on this head, there can be no doubt that all the particular powers requisite as a means of executing the general powers would have resulted to the government by unavoidable implication. No axiom is more clearly established in law or in reason, that whenever the end is required the means are authorized; whenever a general power to do a thing is given, every particular power necessary for doing it is included.

The subsidiary power existing without the clause in question, its insertion in the constitution was no doubt intended, as observed by Mr. Hamilton, to prevent "all cavilling refinements" in those who might thereafter feel a disposition to curtail and evade the legitimate authorities of the Union; and also, I may add, to indicate the true sphere and limits of the implied powers.

But though the subsidiary power would have existed without this clause, there would have been the same perpetually recurring question as now, as to what laws are necessary and proper for the execution of the expressly enumerated powers.

The particular clause in question has at different times undergone elaborate discussions in congress, in cabinets, and in the courts. Its meaning was much debated in the first congress upon the proposition to incorporate a national bank, and afterwards in the cabinet of Washington, when that measure was presented for his approval. Mr. Jefferson, then secretary of state, and Mr. Hamilton, then secretary of the treasury, differed widely in their construction of the clause, and each gave his views in an elaborate opinion. Mr. Jefferson held that the word "necessary," restricted the power of congress to the use of those means, without which the grant would be nugatory, thus making necessary equivalent to indispensable.

Mr. Hamilton favored a more liberal, and in my judgment, a more just interpretation, and contended that the terms "necessary and proper," meant no more than that the measures adopted must have an obvious relation as a means to the end intended. "If the end," he said, "be clearly comprehended within any of the specified powers, and if the measure have an obvious relation to that end, and is not forbidden by any particular provision of the constitution, it may safely be deemed to come within the compass of the national authority." "There is also," he added, "this further criterion which may materially assist the decision: Does the proposed measure abridge a preëxisting right of any state, or of any individual? If it does not, there is a strong presumption in favor of its constitutionality; and slighter relations to any declared object may be permitted to turn the scale." From the criterion thus indicated, it would seem that the distinguished statesman was of opinion that a measure which did interfere with a preëxisting right of a state or an individual would not be constitutional.

The interpretation given by Mr. Hamilton was substantially followed by Chief Justice Marshall, in *McCulloch* v. *The State of Maryland*, when, speaking for the court, he said that if the end to be accomplished by the legislation of congress be legitimate, and within the scope of the constitution, "all the means which are appropriate, which are plainly adapted to that end, and which are not prohibited, but are consistent with the letter and spirit of the constitution, are constitutional." The chief justice did not, it is true, in terms declare that legislation which is not thus appropriate, and plainly adapted to a lawful end, is unconstitutional, but such is the plain import of the argument advanced by him; and that conclusion must also follow from the principle that, when legislation of a particular character is specially authorized, the opposite of such legislation is inhibited.

Tested by the rule given by Mr. Hamilton, or by the rule thus laid down by this court through Mr. Chief Justice Marshall, the annexing of a quality to the promises of the government for money borrowed, which will enable the holder to use them as a means of satisfying the demands of third parties, cannot be sustained as the exercise of an appropriate means of borrowing. That is only appropriate which has some relation of fitness to an end. Borrowing, as already stated, is a transaction by which, on one side, the lender parts with his money, and on the other the borrower agrees to repay it in such form and at such time as may be stipulated. Though not a necessary part of the contract of borrowing, it is usual for the borrower to offer securities for the repayment of the loan. The fitness which would render a means appropriate to this transaction thus considered, must have respect to the terms which are essential to the contract, or to the securities which the borrower may furnish as an inducement to the loan. The quality of legal tender does not touch the terms of the contract of borrowing, nor does it stand as a security for the loan. A security supposes some right or interest in the thing pledged, which is subject to the disposition of the borrower.

There has been much confusion on this subject from a failure to distinguish between the adaptation of particular means to an end and the effect, or supposed effect, of those means in producing results desired by the government. The argument is stated thus: the object of borrowing is to raise funds; the annexing of the quality of legal tender to the notes of the government induces parties the more readily to loan upon them; the result desired by the government—the acquisition of funds—is thus accomplished; therefore, the annexing of the quality of legal tender is an appropriate means to the execution of the power to borrow. But it is evident that the same reasoning would justify, as appropriate means to the execution of this power, any measures which would result in obtaining the required funds. The annexing of a provision by which the notes of the government should serve as a free ticket in the public conveyances of the country, or for ingress into places of public amusement, or which would entitle the holder to a percentage out of the revenues of private corporations, or exempt his entire property, as well as the notes themselves, from state and municipal taxation, would produce a ready acceptance of the notes. But the advocate of the most liberal construction would hardly pretend that these measures, or similar measures touching the property of third parties would be appropriate as a means to the execution of the power to borrow. Indeed, there is no invasion by government of the rights of third parties which might not thus be sanctioned upon the pretence that its allowance to the holder of the notes would lead to their ready acceptance and produce the desired loan.

The actual effect of the quality of legal tender in inducing parties to receive them was necessarily limited to the amount required by existing debtors, who did not scruple to discharge with them their preëxisting liabilities. For moneys desired from other parties, or supplies required for the use of the army or navy, the provision added nothing to the value of the notes. Their borrowing power or purchasing power depended, by a general and a universal law of currency, not upon the legal tender clause, but upon the confidence which the parties receiving the notes had in their ultimate payment. Their exchangeable value was determined by this confidence, and every person dealing in them advanced his money and regulated his charges accordingly.

The inability of mere legislation to control this universal law of currency is strikingly illustrated by the history of the bills of credit issued by the Continental congress during our Revolutionary war. From June, 1775, to March, 1780, these bills amounted to over $300,000,000. Depreciation followed as a natural consequence, commencing in 1777, when the issues only equalled $14,000,000. Previous to this time, in January, 1776, when the issues were only $5,000,000, congress had, by resolution, declared that if any person should be "so lost to all virtue and regard to his country" as to refuse to receive the bills in payment, he should, on conviction thereof by the committee of the city, county, or district, or, in case of appeal from their decision, by the assembly, convention, council, or committee of safety of the colony where he resided, be "deemed, published, and treated as an enemy of his country, and precluded from all trade or intercourse with the inhabitants" of the colonies.

And in January, 1777, when as yet the issues were only $14,000,000, congress passed this remarkable resolution:

"*Resolved*, That all bills of credit emitted by authority of congress ought to pass current in all payments, trade, and dealings in these states, and be deemed in value equal to the same nominal sums in Spanish milled dollars, and that whosoever shall offer, ask, or receive more in the said bills for any gold or silver coins, bullion, or any other species of money whatsoever, than the nominal sum or amount thereof in Spanish milled dollars, or more in the said bills for any lands, houses, goods, or commodities whatsoever than the same could be purchased at of the same person or persons in gold, silver, or any other species of money whatsoever, or shall offer to sell any goods or commodities for gold or silver coins or any other species of money whatsoever and refuse to sell the same for the said continental bills, every such person ought to be deemed an enemy to the liberty of these United States and to forfeit the value of the money so exchanged, or house, land, or commodity so sold or offered for sale. And it is recommended to the legislatures of the respective states to enact laws inflicting such forfeitures and other penalties on offenders as aforesaid as will prevent such pernicious practices. That it be recommended to the legislatures of the United States to pass laws to make the bills of credit issued by the congress a lawful tender in payments of public and private debts, and a refusal thereof an extinguishment of such debts; that debts payable in sterling money be discharged with continental dollars at the rate of 4*s.* 6*d.* sterling per dollar, and that in discharge of all other debts and contracts continental dollars pass at the rate fixed by the respective states for the value of Spanish milled dollars."

The several states promptly responded to the recommendations of congress, and made the bills a legal tender for debts, and the refusal to receive them an extinguishment of the debt.

Congress also issued, in September, 1779, a circular addressed to the people, on the subject, in which they showed that the United States would be able to redeem the bills, and they repelled with indignation the suggestion that there could be any violation of the public faith. "The pride of America," said the address, "revolts from the idea; her citizens know for what purposes these emissions were made, and have repeatedly plighted their faith for the redemption of them; they are to be found in every man's possession, and every man is interested in their being redeemed; they must, therefore, entertain a high opinion of American credulity who suppose the people capable of believing, on due reflection, that all America will, against the faith, the honor, and the interest of all America, be ever prevailed upon to countenance, support, or permit so ruinous, so disgraceful a measure. We are convinced that the efforts and arts of our enemies will not be wanting to draw us into this humiliating and contemptible situation. Impelled by malice, and the suggestions of chagrin and disappointment at not being able to bend our necks to the yoke, they will endeavor to force or seduce us to commit this unpardonable sin in order to subject us to the punishment due to it, and that we may thenceforth be a reproach and a by-word among the nations. Apprised of these consequences, knowing the value of national character, and impressed with a due sense of the immutable laws of justice and honor, it is impossible that America should think without horror of such an execrable deed."

Yet in spite of the noble sentiments contained in this address, which bears the honored name of John Jay, then president of congress, and afterwards the first chief justice of this court, and in spite of legal tender provisions and harsh penal statutes, the universal law of currency prevailed. Depreciation followed until it became so great that the very idea of redemption at par was abandoned.

Congress then proposed to take up the bills by issuing new bills on the credit of the several states, guaranteed by the United States, not exceeding one-twentieth of the amount of the old issue, the new bills to draw interest, and be redeemable in six years. But the scheme failed, and the bills became, during 1780, of so little value that they ceased to circulate and "quietly died," says the historian of the period, "in the hands of their possessors."

And it is within the memory of all of us that during the late rebellion the notes of the United States issued under the legal tender act rose in value in the market as the successes of our arms gave evidence of an early termination of the war, and that they fell in value with every triumph of the Confederate forces. No legislation of congress declaring these notes to be money instead of representatives of money or credit could alter this result one jot or tittle. Men measured their value, not by congressional declaration, which could not alter the nature of things, but by the confidence reposed in their ultimate payment.

Without the legal tender provision the notes would have circulated equally well and answered all the purposes of government—the only direct benefit resulting from that provision arising, as already stated, from the ability it conferred upon unscrupulous debtors to discharge with them previous obligations. The notes of state banks circulated without possessing that quality, and supplied a currency for the people just so long as confidence in the ability of the banks to redeem the notes continued. The notes issued by the national bank associations during the war under the authority of congress, amounting to $300,000,000, which were never made a legal tender, circulated equally well with the notes of the United States. Neither their utility nor their circulation was diminished in any degree by the absence of a legal tender quality. They rose and fell in the market under the same influences, and precisely to the same extent as the notes of the United States, which possessed this quality.

It is foreign, however, to my argument to discuss the utility of the legal tender clause. The utility of a measure is not the subject of judicial cognizance, nor, as already intimated, the test of its constitutionality. But the relation of the measure as a means to an end authorized by the constitution, is a subject of such cognizance, and the test of its constitutionality, when it is not prohibited by any specific provision of that instrument, and is consistent with its letter and spirit. "The degree," said Hamilton, "in which a measure is necessary can never be a test of the *legal right* to adopt it. That must be a matter of opinion, and can only be a test of expediency. The relation between the means and the end, between the nature of a *means* employed toward the execution of the power and the *object* of that power, must be the criterion of unconstitutionality; not the more or less of necessity or utility."

If this were not so, if congress could not only exercise, as it undoubtedly may, unrestricted liberty of choice among the means which are appropriate, and plainly adapted to the execution of an express power, but could also judge, without its conclusions being subject to question in cases involving private rights, what means are thus appropriate and adapted, our government would be, not what it was intended to be, one of limited, but one of unlimited powers.

Of course congress must inquire in the first instance, and determine for itself, not only the expediency, but the fitness to the end intended, of every measure adopted by its legislation. But the power of this tribunal to revise these determinations in cases involving private rights has been uniformly asserted, since the formation of the constitution to this day, by the ablest statesmen and jurists of the country.

I have thus dwelt at length upon the clause of the constitution investing congress with the power to borrow money on the credit of the United States, because it is under that power that the notes of the United States were issued, and it is upon the supposed enhanced value which the quality of legal tender gives to such notes, as the means of borrowing, that the validity and constitutionality of the provision annexing this quality are founded. It is true that in the arguments of counsel, and in the several opinions of different state courts, to which our attention has been called, and in the dissenting opinion in *Hepburn* v. *Griswold*, reference is also made to other powers possessed by congress, particularly to declare war, to suppress insurrection, to raise and support armies, and to provide and maintain a navy—all of which were called into exercise and severely taxed at the time the legal tender act was passed. But it is evident that the notes have no relation to these powers, or to any other powers of congress, except as they furnish a convenient means for raising money for their execution. The existence of the war only increased the urgency of the government for funds. It did not add to its powers to raise such funds, or change, in any respect, the nature of those powers or the transactions which they authorized. If the power to engraft the quality of legal tender upon the notes existed at all with congress, the occasion, the extent, and the purpose of its exercise were mere matters of legislative discretion; and the power may be equally exerted when a loan is made to meet the ordinary expenses of government in time of peace, as when vast sums are needed to raise armies and provide navies in time of war. The wants of the government can never be the measure of its powers.

The constitution has specifically designated the means by which funds can be raised for the uses of the government, either in war or peace. These are taxation, borrowing, coining, and the sale of its public property. Congress is empowered to levy and collect taxes, duties, imposts, and excises, to any extent which the public necessities may require. Its power to borrow is equally unlimited. It can convert any bullion it may possess into coin, and it can dispose of the public lands and other property of the United States, or any part of such property. The designation of these means exhausts the powers of congress on the subject of raising money. The designation of the means is a negation of all others, for the designation would be unnecessary and absurd if the use of any and all means were permissible without it. These means exclude a resort to forced loans, and to any compulsory interference with the property of third persons, except by regular taxation in one of the forms mentioned.

But this is not all. The power to "coin money" is, in my judgment, inconsistent with and repugnant to the existence of a power to make anything but coin a legal tender. To coin money is to mould metallic substances having intrinsic value into certain forms convenient for commerce, and to impress them with the stamp of the government indicating their value. Coins are pieces of metal of definite weight and value, thus stamped by national authority. Such is the natural import of the terms, "to coin money" and "coin;" and if there were any doubt that this is their meaning in the constitution, it would be removed by the language which immediately follows the grant of the "power to coin," authorizing congress to regulate the value of the money thus coined, and also "of foreign coin," and by the distinction made in other clauses between coin and the obligations of the general government and of the several states.

The power of regulation conferred is the power to determine the weight and purity of the several coins struck, and their consequent relation to the monetary unit which might be established by the authority of the government—a power which can be exercised with reference to the metallic coins of foreign countries, but which is incapable of execution with reference to their obligations or securities.

Then, in the clause of the constitution immediately following authorizing congress "to provide for the punishment of counterfeiting the securities and current coin of the United States," a distinction between the obligations and coins of the general government is clearly made. And in the tenth section, which forbids the states to "coin money, emit bills of credit, and make anything but gold and silver coin a tender in payment of debts," a like distinction is made between coin and the obligations of the several states. The terms gold and silver, as applied to the coin, exclude the possibility of any other conclusion.

Now, money, in the true sense of the term, is not only a medium of exchange, but it is a standard of value by which all other values are measured. Blackstone says — and Story repeats his language—"Money is a universal medium or common standard, by a comparison with which the value of all merchandise may be ascertained, or it is a sign which represents the respective values of all commodities." Money being such standard, its coins or pieces are necessarily a legal tender to the amount of their respective values, for all contracts or judgments payable in money, without any legislative enactment to make them so. The provisions in the different coinage acts, that the coins to be struck shall be such legal tender, are merely declaratory of their effect when offered in payment, and are not essential to give them that character.

The power to coin money is therefore a power to fabricate coins out of metal as money, and thus make them a legal tender for their declared values, as indicated by their stamp. If this be the true import and meaning of the language used, it is difficult to see how congress can make the paper of the government a legal tender. When the constitution says that congress shall have the power to make metallic coins a legal tender, it declares in effect that it shall make nothing else such tender. The affirmative grant is here a negative of all other power over the subject.

Besides this, there cannot well be two different standards of value, and consequently two kinds of legal tender for the discharge of obligations arising from the same transactions. The standard or tender of the lower actual value would in such case inevitably exclude and supersede the other, for no one would use the standard or tender of higher value when his purpose could be equally well accomplished by the use of the other. A practical illustration of the truth of this principle we have all seen in the effect upon coin of the act of congress making the notes of the United States a legal tender. It drove coin from general circulation, and made it, like bullion, the subject of sale and barter in the market.

The inhibition upon the states to coin money, and yet to make anything but gold and silver coin a tender in payment of debts, must be read in connection with the grant of the coinage power to congress. The two provisions taken together indicate beyond question that the coins which the national government was to fabricate, and the foreign coins, the valuation of which it was to regulate, were to consist principally, if not entirely, of gold and silver.

The framers of the constitution were considering the subject of money to be used throughout the entire union when these provisions were inserted, and it is plain that they intended by them that metallic coins fabricated by the national government, or adopted from abroad by its authority, composed of the precious metals, should every where be the standard, and the only standard, of value by which exchanges could be regulated and payments made.

At that time gold and silver, moulded into forms convenient for use and stamped with their value by public authority, constituted, with the exception of pieces of copper for small values, the money of the entire civilized world. Indeed these metals, divided up and thus stamped, always have constituted money with all people having any civilization, from the earliest periods in the history of the world down to the present time. It was with "four hundred shekels of silver, current money with the merchant," that Abraham bought the field of Machpelah, nearly four thousand years ago. This adoption of the precious metals as the subject of coinage—the material of money by all peoples in all ages of the world—has not been the result of any vagaries of fancy, but is attributable to the fact that they, of all metals, alone possess the properties which are essential to a circulating medium of uniform value.

"The circulating medium of a commercial community," says Mr. Webster, "must be that which is also the circulating medium of other commercial communities, or must be capable of being converted into that medium without loss. It must also be able not only to pass in payments and receipts among individuals of the same society and nation, but to adjust and discharge the balance of exchanges between different nations. It must be something which has a value abroad as well as at home, by which foreign, as well as domestic debts can be satisfied. The precious metals alone answer these purposes. They alone, therefore are money, and whatever else is to perform the functions of money must be their representative and capable of being turned into them at will. So long as bank paper retains this quality it is a substitute for money; divested of this, nothing can give it that character."

The statesmen who framed the constitution understood this principle as well as it is understood in our day. They had seen in the experience of the revolutionary period the demoralizing tendency, the cruel injustice, and the intolerable oppression of a paper currency not convertible on demand into money, and forced into circulation by legal tender provisions and penal enactments. When they, therefore, were constructing a government for a country which they could not fail to see was destined to be a mighty empire, and have commercial relations with all nations, a government which they believed was to endure for ages, they determined to recognize in the fundamental law, as a standard of value, that which ever has been, and always must be, recognized by the world as the true standard, and thus facilitate commerce, protect industry, establish justice, and prevent the possibility of a recurrence of the evils which they had experienced and the perpetration of the injustice which they had witnessed. "We all know," says Mr. Webster, "that the establishment of a sound and uniform currency was one of the greatest ends contemplated in the adoption of the present constitution. If we could now fully explore all the motives of those who framed and those who supported that constitution, perhaps we should hardly find a more powerful one than this."

And how the framers of the constitution endeavored to establish this "sound and uniform currency" we have already seen in the clauses which they adopted providing for a currency of gold and silver coin. Their determination to sanction only a metallic currency is further evidence from the debates in the convention upon the proposition to authorize congress to emit bills on the credit on the United States. By bills of credit, as the terms were then understood, were meant paper issues, intended to circulate through the community for its ordinary purposes as money, bearing upon their face the promise of the government to pay the sums specified thereon at a future day. The original draft contained a clause giving congress power to "borrow money and emit bills on the credit of the United States," and when the clause came up for consideration, Mr. Morris moved to strike out the words "and emit bills on the credit of the United States," observing that "if the United States had credit, such bills would be unnecessary; if they had not, unjust and useless." Mr. Madison inquired whether it would not be "sufficient to prohibit the making them a legal tender." "This will remove," he said, "the temptation to emit them with unjust views, and promissory notes in that shape may in some emergencies be best." Mr. Morris replied that striking out the words would still leave room for "notes of a responsible minister," which would do "all the good without the mischief." Mr. Gorham was for striking out the words without inserting any prohibition. If the words stood, he said they might "suggest and lead to the measure," and that the power, so far as it was necessary or safe, was "involved in that of borrowing." Mr. Madison said he was unwilling "to tie the hands of congress," and thought congress "would not have the power unless it were expressed." Mr. Ellsworth thought it "a favorable moment to shut and bar the door against paper money." "The mischiefs," he said, "of the various experiments which had been made were now fresh in the public mind and had excited the disgust of all the respectable part of America. By withholding the power from the new government, more friends of influence would be gained to it than by almost anything else. Paper money can in no case be necessary. Give the government credit, and other resources will offer. The power may do harm, never good." Mr. Wilson thought that "it would have a most salutary influence on the credit of the United States to remove the possibility of paper money." "This expedient," he said, "can never succeed whilst its mischiefs are remembered, and as long as it can be resorted to it will be a bar to other resources." Mr. Butler was urgent for disarming the government of such a power, and remarked "that paper was a legal tender in no country in Europe." Mr. Mason replied that if there was no example in Europe there was none in which the government was restrained on this head, and he was averse "to tying up the hands of the legislature altogether." Mr. Langdon preferred to reject the whole plan than retain the words.

Of those who participated in the debates, only one, Mr. Mercer, expressed an opinion favorable to paper money, and none suggested that if congress were allowed to issue the bills their acceptance should be compulsory—that is, that they should be made a legal tender. But the words were stricken out by a vote of nine states to two. Virginia voted for the motion, and Mr. Madison has appended a note to the debates, stating that her vote was occasioned by his acquiescence, and that he "became satisfied that striking out the words would not disable the government from the use of public notes, as far as they could be safe and proper; and would only cut off the pretext for a *paper currency* and particularly for making the bills *a tender* either for public or private debts."

If anything is manifest from these debates it is that the members of the convention intended to withhold from congress the power to issue bills to circulate as money—that is, to be receivable in compulsory payment, or, in other words, having the quality of legal tender—and that the express power to issue the bills was denied, under an apprehension that if granted it would give a pretext to congress, under the idea of declaring their effect, to annex to them that quality. The issue of notes simply as a means of borrowing money, which of course would leave them to be received at the option of parties, does not appear to have been seriously questioned. The circulation of notes thus issued as a voluntary currency and their receipt in that character in payment of taxes, duties, and other public expenses, was not subject to the objections urged.

I am aware of the rule that the opinions and intentions of individual members of the convention, as expressed in its debates and proceedings, are not to control the construction of the plain language of the constitution or narrow down the powers which that instrument confers. Members, it is said, who did not participate in the debate may have entertained different views from those expressed. The several state conventions to which the constitution was submitted may have differed widely from each other and from its framers in their interpretation of its clauses. We all know that opposite opinions on many points were expressed in the conventions, and conflicting reasons were urged both for the adoption and the rejection of that instrument. All this is very true, but it does not apply in the present case, for on the subject now under consideration there was everywhere, in the several state conventions and in the discussions before the people, an entire uniformity of opinion, so far as we have any record of its expression, and that concurred with the intention of the convention, as disclosed by its debates, that the constitution withheld from congress all power to issue bills to circulate as money, meaning by that bills made receivable in compulsory payment, or, in other words, having the quality of legal tender. Every one appears to have understood that the power of making paper issues a legal tender, by congress or by the states, was absolutely and forever prohibited.

Mr. Luther Martin, a member of the convention, in his speech before the Maryland legislature, as reported in his letter to that body, states the arguments urged against depriving congress of the power to emit bills of credit, and then says that a "majority of the convention being wise beyond every event, and being willing to risk any political evil rather than admit the idea of a paper emission in any possible case, refused to trust this authority to a government to which they were lavishing the most unlimited powers of taxation and to the mercy of which they were willing blindly to trust the liberty and property of the citizens of every state in the Union, *and they erased that clause from the system.*"

Not only was this construction given to the constitution by its framers and the people in their discussions at the time it was pending before them, but until the passage of the act of 1862, a period of nearly three-quarters of a century, the soundness of this construction was never called in question by any legislation of congress or the opinion of any judicial tribunal. Numerous acts, as already stated, were passed during this period, authorizing the issue of notes for the purpose of raising funds or obtaining supplies, but in none of them was the acceptance of the notes made compulsory. Only one instance have I been able to find in the history of congressional proceedings where it was even suggested that it was within the competency of congress to annex to the notes the quality of legal tender, and this occurred in 1814. The government was then greatly embarrassed from the want of funds to continue the war existing with Great Britain, and a member from Georgia introduced into the house of representatives several resolutions directing an inquiry into the expediency of authorizing the secretary of the treasury to issue notes convenient for circulation and making provision for the purchase of supplies in each state. Among the resolutions was one declaring that the notes to be issued should be a legal tender for debts due or subsequently becoming due between citizens of the United States and between citizens and foreigners. The house agreed to consider all the resolutions but the one containing the legal tender provision. That it refused to consider by a vote of more than two to one.

As until the act of 1862 there was no legislation making the acceptance of notes issued on the credit of the United States compulsory, the construction of the clause of the constitution containing the grant of the coinage power never came directly before this court for consideration, and the attention of the court was only incidentally drawn to it. But whenever the court spoke on the subject, even incidentally, its voice was in entire harmony with that of the convention.

Thus, in *Gwin* v. *Breedlove*, where a marshal of Mississippi, commanded to collect a certain amount of dollars on execution, received the amount in bank notes, it was held that he was liable to the plaintiff in gold and silver. "By the constitution of the United States," said the court, "gold or silver coin made current by law can only be tendered in payment of debts."

And in the case of the *United States* v. *Marigold*, where the question arose whether congress had power to enact certain provisions of law for the punishment of persons bringing into the United States counterfeit coin with intent to pass it, the court said: These provisions "appertain to the execution of an important trust invested by the constitution, and to the obligation to fulfill that trust on the part of the government, namely, the trust and the duty of creating and maintaining a uniform and pure metallic standard of value throughout the Union. The power of coining money and of regulating its value was delegated to congress by the constitution for the very purpose, as assigned by the framers of that instrument, of creating and preserving the uniformity and purity of such a standard of value, and on account of the impossibility which was foreseen of otherwise preventing the inequalities and the confusion necessarily incident to different views of policy, which in different communities would be brought to bear on this subject. The power to coin money being thus given to congress, founded on public necessity, it must carry with it the correlative power of protecting the creature and object of that power."

It is difficult to perceive how the trust and duty here designated, of "creating and maintaining a uniform and metallic standard of value throughout the Union," is discharged, when another standard of lower value and fluctuating character is authorized by law, which necessarily operates to drive the first from circulation.

In addition to all the weight of opinion I have mentioned we have, to the same purport, from the adoption of the constitution up to the passage of the act of 1862, the united testimony of the leading statesmen and jurists of the country. Of all the men who, during that period, participated with any distinction in the councils of the nation, not one can be named who ever asserted any different power in congress than what I have mentioned. As observed by the chief justice, statesman who disagreed widely on other points agreed on this.

Mr. Webster, who has always been regarded by a large portion of his countrymen as one of the ablest and most enlightened expounders of the constitution, did not seem to think there was any doubt on the subject, although he belonged to the class who advocated the largest exercise of powers by the general government. From his first entrance into public life, in 1812, he gave great considerations to the subject of the currency, and in an elaborate speech in the senate, in 1836, he said: "Currency, in a large and perhaps just sense, includes not only gold and silver and bank bills, but bills of exchange also. It may include all that adjusts, exchanges, and settles balances in the operations of trade and business; but if we understand by currency the legal money of the country, and that which constitutes a lawful tender for debts, and is the statute measure of value, then undoubtedly nothing is included but gold and silver. Most unquestionably there is no legal tender, and there can be no legal tender in this country, under the authority of this government or any other, but gold and silver—either the coinage of our own mints or foreign coins, at rates regulated by congress. This is a constitutional principle, perfectly plain, and of the very highest importance. The states are expressly prohibited from making anything but gold and silver a tender in payment of debts, and, although no such express prohibition is applied to congress, yet, as congress has no power granted to it in this respect but to coin money, and to regulate the value of foreign coins, it clearly has no power to substitute paper, or anything else, for coin, as a tender in payment of debts and in discharge of contracts. Congress has exercised this power fully in both its branches. It has coined money, and still coins it; it has regulated the value of foreign coins, and still regulates their value. The legal tender, therefore, the constitutional standard of value, is establishsd and cannot be overthrown. To overthrow it would shake the whole system."

If, now, we consider the history of the times when the constitution was adopted; the intentions of the framers of that instrument, as shown in their debates; the contemporaneous exposition of the coinage power in the state conventions assembled to consider the constitution, and in the public discussions before the people; the natural meaning of the terms used; the nature of the constitution itself as creating a government of enumerated powers; the legislative exposition of nearly three-quarters of a century; the opinions of judicial tribunals, and the recorded utterances of statesmen, jurists, and commentators, it would seem impossible to doubt that the only standard of value authorized by the constitution was to consist of metallic coins struck or regulated by the direction of congress, and that the power to establish any other standard was denied by that instrument.

There are other considerations besides those I have stated, which are equally convincing against the constitutionality of the legal tender provision of the act of February 25th, 1862, so far as it applies to private debts and debts by the government contracted previous to its passage. That provision operates directly to impair the obligation of such contracts. In the dissenting opinion, in the case of *Hepburn* v. *Griswold*, this is admitted to be its operation, and the position is taken that, while the constitution forbids the state to pass such laws, it does not forbid congress to do this, and the power to establish a uniform system of bankruptcy, which is expressly conferred, is mentioned in support of the position. In some of the opinions of the state courts, to which our attention has been directed, it is denied that the provision in question impairs the obligation of previous contracts, it being asserted that a contract to pay money is satisfied, according to its meaning, by the payment of that which is money when the payment is made, and that if the law does not interfere with this mode of satisfaction, it does not impair the obligation of the contract. This position is true so long as the term money represents the same thing in both cases or their actual equivalents, but it is not true when the term has different meanings. Money is a generic term, and contracts for money are not made without a specification of the coins or denominations of money, and the number of them intended, as eagles, dollars, or cents; and it will not be pretended that a contract for a specified number of eagles can be satisfied by a delivery of an equal number of dollars, although both eagles and dollars are money; nor would it thus be contended, though at the time the contract matured the legislature had determined to call dollars eagles. Contracts are made for things, not names or sounds, and the obligation of a contract arises from its terms and the means which the law affords for its enforcement.

A law which changes the terms of the contract, either in the time or mode of performance, or imposes new conditions, or dispenses with those expressed, or authorizes for its satisfaction something different from that provided, is a law which impairs its obligation, for such a law relieves the parties from the moral duty of performing the original stipulations of the contract, and it prevents their legal enforcement.

The notion that contracts for the payment of money stand upon any different footing in this respect from other contracts appears to have had its origin in certain old English cases, particularly that of mixed money, which were decided upon the force of the prerogative of the king with respect to coin, and have no weight as applied to powers possessed by congress under our constitution. The language of Mr. Chief Justice Marshall in *Faw* v. *Marsteller*, which is cited in support of this notion, can only be made to express concurrence with it when detached from its context and read separated from the facts in reference to which it was used.

It is obvious that the act of 1862 changes the term of contracts for the payment of money made previous to its passage, in every essential particular. All such contracts had reference to metallic coins, struck or regulated by congress, and composed principally of gold and silver, which constituted the legal money of the country. The several coinage acts had fixed the weight, purity, and forms, impressions, and denominations of these coins, and had provided that their value should be certified by the form and impress which they received at the mint.

They had established the dollar as the money unit, and prescribed the grains of silver it should contain, and the grains of gold which should compose the different gold coins. Every dollar was therefore a piece of gold or silver certified to be of a specified weight and purity, by its form and impress. A contract to pay a specified number of dollars was then a contract to deliver the designated number of pieces of gold or silver of this character; and, by the laws of congress and of the several states the delivery of such dollars could be enforced by the holder.

The act of 1862 changes all this; it declares that gold or silver dollars need not be delivered to the creditor according to the stipulations of the contract; that they need not be delivered at all; that promises of the United States, with which the creditor has had no relations, to pay these dollars, at some uncertain future day, shall be received in discharge of the contracts — in other words, that the holder of such contracts shall take in substitution for them different contracts with another party, less valuable to him, and surrender the original.

Taking it, therefore, for granted that the law plainly impairs the obligation of such contracts, I proceed to inquire whether it is, for that reason, subject to any constitutional objection. In the dissenting opinion in *Hepburn* v. *Griswold*, it is said, as already mentioned, that the constitution does not forbid legislation impairing the obligation of contracts.

It is true there is no provision in the constitution forbidding in express terms such legislation. And it is also true that there are express powers delegated to congress, the execution of which necessarily operates to impair the obligation of contracts. It was the object of the framers of that instrument to create a national government competent to represent the entire country in its relations with foreign nations, and to accomplish by its legislation measures of common interest to all the people, which the several states, in their independent capacities, were incapable of effecting, or if capable, the execution of which would be attended with great difficulty and embarrassment. They, therefore, clothed congress with all the powers essential to the successful accomplishment of these ends, and carefully withheld the grant of all other powers. Some of the powers granted, from their very nature, interfere in their execution with contracts of parties. Thus war suspends intercourse and commerce between citizens or subjects of belligerent nations; it renders, during its continuance, the performance of contracts previously made unlawful. These incidental consequences were contemplated in the grant of the war power. So the regulation of commerce and the imposition of duties may so affect the prices of articles imported or manufactured as to essentially alter the value of previous contracts respecting them; but this incidental consequence was seen in the grant of the power over commerce and duties. There can be no valid objection to laws passed in execution of express powers that consequences like these follow incidentally from their execution. But it is otherwise when such consequences do not follow incidentally, but are directly enacted.

The only express authority for any legislation affecting the obligation of contracts is found in the power to establish a uniform system of bankruptcy, the direct object of which is to release insolvent debtors from their contracts upon the surrender of their property. From this express grant in the constitution I draw a very different conclusion from that drawn in the dissenting opinion in *Hepburn* v. *Griswold*, and in the opinion of the majority of the court just delivered. To my mind it is a strong argument that there is no general power in congress to interfere with contracts—that a special grant was regarded as essential to authorize a uniform system of bankruptcy. If such general power existed, the delegation of an express power in the case of bankrupts was unnecessary. As very justly observed by counsel, if this sovereign power could be taken in any case without express grant, it could be taken in connection with bankruptcies, which might be regarded in some respects as a regulation of commerce made in the interest of traders.

The grant of a limited power over the subject of contracts necessarily implies that the framers of the constitution did not intend that congress should exercise unlimited power, or any power less restricted. The limitation designated is the measure of congressional power over the subject. This follows from the nature of the instrument as one of enumerated powers.

The doctrine that where a power is not expressly forbidden it may be exercised, would change the whole character of our government. As I read the writings of the great commentators, and the decisions of this court, the true doctrine is the exact reverse, that if a power is not in terms granted, and is not necessary and proper for the exercise of a power thus granted, it does not exist.

The position that congress possesses some undefined power to do anything which it may deem expedient, as a resulting power from the general purposes of the government, which is advanced in the opinion of the majority, would of course settle the question under consideration without difficulty, for it would end all controversy by changing our government from one of enumerated powers to one resting in the unrestrained will of congress.

"The government of the United States," says Mr. Chief Justice Marshall, speaking for the court in *Martin* v. *Hunter's*

Lessee, "can claim no powers that are not granted to it by the constitution, and the powers actually granted must be such as are expressly given, or given by necessary implication." This implication, it is true, may follow from the grant of several express powers as well as from one alone, but the power implied must, in all cases, be subsidiary to the execution of the powers expressed. The language of the constitution respecting the writ of habeas corpus, declaring that it shall not be suspended unless, when in cases of rebellion or invasion, the public safety may require it, is cited as showing that the power to suspend such writ exists somewhere in the constitution; and the adoption of the amendments is mentioned as evidence that important powers were understood by the people who adopted the constitution to have been created by it, which are not enumerated, and are not included incidentally in any of those enumerated.

The answer to this position is found in the nature of the constitution, as one of granted powers, as stated by Mr. Chief Justice Marshall. The inhibition upon the exercise of a specified power does not warrant the implication that, but for such inhibition, the power might have been exercised. In the convention which framed the constitution a proposition to appoint a committee to prepare a bill of rights was unanimously rejected, and has been always understood that its rejection was upon the ground that such a bill would contain various exceptions to powers not granted, and on this very account would afford a pretext for asserting more than was granted. In the discussions before the people, when the adoption of the constitution was pending, no objection was urged with greater effect than this absence of a bill of rights, and in one of the numbers of the *Federalist*, Mr. Hamilton endeavored to combat the objection. After stating several reasons why such a bill was not necessary, he said: "I go further and affirm that bills of rights, in the sense and to the extent they are contended for, are not only unnecessary in the proposed constitution, but would even be dangerous. They would contain various exceptions to powers not granted, and on this very account would afford a colorable pretext to claim more than were granted.

For why declare that things shall not be done which there is no power to do? Why, for instance, should it be said that the liberty of the press shall not be restrained when no power is given by which restrictions may be imposed? I will not contend that such a provision would confer a regulating power, but it is evident that it would furnish to men disposed to usurp a plausible pretence for claiming that power. They might urge, with a semblance of reason, that the constitution ought not to be charged with the absurdity of providing against the abuse of an authority which was not given, and that the provision against restraining the liberty of the press afforded a clear implication that a right to prescribe proper regulations concerning it was intended to be invested in the national government. This may serve as a specimen of the numerous handles which would be given to the doctrine of constructive powers by the indulgence of an injudicious zeal for bills of right."

When the amendments were presented to the states for adoption they were preceded by a preamble stating that the conventions of a number of the states had, at the time of their adopting the constitution, expressed a desire "in order to prevent *misconception or abuse* of its powers, that further declaratory and restricted clauses should be added."

Now, will any one pretend that congress could have made a law respecting an establishment of religion or prohibiting the free exercise thereof, or abridging the freedom of speech, or the right of the people to assemble and petition the government for a redress of grievances, had not prohibitions upon the exercise of any such legislative power been embodied in an amendment?

How truly did Hamilton say, that had a bill of rights been inserted in the constitution, it would have given a handle to the doctrine of constructive powers. We have this day an illustration in the opinion of the majority of the very claim of constructive power which he apprehended, and it is the first instance, I believe, in the history of this court, when the possession by congress of such constructive power has been asserted.

The interference with contracts by the legislation of the several states previous to the adoption of the constitution was the cause of great oppression and injustice. "Not only," says Story, "was paper money issued and declared to be a tender in payment of debts, but laws of another character, well known under the appellation of tender laws and appraisement laws, installment laws and suspension laws, were from time to time enacted, which prostrated all private credit and all private morals. By some of these laws the due payment of debts was suspended; debts were, in violation of the very terms of the contract, authorized to be paid by installments at different periods; property of any sort, however worthless, either real or personal, might be tendered by the debtor in payment of his debts, and the creditor was compelled to take the property of the debtor, which he might seize on execution, at an appraisement wholly disproportionate to its known value. Such grievances and oppressions, and others of a like nature, were the ordinary results of legislation during the revolutionary war and the intermediate period down to the formation of the constitution. They entailed the most enormous evils on the country, and introduced a system of fraud, chicanery and profligacy which destroyed all private confidence and all industry and enterprise."

To prevent the recurrence of evils of this character not only was the clause inserted in the constitution prohibiting the states from issuing bills of credit and making anything but gold and silver a tender in payment of debts, but also the more general prohibition from passing any law impairing the obligation of contracts. "To restore public confidence completely," says Chief Justice Marshall, "it was necessary not only to prohibit the use of particular means by which it might be effected, but to prohibit the use of any means by which the same mischief might be produced. The convention appears to have intended to establish a great principle, that contracts should be inviolable."

It would require very clear evidence, one would suppose, to induce a belief that with the evils resulting from what Marshall terms the system of lax legislation following the Revolution deeply impressed on their minds, the framers of the constitution intended to vest in the new government created by them this dangerous and despotic power, which they were unwilling should remain with the states, and thus widen the possible sphere of its exercise.

When the possession of this power has been asserted in argument (for until now it has never been asserted in any decision of this court), it has been in cases where a supposed public benefit resulted from the legislation, or where the interference with the obligation of the contract was very slight. Whenever a clear case of injustice, in the absence of such supposed public good, is stated, the exercise of the power by the government is not only denounced, but the existence of the power is denied. No one, indeed, is found bold enough to contend that if A has a contract for one hundred acres of land, or one hundred pounds of fruit, or one hundred yards of cloth, congress can pass a law compelling him to accept one-half of the quantity in satisfaction of the contract. But congress has the same power to establish a standard of weights and measures as it has to establish a standard of value, and can from time to time alter such standard. It can declare that the acre shall consist of eighty square rods instead of one hundred and sixty, the pound of eight ounces instead of sixteen, and the foot of six inches instead of twelve; and if it could compel the acceptance of the same *number* of acres, pounds or yards, after such alteration, instead of the actual *quantity* stipulated, then the acceptance of one-half of the quantity originally designated could be directly required without going through the form of altering the standard. No just man could be imposed upon by this use of words in a double sense, where the same names were applied to denote different quantities of the same thing, nor would his condemnation of the wrong committed in such case be withheld, because the attempt was made to conceal it by this jugglery of words.

The power of congress to interfere with contracts for the payment of money is not greater in any particular difference from its power with respect to contracts for lands or goods. The contract is not fulfilled any more in one case than in the other

29

by the delivery of a thing which is not stipulated, because by legislative action it is called by the same name. Words in contracts are to be construed in both cases in the sense in which they were understood by the parties at the time of the contract.

Let us for a moment see where the doctrine of the power asserted will lead. Congress has the undoubted right to give such denominations as it chooses to the coins struck by its authority, and to change them. It can declare that the dime shall hereafter be called a dollar, or, what is the same thing, it may declare that the dollar shall hereafter be composed of the grains of silver which now compose the dime. But would any body pretend that a contract for dollars, composed as at present, could be satisfied by the delivery of an equal number of dollars of the new issue? I have never met any one who would go to that extent. The answer always has been—that would be too flagrantly unjust to be tolerated. Yet enforcing the acceptance of paper promises or paper dollars, if the promises can be so called, in place of gold or silver dollars, is equally enforcing a departure from the terms of the contract, the injustice of the measure depending entirely upon the actual value at the time of the promises in the market. Now reverse the case. Suppose congress should declare that hereafter the eagle should be called a dollar, or that the dollar should be composed of as many grains of gold as the eagle, would any body for a moment contend that a contract for dollars, composed as now of silver, should be satisfied by dollars composed of gold? I am confident that no judge sitting on this bench, and, indeed, that no judge in Christendom could be found who would sanction the monstrous wrong by decreeing that the debtor could only satisfy his contract in such case by paying ten times the value originally stipulated. The natural sense of right which is implanted in every mind would revolt from such supreme injustice. Yet there cannot be one law for debtors and another law for creditors. If the contract can at one time be changed by congressional legislation for the benefit of the debtor, it may at another time be changed for the benefit of the creditor

For acts of flagrant injustice such as those mentioned there is no authority in any legislative body, even though not restrained by any express constitutional prohibition; for as there are unchangeable principles of right and morality, without which society would be impossible, and men would be but wild beasts preying upon each other, so there are fundamental principles of eternal justice, upon the existence of which all constitutional government is founded, and without which government would be an intolerable and hateful tyranny. There are acts, says Mr. Justice Chase, in *Calder* v. *Bull*, which the federal and state legislatures cannot do without exceeding their authority. Among these he mentions a law which punishes a citizen for an innocent action; a law that destroys or impairs the lawful private contracts of citizens; a law that makes a man a judge in his own cause; and a law that takes the property from A and gives it to B. "It is against all reason and right," says the learned justice, "for a people to intrust a legislature with such powers, and therefore it cannot be presumed that they have done it. The genius, the nature, and the spirit of our state governments amount to a prohibition of such acts of legislation, and the general principles of law and reason forbid them. The legislature may enjoin, permit, forbid and punish; they may declare new crimes, and establish rules of conduct for all its citizens in future cases; they may command what is right and prohibit what is wrong, but they cannot change innocence into guilt, or punish innocence as a crime, or violate the rights of an antecedent lawful private contract, or the right of private property. To maintain that our federal or state legislatures possess such powers if they had not been expressly restrained, would, in my opinion, be a political heresy altogether inadmissible in our free republican governments."

In *Ogden* v. *Saunders*, Mr. Justice Thompson, referring to the provisions in the constitution forbidding the states to pass any bill of attainder, *ex post facto* law, or law impairing the obligation of contracts, says: "Neither provision can strictly be considered as introducing any new principle, but only for greater security and safety to incorporate into this charter provisions admitted by all to be among the first principles of government. No state court would, I presume, sanction and enforce an *ex post facto* law if no such prohibition was contained in the constitution of the United States; so, neither would retrospective laws, taking away vested rights, be enforced. Such laws are repugnant to those fundamental principles upon which every just system of laws is founded. It is an elementary principle, adopted and sanctioned by the courts of justice in this country and in Great Britain, whenever such laws have come under consideration, and yet retrospective laws are clearly within this prohibition."

In *Wilkeson* v. *Leland*, Mr. Justice Story, whilst commenting upon the power of the legislature of Rhode Island under the charter of Charles II, said: "The fundamental maxims of a free government seem to require that the rights of personal liberty and private property should be held sacred. At least no court of justice in this country would be warranted in assuming that the power to violate and disregard them, a power so repugnant to the common principles of justice and civil liberty, lurked under any general grant of legislative authority, or ought to be implied from any general expressions of the will of the people. The people ought not to be presumed to part with rights so vital to their security and well-being without very strong and direct expressions of such an intention."

Similar views to these cited from the opinions of Chase, Thompson, Story, and Marshall, are found scattered through the opinions of the judges who have preceded us on this bench. As against their collective force the remark of Mr. Justice Washington, in the case of *Evans* v. *Eaton*, is without significance. That was made at *nisi prius* in answer to a motion for a nonsuit in an action brought for an infringement of a patent right. The state of Pennsylvania had, in March, 1787, which was previous to the adoption of the constitution, given to the plaintiff the exclusive right to make, use, and vend his invention for fourteen years. In January, 1808, the United States issued to him a patent for the invention for fourteen years from that date. It was contended, for the nonsuit, that after the expiration of the plaintiff's privilege granted by the state, the right to his invention became invested in the people of the state, by an implied contract with the government, and, therefore, that congress could not, consistently with the constitution, grant to the plaintiff an exclusive right to the invention. The court replied that neither the premises upon which the motion was founded, nor the conclusion, could be admitted; that it was not true that the grant of an exclusive privilege to an invention for a limited time implied a binding and irrevocable contract with the people that at the expiration of the period limited the invention should become their property; and that even if the premises were true, there was nothing in the constitution which forbade congress to pass laws violating the obligation of contracts.

The motion did not merit any consideration, as the federal court had no power to grant a nonsuit against the will of the plaintiff in any case. The expression under these circumstances of any reason why the court would not grant the motion, if it possessed the power, was aside the case, and is not, therefore, entitled to any weight whatever as authority. It was true, however, as observed by the court, that no such contract with the public, as stated, was implied, and inasmuch as congress was expressly authorized by the constitution to secure for a limited time to inventors the exclusive right to their discoveries, it has the power in that way to impair the obligation of such a contract, if any had existed. And this is, perhaps, all that Mr. Justice Washington meant. It is evident from his language in *Ogden* v. *Saunders*, that he repudiated the existence of any general power in congress to destroy or impair vested private rights.

What I have heretofore said respecting the power of congress to make the notes of the United States a legal tender in payment of debts contracted previous to the act of 1862, and to interfere with contracts, has had reference to debts and contracts between citizens. But the same power which is asserted over these matters is also asserted with reference to previous debts owing by the government, and must equally apply to contracts between the government and the citizen. The act of 1862 declares that the notes issued shall be a legal tender in payment of *all debts, public and private*, with the exception of duties on imports and interest on the public debt. If they are legal tender for antecedent private debts, they are also a legal tender for such debts owing by the United States, except in the cases mentioned. That any exception was made was a mere matter of legislative discretion. Express contracts for the payment of gold or silver have been maintained by this court, and specifically enforced on the ground that, upon a proper construction of the act of 1862, in connection with other acts, congress intended to except these contracts from the operation of the legal tender provision. But the power covers all cases if it exists at all. The power to make the notes of the United States the legal equivalent to gold and silver necessarily includes the power to cancel with them specific contracts for gold as well as money contracts generally. Before the passage of the act of 1862, there was no legal money except that which consisted of metallic coins, struck or regulated by the authority of congress. Dollars then meant, as already said, certain pieces of gold or silver, certified to be of a prescribed weight and purity by their form and impress received at the mint. The designation of dollars, in previous contracts, meant gold or silver dollars as plainly as if those metals were specifically named.

It follows, then, logically, from the doctrine advanced by the majority of the court as to the power of congress over the subject of legal tender, that congress may borrow gold coin upon a pledge of the public faith to repay gold at the maturity of its obligations, and yet, in direct disregard of its pledge, in open violation of faith, may compel the lender to take, in place of the gold stipulated, its own promises; and that legislation of this character would not be in violation of the constitution, but in harmony with its letter and spirit.

The government is, at the present time, seeking in the markets of the world a loan of several hundred millions of dollars in gold, upon securities containing the promises of the United States to repay the money, principal and interest, in gold; yet this court, the highest tribunal of the country, this day declares, by its solemn decision, that should such loan be obtained, it is entirely competent for congress to pay it off, not in gold, but in notes of the United States themselves, payable at such time and in such manner as congress may itself determine, and that legislation sanctioning such gross breach of faith would not be repugnant to the fundamental law of the land.

What is this but declaring that repudiation by the government of the United States of its solemn obligations would be constitutional? Whenever the fulfillment of the obligation in the manner stipulated is refused, and the acceptance of something different from that stipulated is enforced against the will of the creditor, a breach of faith is committed; and to the extent of the difference of value between the thing stipulated and the thing which the creditor is compelled to receive, there is repudiation of the original obligation. I am not willing to admit that the constitution, the boast and glory of our country, would sanction or permit any such legislation. Repudiation in any form, or to any extent, would be dishonor, and for the commission of this public crime no warrant, in my judgment, can ever be found in that instrument.

Some stress has been placed in argument in support of the asserted power of congress over the subject of legal tender in the fact that congress can regulate the alloy of the coins issued under its authority, and has exercised its power in this respect without question, by diminishing in some instances, the actual quantity of gold or silver they contain. Congress, it is assumed, can thus put upon the coins issued other than their intrinsic value; therefore, it is argued, congress may, by its declaration, give a value to the notes of the United States, issued to be used as money, other than that which they actually possess.

The assumption and the inference are both erroneous, and the argument thus advanced is without force, and is only significant of the weakness of the position which has to rest for its support on an assumed authority of the government to debase the coin of the country.

Undoubtedly congress can alter the value of the coins issued by its authority by increasing or diminishing, from time to time, the alloy they contain, just as it may alter, at its pleasure, the denominations of the several coins issued, but there its power stops. It cannot make these altered coins the equivalent of the coins in their previous condition; and if the new coins should retain the same names as the original, they would only be current at their true value. Any declaration that they should have any other value would be inoperative in fact, and a monstrous disregard by congress of its constitutional duty. The power to coin money, as already declared by this court, is a great trust devolved upon congress, carrying with it the duty of creating and maintaining a uniform standard of value throughout the Union, and it would be a manifest abuse of this trust to give to the coins issued by its authority any other than their real value. By debasing the coins, when once the standard is fixed, is meant giving to the coins, by their form and impress, a certificate of their having a relation to that standard different from that which, in truth, they possess; in other words, giving to the coins a false certificate of their value. Arbitrary and profligate governments have often resorted to this miserable scheme of robbery, which Mill designates as a shallow and impudent artifice, the "least covert of all modes of knavery, which consists in calling a shilling a pound, that a debt of one hundred pounds may be cancelled by the payment of one hundred shillings."

In this country no such debasement has ever been attempted, and I feel confident that none will ever be tolerated. The changes in the quantity of alloy in the different coins has been made from time to time, not with any idea of debasing them, but for the purpose of preserving the proper relative value between gold and silver. The first coinage act, passed in 1792, provided that the coins should consist of gold, silver and copper—the coins of cents and half-cents consisting of copper, and the other coins consisting of gold and silver—and that the relative value of gold and silver should be as fifteen to one, that is, that an ounce of gold should be taken as the equal in value of fifteen ounces of silver.

In progress of time, owing to the increased production of silver, particularly from the mines of Mexico and South America, this relative value was changed. Silver declined in relative value to gold until it bore the relation of one to sixteen instead of one to fifteen. The result was that the gold was bought up as soon as coined, being worth intrinsically sixteen times the value of silver, and yet passing by law only at fifteen times such value, and was sent out of the country to be recoined. The attention of congress was called to this change in the relative value of the two metals and the consequent disappearance of gold coin. This led, in 1834, to an act adjusting the rate of gold coin to its true relation to silver coin.

The discovery of gold in California, some years afterwards, and the great production of that metal, again changed in another direction the relative value of the two metals. Gold declined, or in other words, silver was at a premium, and as gold coin before 1834 was brought up, so now silver coin was bought up, and a scarcity of small coin for change was felt in the community. Congress again interfered, and in 1853 reduced the amount of silver in coins representing fractional parts of a dollar, but even then these coins were restricted from being a legal tender for sums exceeding five dollars, although the small silver coins of previous issue continued to be a legal tender for any amount. Silver pieces of the denomination of three cents had been previously authorized in 1851, but were only made a tender for sums of thirty cents and under. These coins did not express their actual value, and their issue was soon stopped, and in 1853 their value was increased to the standard of coins of other fractional parts of a dollar.

The whole of this subject has been fully and satisfactorily explained in the very able and learned argument of the counsel who contended for the maintenance of the original decision of this court in *Hepburn* v. *Griswold*. He showed by the debates that congress has been moved, in all its actions under the coinage power, only by an anxious desire to ascertain the true relative value of the two precious metals, and to fix the coinage in accordance with it; and that in no case has any deviation from intrinsic value been permitted except in coins for fractional parts of a dollar, and even that has been only of so slight a character as to prevent them from being converted into bullion, the actual depreciation being made up by their portability and convenience.

It follows, from this statement of the action of congress in altering at different times the alloy of certain coins, that the assumption of power to stamp metal with an arbitrary value and give it currency, does not rest upon any solid foundation, and that the argument built thereon goes with it to the ground.

I have thus far spoken of the legal tender provision with particular reference to its application to debts contracted previous to its passage. It only remains to say a few words as to its validity when applied to subsequent transactions.

So far as subsequent contracts are made payable in notes of the United States, there can of course be no objection to their specific enforcement by compelling a delivery of an equal amount of the notes, or by a judgment in damages for their value as estimated in gold or silver dollars, nor would there be any objection to such enforcement if the legal tender provision had never existed. From the general use of the notes throughout the country and the disappearance of gold and silver coin from circulation, it may perhaps be inferred in most cases, that notes of the United States are intended by the parties where gold or silver dollars are not expressly designated, except in contracts made in the Pacific states, where the constitutional currency has always continued in use. As to subsequent contracts, the legal tender provision is not as unjust in its operation as when applied to past contracts, and does not impair to the same extent private rights. But so far as it makes the receipt of the notes, in absense of any agreement of the parties, compulsory in payment of such contracts, it is, in my judgment, equally unconstitutional. This seems to me to follow necessarily from the duty already mentioned cast upon congress by the coinage power,—to create and maintain a uniform metallic standard of value throughout the Union. Without a standard of value of some kind, commerce would be difficult, if not impossible, and just in proportion to the uniformity and stability of the standard is the security and consequent extent of commercial transactions. How is it possible for congress to discharge its duty by making the acceptance of paper promises compulsory in all future dealings—promises which necessarily depend for their value upon the confidence entertained by the public in their ultimate payment, and the consequent ability of the holder to convert them into gold or silver —promises which can never be uniform throughout the Union, but must have different values in different portions of the country; one value in New York, another at New Orleans, and still a different one at San Francisco.

Speaking of paper money issued by the states,—and the same language is equally true of paper money issued by the United States—Chief Justice Marshall says, in *Craig* v. *The State of Missouri:* "Such a medium has been always liable to considerable fluctuation. Its value is continually changing; and these changes, often great and sudden, expose individuals to immense loss, are the sources of ruinous speculations, and destroy all confidence between man and man. To cut up this mischief by the roots, a mischief which was felt by the United States, and which deeply affected the interest and prosperity of all, the people declared in their constitution that no state should emit bills of credit."

Mr. Justice Washington, after referring, in *Ogden* v. *Saunders*, to the provision of the constitution declaring that no state shall coin money, emit bills of credit, make anything but gold and silver coin a tender in payment of debts, says: "These prohibitions, associated with the powers granted to congress 'to coin money and to regulate the value thereof, and of foreign coin,' most obviously constitute members of the same family, being upon the same subject and governed by the same policy. This policy was to provide a fixed and uniform standard of value throughout the United States, by which the commercial and other dealings between the citizens thereof, or between them and foreigners, as well as the moneyed transactions of the government should be regulated. For it might well be asked, Why vest in congress the power to establish a uniform standard of value by the means pointed out, if the states might use the same means, and thus defeat the uniformity of the standard, and consequently the standard itself? And why establish a standard at all for the government of the various contracts which might be entered into, if those contracts might afterwards be discharged by a different standard, or by that which is not money, under the authority of state tender laws? It is obvious, therefore, that these prohibitions in the tenth section are entirely homogeneous, and are essential to the establishment of a uniform standard of value in the formation and discharge of contracts."

It is plain that this policy cannot be carried out, and this fixed and uniform metallic standard of value throughout the United States be maintained, so long as any other standard is adopted, which of itself has no intrinsic value and is forever fluctuating and uncertain.

For the reasons which I have endeavored to unfold, I am compelled to dissent from the judgment of the majority of the court. I know that the measure, the validity of which I have called in question, was passed in the midst of a gigantic rebellion, when even the bravest hearts sometimes doubted the safety of the republic, and that the patiotic men who adopted it did so under the conviction that it would increase the ability of the government to obtain funds and supplies, and thus advance the national cause. Were I to be governed by my appreciation of the character of those men, instead of my views of the requirements of the constitution, I should readily assent to the views of the majority of the court. But, sitting as a judicial officer, and bound to compare every law enacted by congress with the greater law enacted by the people, and being unable to reconcile the measure in question with that fundamental law, I cannot hesitate to pronounce it as being, in my judgment, unconstitutional and void.

In the discussions which have attended this subject of legal tender there has been at times what seemed to me to be a covert intimation, that opposition to the measure in question was the expression of a spirit not altogether favorable to the cause, in the interest of which that measure was adopted. All such intimations I repel with all the energy I can express. I do not yield to any one in honoring and reverencing the noble and patriotic men who were in the councils of the nation during the terrible struggle with the rebellion. To them belong the greatest of all glories in our history,—that of having saved the Union, and that of having emancipated a race. For these results they will be remembered and honored so long as the English language is spoken or read among men. But I do not admit that a blind approval of every measure which they may have thought essential to put down the rebellion is any evidence of loyalty to the country. The only loyalty which I can admit consists in obedience to the constitution and laws made in pursuance of it. It is only by obedience that affection and reverence can be shown to a superior having a right to command. So thought our great Master when he said to his disciples: "If ye love me, keep my commandments."

CHAPTER V.

GOVERNMENT CONTROL OF RAILROADS.

SINCE concluding what we desired to say on the subject of controlling and regulating railroads and railroad corporations, our attention has been directed to a circular from *The New York Nation*, of July 27th, 1873, entitled: "The Railroad Discussion, and Common Sense." This singular article challenges attention. If it is put forth in the interest of railroad corporations, we can readily account for the views expressed, and the covert foreshadowing of national control of railroads; but if it be published and circulated in the interest of the people as *The Nation* would have us understand, it is not calculated to assist them in their efforts at reform, but on the contrary will tend to divide and distract their counsels, and delay the relief sought.

We copy the circular, that the reader may judge of its merits, and to give a more intelligent understanding of our remarks upon it:

THE RAILROAD DISCUSSION AND COMMON SENSE—THE LATEST DEVICE FOR FIXING RATES OF TRANSPORTATION.

(From the Nation [N. Y.] of July 17.)

We have followed, and shall continue to follow, the "farmers' movement with great interest, but it must be confessed that it seems at times of no little difficulty, owing to the very heterogenous composition of the organizations which are carrying it on, and the wide diversity of their character and avowed aims. When Judge Lawrence was turned out of office in Illinois by the "Grangers," and Judge Craig put in his place, we took it for granted that they were going to deliver themselves from the tyranny of the railroads by putting judges on the bench pledged to interpret the state constitution in a particular way, or in other words, as one of the local papers put it, by showing that "the people" were superior to both laws and judges. It has, however, since been stoutly denied that this interference with the bench was anything more than a local accident, and we have been assured that the farmers seek changes of a much more legitimate character, and resting on more solid foundations than the creation of a subservient judiciary. The recent platforms have recently had a much wider sweep than the earlier ones, and, unless language has been gravely abused in making them, embrace grave modifications in fiscal as well as in railroad legislation. But the question how to reduce the railroads to the condition of public highways, controllable by and existing solely or mainly for the convenience of the community, is still apparently as far from solution as ever. It is by no means surprising that this should be the case, but that it *is* the case we are forced to conclude by the extraordinary character of the latest plan propounded by the reformers, which has had sufficient plausibility to command the approval of so sober-minded a paper as the *Chicago Tribune*.

The farmers have been accused, partly in consequence of their escapade about the judges in Illinois, of seeking to rob the railroad companies of their lawful earnings by forcing them to carry on their business at a loss, under the operation of cast-iron rules, drawn up without reference to its peculiar nature. This was a charge of which the farmers soon began to see the gravity, and they accordingly now announce that they have no scheme of spoliation or confiscation in their minds, but that they have at last hit upon a mode of ascertaining what are "reasonable rates," which consists in discovering what was the amount of capital "actually invested in constructing and operating the roads," and treating a fair percentage of this as a proper return to the stockholders, and all charges which bring in more than this as "unreasonable," and therefore open to prohibition by the courts and state legislatures. Under this theory of railroad property, all stock which does not represent money actually invested is treated as "fictitious," and all attempts to earn dividends on such stock as attempts at extortion. For instance—to put a case of frequent occurrence—a corporation obtains a charter for a road which will cost two million dollars to build. It accordingly borrows the two millions on mortgage bonds, and constructs the road, while the members divide among themselves two millions of stock more, and they work the road so as to make it pay interest on the four millions. The farmers now say that no road shall be so worked as to pay interest on anything but the proceeds of the bonds, or, in other words, the actual cost of construction and equipment. This, stripped of details, is the new plan, as gravely propounded by the *Chicago Tribune*.

Now, if anybody will get up and propose a general railroad act of this nature, applicable to all roads hereafter to be built, we think we can promise that he will have the hearty support of everybody who has seriously reflected on the railroad problem. Forbid the construction of any road except with the proceeds of paid-up stock, and forbid any higher dividends than a certain fixed percentage on this amount, and we shall have a rule of which nobody can complain. We do not believe that a single mile of railroad would ever be constructed under such a rule in a new and thinly settled country like the west or south. Safe investments are not so scarce as to induce people to go into one of the most unsafe of investments, and one promising in most cases no return at all for several years, for the mere chance of seven or even ten per cent. at the outside. But we should, nevertheless, be heartily glad to see the plan tried, and believe it would, by stopping railroad construction for the present, bring the western farmers to a healthier comprehension of their relations to the roads, and railroad companies to a healthier comprehension of their relations to the community, and might tend to a solution of the railroad problem which would be both permanent and satisfactory.

But the application of any such rule now to roads *already in operation* would be spoliation pure and simple—spoliation as flagrant as any ever proposed by Karl Marx or Ben. Butler; if any attempt were made to carry it out, it would produce perhaps the greatest financial crash ever witnessed. It has, in the first place, that leading characteristic of Ben. Butler's greenback scheme, that it would not only violate a tacit pledge made by the state to individuals, but it would deprive men of rewards already earned by running great risks. When a railroad constructed for two million dollars is made to earn interest on four millions, the case is precisely similar to that of a government which, in a time of great danger and perplexity, sells seven per cent. bonds at fifty; and the present proposal of the farmers resembles Butler's plan of paying the bondholders in 1870, what they gave for their bonds in 1862. In fact, it is the old-fashioned game on a great scale of "Heads I win, tails you lose." The west has, during the past thirty years, wanted railroads, which there was a very small chance of making profitable for a long time. It encouraged eastern men and foreigners to make them in any way they pleased, running whatever risk there was, and pocketing whatever gain there might be, and they were made. The investment then was one of great danger and difficulty; *to treat it now as one of no danger and no difficulty would be simply swindling.* The word is hard, but the times demand plain speech. This was perhaps a bad mode of securing lines of communication, but the laws allowed it and encouraged it, and the people applauded it, and it is now a contract as binding in morals as in law. It is open to us to turn over a new leaf, and permit no more roads to be made in that way, but it is not open to us to treat those who lent us their money as dupes. As there has been enough of this sharp practice already, more of it would seriously shake the foundations of social order.

In the second place, as regards the older roads, it is not possible for "the people" or anybody else to ascertain what is the exact amount on which, in abstract justice, the earnings ought to pay interest. The stock, whether "fictitious" or not, has in most cases passed out of the hands of the original holders. It has been sold and resold, in open market, under the most solemn guarantees known to civilized society, with the understanding that it represented the *bona fide* ownership of the roads, with all their earnings, possible as well as actual. The laws, the courts, and public opinion, assured to it this character without reservation or qualification. In this character it has passed into the hands of widows, orphans, and helpless people generally, of charitable corporations, of colleges, banks, and institutions of all kinds by which the affairs of the community are administered. To throw any doubt on its value now, would be to cause an amount of misery and alarm which no thinking man could contemplate without a shudder. If the state wants to make the railroads common highways, it has the right to take them, but at their market value, paying the owners what other people would pay them, and not inquiring curiously and knavishly into the original cost. Between honest parties to a bargain, that, to use a homely phase, is "Neither here or there." The people ought, undoubtedly, to have looked forward a little when they first began to grant charters; but not having done so, they ought not to now throw on others the whole damage done by their own laches.

Though last, not least, much of the outcry over the high rates charged by railroads is due to an immense but deeply seated popular delusion as to the value of railroad property. When one puts his newspaper aside, and sits down calmly to examine the receipts which the farmers are so anxious to have cut down, the proposal we are discussing assumes a somewhat ludicrous aspect. We have before us the last issue of *Poor's Railroad Manual*, which certainly ought to be perfectly studied before the minds of the public are filled with wild and revolutionary notions about railroad property. There were in operation last year, in the United States, 57,323 miles of railroad, the net earnings of which bore to the *cost* of the roads the relation of 5.20 per cent., and to the capital stock of 3.21. This means simply that the work of transportation in the United States is, on the average, already done at a loss to the owners of the lines, or, in other words, vastly more cheaply to the public than there is the least likelihood of its being done in any other way—an assertion which anybody may verify by examining the accounts of the New York state canals. Now, fancy anybody seriously proposing to capitalists to construct railroads, as most of the western railroads were constructed, through a howling wilderness, for *the chance* of five and a half per cent., whenever the earnings allowed it; and fancy what subjects for spoliation are presented by the bloated owners of railroad property who pocket on the average less than four per cent. on the face value of their stock. Let us add, finally, that no corporation should be restricted by law to a certain rate of earnings, unless it contracts freely to do the work on those terms or has a minimum guaranteed to it by the state. In short, the railroad question, we would remind the *Chicago Tribune*, is not simply a question of dollars and cents. It is a question of morality in its highest and most important phases, and one the settlement of which must touch the security of all property, and affect the value of constitutions as safeguards of individual rights.

We have gone on for thirty years treating railroads as private property, and permitting and encouraging their construction by private enterprise. Out of this numerous abuses have grown up which ought to be remedied. The corporations have grown too powerful; their influence in politics is corrupting; the power of directors in the management is too great. For the reform of all this, careful legislation *preceded by careful inquiry* is necessary. The prohibition of special legislation would do much to abate the corruption. Some means ought also to be devised for protecting the minority of the stockholders against the despotic power, which, in some cases, amounts to virtual confiscation, of those holding a bare majority of the stock, or, in other words, of giving stockholders the means of actually superintending the management of their own property, and defending themselves against "rings" and "raids." Moreover, the power of directors to do anything but work the road ought to be diminished. Their discretion as regards extensions, combinations, consolidations, leases, and purchases, ought to be greatly reduced, if not destroyed. This involves two things not easily supplied. One is wise legislation, and the other honest government inspection. How far we are from both is best shown by the Illinois attempt at reform, which consists at present in taking the working of the roads out of the hands of the exceedingly able body of trained business men who now have charge of it, and compelling them to use a crazy table of "rates" drawn up by a mob of excited and ignorant politicians. If we are not prepared for this, the alternative, and the only one, is the purchase of the railroads by the state, and their management by our Murphys and Caseys. We shall not argue against this at present, for obvious reasons. But this, whatever difficulties it may present, is the only honorable way of escaping the necessity of such reforms in the present system as we have indicated above. Whatever the evils of our railroad system, they are not to be met or removed by fraud.

First. *The Nation* says that it has "followed the 'farmers' movement' with great interest, and with no little difficulty, owing to the heterogeneous composition of the organizations which are carrying it on, and the wide diversity of their character and avowed aims." The thought suggested is, that because the farmers are not united in their views relative to the best means to effect reform, because of the heterogeneity of their composition, the author of the circular could not understand their objects and aims. Unity of thought and action is rarely found in any body of men, even when few in number, during the discussion of ends sought to be obtained. Such unity cannot be expected in the first stages of the organization and discussions of plans for future action. When the people living in various parts of the country, in different states, with diverse interests, but all having in view the accomplishment of a common end, attempt to unite their efforts, it would be too much to expect that they would harmonize at the outset in their views, or that they would not commit some errors. The "farmers' movement" is in its incipiency; it may be said to be now only preparing for action, and it is yet too soon to look for united effort. The first assertion of the circular is only a covert thrust at the "farmers' movement"—an attempt to impress upon the public mind the belief that it is the effort of an irresponsible *mob* or *rabble* to defy laws and override the rights of other classes, and especially of railroad corporations. Hence *The Nation* is desirous of talking "common sense," and in its opening discloses its "common sense" to be a plea in behalf of railroad corporations.

Second. The circular casts odium on the efforts now being made to correct the abuses practiced by railroad corporations, by the use of the following language: "When Judge Lawrence was turned out of office in Illinois by the Grangers, and Judge Craig was put in his place, we took it for granted that they were going to deliver themselves from the tyranny of railroads by putting judges on the bench pledged to interpret the state constitution in a particular way, or, in other words, as a local paper has it, by showing that 'the people were superior to both laws and judges.'" Is it true that "Judge Lawrence was turned out of office?" He was a candidate for re-election, but a majority of the people voted for another man. Judge Craig was elected to office in the constitutional method, and took the seat formerly occupied by Judge Lawrence. The people did not "turn him out," but in the legal method, when his term had expired, elected another man. But says the circular: "We took it for granted that they [the Grangers] were going to deliver themselves," etc. There were no other judges to be elected, and there was nothing in the election of Craig that would warrant *The Nation* in arriving at the conclusion that control of the state was to be taken, and judges elected pledged to decide constitutional questions in a particular way. The idea is put prominently forth that the people who are attempting reform are a heterogeneous, irresponsible body of men—a mob, who, by the mere strength of numbers, is going to overturn all law, pack the courts, and rule as mere caprice should dictate, This was taken for granted because the people had elected one judge whom they believed was in sympathy with them. By the same rule we are warranted in assuming that the appointment of two judges in sympathy with the railroad interest of the country will revolutionize this whole government, and that all judges to be hereafter appointed will be pledged to decide all constitutional questions in favor of railroads. The author of this circular, however, is forced to admit that he was mistaken in his conclusions, and that the farmers "seek changes of a more legitimate character and resting on a more solid formation than the creation of a subservient judiciary." While the people of the whole country knew and fully understood that the objects the farmers were seeking to accomplish were relief from the oppressions and extortions practiced by railroad companies; while the agricultural, political and religious press of the land had been discussing the various propositions, and conventions of farmers and mechanics were meeting, and platforms and principles were being published, and the Patrons of Husbandry were discussing at public meetings and in the newspapers the best means for adoption, the author of this circular, who is now coming to the front as the champion of railroad corporations, or of the people, or of both, and is scattering his circular throughout the land, had heard nothing of the movement, and took it for granted that all that was sought by the "Grangers" was to elect "judges pledged to decide constitutional questions in a particular way;" and it required the "recent platforms" to admonish him that the Grangers looked to a reform of the abuses connected with the railroads and finances of the country.

With the new light our author received from the "platforms" he hastens to illuminate the public mind on this "vexed" railroad question. Having now mastered the situation, the writer takes it for granted that the all-important question is, "How to reduce railroads to the condition of public highways—controllable and existing solely or mainly for the convenience of the community," and concludes that the question is "as far from solution as ever."

It matters little whether railroads are considered "public highways" or private property. The name by which they are known will not make any difference. The real question is, how to make them subserve the objects for which they were intended, and at the same time afford a fair remuneration to the persons owning them. Some of the courts have already decided that the railroads of the country are public highways, but such decisions afford no relief. *The Nation* does not give us its opinion, nor does it seem to be aware that the supreme court of the United States has decided that railroads are public highways.

Third. The Nation says that "the farmers have been accused partly because of their escapade about the judges of Illinois, of seeking to rob the railroad companies of their lawful earnings, by forcing them to carry on their business at a loss, under the operation of cast-iron rules, drawn up without reference to its peculiar nature; that the farmers virtually acknowledged this charge when they saw its gravity, and that they accordingly now announce that they have no scheme of spoliation or confiscation in their minds, but have at last hit upon a mode of ascertaining what are 'reasonable rates,' which consists in discovering what was the amount of capital invested in constructing and operating the roads, and treating a fair per cent. on this as a proper return to the stockholders, and all charges which bring in more than this as 'unreasonable,' and therefore open to prohibition by the courts and state legislatures." *The Nation* admits that this rule applied to companies hereafter organized, and roads hereafter built, would be just, and assures us that everybody would approve of such a law. Let the road be built with the proceeds of paid-up stock, and restricted to a fair per cent. dividend on such paid stock, and *The Nation* will approve. To verify its hearty indorsement of this plan, it tells us in the next sentence that it does "not believe that a single mile of railroad would ever be constructed under such a rule in a new and thinly settled country like the west and south." It would be glad to see it tried, believing "it would stop builing railroads for the present, bring western farmers to a healthier comprehension of their relation to the roads, and railroad companies to a healthier comprehension of their relation to the community, and might tend to a solution of the railroad problem which would be both permanent and satisfactory." It gives as a reason why no roads would be built, that capitalists would not invest their money on unsafe security, or where the return would be uncertain. The logical deduction is, that if railroad companies are limited in the amount of their stock to the actual cost of the roads, no money can be obtained to build them; but if the company is allowed to add fictitious stock—to "water" it at pleasure—then capital can be had.

We do not discover the force of this reasoning. Railroads are usually constructed with borrowed capital. The capitalist loaning his money, loans it on what he believes to be advantageous terms and good security. If a road cost $2,000,000, and is built with borrowed capital, we cannot readily see how the security is improved by issuing to the stockholders certificates for $2,000,000 of stock, no part of which has been paid. True, it may have the effect to place the road in the hands of men who are experienced in operating roads, capitalizing their earnings and watering stocks, borrowing money on bonds, and loading the road with a burden that can only be supported by extortion; but it does not increase the value of the security held by the lender, nor does it enhance the value of the road. The less burden in the way of debts there is resting on a road, the more valuable are its stocks and bonds. We confess we cannot discover the strength of *The Nation's* argument. It seems to take it for granted that railroads can only be constructed by the class of men who now monopolize the business; in other words, that the class of unscrupulous men who have reduced the organizing of railroad companies and the manner of obtaining capital for the construction of roads to a system, are the only men who can undertake any railroad enterprise. It looks upon the south and west as destitute of men competent to organize a railroad company, or to procure means for the construction of railroads, or to construct them when the capital has been obtained. It regards the home construction of railroads in these sections as out of the question. It concludes that the method now adopted for procuring capital and constructing railroads is the only one that can be adopted. It forgets that in purer and simpler times railroads were built and owned by the parties living along their lines; that the process of adding large amounts of stock by watering was not then discovered, and that without these fictitious additions fair returns were made for the amounts invested. After all, railroads are only built when and where the business of the country requires them, save where large bounties are paid. In the west and south, where the business of certain localities and districts require a railroad, it will be built, even if the legislature should require the owners and stockholders to become so far honest as to limit their stock to the actual cost of the road, and to compel stockholders to pay up before obtaining certificates for their stock. It does not require these professional men to organize and control railroad companies, or the roads after construction.

But for the interference of rings formed to prevent such a consummation, any company of men who desire a railroad in their locality, by pursuing an honest course, could organize a company and build their road. If the amount of stock necessary to build the road was in good faith subscribed, and the same was being paid up as the construction of the road progressed, any reasonable amount of money could be obtained by such company by making an honest showing to capitalists. The demand for railroads would be as regularly supplied as for any other article of necessity. The laws of trade would regulate their construction. In all such cases capitalists would have the best of security, and the roads would pay fair dividends on paid-up capital and interest on the sum borrowed for legitimate purposes. But if there were no legitimate call for the road, if it were intended as a fraud by a set of educated sharpers who desired to receive large dividends on stock not paid up, or to borrow money by the sale of bonds in an amount double the cost or value of the road when completed, then it could not be built under the *new rules*, and *The Nation's* prediction would be verified. Any legitimate business not "cornered" or controlled by combinations or rings can be successfully prosecuted, and to say, as does *The Nation* in substance, that if railroad companies are forbidden to act dishonestly and corruptly no more railroads will be constructed, is an admission that the whole system is a fraud, and is a strong argument in favor of immediate, prompt, and efficient action on the part of state legislatures and of the courts. If men must become dishonest in order to build and operate railroads successfully, the whole system is rotten and should be destroyed, and an honest plan substituted.

Fourth. But says *The Nation:* "The application of any such rule to roads *already in operation*, would be spoliation, pure and simple. * * * It would not only violate a tacit pledge made by the state to individuals, but would deprive men of rewards already earned by running great risks." This is the old argument in favor of railroad companies, but with this difference: It makes the state a party to the dishonest practices of men who have enriched themselves at the expense of the public, and those to whom they have sold their bonds. We venture the assertion that, with few exceptions, all railroads in the United States that have been honestly and prudently managed have earned a fair per cent. on the capital actually expended in building, equipping, and operating them, and that a scale of tariffs greatly less than the rates now charged would, as a rule, afford fair dividends on the actual cost of the roads. No instances can be shown where the states, in granting charters to railroad companies, directly or in the passage of general incorporation statutes, have given to the companies the right to commit frauds upon the parties with whom they deal by using their credit to build their roads, and, without payment of their subscriptions, issue to themselves certificates as for paid-up stock. In all cases, individual stockholders are made liable for the debts to the amount of their stock. In contemplation of law the stock is paid up, and the roads are constructed by using the capital derived from this source. The stock is supposed to amount to as much as the cost of the road. The state, in giving the company a corporate or artificial being, enters into no agreement, express or implied, to make good the contract of the company, or be responsible for their misconduct, further than to exercise such control over them as to prevent or reform abuses, by compelling them to act honestly —being the same control exercised over all other persons within its jurisdiction. The creditors of railroad corporations have no stronger claim on the state in case of the non-fulfillment of contracts by railroad companies, or in cases of fraudulent and dishonest practices, than have the creditors of individuals. If a man worth $2,000 represents himself to be worth $4,000, knowing that his representations are false, and obtains credit upon his property for twice its real value, he violates the law, can be punished criminally, and is also responsible in a civil action; but his creditor has no claim upon the state for payment of the sum loaned or credit given on those representations. Is the claim different when a railroad corporation is the party obtaining the credit? Is the state under any greater obligations in one case than in the other? But *The Nation* says the custom of doing business on this plan has obtained and been in use for thirty years, and from this draws an argument in favor of its legitimacy. Does this fact make it honest, or change the relations of the state to these corporations? A man has followed horse-stealing for thirty years, and is at last detected; he has been in the habit of selling his stolen horses to innocent parties; they have been reclaimed by their owners; can the purchasers, because this thief has so long followed his pursuit, claim compensation from the state? A man obtains goods under false pretenses, and before the owner can reclaim them, sells them to a third party; can the person defrauded claim compensation from the state? We cannot discover the distinction between the cases stated and that of railroad companies, who, by falsely pretending that they have paid up their capital stock, obtain money on their bonds for an amount greater than the value of their entire roads. They all commit crimes for which they are liable to be punished, and all are liable in law to make good their contracts; but in neither case is there any pecuniary liability imposed upon the state or the public. Nor would the application of the rule to railroad companies already in existence, who have built their roads, be "spoliation pure and simple." It never can be wrong to compel men to do right. If railroad companies, by arbitrarily increasing their capital stock, and issuing certificates therefor without payment of any part of it, as is the general rule among them, are receiving dividends on such stock, justice to the public demands that the state legislatures should compel them to purge their stock, and at once cancel all such spurious and illegitimate issues. The duty the state government owes to the public demands this, that the oppressions under which the people suffer may be prevented in the future. But "it would deprive men of rewards already earned by running great risks." What these "great risks" are is not readily seen. They certainly have not risked their money; they built their roads on borrowed capital, and have declared dividends to themselves on stock they have never paid. They extort from the public, in charges for transportation, money sufficient to pay the interest on the money borrowed for building their roads, and to pay dividends on their stock that has not cost them anything, and if they have run any risks they are the same that all men, who violate the law, have ventured upon. The pecuniary risks are all taken from the parties from whom they borrow.

The Nation says that the west during thirty years has wanted railroads, and that there was small chance of making them profitable for a long time. That "it encouraged eastern men and foreigners to make them in any way they pleased, running whatever risks existed, and pocketing whatever gain there might be—and they were made." The people of the west have vivid recollections of the manner in which the means were raised to make their railroads. They took large amounts of stock, and voted large amounts of local aid for which they were to receive stock and dividends. After contributing sufficient to pay at least one-half of the entire cost of their roads, their eastern *friends* mortgaged their roads and sold them out, and the "people of the west" got neither stock nor dividends, but they are to-day paying taxes to discharge debts contracted by them in building their roads after having been swindled by their *eastern friends* out of values, amounting in Iowa alone, to not less than $4,000,000. *The Nation* further says that "the investment then was one of great danger and difficulty; *to treat it now as one of no difficulty and no danger, would be simple swindling.*" This journal evidently knew but little of the real facts in the case, or it would not have made this assertion. But if we admit that the undertaking was both dangerous and difficult, does that exempt from all responsibility the adventurers who came west and *fattened* off of the simplicity of the people? Does it absolve them from the effects of their dishonest acts? Are the states pledged to make good the dishonest contracts of these adventurers because of the danger or difficulty they run?

While the law should regulate the action of all railroad companies, would it be "simple swindling" for the legislature to compel these pioneer adventurers to purge their companies of fictitious or "watered" stock, or limit their rates of charges? We do not believe that the legislature ever intended to charter railroad companies to prey upon the people at pleasure and without restriction, nor is it true that any injustice would be done in compelling companies, whose roads are constructed, to reduce their stocks to the amounts actually invested in their roads, and to limit their rates of charges to a fair and reasonable compensation for the money so invested. Nor would it shake the foundations of social order to compel these men to act honestly.

But another difficulty is suggested in this circular. Our author says: "It is not possible for 'the people' or anybody else to ascertain the *exact* amount, on which, in abstract justice, the earnings ought to pay interest." True, it may be hard to ascertain what is the "exact" amount, but this fact presents no great difficulty. It is now known to nearly everybody about what railroads cost per mile. When a road that we know, in the nature of things, could not have cost more than $35,000 per mile, is by the "watering" process shown to have cost the sum of $75,000, it would not be difficult to approximate the amount of stock that should be cancelled; nor need the fact that the exact amount cannot be ascertained prevent legislative action. In all cases a large margin to cover any doubts might be allowed by the companies, and still great reductions could be made.

Fifth. *The Nation*, as it progresses, becomes more earnest. It takes up the oft repeated cry of "innocent purchasers," "widows and orphans," with their all invested in railroad stock. "Charitable corporations and banks" have invested in railroad stocks and "helpless people generally." It tells us that "this stock has been sold and resold, in open market, under the most solemn guarantees known to civilized society, with the understanding that it represents the *bona fide* ownership of the roads, with all their earnings, possible as well as actual. The laws, the courts, and public opinion, assured to it this character without reservation or qualification. * * To throw any doubt on its value now would be to cause an amount of misery and alarm which no thinking man could contemplate without a shudder." That some parties would suffer financially by compelling railroad companies to reduce their stock to an honest standard cannot be denied, and in some cases it might work absolute financial ruin. But that any considerable amount of railroad stock is held and owned by poor people is rather improbable, and that "helpless people generally" deal in railroad stock is not true. That some purchases are made by innocent parties may also be true; yet in this day and age when the fact that at least one-half of all railroad stock is mere fiction and has no intrinsic value is known to the public generally, a third party must be "innocent" indeed to purchase it without knowing that its value is imaginary rather than real.

Most of the stocks and bonds of railroad companies are sold in Wall street by the owners and managers, acting in their character of brokers and stock gamblers. The innocent third parties are generally the dupes of these brokers who are on the lookout for the unwary. These dupes are caught and stripped and turned loose without remorse, when the managers of the great railroad interests of the country are "loading or unloading," and no complaint is heard. The "innocents" are robbed without exciting a passing remark; but when an attempt is made to relieve the people from the onerous burdens imposed upon them, we hear on all sides the cry of "innocent purchasers!" and of the great wrongs about to be committed. They virtually admit their own dishonesty, but say in substance: "We have duped others and you must permit us to rob the people in order that 'innocent' third parties may not suffer."

This is the pith of *The Nation's* argument. It goes further, and says: The law and the courts have sanctioned this dishonest course, and because of this, the same raid upon the rights of the people must be allowed to continue without interruption.

Neither the people nor the state are in any manner responsible for the acts of these railroad managers. All contracts for the sale of bonds or stocks are in the first instance made with the company or their agents. They are responsible to the parties holding their bonds or stocks. Their roads are liable to their full value, and each stockholder is liable to the amount of stock he owns, and to that extent must make good the contracts made by the managers of the road. The purchaser had the means of knowing the value of the stock he purchased. If he suffer, his suffering is the result of the fraud of the directors of the road, and of his own negligence. None of these causes affect the right of the state to regulate the company, and to compel it to act honestly.

The cry of "innocent purchasers" will not avail. While the people can sympathize with those who are defrauded by the dishonest acts of the companies, and appreciate the helpless condition of widows and orphans who have lost by railroad rascality, the facts will demonstrate that they are few in number, unless we include among the "widows and orphans" Commodore Vanderbilt, Col. Tom. Scott, Daniel Drew, Jay Gould, and the Wall street brokers generally, who own and control most of the railroad stocks. If we admit all that is stated in the circular, the right of the people to be protected against the impositions and oppressions of the railroad companies remains unchanged, and the legislature, acting for the whole people, can control the management of the companies so far as it affects the public. If the doctrine advocated by the circular be true, railroad corporations are now able to defy the government and the people.

Sixth. The Nation, in its circular letter, says: "If the state wants to make the railroads common highways, it has the right to take them, but at their market value, paying the owners what other people pay them, and not inquiring curiously and knavishly into their original cost. Between honest parties to a bargain, that, to use a common phrase, is neither here nor there." We get more light as we advance. As we understand the principles of our government, the states possess the right of eminent domain. But they have no power to buy and sell, like corporations or individuals. They may condemn private property for public use, if the public good requires it. The value of property for public use is ascertained in the manner prescribed by statute. *The Nation* is inconsistent. It says in one paragraph that the state has no lawful right to regulate railroads and restrict the action of railroad companies in the issuing of stock, etc., and then declares that the state can take the railroads from the companies should it desire to do so. But for cool assurance *The Nation* is entitled to the champion belt when it says the state *must* take the roads at their market value—at what other people would pay for them—without inquiring "curiously and knavishly" into the original cost! In other words, these corporations are so potent that should the state attempt to exercise its right of eminent domain, they can dictate the terms upon which they would be willing to surrender their roads to the public. The terms are that the state must pay the companies' value for all the watered stock with which they have loaded their roads, as well as for all the bonds the companies have sold, and do this *without asking questions*. If the people or the states should stop to inquire into their cost, they would be acting knavishly. True, the companies could not build their roads without special grants from state legislatures, but having obtained the privilege of locating their roads where they pleased, and having, by false pretences, obtained local aid and defrauded the people who helped to build the roads; having piled up their fictitious stock by the billion, and by onerous and dishonest charges reduced the farming population to poverty, their champion, *The Nation*, tells the states: "If you want the railroads you can take them, but you must not be curious to know what they cost; this would be a knavish act; you can have them by paying the companies the full amount of money they claim to have invested, including fictitious and watered stock." This kind of impudence is sublime. The railroad companies, through this *hired spokesman*, propose to quit business provided the states will pay them just what they are pleased to call the value of their roads, and ask no questions. It is usual for the thief, when seeking immunity for his crimes, to propose to return a part of the stolen property, but these corporations, who have been robbing the states and the people for years, offer to close their career by forcing upon the parties robbed what is left of their booty, provided the states will pay to them not only the cost of the roads, but allow them par value for all their bogus or fictitious stock.

They propose to compel the states to adopt a new rule—the rule that governs operations in Wall street. They will "bull" their stock to the highest point, and force the states to purchase at these high figures. *The Nation* says that "the people ought undoubtedly to have looked forward a little when they first began to grant charters; but, not having done so, they ought not now to throw on others the whole damage done by their own *laches*." The conclusion is that because they dealt with railroad companies as they deal with honest men, and did not provide in advance for the punishment of all conceivable dishonest practices on the part of the officers of the companies, *therefore* the people are the guilty parties and should reward the innocent railroad companies by paying them real dollars for the imaginary dollars they have added to their stock. The railroad companies took an undue advantage of the people, but that is "neither here nor there;" the companies must get from the states all that they please to demand for their roads. This is the "common sense" *The Nation* presents to the people.

The power of the states, under the constitution, to purchase, is not doubted by this advocate of the railroad interest, nor does he, in his "common sense," consider the immense tax that the purchase of the railroads would entail upon the people.

Seventh. The Nation says that "Much of the outcry over

31

high rates charged by railroads is due to an immense but deeply-seated popular delusion as to the value of railroad property." The reader is then referred to *Poor's Railroad Manual* for the value of railroad property, but *The Nation* fails to state that in this *Manual* the value of all railroads is given as furnished by the companies themselves; it includes all their watered stock and bonds with which the roads are "loaded," and does not purport to give the actual cost of any road. The book, too, is published in the interest of the companies, and for the purpose of inflating rather than giving the true value of the roads. From this *Manual* it appears dividends do not average more than five per cent. on the stock. When it is remembered that every dollar invested in railroads (taking all the roads in the United States) represents two additional dollars, or that by the increase of stock and issuing of bonds, the reported cost is three times the actual cost of the roads, a dividend of five per cent. is equivalent to fifteen per cent. on the actually paid-up honest capital, it would appear that *The Nation*, and not the people, is laboring under "a deep-seated delusion." *The Nation* is not informed upon the subject, or desires to prevent an unfair view of it. In the *Manual* to which reference is made, the New York organ will find the statement that railroads can afford to carry freights for one and one-fourth per cent. per ton per mile. This is their own statement. What *are* their charges? Recently they have been reducing their rates. As published, old rates from New York to Chicago were one dollar per hundred-weight. This has been reduced to seventy-five cents by the managers of the Grand Trunk lines. By the new scale the rates charged are about double what the *Manual* fixes as "paying," and yet *The Nation* thinks that because the farmers desire lower rates, the question of reduction assumes a "somewhat ludicrous aspect." We are advised to examine *Poor's Railroad Manual* before we permit our minds to be filled with revolutionary notions about railroads. The farmer should presume that the advantage is all on his side when railroad companies charge him *only* seventy-five cents for carrying a bushel of wheat from Iowa to New York, and that at present rates railroad companies are making little or nothing, and are running great risks. These are proper deductions from the circular of *The Nation.* Having presented the whole case to its own satisfaction, it gives reign to fancy, and says: "Now fancy anybody seriously proposing to capitalists to construct railroads, as most of the western railroads were constructed, *through a howling wilderness*, for the *chance* of five and a half per cent. whenever the earnings of the road allowed it; and fancy what subjects for spoliation are presented by these bloated owners of railroad property, who pocket on the average less than four per cent. *on the par value of their stock*,"—to which we might add, "including more than one billion dollars for which they never paid one cent." The fact that these self-denying railroad men are constantly extending their roads, buying and leasing all that they can get control of, for the purpose of more effectually controlling the government and enslaving the people, and are devoting all the earnings of their roads to these objects, are not deemed worthy of notice by this champion of the railroad interest. We know as a fact, that the leading and controlling railroad men are spending their whole energy and their money to this end. These men are fast consolidating the whole railroad interest. We also know, that companies that are content to divide their earnings, rather than extend their roads, make large dividends, and leave a surplus to be capitalized. The "common sense" of *The Nation* does not strike us with its intended force. *The Nation* evidently has but a limited knowledge of the west. The fancy sketch of self-denying railroad men constructing railroads "*through a howling wilderness*," is finely drawn; but it exists only in the minds of *The Nation.* If this writer had been speaking of the mountain gorges and desolate pine plains which vex and impoverish the Boston & Albany track from Albany to Worcester, he might be excused for his words; but the "howling wilderness" does not apply to the cultivated prairies, whose enterprising farmers helped to build the roads now so bitterly and justly complained of, and it describes the domain of no western road save where the companies obtained, through legislative and congressional aid, enough of the people's land to construct the roads.

Eighth. As a last point *The Nation* says, that "no corporation should be restricted by law to a certain rate of earnings unless it consents freely to do such work on those terms, or has a minimum guaranteed to it by the state." The state possesses no power to guarantee to any private corporation any rate of dividends; nor would it be just to compel the people to donate a part of their earnings to railroad companies, or to any other private parties. In our judgment, the state has the constitutional right to regulate and control all private corporations, and when the good of the public demands it to restrict the rates charged by railroad companies for carrying freights and passengers. We admit that "the questions connected with the regulations of railroads are questions of morality, in their highest and most important phases, the settlement of which must touch the security of all property, and affect the value of constitutions as safeguards of individual rights." We go further, and say that in the management of railroads, and the favors shown to the companies, the constitutional rights of individuals have already been measurably destroyed, and that the most important question now is, How can those rights be restored and no injustice be done to railroad companies? These questions we have already discussed, and will only add that the sole remedy to be applied is legislative limitation and restriction. The abuses now practiced by railroad companies must be corrected. The legislatures have the power and it is their duty to restrict the scale of charges to such rates as will afford a fair remuneration to the companies on their investments, and at the same time protect the people from the extortions of soulless corporations. This power can be exercised over the companies now in being as well as over those to be hereafter organized.

We have devoted this chapter to an examination of the views of *The Nation* for the reason that, in the form of a circular, they have been widely distributed, and are designed to distract and divide those who are seeking relief from the oppressions

EQUALITY BEHIND THE LAW
OUR
IN UNION THERE IS STRENGTH
CREDIT MOBILIER
BACK PAY TO THE FRONT
STRAIGHT
LIBERT
VOTE EARLY
VIVE LA COMMUNE
LONG LIVE THE KING
LOUISIANA

of this railroad monopoly, and because the writer treats the "Farmers' Movement," the "Grangers," and "the people" with undisguised derision and contempt. The farmers are characterized as a *mob* of politicians—an irresponsible body—ignorant and careless of the rights of others, and represented as claiming a superiority to courts and laws. The idea that the people, farmers, or grangers have not sufficient knowledge to take the lead in any attempt to reform the abuses under which they suffer, is put prominently forth. The attempt at reform in Illinois is referred to in the following words, in speaking of the remedy of the present abuses: "How far we are from both (*i. e.*, ascertaining and applying the remedy) is best shown by the Illinois attempt at reform, which consists at present in taking the working of the roads out of the hands of the exceedingly able body of trained business men who have charge of it, and compelling them to use a crazy table of 'rates' drawn up by a *mob* of excited and ignorant politicians." The prevailing notion which has obtained in some parts of the country, that farmers and working men are not qualified to act in matters of a public nature, is reflected throughout the circular, and the rights and privileges of railroad corporations are spread before the reader in what is termed a "common sense" manner. The object of all this is apparent: It is to impress upon the public mind the idea that the people are not equal to the occasion, and that no reform can be effected.

CHAPTER VI.

THE INFLUENCE OF MONOPOLIES UPON LABOR.

IT is a self-evident proposition, that the wealth of a country lies in its products, and that the quantity of its products depends directly upon the amount of labor employed. The diverse interests and pursuits in our country afford opportunity for the employment of an immense number of laborers. Indeed, the persons employed in manual labor in the various industrial pursuits of the country number more than one-half of the whole population. This great army of laborers is engaged in agricultural and horticultural pursuits; its rank labors in shops, factories, furnaces, mines, stores, and offices, upon railroads and canals, and in vessels, and in the numerous other relations requiring their services. Their right to fair remunerative prices for their labor is admitted by all. Whether that remuneration is paid in money, as when the labor is hired, or shares in the product of its creation, the workman should receive a just reward for his services. No onerous taxes, duties, or restrictions, should be imposed upon labor. The profits derived from labor should belong to the laborer. When capital and labor unite in producing, a fair division of the product should be made. Any system that gives the whole product to the capitalist, except the small stipend paid for the time the labor is employed, is oppressive. We are not an advocate of a division or distribution of the wealth of the country among all classes and pursuits, but contend that it is but just that the operatives in the factory, the forgers of the foundry, the skilled artificers of the machine shop, the miners who extract wealth from the earth, the laborers who build and operate railroads, canals, etc., and, in short, all whose work and skill, combined with capital, produce a profit, should receive a fair proportion of the profit thus created. Prosperity and contentment can only be found where all industrial pursuits prove remunerative; where manual labor not only supports the laborer, but enables him to acquire a competence in process of time. That division of labor and capital which compels the laborer to toil daily to keep want from his door, and is so inflexible that the sickness of a single day entails the loss of necessaries to his family, is a species of slavery. When by the customs of the country, or by its laws, the line dividing labor and capital is so clearly defined, that the laborer, by a life-time of toil, can accumulate nothing, while the capitalist employing him realizes from ten to one hundred per cent. per annum upon the amount invested, the one is but coining the life-blood of the other, and the laborer is but little better than a bond-servant. From time immemorial, those who obtain their support by manual labor have received less attention from government than any other class. Indeed, in all monarchial governments they are left out of consideration, except as their labor can be made useful in advancing the interests of the superior classes. In our own country there has existed a prejudice against the laboring classes. Especially was this so in the south until the abolition of slavery. As a nation, we have been apt to follow old opinions, and look upon labor as degrading, and the laborer as a menial. This prejudice still exists to a great degree, and our boys seek speculative rather than legitimate industrial employments. While in theory all men are considered equal in our country, practically the old feudal distinction is kept up. We have no titled aristocracy in America, but we are fast creating an aristocracy of wealth and pursuits. While labor is the motive-power, and manual laborers the engineers who keep the car of progress moving forward, they receive less consideration from the hands of government than the loungers and speculators. While acts of congress and state legislatures, designed to benefit the wealthy capitalists, are of frequent date, but few can be found designed or enacted in the interest of the laboring classes. Special legislation in favor of the capitalists, corporations, and manufacturers, has been the rule; legislation in the interest of the laboring classes the exception.

The *dignity* that should attach to labor is entirely wanting, and the respect the laborer should command is not accorded to him. Not that he is looked upon as the inferior of other men, but that in all matters affecting the public welfare, the interests of the capitalist, the large operator, the banker, manufacturer, and corporations generally, claim special attention, while the real wealth-producing portion of the people is neglected. This is not the result of any design on the part of those engaged in other pursuits—it results from the fact that capital pays particular attention to its own interests, while labor is content to let other interests take control of the government, of all public matters, and of even its own pursuits, quietly accepting a secondary position, and neglecting to claim the consideration and respect to which it is entitled from its intimate connection with the capital of the country and the body politic.

The laborer's political existence is seldom felt save at elections, when the strongest *vote* decides the day, and then generally in the blind following of its file leaders. The reforms promised to labor on these occasions are seldom realized, and the laborer, without asserting his rights as a freeman, is too apt to continue in the old, beaten track, sometimes complainingly, it is true, but willing and ready to be directed by his party or his employer, whenever his help is needed. All of which is calculated to widen the line dividing capital and labor, and to increase the wealth and power of the capitalist.

Let us illustrate: The capitalist is engaged in manufacturing, and wishes protection from the government. The question of protective tariffs is one of the issues of the campaign. He employs one hundred voters. He makes known to them his wishes, and explains to them the benefits he expects to receive. They wish to oblige their employer and accept his views as correct, and all cast their votes for what they are led to believe will be his benefit. They are not less intelligent than other men, but instead of acting independently they wish to please their employer. By this act, they involuntarily take an inferior place among men, and lower their dignity. While they have by their action enabled the manufacturer to increase his gains, by the success of a protective tariff, they have secured nothing for themselves, not even an advance of wages, unless their employer voluntarily allows such an advance. He is aided by legislative enactment through their votes, and can demand additional profit for the product of their labor; but the act is of no personal benefit to them. All they receive, if anything, is voluntarily allowed by the capitalist employing them. Had they examined for themselves they might have discovered that the act which benefited him was detrimental to their own interests. The same illustration will apply to all pursuits requiring capital and labor. The consolidation of any business so as to destroy or prevent competition is detrimental to the interests of labor. Monopolies, of whatever kind, are encroachments upon the interests of those who depend upon manual labor for support.

Railroad corporations in the United States employ not less than two hundred thousand men. This large number of men have no interest in these corporations excepting the wages paid to them. Subtract the sums they so receive, and their daily labor still adds to the wealth of these powerful corporations. They are employed to perform manual labor; they are free and independent citizens of this republic. Their employers do not have any claim upon them for anything but their labor. Yet, as a general rule, in all matters affecting the interests of railroad corporations, when the issue is made at the ballot box, these men are found voting as their employers desire—too often without giving the matter due attention, and not unfrequently in support of measures which are at war with their own best interests. In thus voting, they are influenced by what they deem proper motives — they desire to gratify their employers. This state of things is also most strikingly presented in local and municipal elections, when certain measures are to be carried. In such cases, as a general rule, the person or officer controlling or employing men votes them "solid" on the side of the question he supports. In the cases we have given, as well as in all others of a like character, where any combination or corporation desires to influence or carry certain measures, the undivided support of the employés is expected. So long has this manner of voting been practiced, it has grown into a custom; for the employé, if he refuses to observe it, does so at the risk of losing his employment. We have referred to these things, not for the purpose of showing that the men engaged in manual labor are inferior to other men, or to prove that they act from improper motives, but to demonstrate our proposition that they do not think and act independently in matters of public concern, and are indifferent to their own best interests. That while other interests procure special favors from government, the laboring classes are content to occupy an inferior position, and even give their support to measures tending to degrade rather than to ennoble them. Because of these things, the laboring classes, as a general rule, are treated by those who are getting control of the capital and business of the country as inferior beings, and labor is not classed by them as of honorable calling.

The creation of privileged classes in our country is to be deprecated. The centralization of wealth and the grading of the standing of men by the amount of money they possess; the creation of great corporations with power to control the business and finances of the country, now threaten to overthrow our republican institutions. But equally to be dreaded is the indifference manifested by the laboring classes in asserting and protecting their rights. Practically, so far as the business of the country is concerned, the line between capital and labor is now sharply drawn, and in the administration of the government, the old-time dogma that the class controlling the wealth of the country should rule, while those who labor for a support are to remain "hewers of wood and drawers of water," is fast assuming tangible form, and unless the far-reaching and grasping policy of monopolies is checked by the laboring and producing classes, the absolute control of the government will pass from the people into the hands of their oppressors. By the action of railroad corporations, the special legislation in favor of certain interests; the monopolies given to manufacturers, and the action of the Wall street brokers, the wealth of the country has become centralized, and is controlled by and in the interests of the monopolists, who, because of their combinations, also control the value of labor throughout the country. The influence of the laboring classes is made to subserve the purposes of monopolists. The manufacturer, protected by government, enjoys all the profit accruing from the labor of the operatives, and uses the influence incident to his position to strengthen his interests by controlling their suffrages.

In all the different labor-employing pursuits, the political privileges enjoyed by the employé are directed and controlled by the employer in his own interest; the whole mental and physical structure of the laborer is used in advancing his employer's interest. Because of this law of capital the comparatively few men now controlling the railroads of the country, our manufacturers and other great interests which have become the special favorites of those in power, have obtained an almost unlimited influence over the best interests of the country. They have been able to entrench themselves in their strongholds, and compel all the agricultural, the commercial, and other industrial pursuits to contribute to their already dangerous power. The great army of laborers, instead of controlling the political affairs of the country in their own interest, become the instruments in the hands of the monopolists of their own oppression. With sufficient strength to shape the whole policy of the government, they are content to let others control them, while they toil from day to day for the small compensation allowed them, and derive no benefit from the proceeds of their labor.

If the capital and labor of the country were combined, so that the products could be divided and a fair proportion allowed to the laborer, his social and financial condition would be improved, and the power of the few men who now control the government in their own interest would be destroyed. While the duty of providing for himself and family is imposed upon every one, *in this country* every citizen has another important duty to perform — the duty of aiding in the preservation of republican government and the equal rights of all the people. Those who become indifferent to these objects and duties, and allow selfish or ambitions men to get the control of the government, and prostitute it to their own purposes, are the authors of their own sufferings. And those who permit themselves to become instruments in the hands of the people's oppressors for the continuance of oppression, commit great wrongs to themselves and their country.

The public opinion that accords to the Wall street stock gambler a place among honorable men, and allows him to shape the financial policy of the country, that allows him to live outside of prison walls, is corrupted and perverted. Yet there is no class of men in the whole country who have so great an influence over the government and the commercial and financial interests as the Wall street brokers.

No class of citizens should command greater respect than that engaged in manual labor, nor should any other class exercise a more potent influence in the nation; yet, as a matter of fact, no class receives so little consideration or has less influence in national affairs. While great interests with concentrated wealth, requiring no special aids from government, are constantly receiving them, the interests of the laboring and producing classes receive no special care or attention. While railroad corporations and other great monopolies are vigilant in protecting and strengthening their interests, the laboring classes are indifferent as to what is to be their future.

While other interests are extending their influence, the interests of the laborers are neglected, and the laborers themselves are content to occupy inferior places in the body politic. While labor is the means, and the *laborer* the *power* that develops and enriches the country, the *interests* of the laborers languish, while those of the speculator, the stock broker, and capitalist, *prosper*. Before we can become a prosperous, contented, and happy people, all honorable pursuits must have equal rights before the law. Special and class legislation must be abandoned, and the *dignity* of labor must be fully vindicated.

But it may be asked, "How are these things to be accomplished?" We answer: 1st. By laborers asserting their right to think and act as independent men; by giving their employers to understand that they do not hire their intellects, their *rights* as citizens, but only their physical force; that while they labor for their employers, they preserve their individuality and self-respect; by giving their employers to understand that they are only paid for manual labor, and that they are not bondsmen. 2d. By demanding for labor such remuneration as will allow the laborer to share in the profits resulting from his toil, either by treating it as an investment in the business in which it is employed, or by the payment of such compensation as will allow a surplus for investment—refusing to wear out their lives in procuring a bare subsistence. 3d. By the diffusion of knowledge among the laboring classes, especially of the theory and objects of our government, and the relation sustained by the laboring classes to the government, and by demanding for themselves due respect and consideration on the part of those engaged in other pursuits; by demanding of legislatures and of congress the enactment of such statutes as shall not impose taxes upon their labor for the benefit of other pursuits, and such as shall require all taxes levied for any purpose to be levied upon the *property* and *not the labor* of the country. 4th. By demanding the unconditional repeal of all statutes which confer upon individuals, classes, companies, corporations, or callings, special bounties, grants, privileges, or profits, which in their operations act oppressively upon the laboring and producing classes. And lastly, to strive to eradicate the ancient and continuing prejudice against labor, and to vindicate the truth of the often repeated declaration of eminent men: "That the person engaged in manual labor is following the most ancient as well as the most noble calling."

Those objects can all be accomplished by united and intelligent action. The false, yet popular, idea that a man's respectability among his fellows is graduated by the extent of his possessions, and his political standing scaled, by the amount of his money, can be obliterated, and merit alone will become the rule by which to measure the man. The laboring man with intellect and personal merit will supersede the man who has money, but lacks mind, in the social and political world.

When the laboring classes, including the farmers and mechanics, shall boldly step into the front ranks they will make their influence felt; reforms will be the order of the day; trading and dishonest politicians will be suffered to go into retirement; courts committed to the interests of monopolies will be reformed, and the law will be administered by judges who will not pervert the plain letter and spirit of the constitution for the purpose of upholding unjust laws; the monopolists who now rule and ruin the country will be shorn of their power, the producer and laborer will receive for their labor and products fair value in money, and will not be obliged to receive payment in depreciated paper, while the speculator, the broker, and the government buy and sell gold and silver as articles of commerce. The agriculturist, the mechanic, and laborer will be the *peers* of the men who are now forming an aristocracy of wealth; the laws will be faithfully and honestly administered, and peace and prosperity will fill the land.

CHAPTER VII.

THE FINANCIAL POLICY OF THE GOVERNMENT PRACTICALLY DEVELOPED.

IN our principal work, we stated that the financial policy of the country, backed and supported by the legal tender decisions, placed the entire commerce of the country in the hands and under the control of a few men, who were not engaged in any legitimate business, but were assembled in Wall street, engaged in what they term dealing in money, stocks and bonds, but who were only engaged in gambling and reckless speculation, that they had obtained the entire control of the finances of the whole country, and that even the secretary of the treasury, who had nominally the control of the currency, was unable to dispute the supremacy with them, and that it was only a question of time as to when he would be compelled to yield to their demands, and pay them tribute. This is now, (Sept. 25, 1873,) being demonstrated. The further fact is shown that the persons, firms and banking houses selected by the secretary of the treasury, with and through whom the business of the government is being transacted, and who were supposed to have made large fortunes in handling government money, selling government bonds, etc., are engaged in the same reckless speculations as other Wall street gamblers. The failure of Jay Cooke & Co., with their principal house in Wall street, New York, another house in Philadelphia, another in Washington, and also owning the First National Bank in Washington City, in which the government officials keep their deposits, but illustrates the defective financial system of the country. As a closing chapter to the appendix of this edition of our work, we deserve to call attention to the recent financial disturbance, its causes and effect. The whole country was startled a few days since by the announcement of the failure of one financial firm in New York. This caused general alarm. It was followed by like announcements as to other firms in the same and other cities, in different parts of the country, and some in other countries. This happens at a time when the granaries of the north and west are full, and when pastures and prairies are dotted over with immense herds of cattle; when pork is abundant, when the south has an abundant supply of cotton, and when no unusual cause exists in the ordinary routine of legitimate business for failures, for a money crisis, or for any alarm. Yet the facts are telegraphed over the whole country, and to Europe, that failures are frequent, that banks refuse to discount, or do a legitimate business, some have suspended, that money cannot be had, and that honest dealers and depositors are being ruined.

Dispatches like the following of September 20th, are flashed to all parts of the old and new world, and business is suspended:

THE STOCK PANIC! — MORE FAILURES AMONG BROKERS AND BANKERS! — THE SITUATION IN NEW YORK AND PHILADELPHIA.

NEW YORK, Sept. 20, 1873.—The Union Trust Company suspended at half past ten.

Great crowds are in Wall and Broad streets, and the policemen are busy keeping free the entrances and exits of the Stock Exchange.

The failures of Ketchum & Belknap and E. C. Morehead are the latest reported.

The National Bank of the Commonwealth has suspended.

Saxe & Rogers have suspended.

A meeting of the creditors of Jay Cooke & Co. is to be held on Monday.

Edward Haight & Co., it is just announced, have suspended.

NEW YORK, Sept. 20.—New suspensions: Toussig & Fisher, P. M. Meyers, Miller & Walsh, Laurens Josephs, Fearling & Dillinger, Williams & Bostwick.

The sub-treasurer has posted a notice stating that he has been instructed by the secretary of the treasury to purchase $10,000,000 in bonds to-day. This prompt response of the government to the request made for relief by the bankers yesterday, gives apparently additional strength to the strong and encouragement to the weak. A better feeling prevails, and it looks as if the worst is over. The stock market shows an improvement of five per cent.

The suspension of Fisk & Hatch is said to make probable the embarrassment of the Hoboken bank for savings. A defalcation of nearly $70,000 was discovered in the bank lately, and the directors disposed of the securities to make up the deficiency, depositing with Fisk & Hatch for safe keeping $94,000 of the amount realized. The suspension of the firm makes this sum unavailable at present.

NEW YORK, Sept. 20.—Brown, Wadsworth & Co. have failed. A special from Washington says: "It may be stated, on the highest authority, that should the order to purchase $10,000,000 of bonds fail to check the financial excitement, it has been decided on by secretary Richardson to issue any part of the $44,000,000 reserve that may be necessary to restore confidence."

There were thirteen proposals to sell bonds to the government, at the sub-treasury, aggregating $2,672,650, at from 109 to 112.

The National Trust company has just closed its doors.

At nearly one o'clock the $10,000,000 promised from Washington cannot be made available, owing to "red-tape" requirements, opening and reading, offering to sell bonds, and telegraphing to know if the rates are acceptable.

The tills of the best and strongest banking houses must be getting low, having stood a run now of nearly three days. Under the order issued by the president of the stock exchange, forbidding members, under the penalty of expulsion, to engage in operations outside, it is not possible to realize on securities, and each man's own vault is now his only stand by.

PHILADELPHIA, Sept. 20.—The Union banking company has

failed. This bank has a state charter, and bore a heavy run yesterday.

Third street is comparatively quiet this morning.

The run on the Fidelity Trust company has almost entirely subsided.

At Jay Cooke's the clerks are preparing a statement to be laid before the members of the firm on the arrival of the steamship Prussia, on board of which are two of the partners.

NEW YORK, Sept. 20.—The bank presidents have passed a resolution to issue immediately ten millions in loan certificates.

The defalcation in the Union Trust company is said to be $500,000, and the secretary, Charles Carleton, is the reported defaulter.

The Manhattan bank honors the Union Trust company's drafts as fast as presented.

Gold, $1.11⅞.

A special dispatch from Washington says secretary Richardson leaves Washington this evening for New York. A conference will be held to-morrow morning at the sub-treasury to determine what action he will take in the matter.

Toussig, Gemp & Co., of this city, closed doors this afternoon, after the announcement of the failure of their New York house, Toussig, Fisher & Co.

A number of telegrams were received at the postoffice, requesting the postmaster to withhold from delivery letters bearing the stamp of the firm sending messages and which were addressed to Jay Cooke & Co. The postmaster could not comply with the request, as the postal regulations provide that, after a letter has passed from the mailing office, the delivery of it cannot be prevented or delayed by the alleged writer.

The excitement and panic, which followed the announcement in the stock exchange of the suspension of the Union Trust company, and the bank of the Commonwealth, were beyond description. The stock exchange resembled a mad-house, and the streets were blocked with people, all laboring under great excitement and frenzy. Prices tumbled from two to sixteen per cent., and stocks were slaughtered without any regard to values amid the surging of the excited crowd.

In the stock exchange amid continued destruction of values, there were some few cool and level heads. These men conceived the idea of imitating the Vienna plan of closing the exchange, and immediately a governing committee was convened to take action therein. In a few moments the board was called to order and the announcement made that the exchange would be closed until further orders from the president. This was received with great joy and the exchange resounded with cheers. The gong sounded and in less time than it takes to record the fact, the wild excitement was over, the surging crowd of frantic brokers disappeared, and the stock exchange was a deserted hall.

London, Sept. 20.—The London *Times*, commenting on the financial panic in New York, says: "In view of the extraordinary prosperity in the United States, and the high price of its government bonds, the present gust can but be remarked as simply an effort of the financial system to get rid of its dishonest element."

The *Daily Telegraph* says: "Such local troubles as the suspensions in New York seems to be, are merely the rank outgrowth of an exuberent prosperity, and the accessories to a progress which does not for a moment halt."

London, Sept. 20.—The continental bourses are disturbed by news from New York.

Montreal, Sept. 20.—The only effect here of the panic in New York has been to make bankers more cautious.

Toronto, Sept. 20.—H. J. Morse & Co., bankers and brokers, in this city, have suspended, owing to the failure of Jay Cooke & Co.

Boston, Sept. 20.—The financial alarm in New York is the principal topic of discussion, but so far does not interfere with business.

Albany, Sept. 20.—T. C. Squire & Co., announce their temporary suspension until further advices from New York.

CINCINNATI, Ohio, Sept. 20.—The New York financial news is the absorbing topic on 'Change, and trade is generally quiet in consequence.

CHICAGO, Sept. 20.—The Franklin bank of this city suspended to-day, being unable to meet a debt balance of nine thousand dollars at the clearing house. It is one of the small savings banks and declares its ability to settle when the panic ends. The only unusual item in the course of trade here is the difficulty experienced in negotiating grain bills in the east.

BURLINGTON, Iowa, Sept. 20.—The Orchard City savings bank suspended at 12:20 P.M.

The shipper whose produce is on the way, or has reached the market place, must wait; the man with his car-loads of live stock must be content to sacrifice the whole or wait at great cost until the Wall street gamblers can resume their dishonest business. The honest creditor must suffer financial ruin, and the national treasury must be open with an unsparing hand in aid of these reckless and dishonest speculators. Those in the interests of the rings announce that the crisis is past and confidence restored; yet, notwithstanding these announcements, on the 24th day of September we have sent over the country dispatches like the following:

BALTIMORE, Sept. 24, 1873.—McIlvaine & Co., of Petersburg, one of the largest commission firms in the state, is reported suspended.

The directors of the Citizens' bank of Petersburg, at a meeting yesterday, decided to suspend to-day.

The Dollar Savings bank closed this morning, and Isaac Taylor and Williams, bankers, have suspended.

LONDON, Sept. 24.—The house of Clews, Habecht & Co. have decided to suspend.

A dispatch from Berlin announces the failure of a bank in that city.

The £138,000 drawn from the bank of England on balance to-day was for shipment to New York; £20,000 in addition to the above amount was also shipped to the same place to-day.

New York, Sept. 24—10.30 a.m.—The governing committee has decided not to open the stock exchange to-day.

The feeling on the street is rather nervous. Brokers are congregated in front of the stock exchange, but are doing little or no business.

Howes & Macy have suspended. This is the first effect of the suspension, yesterday, of Henry Clews & Co. This morning Mr. Macy said the only explanation of their suspension was that which applied under existing circumstances to all the firms having a large number of depositors. He says such houses must suspend. His firm had yielded to the inevitable result of the present financial alarm, and would resume when quiet was restored.

New York, Sept. 24—2 p.m.—All is quiet about the savings banks throughout the city, and there seems to be no suspension of payment, and depositors appear to be more confident.

Brown & Watson, gold brokers, have suspended. Very little excitement followed this suspension.

New York, Sept. 24 — noon.— The bank presidents have decided to issue another $10,000,000 of loan certificates.

Gold is quoted $111\frac{5}{8}$@$111\frac{2}{8}$.

The clearing-house banks, at a meeting to-day, resolved not to pay out any more currency, but to certify all checks payable at the clearing house only. This is intended to prevent any lock-up of greenbacks.

New York, Sept. 24.—The sub-treasury purchased a million and a half of bonds up to this hour — 12:30 this afternoon. An effort is making by the sub-treasurer to distribute the greenbacks as much as possible, and no more is being supplied to the savings banks than their needs require.

New York, Sept. 24.—The banks—members of the clearing house—have also resolved to stand by each other with all their interests, and to expel any bank failing so to do. Each member of the loan committee was made a committee of one to find out where the $10,000,000 of government bonds, or any part of that amount, can be purchased. The president and secretary of the treasury have been asked to anticipate the payment of the bonded indebtedness of the government not yet matured.

A committee of the stock exchange to-day sent the chairman of the clearing-house committee their views as to the proper course to be pursued by banks to save themselves from future complications, to enable the stock exchange to resume operations with safety to the banks, themselves, and to those whose interests they represent. The committee say: "The true plan in the present emergency, in our opinion, is that those banks who were content to make clearances with each other, should, to the extent of their associated capital, guarantee the payment of checks certified by banks allowed to enter into the clearing house."

New York, Sept. 24.—The banks are paying the manufacfurers' pay-rolls in greenbacks.

The cashier of the Fourth National bank expresses the opinion that the issue of the ten million additional loan certificates by the clearing house, and the promise to repeat this action, if necessary, placed the banks on a sure foundation, and that no further trouble need be apprehended at the various savings banks throughout the city. Matters were extremely quiet to-day. Persons appear to be regaining their senses and to have confidence in the stability of the banks. The leading grocers, petroleum and hardware dealers throughout the city deny that the present financial excitement has had the slightest effect on their business.

The secretary of the treasury this morning suggested to the president that the purchase of bonds now being made should cease when the twelve millions have been purchased. He says the treasury cannot fu[illegible] all the currency that a frenzied people may want, and that the treasury must be kept strong, so that it may be in a condition to assist commerce after the financial crisis passes.

The money panic blocked business. Shippers experience great difficulty in selling and exchange, and there is not enough doing at the produce exchange to establish prices. Cash buyers can obtain material concessions. An effort is making by the sub-treasury to distribute the greenbacks as much as possible, and no more is being supplied to the savings banks than their needs require.

The bank presidents have another meeting at half-past three this afternoon. The banks have made their clearings in good shape, and their differences are settled.

Brokers are beginning to think they can see daylight.

Money is about one per cent. per diem.

Mr. Henry Clews was early in the street to-day. Multitudes of sympathizing friends were eager to shake hands with him, and it was the general expression that the fight made by the house during the last few days was indeed a brave struggle against the suspension which came at last.

It seems to be an accepted plea of suspension that a suspension of a solvent house, induced by a general complexion of unavoidable necessity of the present panic, is a matter of precaution rather than an evidence of permanent disaster.

PHILADELPHIA, Sept. 24.—No failures are reported at Allentown or Harrisburg, Pennsylvania, or Trenton, New Jersey.

Brown & Gray, bankers at Wilkesbarre, suspended this morning.

BALTIMORE, Sept. 24.—Brown, Lancaster & Co., well known bankers and brokers in this city, and the agents of the Chesapeake & Ohio railroad, having branch houses in New York and Richmond, suspended this afternoon.

This, perhaps, to be followed by others of like character: "Suspensions are only temporary;" "unforseen causes compelled suspension." "The parties suspending have the confidence and sympathy of the public." These and like expressions are the "sugar-coated pills" administered to those unfortunates who have been robbed by the reckless speculators, who fail during a time of profound peace and plenty; and as a general rule this is about all the pay they ever receive from the "honorable men" who have robbed them. On the 25th September, 1873, comes the annoucement that the banks in almost all parts of the country are either suspending payment, or only paying small checks, and the whole country is in an unsettled state. No one can tell what is yet to follow. What is the cause of all this commotion? *First.* The financial system of the country, that limited the amount of the circulating medium of the country, and pretended to say how much of that currency shall be placed in each state, county and city, thereby advising the stock and gold speculators of the amount it is necessary to corner, in order to produce a crisis and panic in the business of the country. *Second.* The legal tender decisions, which make the resumption of specie payment impossible, and drains our country of its coin. *Third.* The action of state legislatures and of the federal congress, in conferring upon corporations, and particular persons and classes, special privileges not allowed to the whole people. *Fourth.* The aid and approval given to these speculators in selecting them as the medium, through whom the business of the general government is transacted, thus giving them undue prominence and respectability. All these causes combined have enabled the men who build and operate railroads and speculate in stocks, bonds and money to get the control of the finances of the country and use them for illegitimate purposes, to the destruction of the legitimate business of the country. With all these facilities afforded these men, for amassing fortunes by reckless speculations, they have gone systematically to work. They have extended their ramifications throughout the whole country, have formed partnerships with European and provincial houses all leagued together, for the purpose of controlling the gold, stock and bond markets. An international alliance seems to have been formed for the purpose of depleting the nation of gold, and the people of the country of currency, sending the coin to Europe, or cornering it in Wall street, and at the same time controlling the currency of the country. Under the present system, it is not difficult to deplete the country of coin. This is easily effected in our commerce and dealing with Europe.

The imports for the year ending June 30, 1873, amounted to $660,000,000 in round numbers, while our exports, exclusive of coin, amounted to little more than $580,000,000. Coin was used to supply the deficit. The balance of $80,000,000, withdrawn from the country, went to fill the coffers of foreign nations. This amount was about equivalent to the product of our mines and the value of petroleum exported, adding the export of coin required to pay interest on government and other bonds held and payable in Europe, and the drain of specie for that year, for which we received no return was not less than $250,000,000. Much of this amount had to be taken from the coin of the country, and has not been returned. The amount that remains abroad is permanently lost to us, and under our present financial policy no substitute is supplied, but we are left with a money deficit of the amount so withdrawn. Back also of this is the policy that places the gold market under the control of the gold brokers of Wall street. How, under such circumstances, can coin be made available as a means of relief, when Wall street operators determine to bring on a stringency and unsettle values! Yet if they controlled only the gold market no great financial disaster would visit the country. The fault lies in the present banking system. Not that the currency is not as good and valuable as it is possible for it to be, but because it may be controlled in the interests of those who, in the pursuit of their illegitimate purposes, determine to profit at the sacrifice of all legitimate pursuits.

The bank currency, exclusive of reserves, is not much in excess of $300,000,000. In the prosecution of a legitimate business, banks have the right to receive deposits, make loans and discounts, and to deal in exchange. In contemplation of law, they are prohibited from loaning to the stockholders of their respective banks, save in limited amounts, and also from dealing in real estate, save where it becomes necessary in the collection of claims due them. Unfortunately, for the best interest of the country, many of the banks are owned and controlled by men, who are engaged in business as private bankers and brokers, who are large dealers and operators in stocks and bonds, who are stockholders and directors in railroad companies, and are engaged in building railroads and selling their bonds. In the prosecution of their business, they not only deplete their banks, but acting the double role of corporate and private bankers, they use the money of depositors in the construction of their railroads. As a necessary result, the banks controlled by this class of men cannot in an emergency meet the demands of the depositors. This state of facts is known and understood by the "bears" who are planning a raid upon the "bulls." The legitimate avenues of trade must also be supplied with loans from banks or bankers, and thus they are weakened. All that is now necessary to be done to bring on the crisis is for the "bears" to borrow and corner a few millions in the commercial centers, especially in New York, and the financial interests of the whole country are at once under their control.

To make this more plain, and apply the practical test, let us see how the bank account of the whole country stands with the people. The entire banking capital of the country is, in round numbers, $400,000,000. We have not the figures before us showing how their loan account stands at the present time, but can approximate it by taking the account as it stood last April. The whole amount of reported loans in April, 1873, was $908,000,000. It has fluctuated since that date, but is at the present time not any less; probably more. It will be seen that the banks have not only loaned their entire capital, reserved funds included, but have also loaned $508,000,000 of their deposits, and $60,000,000 more than the entire currency of the country, greenbacks included. Much of this vast sum, perhaps the greater part, has been invested in railroad bonds, or stocks, and cannot be made available by the banks. The firms of Jay Cooke & Co., undertook to supply the means, by sale of bonds and otherwise, to build the Northern Pacific railroad. They used their own means and the deposits of their four houses, including the First National bank at Washington City, where the president and ex-president of the United States kept their deposits. These banks were all depleted, and when calls were made upon them they were forced to suspend. The "bears" began to squeeze the "bulls," who applied to the banks for aid. The banks having already used their own money, and over five hundred millions of that belonging to depositors, were not in a situation to afford relief to the "bulls." That struggle for the mastery between the "longs" and "shorts" in Wall street, has spread panic throughout the country, and has caused losses of untold millions to those who are engaged in honest pursuits. The government at Washington had such a realizing sense of the impending ruin that the secretary of the treasury went to New York with $12,000,000 of treasury notes to fight the "bears," and after he had expended that in the purchase of bonds, without affording relief, retired from the field. The desperate "bulls" demanded that the president and secretary of the treasury should disregard the law and lay themselves liable to a criminal prosecution, by the issue of $44,000,000 of legal tender notes to relieve the money market. This they refused to do, notwithstanding the threats of the enraged, arrogant "bulls." The action of the president and secretary in refusing to afford further aid to these Wall street gamblers will be applauded by all the honest dealers in the country, while the wisdom of purchasing twelve millions of bonds, unless the same was done in the interest of the government, and not to aid Wall street speculators, will not be heartily endorsed.

As will have been noticed, the currency in the vaults of the banks was not sufficient to relieve the embarrassment of the time, and an attempt to this end would have involved the business of the whole country. There is no specie basis upon which to rely, nor is there any present means for the increase of the volume of currency. If the banks ever had the means, the legitimate business of the country would not have been benefited by there making additional loans to the stock operators. The course adopted by the banks that are pursuing a legitimate business, in refusing to sell exchange, and even suspending business, will meet the approval of most men who are not speculating in stocks and bonds. Besides all this, an attempt on the part of the banks to go to the aid of Wall street brokers, would only afford temporary relief, and defer for a time a calamity that must sooner or later overtake those who are dealing in stocks and bonds, which are in the main pure fiction. When it is remembered that most railroad stocks and bonds have no real value beyond one-third of what they represent, and that many of the banks are already loaded with this class of security, all must become satisfied that the sooner the bubble bursts, the sooner will prosperity attend the honest business of the people. If all sound business men, who wish to avoid financial disaster, will keep out of Wall street, and let the "bulls" and "bears" fight it out, no great calamity will overtake the country. The result will be the destruction of rotten railroad schemes, and bond speculations, and those banks that have departed from a legitimate business to carry through worthless railroad projects, must pass into the hands of a receiver. A further result will be a strengthening of sound institutions and prosperity in honest pursuits.

But we cannot loose sight of the fact, that under the present financial system, there is a lack of confidence throughout the country. A defalcation by a bank officer or the failure of a single prominent firm, creates general alarm. There seems to be a realizing sense of the fact that the entire business of the country is transacted on credit; that we have no money standard, nor any circulating medium that can be converted into money without a great sacrifice, and that the men who frequent Wall street have had almost unlimited control of the business of the country, because of the ease with which they can absorb its currency, acting on the theory that our circulating medium is not of equal value with the money of other countries. The estimated cost of building railroads has been largely increased of late years, and bonds have been issued and put upon the market largely in excess of the actual cost of the road. As a necessary result those who invest in these bonds must suffer loss. To this cause may be attributed the failure of Jay Cooke & Co. They were the financial agents of the Northern Pacific railroad company and made large advances to forward the work, and took the bonds of the company as security. In so doing they absorded their own and their depositors' money. Two members of the firm were directors in the railroad company. It had a grant of land amounting to about 50,000,000 acres. The firm believed that the grant would help them to sell the mortgage bonds of the company at a fair rate and make large profits. They became a party to a base fraud upon the government and the people. The company issued its bonds secured by mortgage upon its land and its road when built at the rate of $50,000 per mile. With the proceeds of the sale of these bonds the road was to be built. With their reputation acquired as bankers and in the negotiation and sale of government bonds, they expected to be able to realize on the bonds of the company. Acting upon this belief and relying upon their ability to replace the amounts, when needed by depositors and creditors, they used their fund in bank for a purpose forbidden by statute, and went into Wall street as venders of bonds. They were attacked and squeezed by the "bears" and became bankrupt. The desire to enrich themselves by realizing on bonds issued largely in excess of the cost of the road, and before its construction was commenced, controlled their action. The actual cost of the road to the company when 519 miles were completed was $31,500 per mile, leaving a large margin for division among the stockholders, provided their bonds could be sold at usual rates. The influence of the firms of Jay Cooke & Co. in New York, Philadelphia and Washington city, and as owners of the First National Bank of Washington city, were all used to "bull" these railroad bonds in Wall street. The "bears" having scented their prey, pursued it until it was captured. It is noticeable that the money of ex-president Johnson and of president Grant and other officials who patronized this firm, have all been used in *constructing the Northern Pacific railroad* and that the firm once made rich by government patronage, is the firm that has robbed its patrons.

The absolute control of the brokers of Wall street over the financies of the country, cannot be more forcibly illustrated than by a careful examination of the case of Jay Cooke & Co. It demonstrates the fact that stock speculators supported by railroad corporations, not only control the commerce of the country, but that they are so potent, that they can reach out their arms to Washington city and compel the bank, that is the recognized government bank to suspend, and at the same time destroy the firm that above all others had the confidence of the country. It demonstrates the further fact, that a policy that is so shaken by a fight between the "bulls" and "bears" of Wall street, as to cause the interfering of the secretary of the treasury and create alarm throughout the country, is not sound.

The prosperity of the country can only be secured by allowing the people to have and use coin *as money* or by so amending the banking law, as to make it impossible for a few men to control the entire currency of the country. This can be effected by so amending the laws as to allow a resumption of specie payment and free banking. But if the present system is to be continued, the coin of the country will continue to diminish, the business of the country will continue in an unsettled and feverish state, with frequent recurrences of the disasters through which we are now passing.

The present financial crisis demonstrates the fallacy of the system that attempts to place the circulating medium of the whole country under the control of one man, and to limit the amount. Whatever may have been the necessity for the present banking law, as a war measure, that necessity no longer exists, and the interests of the country demand a thorough and radical change. It is now announced that certain banks have suspended. Suspension implies the failure of a bank to redeem its bills. The issuing of bills or notes for circulation by banks is supposed to be based upon the fact that the banks are supplied with coin or greenbacks with which to redeem their bills on presentation. Under the present law they have neither. Coin is out of the question, and the banks are not supplied with greenbacks. The law creating banks is nothing more or less than an attempt to substitute an organized national association of private bankers and brokers for legitimate banks. Whatever may have been the anticipations of congress as to the effect of the system upon the business of the country, recent developments prove that what are in law termed National Banks are really nothing more than legalized brokerage and loan offices, with no pecuniary obligations to the government except to redeem the amounts received for circulation, or to permit the government to do so from the proceeds of the bonds deposited with the comptroller. To prove our assertion that they are only brokers, receiving from government its promises to pay, and loaning them to other parties, let us look at the facts as they exist.

The private corporation deposits its bonds, and in return receives from government its promises to pay in what is called "currency," with authority from the government (the principal) to loan these promises to pay. There is not any money in the transaction, save the gold interest the principal (the government) pays to its agents (the brokers) on their security deposited with their principal. They are organized under the laws of congress, but do not add a dollar to the amount received for circulation, or to the currency of the country. They receive money on deposits, and become the agent of their depositors, with the implied or expressed agreement that they will safely keep, and on demand return, these deposits. Without a dollar of their own, save the bonds deposited with the comptroller of the currency, as collaterals for the return of the currency received, they transact the business usual in their line. They make loans, and not unfrequently buy and sell stocks. Of course they are expected to be able to account to their principals (the government and depositors) when called upon for the amounts received of them respectively. With the government they have agreed to redeem in treasury notes the amount of currency intrusted to them. With their depositors they have agreed to return the amounts deposited when called upon for that purpose. They are not required to settle with the government until they fail to redeem with treasury notes the currency paid out at their respective counters. Prudence in the management of their agencies, and the pursuit of legitimate business, would preclude their inability to pay their deposits. As we have already shown, these *government agents* had loaned more currency than there was in the whole country, treasury notes included. While many of these agencies had acted honestly, and pursued a legitimate business, many had dealt recklessly in bonds and stocks, while not a few had gone into worthless and dishonest railroad schemes, and, as a natural consequence, at the present time, when depositors want their deposits, these banks have nothing for them, and announce that they have *suspended payment.* Suspension means that the banks have not the means with which to fulfill their contracts. The peculiarity of the system is, that they have neither currency nor dishonored treasury notes with which to pay depositors. The distinction between suspension and failure is this: when a bank suspends it refuses to pay out one class of irredeemable paper for another; a failure occurs when the bank has neither class of irredeemable paper to pay. Suspension formerly meant a refusal to pay coin in redemption of bank paper. The reckless and dishonest conduct of some of these government brokers or bankers has made it necessary for those who are pursuing a legitimate calling to refuse to pay out greenbacks as a matter of self-preservation, and to save their customers and depositors from loss.

An amendment to the banking laws so as to allow all who desire to do a banking business, the privilege of banking upon the condition that they purchase from government currency to the amount desired, paying therefor in coin, or government bonds, without limiting the amount of currency would render it impossible for Wall street, and dishonest and reckless speculators elsewhere, to get control of the finances of the country, for they could not know what amount they would have to control in order to unsettle business, and create a stringency in the money market. But as the *measure of values* in this country, as announced by the supreme court, is not coin, but treasury notes, a preferable plan would be to so amend the laws as to use treasury notes as currency instead of the paper now used, and provide for its redemption in coin. Nor need there be any limit to the volume of treasury notes so issued, provided the banks receiving them gave ample security for their redemption in coin. To this plan it might be objected that the volume of the circulating medium would become too great. The answer is that it is impossible to limit the amount of coin: demand and supply is the only law that can control it. The same law of demand and supply would fix the volume of currency. When banking ceased to be remunerative, because of an oversupply of currency, bankers would do like other men in other pursuits that ceased to be remunerative—they would engage in other business. No loss would result from this system of banking. Government would be secure for the amounts of bank notes, and the holders would be secure for two reasons: 1st. The banks would be compelled to redeem in coin, or suspend business. 2d. In case they failed to redeem, the holder could call upon government for payment. There would be no difference between this class of currency and coin, and specie payment would be resumed without any disturbance of the legitimate business of the country. Money panics would be impossible; the legal tender decisions would be harmless, the measure of values would be stable, and the occupation of coin brokers would be gone.

The present financial disturbances demonstrate the fact, that the present banking system instead of affording aid to legitimate business, has become the most powerful auxiliary in the raids upon the honest industry of the country by that class of men whose only employment is to prey upon the public. The ingenuity of man could hardly devise a more perfect plan for placing the finances of the country under the control of a few men. They know how much money there is in the whole country; they know where it is; they know from bank reports the amount of aid to be expected from that source, and what amount of the circulating medium must be cornered, or withdrawn from circulation, in order that the desired object may be accomplished. So well had their plan been formed and executed that the distribution of ten or twelve millions of greenbacks in Wall street had no perceptible effect upon them. Availing themselves of the facilities afforded them by the present banking system, they were able to defeat the secretary of the treasury in his attempt to relieve the people. The lesson we learn from these recent developments, is, that while the general government has the power to coin money and fix its value, it cannot successfully manage the commerce of the whole country by attempting to drive coin from circulation, and supplying its place with a *limited* amount of irredeemable paper.

It will not be out of place to remark in closing, that if it is not within the wisdom or power of congress to devise some better financial system for the country, the policy of intrusting it with the management and control of all the railroad corporations of the country might result in general disaster to the people. We ought not to expect any real relief from national legislation on this subject after, as we have shown in our examination of the action of congress on the subject of railroads, that the greatest monopolists among all railroad companies are those chartered by the general government, and that bounties, subsidies, and favors have been bestowed upon these corporations by congress with an unsparing hand. The attempts thus far made by congress to fix the amount and the kind of money the people shall be allowed to have, and to charter and regulate railroad corporations, do not commend that body of law givers to the people as being the best and safest guardians of their rights and privileges. The present and future well being of our country, as well as the continuance of our republican form of government, imperatively call upon the people to remember that they are sovereign, and that they who assume to act as their *masters* and *guardians*, are but their *servants*, and that, as a sovereign people, they will resist all efforts made by congress for the purpose of *centralizing* power in the general government, ever remembering that the tendency of all power is to encroach, and that our general government has proved no exception to this rule; and also remembering that the first encroachment made by the general government upon the reserved rights of the states and the people, is fraught with more danger to their liberties than all subsequent acts of like character.

INDEX.

APPENDIX.

www.ingramcontent.com/pod-product-compliance
Lightning Source LLC
LaVergne TN
LVHW021307110826
845150LV00003B/510